Violence and the State
in Suharto's Indonesia

Benedict R. O'G. Anderson, editor

Violence and the State in Suharto's Indonesia

SOUTHEAST ASIA PROGRAM PUBLICATIONS
Southeast Asia Program
Cornell University
Ithaca, New York
2001

Cornell Southeast Asia Program Publications
640 Stewart Avenue, Ithaca, NY 14850-3857

Studies on Southeast Asia No. 30

Printed in the United States of America

ISBN 0-87727-729-X

Cover art: Design by Marie Tischler. Photograph of a Jakarta shopping center torched during the May 1998 riots, by Benedict R. O'G. Anderson.

TABLE OF CONTENTS

INDONESIA

INTRODUCTION

Benedict R. O'G. Anderson

A seventy-year old Indonesian woman or man today will have observed and/or directly experienced the following:

1. As a primary school age child—the police-state authoritarianism of the last calm days of Dutch colonial rule and the abrupt collapse of this regime in March 1942 at the hands of Hirohito's armies.

2. As a young teenager—the wartime Japanese military regime, which regularly practiced torture in private and executions in public, which brought about mass starvation, and sent hundreds of thousands to their deaths in forced labor gangs in Indonesia itself and in other parts of Southeast Asia (including gangs sent to work on the notorious Death Railroad constructed between Thailand and Burma).

3. On the eve of adulthood—four years (1945-49) of popular struggle for national liberation against the reimposition of Dutch rule. This was a time of violent social revolution against aristocrats and colonial collaborators, local pogroms against people of Chinese descent, as well as anticolonial warfare carried on by a semiregular Republican army, officered mainly by young men trained by the Japanese, as well as dozens of private militias, armed gangs, and supporters of an Islamic State—all at the cost of hundreds of thousands of lives.

4. As a young adult—in the time of a fragile Liberal Democracy (1950-57), armed rebellions of different types in the Moluccas, in Aceh, in South Sulawesi, and in West and parts of Central Java.

5. As a young mother or father—the CIA-instigated and supplied civil war of 1958-60, and the spreading social violence of President Sukarno's Guided Democracy, culminating in the cataclysm of 1965-66, when at least 600,000 and perhaps as many as two million people regarded as affiliated with the Indonesian Communist Party were slaughtered by the military under Suharto's leadership, in alliance with murderous gangs of Muslim, Protestant, Catholic, and Hindu-Balinese youth groups. Meanwhile hundreds of thousands of others were imprisoned without trial for many years, often tortured, starved, and lawlessly deprived of their property.

6. In middle age—the New Order police-state, and its bloody attempt to annex East Timor, which cost over 200,000 East Timorese lives, as well as those of an as yet uncounted number of Indonesian soldiers.

7. In old age—the spread of armed resistance to the state in Aceh and West Papua, the savage riots of May 1998, which involved more than a thousand deaths and brought about Suharto's fall from power, and the recent outbreak of ruthless inter-confessional warfare in the long peaceful Moluccas.

8. And???

According to a theoretical tradition which comes to us primarily from Max Weber, one of the peculiar features of the modern state is that it claims and exercises an absolute monopoly of legitimate violence within its internationally accepted territory, and that this legitimation comes primarily from the law from which the state derives its fundamental shape. Thus when a citizen of such a state commits a heinous crime like murder, he is not punished by the family or friends of his victim, but by the State. In the process that may lead to his execution, neither judge nor jury, policeman nor prison warden, not even the executioner himself, is committing or abetting murder. The same goes obviously for war, in which the most frightful killings are also innocently performed by soldiers, bomber pilots, rocketmasters, and so forth. Such rules exempt the secret services from the usual punishments for bribery, extortion, blackmail, forgery, assassination, and the like. But the history of what is euphemistically called "state-building" in Europe— and, by later extension, the European empires outside Europe —shows that it has been a long, slow, and difficult process over several centuries, and that its modern "perfection" was impossible without the kind of financial and technological resources that high-industrial capitalism made available. Even "advanced" Great Britain achieved a modern police force only in the middle of the nineteenth century. We also know that the authority of the Law—which permits the hangman to have a good lunch with his family after his day's work is done—is never complete, and long periods of political, economic, and social stability and peace are necessary for its fragile, general acceptance.

Our seventy-year-old Indonesian has never seen such a modern state exist in her/his country and will certainly die without seeing any significant change in this regard. The United East India Company established its presence in the Indonesian archipelago at the start of the seventeenth century, but reasonably standardized police forces had to wait till the turn of the twentieth century (and a secret political police another twenty years, after the arrival of the fingerprint). Till then, most of the non-European quarters of the colony's cities and towns were "policed" by volunteer neighborhood watches, known as *ronda*, who routinely treated suspected thieves, burglars, and other undesirables with vigilante violence. In many rural areas, the colonial regime found it necessarily to farm out policing to assorted groups of plantation guards, the personal spies and bullies of native administrators, and charismatic toughs (known variously as *jago, jawara,* etc.), on the Vidocquian principle of "set a thief to catch a thief."

Over the first forty-two years of the twentieth century, the growing power of the autocratic, and now modernizing, colonial state—which was made possible by The Netherlands' own late industrialization, by colonial agribusiness, and the boom in rubber and petroleum that the arrival of the automobile ensured—did not fail to produce dialectically new forms of resistance. Out of the rapid growth of the print media, out of the significant increase in state and private modern education, and out of that world history-making generation that included Mahatma Gandhi, Vladimir Ilyich Lenin, and Sun Yat-sen, came the beginning of modern-style mass political movements in the colony—Islamic, Communist, and, eventually, nationalist too. In the face of the colonial regime's resolute refusal to permit any form of legal, mass democratic politics, let alone to entertain any idea of ultimate independence for the natives, it was not long before the fragile authority of colonial Law began to crack. In the name of Islam, world-revolution, and/or national independence, activists appeared who made it a point of pride and of tactical necessity to break this Law—with illegal strikes, riots, circulation of banned writing, embezzlement here and there, certainly seditious meetings and secret planning. The Communists even launched a brave, but foolhardy, armed uprising in 1926-27. When activists ended up in jail, as often happened, they learned from the professional criminals detained alongside them some useful tricks in the business of illegality, and at the same time they attempted to recruit these criminals to their respective political causes.

The extreme ease with which the Japanese military destroyed the colonial regime in just a few weeks was a huge, and, on the whole, welcome shock to the Indonesian population. The sight of once arrogant Dutch officials and their haughty wives in flight, even begging "their" natives for help and protection, had its agreeable aspects. After some months, most of the Dutch who did not escape to Australia were sent to harsh detainment camps where their guards were usually Japanese-trained natives. This recruitment of native "security forces" was, of course, made necessary by the scarcity of Japanese (and/or Korean) personnel at a time when the Empire was at war with the Allies from the Indian borders of Burma to the northern periphery of today's Papua-Niugini, to say nothing of a wide arc across the Central and Northern Pacific. And when the tide of the war turned decisively against Tokyo in the spring and summer of 1943, Japanese authorities in the former colony, especially those in charge of Java and Sumatra, began mobilizing a vast number of youths into various anti-Allied auxiliary-military and paramilitary organizations, anticipating the day when the enemy would bring the war directly into the archipelago. The most important of these organizations, the Fatherland Defense Force, or Peta, would, from October 1945 on, provide the bulk of the officers for the army of the revolutionary Republic of Indonesia, and, indeed, for the post-1949 internationally recognized unitary state of Indonesia right up to the end of the 1970s. (Suharto himself was trained in the Peta after a short stint as an NCO in the Dutch colonial military.)

Brief as it was, the period of Japanese occupation (March 1942-August 1945) had decisive long-term consequences for Indonesia. It gave Indonesians their first taste of a militarized state with a militaristic ideology by which they became, also for the first time, "Asians." In other words, they would be the "younger brothers and sisters" of the rulers, not simply radically alien natives. They were also to become hand-to-hand combatants with the "white" enemy. As the popular rhyming slogan went, *Inggris kita linggis, Amerika kita sterika* (We'll take a crowbar to the English, and a hot iron to the Americans). Finally, partly by accident and partly by intent, the Japanese accelerated a profound transformation of values that had begun in that late Dutch colonial time.

Nothing is more striking, if one looks at the early social movements of the twentieth century, than the prominence of the figure of Youth. Young Ambon, Young Muslim League, Young Indonesia—in opposition to which there was never any Old

Ambon, Adult Muslim League, or Middle-Aged Indonesia. The first substantial generation to get a "Western education" and to absorb the teleology of Marxism understood itself as possessed with the power of the Future, where freedom lay waiting. Japanese distrust of colonial civil servants shaped by Dutch bureaucratic culture, and the Japanese belief that by mass indoctrination of the youth of Indonesia the Emperor would gain an uncontaminated force of dedicated servants of the Greater East Asia Co-Prosperity Sphere, vastly expanded the population of "political youth" (*Pemuda*). No previous regime had ever placed such heady political emphasis on the young.

The abrupt Japanese surrender on August 15, 1945, as a result of the atomic bombing of Hiroshima and Nagasaki, and the Soviet Union's declaration of war —thousands of miles away from Indonesia—was even more abrupt than the fall of the Dutch colonial regime three years earlier. It also produced an astonishing vacuum of local power. Holland, itself only recently liberated from Nazi occupation, was in no position yet to reoccupy the archipelago. Lord Mountbatten, the commander of the recently established Southeast Asia Command headquartered in Ceylon, and with the primary task of restoring British power in Burma, Malaya, and Singapore, could not do much to help for several months. Yet the older Indonesian politicians, most of whom had worked with the Japanese with varying degrees of sincerity, hesitated, fearing looming Allied retribution. The moment was seized by radical youths in the capital city of Jakarta, who briefly kidnapped the two top leaders, Sukarno and Hatta, with the idea of forcing them to make a declaration of independence. On August 17 this historic proclamation was then made: in the name of the People of Indonesia.

In the next months, the colonial state in its Dutch and Japanese forms came very close to collapse. Officials regarded as collaborators and exploiters were frequently kidnapped, publicly humiliated, beaten, and sometimes killed by armed youth groups. In various places aristocracies were expelled or physically exterminated by competing bands of revolutionary youngsters. People suspected of being black-marketeers, traitors, or spies often came to miserable ends. The power behind this violence derived from what Indonesians since the first days of free publication at the end of September 1945 were already calling Our Revolution. It did not emanate from the feeble new state, but from a profoundly politicized, radicalized, and pauperized society. When the British, and later the Dutch, appeared, it was this same power, the power that created the mass resistance by official and irregular armed groups, as well as by the population, that doomed the colonial restoration project. After four years of intermittent negotiations and bitter fighting, The Netherlands formally transferred sovereignty to the Federal State of Indonesia at the very end of 1949.

The Indonesian Revolution was the decisive event of twentieth century Indonesian history, not because it achieved many social or economic objectives, but because it made morally possible the massive participation by ordinary Indonesians in the half-millennial reconfiguration of their futures and their nation. The Republican government could stop almost nothing, and its coalitional composition shifted constantly. Well-known gangsters could become revolutionaries, and young prostitutes could be turned into well-trained units of a women's militia. Boys from conservative rural Muslim schools could become Soldiers of Allah. Youngsters still on school benches could leave them for the progressive heroism of membership in the armed Indonesian Socialist Youth—or for the Wild Tigers, the Dare-To-Die League, The Black Dragons, and so on. These organizations, insofar as they were real organizations, were private, arming themselves from seized arsenals of Japanese weapons, from their competitors, or from village smithies, and financing themselves "in the revolutionary way," which meant by almost any means: through appeals to villagers, subscription, revolutionary taxation, extortion, patriotic blackmarketeering, strategic looting, and the spoils of war.

The symbolic significance of Youth as the engine of national liberation appeared also to be confirmed in two aspects of the revolutionary state. President Sukarno and Vice President Hatta took office at the ages of forty-four and forty-three; the first Prime Minister, Sutan Sjahrir, formed his cabinet at age thirty-six; the Commander of the Indonesian Armed Forces, Sudirman, took up the position at the age of twenty-nine. And in these armed forces, formed out of debris of Japanese-period paramilitary organizations, everyone was young, no matter whether they were generals or sergeants. And, even more astonishingly, they were mostly elected by their comrades rather than appointed by their superiors.

The Revolution officially came to an end at the close of 1949, but in a certain sense it has never come to an end. The prestige of this sustained explosion of patriotic popular violence has continued to reecho till the present. During the Revolution, Aceh was the one region that the Dutch never tried to reoccupy, and it was a stalwart military and financial bulwark of the revolutionary Republic. Today, a substantial part of Aceh's population, alienated by the greed and savagery of the Suharto regime, supports an armed popular insurrection for an Aceh Merdeka (Free Aceh) which descends from the Indonesia Merdeka of the Revolution. The same line of descent formed the name of the much less strongly armed insurrectionary group of West Papua, which calls itself the Organisasi Papua Merdeka. During the Suharto regime's frightful attempted annexation of East Timor, nothing was more painful to Indonesians of good conscience than the recognition that their state was playing the role of Dutch colonialism in East Timor, while the heroic part played by their revered revolutionary ancestors was taken by Xanana Gusmaõ and his dedicated, armed and unarmed, "revolutionary" followers.

In 1965, when the vast pogroms against the legal, and mostly unarmed, Communist Party and its affiliates and allies took place, nothing was more striking than the role played in the massacres by "private" youth groups, mostly affiliated with other legal political parties. This role was not justified by "orders from Suharto," though such orders existed, but by the right of the People itself to save the nation, the country's future, religion, and so on. It was not a role that was permitted by the military to exist for more than a short time; and it should in no way be confused with or merged into the icy institutional violence that followed (an institutional violence that imposed on its victims massive illegal expropriation of property; imprisonment without trial under terrible conditions for many years in Suharto's tropical gulag; and systematically organized economic discrimination and social pariahdom after eventual release). But even this vast machine of state violence never stood either alone or uncontested, as Indonesia's present troubled circumstances make only too plain. If the present book is entitled *Violence and the State in Suharto's Indonesia*, it is exactly for this reason. Indonesians, of course, are familiar with the modern state's presumptive monopoly claims to the "right to violence." But they have seen such states founder and disappear, unregretted. They also have good reason to think, from experience, that the violent potential in civil society has had plenty to be said for it, depending on circumstance and moral stance, and by no means always only after the fact.

The contributions to this volume are thus linked together by Indonesia's modern history and by the complexity of the violence it contains. For this reason it is a matter of special gratification that the contributors come from the two disciplines of political science and anthropology, disciplines that rarely meet except, most productively, "in the field." There one sees most clearly the structures, policies, and macroinstitutions that fascinate the first and are entangled with the identities, cultures, and microeconomies that engage the second.

We open with anthropologist Joshua Barker's remarkable study of the culture of the Indonesian police, as observed on location in the city of Bandung and followed nationally in the archives of public documents and newspapers. The most striking contribution this essay makes is to show how, from the early 1980s on, the National Police tried systematically to appropriate, control, survey, and "train" competing, "private" purveyors of security/violence—traditional neighborhood watches and patrols, ex-convicts working in private security firms, petty hoodlums engaged in protection rackets, and the security staffs of major businesses, associations, and professional offices. (This marked a major step beyond the informal networks of collusion with the underworld that were already visible under Guided Democracy's authoritarianism.) At the same time, the formal campaign to "professionalize" the private security sector along police guidelines was, at the same time, accompanied by tendencies in the reverse direction, with the growth of unofficial "fraternities" inside the police mimicking the illegal activities—extrajudicial killings, beatings, and extortion—of brotherhoods of excons and hoodlums. Barker further shows, at least at the precinct level, how close the culture of the police was/is to that of the neighborhoods in which it worked; the shared beliefs in the occult powers of certain criminals and the need to use occult methods against them are particularly striking.

Barker's often alarming scrutiny of the practices of " security" at the level of the street is then followed by—and stands in striking contrast with—political scientist Jun Honna's detailed and careful study of the changing doctrines of national security propagated officially by the Suharto regime over thirty years, and especially developed and implemented by the top leadership of powerful Indonesian Armed Forces (in its own interests, needless to say). Honna argues that the dictatorship's "security state" and "security doctrine" were originally created to manage and justify the physical destruction of the Communist Party, and the incarceration of huge numbers of members who survived the massacres of 1965-66. But once this objective was achieved, the doctrines were used to crush any group thought by the Suharto circle to threaten the dictatorship, and also to institutionalize military control over most organized aspects of state and society. Of special interest is Honna's subtle analysis of how the military tried to manage the transition from the Cold War to the era of "globalization," the Internet, American planetary domination, and the hazardous flows of finance capital, by reinterpreting the "latent danger of communism" to refer to the "communist methods" used by human rights groups, dissident writers, ecological NGOs, hackers, liberals, and even organized Muslim associations. Honna concludes that the fall of the Suharto regime, and the public exposure of the dreadful record of the military's human rights abuses, has divided and demoralized the army in particular. Certain groups of officers now believe that serious reforms are essential and that the military must largely remove itself from everyday politics, while others continue to argue that the massive rise of popular violence in Indonesia (in which, of course, they have had their own half-concealed hand), shows that the State is in such fundamental danger that only tried and tested Suharto-era methods will save it.

The next pair of essays—by anthropologist James Siegel and young political scientist Loren Ryter—are also usefully juxtaposed, but share in common their concern with the residues of the Revolution (and Counter-Revolution 1965). The horrific May 1998 riots in Jakarta that helped bring about Suharto's abdication were marked not only by the "usual" massive trashing and looting of businesses owned by Indonesians of Chinese descent, but also by the burning alive of hundreds of poor looters trapped in ransacked premises, and especially by the unprecedented rape of Sino-Indonesian women. This last feature of the riots has widely—but without clear proof—been attributed to elements of Suharto's security apparatus —paratroopers and/or elite police in mufti, or state-sponsored and protected criminal elements—who purportedly intended to create the basis for a declaration of martial law. Building on his remarkable three earlier books about the New Order, Siegel acutely analyzes how the May violence of the various parties was understood by different class and ethnic elements. He shows, for example, how a well-off woman student at Trisakti University reacted to police sharpshooters killing four of her fellow-collegians, with a characteristic middle-class ambiguity. Distress at the killings never overcame a fundamental idea that the people one has to be afraid of in Jakarta are the "masses" and not the police. The "masses" turn out to be a contemporary middle-class reimagination of the People (*Rakyat*) of the time of the Revolution. Siegel also shows how misconceived it is for anti-Chinese riots to be understood as analogous to anti-Semitic pogroms in an earlier Europe. The peculiarity of the Chinese position is that few Indonesians dream of wiping them out or of expelling them wholesale from the country (and many are genuinely sympathetic to their situation). Looters who ransacked small Chinese neighborhood stores allowed themselves to feel surprised and even annoyed when they discovered that the stores had not reopened for business the following week. After all, they believed, Chinese have unlimited access to goods. But a woman's body is not a replaceable and disposable commodity, and Siegel considers why the unprecedented rapes caused real moral shock, above all among women's groups, but even among typically anti-Chinese elements (not, however, inside the state apparatus).

Ryter's chapter investigates the history, politics, and culture of the New Order's most notorious "official gangsters," the Pancasila Youth/Pemuda Pancasila, who have done a great deal of Suharto's dirty work over the last decades: organizing riots or looting where needed, helping to strong-arm the "right" results in national elections, arranging rent-a-crowds for official rallies, intimidating dissenters, guarding the Suharto children and their hundreds of businesses, as well as engaging in extortion and protection rackets, to say nothing of occasional torture and murder. Yet until Suharto's fall, this organization had impressive offices, published its own books and a glossy magazine, placed its national and regional leaders in the respective legislative bodies, showed up for official receptions and ceremonies, and proclaimed its success in rescuing street-people from criminality by training them and finding them work in the informal sector. The most striking feature of Ryter's analysis of Pemuda Pancasila—and it is one that cannot easily be imagined fitting any other Southeast Asian country—is his historical framing. PP's origins can be traced to the middle-1950s, when the recently dismissed, highly influential Army Chief of Staff, General Abdul Haris Nasution, decided to set up a "non-party" party, which he called the IPKI (League of Supporters of Indonesian Independence) to contest the 1955 elections. The IPKI was meant to draw its strength from youthful veterans of the recent Revolution, to serve the interests of the Army in the civilian political sphere, and to sustain the nationalist spirit. The non-party party was quite unsuccessful in the elections, but it survived liberal democracy and did better under joint rule of the Army and Sukarno during Guided Democracy. Its youth wing, Pemuda Pancasila, got its initial impetus from ex-revolutionary young gangsters in Medan, who came to control various lucrative "turfs" in the city's center, and later was used by local anti-communist army officers and politicians against the Communist party's labor and plantation-worker unions. In North Sumatra and elsewhere, it played a significant role in the massacres of 1965-66.

Ryter raises the interesting question of why the Suharto dictatorship, with so many other formidable instruments of repression to hand, bothered with the PP at all. Part of the answer, he suggests, is that Suharto himself, who had fought actively for the Revolution like so many of his generation, in the end could not bury it. His own regime had been installed with the help of a sort of sinister parody of the popular explosion of 1945, the rightwing youths of the so-called Generation of 1966, and that legacy made its own demands. Pemuda Pancasila, bastion of a thoroughly counter-revolutionary regime, nonetheless came, in the 1980s and 1990s, to be constructed as a perfection and historically final expression of the tradition of National Youth activism.

The last three chapters of the book focus on the experiences of violence in the late New Order's most famously *rawan* (troubled) provinces: East Timor, Irian Jaya/West Papua, and Aceh. Political scientist Douglas Kammen gives a superbly detailed account of policy-making for East Timor in the last decade of Suharto's rule, leading to the final orgy of violence, after Indonesia decisively lost the UN-imposed referendum on independence at the end of August 1999. Once again the most striking feature of the one-sided violence, which destroyed almost all the urban infrastructures of the little country, was that it was carried out prosthetically. While the military held all the strings of money, weapons, and intelligence, the visible actors were "private" anti-independence militias, many of them with bizarre uniforms and spectacularly lurid names, that once again appear as a blackly parodic replay of the Wild Tigers and Black Dragons of the heroic Indonesian Revolution.

Kammen offers a thoughtful discussion of why the militias became so necessary just as the last military resistance of the East Timorese seemed crushed and the legendary leader Xanana Gusmaõ had finally been captured. The Suharto regime was caught by the paradoxes of its own project. If the resistance had finally been destroyed, then the province should become normalized, open to foreign dignitaries, tourists, and the local press. It should also have a university capping an extensive educational system, satellite television, shopping centers, computers and so on. But young East Timorese, aware that a third of their country's population had untimely died in the first years after the 1975 invasion, were able, over and over again, brilliantly to outmaneuver the Jakarta regime in the political sphere.

By the late 1990s, and especially after the financial crash of the summer of 1997, Jakarta had little left to sustain itself in East Timor other than the prosthetic violence of the militia mercenaries.

Anthropologist Danilyn Rutherford, who did her dissertation fieldwork on the island of Biak, offers a contrasting picture of the complexities of Papuan resistance to the New Order State's racism and crony pillaging of the territory's vast natural resources. It has to be remembered that when The Netherlands transferred sovereignty to Indonesia at the end of 1949, it refused to let West Papua be included, partly out of sheer spite, partly so that it would be able to maintain at least some presence in Asia, and partly out of dreams of settling many Eurasians there, who did not want to stay in free Indonesia and whom the metropolitan Dutch did not want moving to Holland. All serious Indonesian attempts to negotiate the integration of West Papua failed in the presence of Dutch intransigence, leading to ever more bitter recriminations and eventually, late in 1957, to the nationalization of almost all Dutch corporate property in Indonesia and the expulsion of Dutch citizens. These steps greatly increased political polarization in Indonesia and helped to precipitate the civil war of 1958-60 and the emergence of the populist-authoritarian Guided Democracy regime of 1959-65. Fearful that the issue was helping the Indonesian Left, and anticipating Indonesian military incursions into West Papua, Washington finally decided to shift its tacit support from The Netherlands to Indonesia. Dutch colonialism was forced to yield to a temporary United Nations authority which was supposed to ensure a fair assessment of the Papuans' political preferences. Unfortunately for West Papua, these sudden shifts took place very shortly before the bloody overthrow of the Sukarno regime and the installation of Suharto's dictatorship. Suharto's political intelligence operatives coerced and faked a declaration of support for integration with Indonesia by traditional chiefs, and the United Nations looked the other way. West Papua was thus the only part of the former Netherlands Indies which had no experience of the liberal democracy of the 1950s, or even much of the populist-authoritarian regime that followed it. For Papuans, integration with Indonesia has been synonymous with dictatorship.

If in Kammen's account the East Timorese resistance (to be sure, treated mainly in passing) appears as a mainstream national liberation movement, Rutherford's close-in ethnography shows that the now popular notion of a Free Papua cannot be understood apart from the millenarian traditions for which Melanesia generally is famous, and the outbursts of popular violence through which they have frequently been expressed. She also considers the warrior cultures of the quite recent past, and the strange way in which, for many Papuans, power is seen to be obtained by visible possession, and/or absorption, of the "foreign"—something that, at least on the surface, runs radically against any conventional idea of nationalism.

Finally, political scientist-turned-historian Geoffrey Robinson gives an absorbing account of the tragic experience of Aceh. Scene of the longest (c. 1873-1903) and bitterest war of Dutch colonial conquest, the province was never fully pacified, even though the sultanate was abolished and the aristocracy thoroughly coopted. At the outbreak of the Revolution, a coalition of nationalist youth and revered Islamic teachers organized a social revolution which killed or expelled almost the entirety of this class. The reputation of the Acehnese as warriors, as well as very serious Muslims and nationalists, meant that after 1945 the Dutch never tried to reconquer the province. Two rebellions against central authority occurred in the 1950s, but neither was separatist in intent; both were expressions of opposition to administrative and economic centralization, as well as of political hostility to the declining position of Muslim parties vis-à-vis Sukarno, secular nationalists, and the communist party. Both were ended by negotiations. In 1965-66, at the instigation of the (non-Acehnese) military commander, Acehnese Muslim and other youth murdered or expelled all known Communists (also mostly non-Acehnese) in the province, to say nothing of thousands of Sino-Indonesians. Yet, in the 1970s and early 1980s, Aceh seemed a model province, calm, quite prosperous, and under a civilian administration.

Robinson provides us with a powerful and convincing explanation of why all this disappeared in the late 1980s and the 1990s. The discovery of huge deposits of natural gas and their subsequent development by foreign corporations and the Indonesian state monopoly created fabulous wealth for the Suharto circle in Jakarta and for its local henchmen; but the Acehnese themselves were largely excluded from the enclave gas economy and from its benefits. Expressions of dissatisfaction were met with massive repression by paratroopers who had learned their cruel tricks-of-the-trade in East Timor and in Papua. Out of this has come the strange situation that the province, which was for long regarded as a fortress of the Republic of Indonesia, is widely viewed as heading for secession from it, either as a Republic or as a revived Sultanate. In Aceh, too, there are obvious residues of East Timor: "fanatical" militias, paratrooper violence disguised as separatist outrages, scorched earth policies, and so on. But the disjointed Acehnese Independence Movement has not failed to respond in rather similar ways, a fact less surprising, perhaps, once we recall that its commander-in-chief is himself a former Red Beret Suharto paratrooper.

It goes without saying that a book of this type can not be comprehensive. We acknowledge several striking absences or unjustifiably diminished considerations. The biggest omission is a chapter on the great massacres of 1965-66, about which more and more information has been coming to light with the fall of Suharto. The book also has no chapter on the grim sectarian war of the past two years in the Moluccas. Nor does it devote more than passing reference to the Petrus ("Mysterious Killers") campaign in 1983, directed by Suharto and General Benny Murdani, which achieved the extrajudicial assassination of several thousand petty criminals and street people. Yet the methods used by Petrus—night-time kidnappings by paratroopers in mufti, brutal executions sometimes accompanied by mutilation, bodies left for display with thumbs tied together with plastic cord behind the victims' backs—emerged from 1965-66, and East Timor, and showed up in the 1990s again in Aceh.

But the central motif of the book, which marks it off from some very fine accounts of military repression and human rights abuses under the Suharto dictatorship, is that violence in twentieth-century Indonesia has never been a legitimate monopoly of the State. It has been deployed, under differing circumstances, with differing kinds of legitimation, by revolutionaries, middle classes, villagers, ethnic groups, "privatized" corporate apparatuses, quasi-official gangsters, the CIA, and so on. The absence of a full state monopoly of legitimate violence has many causes, not to speak of effects. But it is also a manifestation of the absence of a Law by which the monopoly could be generally justified. In the Revolution and its immediate aftermath the Law, or rather its sources, was a controversial matter. Yet the issue was taken quite seriously, and a sizeable part of the political elite was even committed to constitutionalism. Today, after three decades of corrupt, cynical, and arbitrary dictatorship, under which elites were completely immune to legal punishment, while judges, police, prosecutors, and even defense advocates treated cases simply as commercial transactions or as political shows of force, very little of this seriousness still exists, except among some young intellectuals, professionals, and middle-class reformers. Nothing shows its general marginality better than the spread of vigilante justice, "mob attacks" on police-stations and jails, and ever-increasing middle-class demands for stepped up "security." These middle classes are quite aware of what has happened here and there to the Chinese, and how "structurally Chinese" they have themselves become. There is not much in modern Indonesia's history to give them many long-term assurances. Probably one does not need to be seventy years old to understand this strangeness.

STATE OF FEAR: CONTROLLING THE CRIMINAL CONTAGION IN SUHARTO'S NEW ORDER

Joshua Barker

In keeping with the overt symbolism that marked political monuments in Suharto's New Order, the Department of the Interior on Jakarta's main square was ornamented with a giant *kentongan*. A *kentongan* is an instrument made from a hollowed branch that is struck to give off a sound. *Kentongan* have been used by neighborhood night-watches (*ronda*) in Java's towns and villages for centuries as devices to keep thieves away, to call forth populations for territorial defense, and to keep people alert and ready to ward off threats to community well-being.[1] Hung by a mosque, in a guard house, or in front of the village head's home, it is the quintessential technology for community policing. The *kentongan* at the Department of the Interior, by virtue of its size and location, would seem to represent a departure from the strictly local connotations of village *kentongan*. This grand *kentongan* was undoubtedly meant to provide the many thousands of *kentongan* in the nation's villages and towns with a new center with which to resonate. Through a sort of crude symbolism, the installation of this *kentongan* signified the subordination of local security apparatuses to the overarching security framework provided by the state.

The buildings that comprise the Department of the Interior are themselves representative of what is a characteristically New Order architectural style: large structures which appear top-heavy since their upper floors, supported by long

---

[1] On the various functions and meanings of the *kentongan* and the *ronda*, see Joshua Barker, "Surveillance and Territoriality in Bandung" in *Figures of Criminality in Indonesia, the Philippines, and Colonial Vietnam*, ed. Vicente L. Rafael (Ithaca: Cornell Southeast Asia Program, 1999).

concrete columns, extend out beyond the lower ones. Such a style—most commonly seen in the thousands of banks that sprang up in all of Indonesia's towns and cities during the boom periods of recent decades—emphasizes two features of the building: the entranceway and the upper floors. The entranceway can be of monumental proportions, with a ceiling several stories high, giving the visitor a distinct feeling of being very small. The upper floors, in contrast, allow their inhabitants to sit atop the structure and survey the scene below, often from behind a wall of one-way glass. On the occasions between 1995 and 1997 when I was forced to visit the Department of Interior (to report my research plans to the Socio-Political Affairs bureau), I could not help but notice that the coupling of this architecture of surveillance with the *kentongan* did not quite work. Although the *kentongan* was given monumental proportions and carved with intricate designs to make it stand out to visitors, it was clearly added after the building was constructed, for it had been pushed off behind a column so as not to get in the way. Without a spot of its own, it simply hung there, looking uneasy and out of place.

*   *   *

This essay will examine the New Order state's attempts to appropriate local, territorial power and to give it a place within the confines of the state.[2] Specifically, it will focus on the effects of two initiatives pursued by the New Order state to use surveillance to eliminate or discipline representatives of territorial power: Petrus and Siskamling. Petrus is the acronym given to an early-1980s paramilitary operation known as the Mysterious Killings[3] (Pembunuhan Misterius) in which thousands of people labeled criminals were murdered in a number of Indonesia's main cities. Siskamling, or *sistem keamanan lingkungan* (environment security system), is a term that was first coined by the head of the Indonesian police in the early-1980s to describe a new way of organizing the local security apparatus so as to give police the responsibility for coordinating and supervising neighborhood *ronda*, and for training and supervising private security guard units (*satpam*) for use in commercial and public settings.[4] Both of these initiatives were means of dealing with fears regarding a wave of violent crime that peaked in the early-1980s. At a policy level, the two initiatives moved in two different directions since one implied the eradication of the criminal element through what the government referred to as "shock therapy," while the other implied the development of a better system of law enforcement through an extension of the reach of the Police. According to David Bourchier, officials in

---

[2] Territorial forms of power are here represented by the *kentongan*, the *ronda*, the tattoo, and figures like the *jawara* and *preman*. For an account of how territorial power is constructed by the *ronda* and the *kentongan*, see my ibid.

[3] Also meaning Mysterious Shootings (*Penembakan Misterius*) or Mysterious Shooters (*Penembak Misterius*).

[4] Among the police it is also frequently called the *sistem swakarsa* (spontaneous system). The Police have defined it as: "Unity and sameness of people's understanding, attitude, and behavior within various living environments that arise in the shape of care toward preventing, prohibiting, tackling, and responding in an appropriate and speedy way to tendencies and/or cases of disturbance of order, crime, and calamities that could or are striking at their interests, themselves, or their surroundings, along with being able to take care of themselves in accordance with changing circumstances." Pusat Pengembangan Ilmu dan Teknologi Kepolisian, *Laporan Akhir Penelitian Industrial Security dan Permasalahannya* (Final Report of a Study of Industrial Security and Its Problems) (Jakarta, 1994), p. 4.

government were divided as to which strategy to pursue: some advocated the rule-of-law approach represented by Siskamling, others advocated the extra-judicial approach represented by Petrus.[5] In retrospect, however, it seems clear that the two solutions to the crime problem were effectively part of a single process. This process had as its object the "deterritorialization"[6] of local security practices in a manner that was conducive to central state control. In the case of Siskamling, this was largely an institutional question, and depended on subjecting gangs, security guards, and "criminals" to surveillance. But in the case of Petrus, it was a question of appropriating the power that "criminals" and gangs represented, a complex process that involved mimicry as well as surveillance.

This essay is based on a combination of textual sources and field research.[7] It begins with a brief account of crime, security, and state power in the period immediately leading up to Petrus and the introduction of Siskamling. This is followed by a description of the changes to local security brought about by the implementation of Siskamling, changes that would only really get underway once Petrus had scared competitors away or killed them. The bulk of the text is then spent analyzing Petrus itself: its lists, its ambivalence in defining the "criminal," and its attempts to recuperate the power that gangs and their leaders represented. Finally, I describe the legacy of Petrus and Siskamling for the relation between local security and state power.

CRIME, SECURITY, AND STATE POWER IN THE EARLY-1980 S

The raging crime at the beginning of the 1980s, especially armed robbery directed at gold shop owners and bank clients, was a hot story in Bandung's media. The news was consumed by the people via the mass media so that it became a specter [*momok*] that caused the people fear. The criminals' actions were in fact performed not just at night but also in broad daylight and in the middle of public crowds.[8]

---

[5] David Bourchier, "Crime, Law and State Authority in Indonesia" in *State and Civil Society in Indonesia*, ed. Arief Budiman (Clayton, Victoria: Monash University, Asia Institute, 1990), p. 183.

[6] For definitions of deterritorialization, see Gilles Deleuze and Felix Guatarri, *A Thousand Plateaus: Capitalism and Schizophrenia* (Minneapolis: University of Minnesota Press, 1991), especially pp. 61, 141-144, 453-456. My use of the term is somewhat analogous to Weber's use of the term "transpose" as in the following: "Bureaucratic and patriarchal structures are antagonistic in many ways, yet they have in common a most important peculiarity: permanence. In this respect they are both institutions of daily routine . . . The patriarch is the 'natural leader' of daily routine. And in this respect, the bureaucratic structure is only the counter-image of patriarchalism *transposed* into rationality. As a permanent structure with a system of rational rules, bureaucracy is fashioned to meet calculable and recurrent needs by means of a normal routine." Max Weber, S. N. Eisenstadt, ed., *On Charisma and Institution Building* (Chicago: University of Chicago Press, 1968), p. 18 (emphasis added).

[7] Fieldnote citations are indented and signaled by the phrase [Fieldnotes] at the beginning of each section. The statements of informants were not recorded verbatim (unless in inverted commas) but were reconstructed shortly afterward from contemporaneous notes. Names of informants have been changed for obvious reasons.

[8] W. P. Nainggolan, "Penggunaan Lokasi Pertokoan yang Dilaksanakan Oleh Satpam dalam Rangka Menunjang Tugas Poltabes Bandung" (Utilizing Concentration of Shops as Implemented by Security Units in the Framework of Supporting the Mission of the Bandung City Police) (BA thesis, Jakarta: Perguruan Tinggi Ilmu Kepolisian, 1984), p. 44.

The criminal specter came out of the shadow into the light of day at a particular time: the early-1980s.[9] It appeared first in the mass media, then among the crowds, and soon after in Police theses like the one from which the above quotation is taken. There are several ways to explain why criminality appeared as a threat when it did. In the broadest terms, one could point to the fact that, in the history of the New Order, the early-1980s was a watershed period in both economic and political terms. Economically, 1973 to 1981 witnessed a tremendous oil boom which gave the state unprecedented revenues and leeway in pursuing policies of economic nationalism.[10] By 1982, however, the first signs of the oil bust began to appear, leaving the state in a weakened position with respect to foreign capital. As a result, 1982 and 1983 saw the introduction of liberalization policies, significant cuts in subsidies for energy and food, and a 27.6 percent devaluation of the currency.[11] Politically, the regime was also beginning to show the possibility of fracture.[12] Student demonstrations against the New Order in the late-1970s were followed in mid-1980 by the Petition of Fifty, in which many former supporters of Suharto expressed their opposition to the regime. Proponents of human rights and legal reform also managed to push through a new Code of Criminal Procedure which—on paper at least—curtailed some of the powers of the Police. In addition, beginning in 1979, a new, more professionally trained generation of military officers started to be appointed to command positions, a development that had the potential to undermine Suharto's monopolistic control over the military.[13] Finally, enough time had passed since the killings of 1965 that the specter of a re-emergent PKI (Indonesian Communist Party) had begun to lose some of its currency: threats to public order were increasingly portrayed as being "purely criminal" rather than as being manifestations of underground "political" opposition. Against the backdrop of these wider developments, the criminal specter can be seen both as the symptom of a structurally weakened state (and society) and as a convenient excuse for actions aimed at overcoming this weakness.

When the specter of crime appeared, it took very particular forms: *gali-gali* and *jawara* (or *jegger, jago, bromocorah*, etc.).[14] The former term, an acronym for "gangs of wild kids" (*gabungan anak-anak liar*), refers to organized gangs of young people involved in criminal behavior, while the latter terms refer to professional criminals or

---

[9] On the way in which the solar eclipse of 1983 was used to justify the mysterious killings, see John Pemberton, *On the Subject of "Java"* (Ithaca: Cornell University Press, 1994), pp. 314-316. On the shadowy world of crime during the colonial period, see Henk Schulte-Nordholt, "The Jago in the Shadow: Crime and 'Order' in the Colonial State in Java," *Review of Indonesian and Malaysian Affairs* 25: 1 (Winter 1991): 74-92.

[10] According to Jeffrey Winters, 1981 saw the peak in availability of state discretionary funds. See his *Power in Motion* (Ithaca: Cornell University Press, 1996), p. 122.

[11] Richard Robison, *Indonesia: The Rise of Capital* (Sydney: Allen & Unwin, 1986), pp. 125, 382-384.

[12] For a detailed account of tensions between members of the political elite and how they played themselves out in the Petrus campaign, see the excellent analysis by Bourchier, "Crime, Law and State Authority."

[13] Harold Crouch, *The Army and Politics in Indonesia*, rev. ed. (Ithaca: Cornell University Press, 1988), p. 357.

[14] In East Java they were known as *bromocorah*, in Sundanese as *jegger*. A *jegger* is not too different from a *jawara*, except that the term has more criminal connotations. *Bromocorah* has closer connotations with black magic.

charismatic toughs.[15] Taken separately, there was nothing new about these fears and their objects. As numerous studies have demonstrated, *jawara* and their ilk had been a source of dread in Java for many generations.[16] Similarly, at least during the New Order, the existence of youth gangs in urban areas had periodically been a matter of concern.[17] With the rise in violent crime at the beginning of the 1980s,[18] however, both *jawara* and *gali-gali* came under increasing scrutiny by the press and the government. Attracting particular concern were those *jawara* and *gali-gali* that were active in businesses or gangs providing "security services": debt collection, bodyguard rentals, security guard rentals, and the like. Such groups were thought to be taking crime into a new, organized, and supra-local realm. Both Siskamling and Petrus took these organizations as their object of attention.

SISKAMLING[19]

Siskamling was started in 1980 as an off-shoot of a larger government program called Kopkamtib (Komando Pemulihan Keamanan dan Ketertiban, or Command for the Restoration of Security and Order).[20] It represented an attempt by the New Order government to impose overt state control over local security practices by taking them out of the hands of organized private gangs. As the then Chief of Police and founder of the program, Awaloedin Djamin, explained in his autobiography:

> We definitely did not want to have the same thing happen in Indonesia that happened in other countries. In Japan, for example, the Yakuza forced protection on business people. Such a situation can give rise to excesses that are difficult to

---

[15] According to James Siegel, contemporary newspaper accounts of Petrus portrayed *gali-gali* as having the following characteristics: they were excessively violent (*sadis*), they were organized, they took in a lot of money, they had an uncontrolled force of expression, and they desired what everyone else desired. James T. Siegel, *A New Criminal Type in Jakarta: Counter-revolution Today* (Durham: Duke University Press, 1998). For a description of *preman*, see Loren Ryter's essay in this volume.

[16] Onghokham, "The Inscrutable and the Paranoid: An Investigation into the Sources of the Brotodiningrat Affair," in *Southeast Asian Transitions: Approaches Through Social History*, ed. Ruth T. McVey (New Haven: Yale University Press, 1978), pp. 112-157; John Smail, "Bandung in the Early Revolution, 1945-1946" (PhD dissertation, Cornell University, 1964); Sartono Kartodirdjo, *Protest Movements in Rural Java: A Study in Agrarian Unrest in the Nineteenth and Early Twentieth Centuries* (London: Oxford University Press, 1973); Schulte-Nordholt, "The Jago in the Shadow"; Robert Cribb, *Gangsters and Revolutionaries: The Jakarta People's Militia and the Indonesian Revolution 1945-1949* (Honolulu: University of Hawaii Press, 1991).

[17] For the most part, however, the Police regarded such gangs as a problem of juvenile deliquency and not as a serious threat.

[18] For the statistical characteristics of this crime wave, see Bourchier, "Crime, Law, and State Authority."

[19] Parts of this section have appeared in my "Surveillance and Territoriality in Bandung."

[20] Kopkamtib was initiated in October 1965. Headed first by Suharto, and later by General Sumitro and Admiral Sudomo, its aim was to "restore national security and order" by establishing a group within the military which had extraordinary powers and did not have to follow the procedures of criminal law. During the 1960s and 1970s, Kopkamtib was primarily used to suppress "communism" and repress political dissent. Siskamling and Petrus marked a shift in Kopkamtib's activities away from political to "criminal" threats.

overcome. The same was true in the early days of the mafia in the United States.[21]

The Indonesian "security" groups to which Awaloedin was probably referring were mainly of two types. The first were local, territorial gangs, based in residential districts, which had, over time, spread to adjacent bus terminals, markets, or shopping centers. In most major cities there were dozens of such gangs and turf wars were common. Many of these gangs were formed in the early days of the New Order and had been active in providing local "defense" in the context of the anti-communist pogroms.[22] Some derived their authority from charismatic leaders, some from the fact that their members' parents were prominent civil or military officials, and others from their successes in turf warfare.[23] By the beginning of the 1980s, some of these local gangs had actually become quite large, and as their members grew older, had become rather professionally-minded in their provision of "protection" to local businesses.[24] The second set of groups consisted of legal organizations rather than gangs. One of the most prominent of these was Pemuda Pancasila, the nation-wide youth group described elsewhere in this volume. Others included foundations and businesses formed by ex-convicts and similar people with few job possibilities. These groups—like Prems, Massa 33, etc.—provided security services to shops, transport companies, and wealthy business people, by hiring out "guards" for the protection of particular locales, individuals, events, or traffic routes. Some of the larger groups, like Massa 33, claimed memberships of as many as fifty thousand people, almost all ex-convicts and street-people.[25]

The growth of such private security services constituted a serious threat to the authority of the Police, since not only "protection" but even the pursuit, capture, and

---

[21] Awaloedin Djamin, *Pengalaman Seorang Perwira Polri* (Experiences of a Police Officer) (Jakarta: Pustaka Sinar Harapan, 1995), p. 240.

[22] In 1970, the Police listed thirty-nine gangs in South Jakarta alone. The names of some women's gangs: The Fu Man Chu, The Single Girl, The Pretty Doll, Monalisa, The Hunter Boys, Amigos. Regional gangs: Banten Boy, Batak Boy, AMS (Ambon-Maluku-Seram). ABRI (Armed Forces of the Republic of Indonesia) gangs: Gang Siliwangi, Gang Beerland, Gang Panser. Mixed gangs: Santana, The Trouble, SBC (Santa Barisan Setan), MBC (Manggarai Boy's Club), Sarlala (Sarang Laba Laba), Kasko (Kami Selalu Kompak), Kobel, Tjablak, Scarlet BCD, Motor Scarlet, Flamboyant, Devil Kids, The Casanova SK 700, Provost, Chabreek, 9 AK, Mr. Lonely Heart, The Bat Boy MDC, The Flaming Gos, Leo Patra, The Legos. In Bandung: Mexis, AMX, BBC (Buah Batu Boy's Club), Melos (Menak Lodaya Sadis), Megas (Menak Galunggung Sadis), Amek (Anak Muda Emong Karapitan), Hippies Dago, Dollar, Patorados, Bexis, TXC. See Soenarjo, "Suatu Analisa Tentang Tumbuhnya Gang Anak-Anak/Pemuda di Djakarta" (An Analysis of the Growth of Youth Gangs in Jakarta) (BA thesis, PTIK [Perguruan Tinggi Ilmu Kepolisian], 1970), pp. 59-63.

[23] For a study of a *jawara*-based gang, see Ayip Muflich, "Mardy Pelindung Gang (Suatu studi kasus)" (Mardy, Gang Protector—A Case Study) (BA thesis, Criminology Department, Universitas Indonesia, 1979).

[24] See, for example, the study of Gang "X", a gang which showed strong tendencies toward bureaucratization, in Leonard Tomasoa, "Kepemimpinan dalam Gang X (Suatu Studi terhadap Kehidupan Gang di Daerah Kebayoran Baru)" (Leadership in the X Gang—A Study of Gang Life in Kebayoran Baru) (BA thesis, Criminology Department, Universitas Indonesia, 1981).

[25] On Massa 33, see Farid Mappalahere, "Organisasi Massa 33 (studi kasus organisasi pengamanan swasta di Surabaya)" (The Massa 33 Organization—a Case Study of a Private Security Organization in Surabaya) (Surabaya: Airlangga University, PLPIIS, 1981/1982); see also *Surabaya Post*, March 18, 1995, p. 2.

punishment of suspects was increasingly being entrusted to these private groups. Siskamling aimed to counteract this tendency by establishing clear control over such non-state security businesses; it was hoped that Police control would prevent them from becoming mafia-like protection rackets (or at least that the Police would have a stake in these protection rackets). But Siskamling did not just target security businesses. In the domain of volunteer residential security as well, it aimed to establish a system for centralized monitoring and control, one of the goals of which was to discourage acts of communal violence against suspected thieves, sorcerers, and adulterers (and, undoubtedly, the Police themselves, as they were often targets of such violence). Moreover, Siskamling had purposes beyond just the monopolization of violence and the recuperation of "police" repressive powers. Both gangs and neighborhood watches were extremely effective tools for day-to-day surveillance of the population, and Siskamling provided a rubric for integrating them into the bureaucratic surveillance machine. In all these respects, then, Siskamling was viewed as a handy concept for increasing Police power in a society with an extremely low police-to-population ratio; and for doing so at little or no added cost to the state.[26]

Siskamling's system of control worked by dividing local security guards into three types: Satpam (*Satuan Pengamanan*, or Security Units), Kamra (or "Hansip"),[27] and *ronda*. In general, Satpam were responsible for protecting commercial and public buildings and spaces, while Hansip and *ronda* were responsible for patrolling residential neighborhoods. Satpam and Hansip were composed of salaried and uniformed guards, while the *ronda*, a far older institution, was still based on community obligation and used no uniforms. All three elements of the security system were brought under the control of the "Guidance of Society" (Bimbingan Masyarakat, or Bimmas) division of the Police.[28] Because the guards were not paid by the Police, however, Bimmas's sole functions were surveillance and training. This new system, which was centered on the Satpam, was explicitly meant to represent a departure from older forms of territorial security like the *ronda* and the *jawara*. As the head of Bimmas in Jakarta summed it up:

> A Satpam member has two "heads"; the firm, house or office at which he or she is employed, and the Police, from whom he—or she—gets training . . .
>
> Being in a Satpam is a profession. A Satpam member is not a *tukang ronda malam* [voluntary neighborhood night-patrol], nor are they *centeng* [night-watchmen]. They don't just open the door for people . . .
>
> What Satpam basically do is the Police's job, that's why we train them and are responsible for them.[29]

---

[26] In 1994, the ratios of police agents to population in various countries were as follows: Hong Kong: 1:220; Thailand: 1:228; Malaysia: 1:249; Singapore: 1:295; New Zealand: 1:416; Japan: 1:563; Philippines: 1:665; Indonesia: 1: 1,119. *Asia Week*, April 20, 1994.

[27] While technically called Kamra (Keamanan Rakyat, or Peoples' Security), these guards are generally referred to as Hansip.

[28] In addition to its work with Siskamling, Bimmas is also involved in training and working with youth groups.

[29] *Jakarta Post*, October 13, 1996.

The Satpam member was defined by what he or she was not: a thug, an old-fashioned voluntary *ronda*, or some kind of doorman. Like the Police, he or she should be treated with respect, and should consider himself or herself to be a professional.

In the new system, Bimmas would ensure, in the first place, that all schools, neighborhood organizations, markets, businesses, and so forth had an individual or committee responsible for overseeing "security"; this would facilitate co-ordination between the Police and those who paid the guards' salaries. The Police would also, however, survey the guards themselves. As part of this surveillance, Satpam and Hansip guards were to be counted and classified according to the education and training they had received. There were to be one-month and three-month courses provided for Satpam by the Police.[30] Such courses would include training in military formation, marching, self-defense, and how to guard a vital industry, combined with some lessons on how to make reports to the police, how to keep track of the identities of those coming and going from offices, factories, or housing complexes, and what procedure to follow when one caught a suspect in a crime. Those who passed the basic training course would be allowed to possess knives; and those who went through a special screening process would even be eligible to have guns. While Hansip members did not have to undergo such a special training course, in principle they were to join the Satpam at the local police station each week for training. Moreover, all three types of guards—the *ronda* included—were to be "controlled" at their posts on a regular basis by patrolling members of Bimmas. On these more informal occasions, the police could make sure that the guards were well-organized, gather information about threats for their intelligence reports, and give advice. Finally, to distinguish them from the public and from other security services, Satpam and Hansip guards were to wear standardized uniforms and carry identification issued by the Police. The Satpam's uniforms would consist of black pants and smart white shirts with logos on the arms and labels on the front saying "Satpam"; those of the Hansip were comparable but all in army green.

It was not just the guards themselves who were to be revamped. The security posts that used to be known as *gardu* or *pos ronda* were to become "*pos kamling.*" They were now to be counted, inspected, and classified according to their facilities; it was to be noted, for example, what building type the *pos* had (i.e. from what materials it was constructed), and whether it had weapons, maps, flashlights, beds, and so forth. Based on this information, the Police could then work together with Hansip and *ronda* guards to improve the facilities by making recommendations to the heads of RT's and RW's (Neighborhood Associations at different bureaucratic levels) about what had to be purchased (it was they who had to find a way to pay for improvements). Through a process of *kentonganisasi*, every *pos kamling* would be obliged to have a *kentongan* and a standardized code for warning of danger, as well as a list of who was responsible for guarding at what times. Ideally, *pos kamling* should also have handcuffs, weapons, and a phone, along with maps of the area they patrolled, lists of important residents, lists of so-called *residivis*,[31] and rules for the

---

[30] In Bandung in 1996, more than half of the Satpam guards working had attended these courses.

[31] *Residivis* has a broader sense than the English word recidivist: it refers not just to "repeat-offenders" but often to ex-convicts generally.

patrols.[32] These visuals and lists would mimic those found at the local police station. Similarly, the *pos keamanan* (security post) usually to be found in the parking lot or lobby of commercial establishments was to be subject to the same sorts of monitoring and recommendations made to Satpam employers if facilities were lacking.

In sum, if the program was a success, every locale—be it a neighborhood, a shop, a mall, a restaurant, a bus terminal, a government building, a parking lot, a school— would have at least one designated guard and an individual or committee responsible for working with the Police to supervise and organize both the watch and any other security measures. The guards themselves—through their training and use of Police modes of surveillance—would act as local representatives of Police authority.

The only real problem with this plan as it was introduced in the early-1980s was that people would not choose Satpam and Hansip over existing commercial security services. Not only did ex-convicts and gangs instill fear in potential robbers and thieves, they instilled still more fear in businesses and communities. In its earliest manifestation Siskamling thus tended to work not directly with the buyers of security services but with the sellers: those who controlled the gangs. Agreements were made with many of the emerging businesses run by ex-convicts and others, all of whom undoubtedly liked the idea of being legitimized by the state in return for submitting their members to training and guidance. For a brief period between 1980 and 1981, the Police, local government, and businesses created by gangs and ex-convicts thus enjoyed an openly co-operative arrangement that was probably economically beneficial for all involved. It was probably also politically beneficial to the ruling party, Golkar, which reportedly made use of these groups for strong-arm tactics in the run-up to the 1982 elections. The honeymoon was short-lived, however. In June 1982 the Chief of Police, under the banner of Kopkamtib, put out an order that effectively banned private security businesses.[33] While it remained legal to offer security consultation to businesses, to train prospective security guards, and to sell security devices, it was prohibited to rent out employees as guards. Furthermore, those businesses that continued to operate in the more restricted domain set out for them were subject to increased regulation. One new regulation was that employees had to be able to provide a "Letter of Good Behavior,"[34] meaning that no ex-convicts would be eligible to work in such firms; another forced firms to receive permission for their businesses from the provincial Police commander, and, if they intended to serve areas outside that command, from the national Chief of Police.

As a result of this new policy, many of the newly-established private security firms shut down or were driven underground. *Prems* Surabaya, for example, which in February 1982 had met with members of the provincial legislature (DPRD, Dewan Perwakilan Rakyat Daerah) and optimistically claimed that it anticipated a membership of fifty thousand people, about 60 percent of whom would be ex-

---

[32] Much of this mirrors the type of intelligence apparatus set up in East Timor. Compare, for example, the account found in Richard Tanter, "The Totalitarian Ambition: Intelligence Organisations in the Indonesian State" in *State and Civil Society in Indonesia*, pp. 244-245.

[33] Surat Keputusan Kapolri No. Pol. SKEP/220/VI/1982. June 14, 1982.

[34] The police-issued "Letter of Good Behavior" is a required document for almost any employment outside the informal sector (with the exception of foundations and businesses set up for employing and reforming ex-convicts). This regulation thus closed off one of the few avenues ex-convicts had to regain the rights of ordinary citizens, condemning them to a life of economic—as well as social—exile.

convicts, officially broke up less than a month later.[35] *Prems* Jakarta, on the other hand, restricted its official activities to providing legal aid and job-training to ex-convicts, while nonetheless continuing to offer illegal debt-collection and security services.[36] In Bandung, where the first official security guards were known as Satpamsus (Satuan Pengamanan Khusus, Special Security Unit), the new policy had the effect of reducing the powers of the *camat* (head of the *kecamatan*, or sub-district). Initially, Satpamsus had been under the control of the *camat* and the heads of the RT/RW, with some oversight from the Police and the Army. Under that system, the *camat* and RT/RW officials had been the ones profiting from commercial security, since they collected money from shops and factories in their areas and hired out local toughs as guards. With the new regulations, however, the *camat* and RT/RW were restricted to involvement in residential security, while control over commercial security became the responsibility of an alliance between business owners and the Police.

Perhaps the most interesting case, however, was Massa 33, which had been started in the early-1970s by a gang of *calo*[37] but had grown to be one of the largest of the ex-convict organizations, with branches throughout East Java. It continued to operate illegally for a time, but was eventually the target of a Police operation. As a result of this operation (and with permission from the Army and Surabaya's mayor) the Police, working together with the head of the bus terminal, took down personal data on everyone, supposedly screened-out the hardened criminals, and arranged for some of the others to undergo training to become Satpam. At Surabaya's bus terminal, where Massa 33 had been started, reformed gang members were then mixed in with an equal number of non-Massa 33 Satpam people and all became employees of the terminal.[38] In other words, Massa 33's organization was destroyed, but its reformable elements were integrated into a new organization based on co-operation between the Police and the terminal head. To ensure that the gang did not survive as a force within this new organization, it was diluted with non-gang members. Furthermore, since the remaining members of the gang were considered to be employees of the terminal rather than members of an outside organization, they could be subjected to all sorts of governmental and firm-based controls.

In sum, the overall result of the government's policy was to deny gangs and private security firms their economic and legal bases, and to appropriate, and subject to Police surveillance, their "reformable" elements. This policy—in combination with the "systematization" and regulation of existing *ronda* practices—set the stage for a massive expansion of Siskamling into all domains of urban life, a process that would

---

[35] *Surabaya Post*, February 22, 1982, p. 2; *Surabaya Post*, March 8, 1982, p. 2.

[36] Teuku Ashikin Husein, "Jasa-Jasa Keamanan oleh Yayasan Prems di Wilayah Pertokoan Blok M" (Security Achievements of the Prems Foundation in the Shopping District of Block M) (BA thesis, PTIK, 1983).

[37] *Calo* is a term meaning scalper, broker, or go-between. *Calos* at bus terminals approach customers with scalped tickets, outflanking queues and regular prices. They usually demand a cut from bus drivers or bus companies.

[38] One of the reasons ABRI was in favor of Satpam was that they would provide employment opportunities for low-ranking retirees whose pensions were very small (and perhaps would keep them out of trouble).

continue throughout the 1980s and 1990s.[39] It also created a situation in which gangs that continued to operate were criminalized (with notable exceptions like Pemuda Pancasila), while members of those which had disbanded were divided into two clear groups: corrigibles and incorrigibles. In other words, it set the stage for Petrus.

PETRUS

According to David Bourchier, who has analyzed the way the Petrus campaign unfolded, the killings of "criminals" began in earnest in March 1983 in the Central Javanese city of Yogyakarta and lasted for at least two years.[40] During that time, at least five thousand and perhaps more than ten thousand people deemed *bromocorah*, *preman*, or *gali* were killed. The killings were concentrated in the larger cities, like Jakarta, Surabaya, Bandung, Medan, and Semarang. Although the murders were condemned by international human rights groups, many press accounts were more or less approving of the government's methods for much of the campaign. While there were critics who complained that such extra-judicial punishments would undermine the rule of law, press interviews with people "on the street" almost invariably indicated a certain relief that "criminals" were being eliminated from city bus terminals, train stations, markets, and squares. (Fifteen years after the bulk of the killings took place, such sentiments seem to have changed very little.)

Surveillance or Death: Lists, Operations, Tattoos

From the standpoint of its organization, Petrus was rooted in the tradition of surveillance. It depended first of all on a process of identification, which provided a representation of the "criminal" element in society, and secondly on an *operasi* that targeted particular people in the world "out there" based on the labels that had been attached to them. It was centrally planned and organized most likely by General Benny Murdani who then had control over the Armed Forces, Kopkamtib, and military intelligence; and it employed a discourse borrowed from hygiene operations, claiming to be aimed at "cleansing" the nation's cities of the criminal "cancer" that threatened them. [41] Bourchier describes the way the killings took place as follows:

---

[39] The non-gang guards hired were initially mostly low-level ABRI retirees, but as the program expanded they came to include young men and women, almost all of whom were either villagers or people who came from the poorer areas of town.

[40] Bourchier, "Crime, Law and State Authority," p. 185. In September 1982, before Petrus began, the family of a military commander in East Java had been murdered by thugs. The military's response was to avenge the killings by executing the suspects and throwing their corpses in a river. Nico Schulte-Nordholt, "Violence and the Anarchy of the New Order State" (unpublished). It is likely that this event and similar killings in the Jember-Bondowoso area some months before were the immediate models for the Petrus killings. See Bourchier, ibid. One wonders, however, if these East Java commanders got their idea from a wave of killings they had handled in Jember in 1981. The victims of these killings, of which there were twenty-seven, were accused of being sorcerers and *bromocorah*, and were killed by the "masses" in the villages where they lived. They too were tied-up or placed in sacks and thrown into rivers. *Surabaya Post*, March 2, 1981.

[41] Bourchier, "Crime, Law and State Authority," p. 184.

Criminals, gang members, or ex-prisoners, frequently tattooed and almost always young and male, would be met in their houses or in the street by a group of four or five heavily built men. In many cases they would shoot their victim where they found him. More often they would bundle him (or them) into a jeep or Toyota Hardtop and drive off into the night. The victim would be taken to a quiet place and shot through the head and chest at close range with .45 or .38 caliber pistols. His corpse would then either be tossed into a river or left in some public place, outside a cinema, a school, or on a footpath of a busy street. Victims frequently had their hands bound, and often bore marks of torture. The following day there would be a short report about the finding of a *"mayat bertato,"* (tattooed corpse) in the local paper, usually accompanied by grisly pictures.[42]

Bourchier goes on to note that there were also a number of mass graves into which were dumped the corpses of large numbers of murdered men. This was done on a highly routinized basis: every Friday and Sunday, for example. In the early part of the campaign, people living near the graves were permitted to witness the killings.

From this description, it is clear that the killings followed a pattern very similar to the less violent operations which were such a prominent feature of New Order life: operations against pedicab drivers, drug dealers, prostitutes, vagrants, women's fertility (i.e. coercive family planning), and the like. Just as in the *operasi* aimed at drug pushers, for example, the agents descended on their targets and removed them from the scene in order to maintain an image of order. The removal was then followed by the staging of a spectacle in which the targeted objects or people were shown to have truly been eliminated (the dead bodies displayed for all to see and the drugs crushed or burned).[43] Furthermore, as with *operasi* like those conducted under the rubric of Family Planning, the solution Petrus posed for the criminal contagion was not just local elimination but heightened surveillance. Bourchier's description of the mechanics of Petrus in Yogyakarta highlights these two objectives:

The procedure in Yogyakarta appears to have been that police intelligence supplied the garrison commander with a list naming hundreds of suspected criminals and ex-prisoners in the region. The garrison then put together a blacklist and issued a public ultimatum to all *galis* (without, however, naming names) to "surrender immediately" to garrison headquarters. Those who did, and these numbered several hundred, were required to fill out detailed forms, providing their life history as well as data on all their family members and friends. They were also required to sign statements agreeing to refrain from criminal activities or face "firm action" from the authorities. Each *gali* was obliged to carry a special card and report to the garrison on a regular basis. Those who did not turn up to be registered, or did not keep their appointments with the garrison, were hunted down and killed by squads of military men.[44]

---

[42] Ibid, p. 186.

[43] Pemberton, describing the killings in Solo, notes that the Solonese morgue during this period, which was inundated with corpses, had a kind of open-door policy for people to come and look. Pemberton, *On the Subject of "Java,"* p. 312. For a description of the logic of more mundane *operasi*, see my "Territoriality and Surveillance in Bandung."

[44] Bourchier, "Crime, Law and State Authority," pp. 185-186.

In making its ultimatum public, the garrison was saying that it already had completed the process of identification and had a list of "criminals" in its possession. How were these criminals identified? Bourchier notes that the source of this list was the Police. The existence of such lists was, in fact, nothing new, since police and village heads have been compiling lists of so-called "butterflies," *bromocorah*, and *residivis* in their regions since the early part of the century.[45] With the Petrus ultimatum, however, these lists took on a new significance. In the past, *residivis* subjected to heightened surveillance were clearly listed by local authorities and the rules of reporting laid out. There was no mystery about such lists and there was actually a fair amount of flexibility about who was listed, since a person who behaved well in his community might well be left off the lists because of a local official's "oversight." Moreover, the lists themselves served a primarily administrative function, with the work of actual surveillance being carried out by the *ronda* and spies. This meant that a "butterfly" was kept aware of his status as a suspect by being subjected to repetitive monitoring by his peers. The Petrus ultimatum changed this state of affairs in three ways. In the first place, it said that the lists had already been compiled and so there would be no flexibility in the process of identification. Second, it made a point of keeping the contents of the lists secret. Third, it proposed an unprecedented equation: an unsurveilled "criminal" was equivalent to being dead. Each of these points will be discussed below.

In Indonesia, the idea that a government decision cannot be changed is usually greeted by cynicism accompanied by statements to the effect that in Indonesia anything is possible with money and influence. Indeed, one of the more common mantras recited by everyone from coolies to elite lawyers is that: "In Indonesia, everything can be bought." Yet when speaking of blacklists such an attitude is far less prevalent; even people who are otherwise unimpressed by state power show a certain anxiety and respect when the topic comes up. Consider, for example, Mr. Yanto, an older man living in Bandung who fitted very closely the definition of a Petrus target. As a youth he had been a member of street gangs, become known as a fighter, and later joined a group of armed robbers. Just after Petrus he completed a seventeen-year prison term for murder and armed robbery, and when I met him he was working as a bodyguard for an ethnic Chinese businessman. He was a gruff man and prone to sudden outbursts of anger, but he was also past middle-age, a bit weary, and not as good at hiding his kindness as he undoubtedly had been at one time. Nonetheless, he was always extremely self-confident and felt capable of manipulating all sorts of outcomes in his relations with the police, judges, and others. When I raised the topic of Petrus, it was he who mentioned the lists and became visibly frightened by the possibility that he might be on a post-Petrus blacklist. When I suggested that he might be able to pull some strings to make sure his name did not appear on such a list, he responded that it was impossible: "Once your name is on that list, it's done. You can't do anything about it."

That blacklists might be taken to be immutable—and could actually be so in many cases—shows that they are close to the heart of the state's power. At stake for the state in such lists is something far greater than the fate of the individual in

---

[45] For a description of list-taking practices at the start of the century, see my "The Tattoo and the Fingerprint: Crime and Security in an Indonesian City" (PhD dissertation, Cornell University, 1999), chapter 3.

question and greater even than the benefits derived from establishing interpersonal debts. It is something important enough that to subtract a name from the list would constitute a threat of the first order to state power.[46] A clue as to what this might be is provided by a story not about the Petrus blacklists but about their political counterpart. It was told to me by a wealthy businessman in the private sector. As a person with some influence, he had gathered together some high-level military men in hopes of getting political charges against an old friend from his hometown dropped. Accustomed to dealing with such figures in the context of his business, he thought he might at least be able to make sure that his friend was faced with lesser charges. But, when he explained that his friend did not pose a threat and that his offending actions had been a mistake, his guests asked him: "Do you know who [your friend] really is?" They then proceeded to ask him questions about his friend's daily activities, which he could not answer. Finally, they refused to do anything in the case, saying, "Even if you've known [*kenal*] him for a long time, you can't be certain you really know [*tahu*] who he is." It was an event that clearly made a lasting impression on the man, since he told the story to me more than once; moreover, the way he told it made it clear that the questions had genuinely caused him to doubt whether he knew his friend or not.

The story shows that what was at stake for the state in its blacklisting was nothing less than its power of recognition. The state needed to privilege its own "truth" about peoples' identities over competing claims about *who* people really are. By making the lists immutable, state representatives establish a domain where the authority of local knowledge, familiarity, and the like are ultimately denied, and where the knowledge produced using state surveillance techniques is stated to be "true." In the years before Petrus, it might have been possible to use one's own perception of oneself or one's neighbors' perceptions of one to influence the way one was identified by the state. Certainly, it was possible to maintain a local identity that did not directly correspond to that on the files in the state archive. In this respect, many "criminals" were actually regarded as heroes in their local communities. With the Petrus ultimatum, however, any other sources of recognition were denied. In the end, the ultimatum asserted, the state knows people better than their friends do; better even than they know themselves. And although all sorts of other "truths" dictated by the government may be subject to localization and corruption, this domain is untouchable.

The Petrus lists were not only immutable, they were also secret. Secrecy was important not only because it asserted the exclusivity of state knowledge but also because it demanded that all citizens ask themselves if they might be "criminals." In principle, at least, the situation was not so different from that during the killings of "communists" in 1965 and 1966 when people were forced to ask, "Am I PKI or non-PKI?"; only now they were forced to ask themselves about their "criminality."[47] To answer this question they had to imagine what the state perceived criminality to be and how the state imagined them to be. And since the contents of the lists were not made public, the implicit demand was that anyone who had ever been remotely suspected by the state, had been in prison, or had committed a crime, should

---

[46] Adding names, because of local and personal politics, was probably easier.

[47] See the famous article by Pipit Rochijat, "Am I PKI or non-PKI?" in *Indonesia* 40 (October 1985): 37-56.

voluntarily recognize himself as suspect, even if the person immediately judged himself to be innocent in this regard.[48]

Failing to recognize oneself as the state did could prove fatal: if one's name was on the list and one did not submit to heightened surveillance, one could be killed.[49] It was above all those people who hid from the state, or even worse, asserted another identity against that given to them by the state who would be killed. Lieutenant Colonel Hasbi, the Acehnese head of Yogyakarta's garrison, put this in the starkest terms when explaining why the shootings were necessary: "Why shoot? Basically we want to work in a humane way. But there are those who want to fight back. They want to show off their self-identity [*identitas dirinya*]."[50] It was these types, those who refused to submit to registration and monitoring, choosing instead to "show off" their own identities, that the campaign targeted. The state was thus reserving the ultimate power of recognition for its surveillance apparatus: the power over life and death. In theory, at least, agreeing to suspect one's own criminality, not just one's politics, was the new condition of survival for subjects of the New Order state.

That Petrus identified its "criminal" victims through blacklists and that the campaign was designed to demonstrate the overwhelming power of surveillance is only one side of the story. The other side is more interesting and difficult to understand, and it concerns a quite different impression that developed in many quarters regarding how victims were identified. In brief, it was the impression that targets for the killings were identified not by hidden lists but by the very visible markings on their bodies: tattoos. Certainly many ex-convicts had tattoos, but rumors seemed to suggest that having tattoos was sufficient in itself for identifying a criminal, and that the mysterious shooters were hunting down anyone with tattoos. Such rumors might well have originated in press reports about the discovery of corpses, in which frequent reference was made to the victims' tattoos. In any case, many people with tattoos were sufficiently frightened by such rumors that they tried to get rid of their tattoos. During a period of just two weeks in June 1983, two hospitals in Bandung recorded sixty-three people who paid to have plastic surgery to remove tattoos. Others tried to remove their tattoos themselves. Many inmates at Bandung's prison cut their skin off with razor blades or tried to burn their tattoos off using caustic soda; others outside the prison used hot irons (nowadays, one frequently sees bus conductors and the like with huge scars where their tattoos used to be).[51]

How are we to understand this alternate explanation for how Petrus targets were identified? What is the relation between visible tattoos and hidden lists? The relation between lists and tattoos as methods for identifying "criminals" and targets for killings could be understood to be an unproblematic supplemental relation. This is, at least, the gist of the following remarks, which were made toward the end of the

---

[48] In Yogyakarta, the people *Tempo* mentioned as being worried about this ultimatum were all members of protection rackets and gangs. *Tempo*, April 16, 1983, p. 54.

[49] Of course there was no guarantee that those who reported to the authorities would not be killed (for a case of this in Yogyakarta, see *Tempo*, April 16, 1983, p. 54). And we will never know how many people failed to report because they were *too* frightened of being killed and how many failed to report because they did not see themselves as suspect and thus were not frightened at all.

[50] *Tempo*, May 14, 1983, p. 55.

[51] *Surabaya Post*, June 18, 1983, p. 1.

Petrus campaign in 1983 by a member of Reserse's (Criminal Investigation Division of the Police) Identification section in Jakarta:

> It is clear that a tattooed person is not [necessarily] a criminal, but as I often handle the various types of criminals there are, there has at last arisen an indirect impression when I see a tattooed person, such that my inner voice says, "Why it's just like a criminal." And the majority of those who often wear tattoos are those who really are criminals, which is to say, those who have been in and out of prison or who have been blacklisted by the police. And in connection with my work, it is clear that tattoos are special signs that have to be noted in people's identity files, particularly those who have business with the police. And as a matter of fact, historically, before the discovery of a fingerprinting system, tattoos were used as a means for identification just like brands made with hot iron.[52]

This police officer, at the nation's center of criminal identification and registration, conveys his belief that tattoos are an "indirect" sign of criminal identity. Someone like him, he suggests, who has had countless occasions to look back and forth between the lists of convicts and the bodies before him, can pretty safely say that there is a correspondence between "criminals" defined by technologies of surveillance and bodies with tattoos. In this initial comment, we see one possible way in which tattoos might have functioned as a support of the state's claims that its lists and its operations were very precise. For as soon as doubts about precision emerged, people could be reassured by the evidence that the bodies that were turning up in rivers and on the streets were not just any bodies, they were tattooed bodies. For the officer, reassurance comes not just from experience but also through a chain of associations that allows him to get from criminals to tattoos via identity cards and back to criminals again via fingerprints. This chain of associations runs as follows:

criminal —> prisoner —> blacklist —> identity file —> tattoo noted in file —> tattoo on body —> brand on body —> fingerprint —> criminal.

The chain ensures that the gap between the bodies in the world "out there" and the identities on file is bridged by an intermediate figure: the fingerprint or the tattoo. Yet two things about the policeman's statements suggest that he is giving tattoos more significance than would the files. First, he notes at the end of the chain of associations that brands and tattoos historically preceded identity files (fingerprints, lists, etc.) as a way of signifying the "criminal," thereby giving the latter a primacy over the former. Second, he says that whenever he sees tattoos his inner voice (*hati*) says, "Why it's just like a criminal." These statements work against what he started off saying, which was that tattoos signify criminality only by virtue of a statistical correlation. Rather, it turns out that they are "special signs" that in him

---

[52] Cited in Arief Sumarwoto, "Latar Belakang Kebiasaan Pelaku Kejahatan Tertentu Memakai Tatto Sebagai Salah Satu Ciri Penampilannya" (Background on the Custom Among Certain Criminals of Using Tattoos as One Kind of Self-Presentation) (BA thesis, PTIK, 1984), p. 77. This thesis itself raises the question of whether a person wearing a tattoo is necessarily a criminal. It indicates that the association between the two—and their life or death implications—did not always sit well with the Police.

provoke an immediate equation with criminality even when they appear on someone not being processed for heightened surveillance. If this is the case, might it not then be possible that the lists used in Petrus had a similar re-enforcing effect on what had been a prior suspicion of tattoos? Consider the statements of a food seller at a market in Jakarta:

> It's clear that people with tattoos are criminals [*penjahat*] *Pak*, or at least that their hearts and actions aren't good. Before, almost every night the small traders here were asked for money. It's true it wasn't a lot, *Pak*, but that money meant a lot to us. After a time I came to know the person, but didn't know him really well. He turned up only asking for money and then left again. He and his friends indeed had tattoos as their distinguishing marks. So that this gave rise to a hunch that tattooed people are criminals. What's more when meeting those guys, at least I had to be careful, maybe they could be criminals [*jangan-jangan orang ini penjahat*]. My hunch was strengthened after I read in the papers that lots of tattooed people were shot to death, and they said all of them were criminals. But now we here are all calm because those guys who asked for money each night are no longer. Maybe they ran away or were shot by someone.[53]

Here one finds what is probably the most ubiquitous local description of a *preman* or *jegger*: someone who is known, but to whom one would not admit being close, who wears tattoos, and who turns up asking for money. With respect to the tattoos, this man's answer shows a movement from (at most) a hunch to something near certainty that the tattoos he sees mean criminality (and therefore someone whose death is meaningless). One can see in the *"jangan-jangan orang ini penjahat"* that the recognition of whether this person really is criminal, rather than just being "not good," is something that has to come from outside (or perhaps, that if it came from inside the local sphere the man would already have been killed). The confirmation of his suspicion comes from the reports he reads about Petrus.

In sum, while the formal targets of the Petrus campaign were professional and violent criminals, the way in which these criminals were identified was subject to two interpretations. One interpretation suggested that identification primarily followed the logic of surveillance. Hence tattoos were merely a supplemental form of identification (found on corpses) that could have the effect of containing fears about who criminals were. You could see with your own eyes that not just anyone was being killed. Another interpretation suggested that the targets of Petrus were not ex-convicts and repeat offenders as defined by law and by the surveillance apparatus, but people with "special signs" on their bodies. In this interpretation tattoos were already cause for suspicion about someone's "criminality" and the state's lists and dead criminals acted to confirm what—in retrospect at least—one already knew. The fact that tattoo-wearers might be the real targets of Petrus caused Arief Sumarwoto, the policeman who wrote the thesis from which the above quotations were taken, some consternation. For his thesis he interviewed convicts, police, and others, and did statistical analyses to determine what percentage of so-called *residivis* wore tattoos and what percentage of tattoo-wearers were *residivis*. Writing during Petrus, he was clearly bothered by the fact that targeting tattooed bodies might lead to killing the wrong people. Perhaps he was disturbed by the operation and had to

---

[53] Ibid., p. 75.

write about its injustices even if they were defined merely as a technical failure of reference; or perhaps he had a tattoo himself.

By suggesting that blacklists were not the only way "criminals" were identified, I am not trying to argue that Petrus targeted tattoo-wearers rather than repeat-offenders. Although it is possible that the above thesis-writer's fears (fears shared, as we have seen, by tattoo-wearers) were justified, and that people were killed simply for having tattoos, the centralized, bureaucratic form Petrus took makes it likely that lists were what actually determined who was killed in most instances. Nonetheless, the centrality given to tattoos as a supposed form of identification during the campaign should not be dismissed. While it may not tell us the names of who was killed, it provides an important clue as to what people believed the campaign was targeting and its symbolic importance. The final two sections of this essay will address these questions, first, by way of a rather extended digression on the different meanings attached to tattoos at the time of Petrus; and second, by interpreting a few stories told about Petrus and Petrus-like killings by participants and observers of the campaign.

Tattoos and Identity

In their descriptions of what led them to wear tattoos in the first place, some of Sumarwoto's tattoo-wearing respondents suggest how these bodily inscriptions relate to identity, and why they may indicate to outsiders an anti-social or even criminal identity.

> When I first became a sailor, sailing many seas, months in other countries, there arose a feeling of longing for my parents, relatives, and friends . . . so I tried to look for something to do just for the fun of it. I noticed among my friends those who wore tattoos. I was interested and made some just for fun. And it's true that it can chase away the feeling of loneliness. To fill empty time it was better than just daydreaming, thinking about impossibilities [*yang tidak-tidak*].[54]

Tattoos, in this context, provide a distraction from desires that cannot be realized by focusing one's attention on what is present. They give shape to a self that is based on a disavowal or a postponement of desires for others (family, friends).[55] This explanation of tattoos was expressed by several of Sumarwoto's respondents, who linked the power of distraction to the pain that making the tattoos caused. For the mariner above, tattoos also became the basis for a collective memory shared among those who were on his ship; after the passage above he went on to describe how they exchanged tattoos as "mementos" (*kenang-kenangan*) so that when they got home they would not forget their times together.

---

[54] Ibid., p. 68.

[55] This is not to say that the self is necessarily an "individual" person; it can be a collectivity too, as in the following: "I first started wearing tattoos because that is what my friends did. Even though our group didn't have a specific name, between us we had customs that we all followed. Because my friends all wore tattoos, I too joined them in wearing tattoos." Ibid., p. 70. Here the group shares its desires but in a way that does not involve taking on a name. It is not a group that is "looking for a name" (as people often say about gangs in Indonesia) by challenging others to duels and by displaying its power.

That tattoos are a way of defining a personal or collective self by localizing desires and by creating a memory of these desires, means that they have an affinity to language. In the following statement from a prison inmate, this affinity is exemplified by the fact that tattoos can actually become symbols of what one desires.

> The first time I came into the prison in 1979 I saw that many of the inmates had tattoos with all sorts of different pictures. I was attracted and made some myself with the help of some friends who knew how to do it. After I got out of prison the first time I realized that these tattoos were not liked by my parents and they immediately treated me as a son without value. Because of that I felt there was no use any more in doing good and I made more tattoos on this body of mine. To get money I committed more crimes. Finally I often came in and out of this prison. With all these tattoos I wanted to be valued by my friends. Although my body is small as you can see, in other peoples' eyes I want to be seen as terrifying [*serem*]. I made these tattoos while I was fantasizing [*berangan-angan*], fantasizing about things that couldn't be had at the time. Like the picture of the bottle shows that I am a drinker, and the picture of the syringe shows I am a drug addict; and you can see all the other tattoos on my arms, legs, chest, and back that can't even be counted anymore [they are so many]. Me and my friends in the prison already feel that with tattoos on our bodies we are treated as people who are in and out of prison. I feel like I've already been stamped as a criminal.[56]

Here tattoos do not merely localize desire by preventing it from straying beyond the attainable; they actually provide a symbolic representation of what these desires are. (For this man, the desires are so many they cannot even be counted.) While there is undoubtedly some satisfaction in this for the inmate, he also learns that his tattoos make him a bit of a pariah in the eyes of his family. They treat him as a "son without value," and, it seems, refuse to give him money, thereby forcing him to find it by committing more crimes. A good son, presumably, would channel desire through the family and by virtue of this would be repaid by being given money (the parents' way of indicating their desire). But the tattoos connote a channeling of desires that either stop with his body and its addictions or else lead back to other tattoos worn by inmates and gangs. Either way, the language of tattoos is an alien language that is anathema to the language of kinship,[57] and not just kinship but sometimes religion too. The head of the national Council of Ulama (Islamic scholars) said this to Sumarwoto:

> Allah created the human body with perfection. If making tattoos is done by causing the body pain, by wounding it and then inserting ink in the scars, then such an action is wrong, and even more so if this is done without a meaningful aim. These things are reminiscent of the time before people knew religion. They made tattoos as a tool of worship, or as a reason for bodily invulnerability, bodily beauty, and so on . . . And I hear that people who have tattoos can't be made wet by water. So this will disturb the flow of *wudlu* [water of ritual

---

[56] Ibid., p. 62.

[57] This is obviously not the case when the tattoos are a rite of passage for members of kin groups; but then the tattoos are given by the kin community, not self-inflicted or gang-inflicted.

purification] or can cause the failure of the obligatory bath. It's clear that all of this cannot be brought to prayer.[58]

One presumes that a meaningful aim of bodily harm would include ritualized circumcision, which takes place at the hands and under the gaze of selected members of the familial, religious, and neighborhood community. But tattoos do not have such meaningfulness, since they are done "just for fun"; or even if they do have significance, it is a pre-religious, primitive, idolatrous meaningfulness, of which one should be suspicious. As was true in the case of the son and his family described above, desires are channeled in the wrong way; in this case the head of the Council of Ulama asserts that the desires of a tattooed man are channeled to escapism and fetishes instead of to prayer and to God.

In sum, there is indeed a sense in which tattoos assert a certain "self-identity." Both family authorities and religious authorities can find them to be signs of a lack of attention to their respective hierarchies and therefore signs of a misplaced channeling of desires. Undoubtedly the assertion of identity through tattoos is all the more powerful for being territorial: impressed on the body in a permanent form. Especially when they are visible, tattoos serve as a constant reminder to those who see them of an improper channeling of desires.

For the state, in the 1980s, tattoos were additionally offensive because they seemed to assert an identity that could not be traced back to state systems of identification. They were precisely not fingerprints or brands, both of which would be stamped using the hands of the Police under the watchful eye of the state. Tattoos, rather, were self-inflicted, and in prisons at least, were done in hiding from the guards since such practices were against regulations.

With Petrus, however, all this changed. By virtue of the secret lists of criminals, the corpses displayed for all to see, and the hundreds of newspaper headlines emblazoned with the term "tattooed corpse," tattoos were now both criminalized and indelibly associated in people's minds with a form of death that clearly led back to the state. They had become brands, or as the inmates called them: stamps (*cap*). The people who found themselves unexpectedly recognized by the eye of eyes had either to accept the omnipotence of that eye by submitting to perpetual surveillance or to risk death. Some tried a different tactic: to rid themselves of this stamp. The scars they created in the process are perhaps the most vivid reminders of what battles over identities entail when they are fought on the surfaces of bodies. And although these scars necessarily point back to Petrus they do so in a way that does not lead back to death but to survival; they indicate someone who was confronted by the state (at least in their thoughts) and lived to have their scars tell the story.

The Power of Tattoos

While tattoos may assert "self-identity" against kinship, religion, and the state, this only scratches the surface of their apparent power. Tattoos are often associated with something far greater, like invulnerability. In this regard, they make greatest sense when inscribed on the bodies of *jawara*, or *jago*, who are known for their courage and fighting skills. Their ability to "horrify," in the words of the inmate respondent above, fits well with what the *jago* and *jawara* stand for. In the responses

---

[58] Ibid., p. 74.

given to Sumarwoto, this power of tattoos to cause fear is a constant theme. Some indeed craved this power. Another inmate:

> My attitude has always been that I want to be considered a *jagoan*, so not long after going to prison I often stood out in various activities, and in tattoos too I made as many as possible. With so many tattoos on my body many people pay attention to me.[59]

Here tattoos are part of a larger "attitude of acting like a game cock" (*jagoan*). They make him stand out by making people pay attention to him. Not all people wanted this extra attention. One of the respondents actually feared that he would be recognized as someone too powerful: "I felt scared [coming into prison with so many tattoos] that I would be stamped as the most *jagoan*."[60] Those who did want the power tattoos provided them, however, got many and put them in the most visible places. Magically, these were not merely seen as attributes of the *jago* character, however, but as powers in their own right. Another inmate:

> Those inmates who truly [*betul-betul*] are not bad/criminal [*penjahat*] usually they only wear a few tattoos and these are in hidden locations. It's like after having tattoos there arises a feeling of pride so that it gives off an impression of being admired [*dikagumi*], respected [*disegani*], and all this gives a push to increase one's daring to be determined no matter what [*keberanian untuk berbuat nekad*].[61]

Having visible tattoos, by giving an impression of being admired, actually pushes one to be *nekad* or determined. It is as if they have a force of their own that creates a determination with no bounds. An "unlimited power of expression," as James Siegel has called it. This force comes from the ability of tattoos to capture others' attention, to implicate their desires in one's own. The appropriation of such power begins with a process of mimicry:

> It felt good to have tattoo-capital on the body [*modal tatoo di badan*], there was a feeling of being respected, especially by those who just entered the prison. I remember the first time I entered prison, if I saw someone with lots of tattoos, in my gut I felt fearful too, and even more so if his body was big. After I got out of prison for the second time, the capital I had from having been in prison, along with the large number of tattoos on this body of mine, added to my confidence to do crimes.[62]

Seeing himself (and others) fearing and paying attention to tattoos, this inmate wants this attention for himself. He mimics them so that he too will have the power he desires: the fear and respect of new inmates. The power that he gets from this mimicry is a form of capital that gives him the courage to commit more crimes which

---

[59] Ibid., p. 65.

[60] Ibid., p. 66. This respondent also noted that he did not put the tattoos on all at once because there was no way he could have stood the pain.

[61] Ibid., p. 66.

[62] Ibid., p. 63.

makes more people admire him, which makes him commit more crimes, etc. It is difficult to see where this process would end (except, perhaps, in Petrus).

With this man, it is not just that he "desires what everyone desires" (money, a nice house, etc.), as Siegel has noted,[63] but that he desires what some people do not desire: other people's attention. His command over other people's attention, by virtue of his fetishized tattoos, is what makes him such a fearsome character and makes them respect him. Everyone is looking at him. And insofar as they share his desires too, he has charisma. At least he does for as long as inmates are "new" and he can still command their attention.

*   *   *

When the specter of crime appeared in the light of day in the early-1980s, its effect was not unlike the effect tattoos had on new inmates. Or at least that is how the media and the government portrayed it. The *gali-gali* seemed *nekad* in their audacious crimes, and through the press everybody was looking at them, admiring and fearing their power. Their organization of protection rackets, moreover, seemed to give their power currency which they could trade for economic gain. It was as if a hierarchy based on tattoos, duels, and territorial authority was taking shape alongside established hierarchies based on kinship, office, and rank. This was not merely a question of "self-identity" but a question of political power. Of course, it is difficult to imagine that these organizations posed any genuine threat to President Suharto's authority. Most of the organizations were more like unions of the disenfranchised than true mafias. Furthermore, even those organizations that had not been formed under the auspices of the military were quickly subordinated, through Siskamling, to Police and government authority. So why did President Suharto opt for Petrus? It may have been, as Bourchier has suggested, that such organizations were tied to a particular fraternity[64] within the military and that Suharto felt threatened by this alternative power base; or that their ties to local authorities threatened to undermine Jakarta's ability to control the regions.[65] Whatever the immediate political reasons were, we shall see below that Petrus did indeed have consequences both for the power of fraternities and for that of local communities. In different ways, both were implicated in, and transformed by, the killings whose overall symbolic effect was to appropriate the power represented by "criminals" and embed it within the hierarchy of the state.

Mimicry and Appropriation in the Killings

1. "Criminals" and the State

The tendency of the Petrus killings to mimic the violence attributed to the figure of the *gali* has been analyzed by James Siegel. According to Siegel, this mimicry is especially apparent in the excessive (what the Indonesian press calls *sadis*, or sadistic)

---

[63] See Footnote 15 above.

[64] My terminology, not his. I use the term "fraternities" to describe such intra-institutional gangs partly because they are overwhelmingly male and partly because—especially within ABRI—they often trace their alliances (and rivalries) back to the Military Academy.

[65] Bourchier, "Crime, Law, and State Authority," p. 195

violence used to kill the campaign's victims. This sadism was particularly odd since the express objective of the campaign was to rid society once and for all of such excesses. If that was the objective, why did the state use the methods that it supposedly deplored?

> [B]y multiply wounding these *gali* and accusing the *gali* of acting in just that way, the government, and President Suharto himself, implicitly identified themselves with their victims even as they asserted their differences from them. It is the imitation of the criminal that is predominant while the assertion of difference at this point was mere camouflage.
>
> . . . The government . . . turned *gali* into corpses intended to indicate not merely the danger of anyone daring to act as they were presumed to act, but also the unlimited power, inherent not merely in the sadistic quality of these criminals but in something beyond it that made it necessary to kill each criminal several times. When it is unrestricted, the power of the government is claimed to be equal to the power of its adversaries. The force of the government was made equivalent to the power attributed to these corpses precisely when the victims were murdered multiple times.[66]

Exactly how this works on a local level is apparent in the following summary of what happened during Petrus in a neighborhood in Bandung. It was told to me by a young man who was familiar with street culture in that neighborhood.

> [Fieldnotes][67] In this area alone there were three killed [during the Petrus campaign]. Everyone knows who the *preman* are because they have their own *lokasi* [place] from which they collect money. If they aren't paid they will stab people, burn the store, etc. They will often ask people for their watches. People are scared of them and do what they say. To find the *preman* the military used lists of ex-cons (*residivis*). The usual way of picking them up was with a Land Rover. If kids saw a green Land Rover with yellow on the door enter the neighborhood they would run in fear. The military would then go to the *preman*'s house and haul him out into the car (he repeats Land Rover as it clearly stood out in his mind). It didn't matter if the *preman* had already stopped doing bad things, lived with his family, prayed or whatever. He would still be hauled off. One was even a *kepala* [head of an] RT. When they started turning up dead, people talked about how they were being killed. Some of them were shot but wouldn't die because they had *ilmu* [magical powers]. If they were shot the bullets would enter and they wouldn't be able to get up, but they wouldn't die. The only way to kill them was to tie their feet with *benang plastik* [plastic string] and to tie their neck with *benang plastik*, and then to pull (or tie one end to a tree) so that they were held off the ground. It was said that if they touched the ground they wouldn't be able to be killed. Kind of like electric wires which must be suspended in mid-air. The corpses were then always put in a rice sack and dropped in the river or at the outskirts of the city.

---

[66] Siegel, *A New Criminal Type in Jakarta*, pp. 108-109.

[67] Interpolations written down contemporaneously with the fieldnotes are in parentheses. Those that have been added since are bracketed.

This local perspective on Petrus shows the sense of powerlessness in the face of agents of death who come from without. We must assume that when he says "everyone knows who the *preman* are," he is not only referring to local knowledge, for when he then describes the victims that were chosen, it turns out that they might have been good and respected members of the community (praying, family, etc.). The lists of the center are portrayed as having an inevitable referentiality about them that the local sphere can do nothing about.

As soon as this misgiving is out of the way, however, the story turns to how these powerful figures were killed. Here, as in other stories we shall consider later, the killers are said to believe they are confronting someone who is invulnerable. "*If they were shot the bullets would enter and they wouldn't be able to get up, but they wouldn't die.*" The victims do not die an ordinary death. Rather, their death is one that comes from outside the local sphere and achieves its ends by finding the weaknesses in magical invulnerability. (In this story, the weak point in a man's invulnerability is that he loses his invulnerability when he is lifted out of his territory.) Had it been the case that the victims simply died ordinary deaths, this fact alone might conceivably become grounds for questioning the very existence of their powers of invulnerability and charisma. But what the story shows is that in fact the people being killed *were* invulnerable in relation to ordinary death; the type of death they experienced was supernatural. The killers had confronted the magical power of their victims with a magic of their own.

It is the continued existence of the supernatural power that makes the story worth repeating, for an ordinary death would be of little or no interest so long after the fact. But as Siegel has shown in an analysis of stories surrounding the discovery of Petrus corpses, the logic of such stories—and therefore, perhaps, the "reason" for making the killings themselves into public spectacles—was such that it shifted the focus of interest from the *preman* back to the state.[68] Rather than being fascinated by the criminal specter, people became fascinated with the power of the killers; rather than tracing the source of power back to gangs and other forms of hierarchy, people traced this power back to the state. At least this was the case for as long as the corpses of "criminals," like the tattoos we saw above, had the effect of powerful signs.

2. Territorial Communities and the State

Besides identifying itself with the power attributed to the criminal specter, the state also used Petrus to identify itself with the power of territorial communities (or the *massa,* as it were). This somewhat more explicit identification was based on the supposed similarity between the Petrus killings and cases of *main hakim sendiri* (taking justice into one's own hands, lynch-law) that preceded Petrus and continued both during and after the campaign.[69] In cases of *main hakim sendiri*, members of a

---

[68] Ibid., pp. 120-124.

[69] Regarding highly publicized cases before Petrus and the possibility that Petrus mimicked these cases, see footnote 40. For cases after Petrus see, for example, "Dua Mayat Dalam Tarung Ternyata Recidivis Yang Dibantai Warga" (Two Corpses in a Sack Turn Out to be Recidivists Killed by Villagers), *Media Indonesia*, September 20, 1996; "Dituduh Curi Celengan 'Jegger' Desa Dewas Dahikimi Massa" (Accused of Stealing Piggy Bank, Village 'Jegger' Dead by Mass Punishment), *Suara Karya*, December 15, 1995; "Preman Dilempar Ke Sungai" (*Preman* Thrown in River), *Suara Karya*, August 20, 1996.

community beat and often kill either outsiders caught in a criminal act, such as theft or robbery, or people from the community who are thought to have done something wrong, like having sex out of marriage, committing sorcery, or just being bad characters (i.e. *bromocorah, jegger, gali,* etc.). In many of these cases, the violence also knows no limits, the targets are the same as those of Petrus, and sometimes the body is even disposed by methods analogous to those of Petrus. Certainly cases of *main hakim sendiri* and Petrus are reported in a very similar way. Consider, for example, the following episode which occurred during Petrus and was reported under the title (translated from the Indonesian): "Recidivist with 'Sweet Memory' Tattoo Killed after being Mobbed by Inhabitants of Kampung Krendang."

> The brain of a criminal gang in the area of Kampung Krendang named Miming (25 years old), just released from Cipinang prison, was killed as he was discovered to be about to commit a crime in the same area last Saturday. The suspect, whose body was full of tattoos, was sprawled out bathed in blood in front of Gang Janda in East Krendang.[70]

Main hakim sendiri cases are subject to the sometimes loose notion of "catching people redhanded." Petrus, on the other hand, targeted people at any time, in any place. Nonetheless, the similarity with Petrus in the reporting of such cases is unmistakable. Indeed, *Tempo's* article on Lieutenant Colonel Hasbi, explaining who Petrus in Yogyakarta was targeting, was placed on the same page as a discussion of all the recent cases where *kampung* in Central Java had punished "criminals" with death. The reasons analysts gave for these cases were: "the culture of violence among the people," "letting emotion speak rather than rationality," and "an excess of solidarity."[71] It was an identification that did not escape critics of the government's policy. Adnan Buyung Nasution, who was then head of the Legal Aid Institute, rhetorically asked: "If the people act to *main hakim sendiri* it's considered anarchy, but if it is the security forces that do, well?"[72]

While the story about Petrus in Bandung throws doubt on how far this identification was successful, there was a sense in which Petrus could be interpreted as the government acting on the behalf of territorial communities, disregarding the law as they did, and establishing an "excess of solidarity" with the people. At the same time, for its symbolic effect the state's violence depended on being distinguishable from that of *main hakim sendiri* in its local territorial sense. Otherwise, one might really have anarchy since the violence would appear as a contagion with no clear source and the state would not be representing the violence but merely participating in it. This could explain why the state, in many cases, found it necessary to claim authorship for the killings and why the killings were conducted in a manner that left no doubt as to who was behind them.

Yet, insofar as the killings did involve an identification with communal violence, they would be comparable to Siskamling's process of *kentonganisasi,* which as we have seen, was meant to bring all the local territories into one giant security system that derived its meaning from its supposed source in the state. However, with

---

[70] *Harian Berita Buana,* July 25, 1983, p. 7.

[71] *Tempo,* May 14, 1983, p. 55.

[72] *Tempo,* May 21, 1983, p. 12.

Petrus, not just the community's solidarity was to be identified with the state, but also its violence and its power.

3. The Locus within the State: Fraternities and Individuals

Within the state itself, the degree to which the power associated with such killings achieved currency, and the tendency to trace the source of that power upward through the hierarchy to some higher authority or power, varied. The story below was told by Prasetyo, a mid-ranking police officer in Bandung.[73] Prasetyo himself was probably the most ambitious, and also the most successful, young officer I met in Bandung's police. In contrast to the jaded Reserse agents at the precinct, for example, he was radiant in his appearance and gave the impression that he was someone who worked hard and did things by the book. It was thus quite disturbing to hear him tell this story in a tone of youthful exuberance and pride. It concerns a killing not in the Petrus campaign itself, but one of the many that have followed in its wake.[74]

[Fieldnotes] Prasetyo and I sat on the couch in the division head's office and the two of them discussed who I should talk to from the division for my research on *ilmu*. Suddenly Prasetyo remembered a story about a case he had had during one of his former postings. When he first started telling the story he was directing it to me, but as he went on he increasingly looked expectantly for responses only from his boss. The story was about a man who was being held in a lockup by the police for having committed some crime (he didn't say what). He was known to the locals as an *orang pintar* [a person with special powers] and indeed it turned out that he was able to use an *ilmu* so that he not only talked the police into letting him out of his cell, but even to giving him a gun and letting him go. When the police realized (*sadar*) what had happened they called for help in finding him. This is how Prasetyo got involved, as he was part of the team that was sent to search for the man. The police who had let him escape told Prasetyo to be careful of his *ilmu* and also said that this man was famous for his huge penis. They caught him at the home of one of his many wives. And it was true, his *alat* [tool] was bigger than anything that could be imagined (showing with his hands) . . . Almost as an afterthought but conveying a sense that this is what really made the story important (not the magic), Prasetyo then looked knowingly at his boss and said in a soft voice (so I wouldn't hear) something that sounded like, "It was a 486." His boss didn't catch it and asked, "What?" "486. We got an order."[75] As he said this Prasetyo made a cutting motion at his throat. "Had to be separated (*dipisahkan*)," he said, still speaking softly.

---

[73] Because of the nature of Petrus, it is difficult to obtain first-hand accounts of what those who conducted the killings thought about it. For the most part, the police I asked denied any knowledge about the campaign or made it clear that it was not something that should be discussed. Nonetheless, I was told some stories about similar events.

[74] The impression I was given was that Petrus-like killings have become a standard Police tool for fighting violent crime.

[75] I could not be sure I had caught the actual code number, but I think it was 486.

In this story, the potency of the victim is described in overtly phallic terms. Not only does he have a huge penis, but he can control language, disarm a policeman, and he is the center around which women circulate. An order is received for the man to be killed but the killing "has to" be done in a particular way, namely, the man must be beheaded. It is common lore in Indonesia that someone with magical powers will not actually die unless his head is detached from his body and the two buried separately.[76] In Prasetyo's story, this beheading seems to take on the significance of a castration. It is as if the state, for fear of its own loss of potency, is responding not just by killing the victim but by emasculating his power.

That Prasetyo took part in this symbolic castration could well have been a source of personal pride quite apart from the recognition that he received from his superiors. But the way Prasetyo told the story suggested that he himself did not lay claim to some superior phallic power. His task was not a personal accomplishment but something that "had to" be done because that is what the orders were. Insofar as the killing was a feat of superior potency, it represented the state's potency, not his. This is not to say that the killing did not serve a purpose for him. One could see that he felt a certain pride, but this pride was the result of having been entrusted with such an important mission. It was as if telling the story was a kind of showing-off about his successes, not in terms of the killing itself, but in terms of the recognition it implied he enjoyed from his superiors. This showing-off was not for my benefit at all but solely for that of his boss, whom he kept looking to for approval as he told the story. This culminated in his use of the coded term ("486") for an order to kill, which had the purpose of acting both as a euphemism and as a way to establish a solidarity with his boss by highlighting a "secret" that they shared (and from which I was excluded). In this regard, the story seemed to be part of the currency of "secrets" that helps to constitute fraternities in institutions like the Army and Police. Interestingly, his boss did not give Prasetyo the reward of recognition he sought; rather, he chose not to look directly at Prasetyo and to "not understand" what he meant by the code. My impression was that this failure to recognize the killing as deserving of recognition was not caused by a feeling that Prasetyo had committed an indiscretion in front of a foreign visitor, but was actually Prasetyo's boss's way of quietly refusing to use that particular form of behavior as any measure of success. Without explicitly opposing such killings, he was nonetheless implying that his subordinate was not going to improve his status through "accomplishments" in those terms. Other officers, of course, might be far more responsive to Prasetyo's desire for recognition; and it is easy to imagine how such killings, by virtue of being clandestine and risky ventures, could become an important currency in fraternal alliances.

The second story to be recounted also concerns post-Petrus killings but was told by Joni, a person quite different from Prasetyo. Joni was from military intelligence, rather than from the Police, and moonlighted as a debt collector specializing in collections from military debtors. Talking to Joni, one had the impression that the quotidian aspects of life had receded entirely from his awareness. He looked at everyone as if they were strangers, even his wife and kid. He lived in fear and in an unsettling but not overt way he imparted fear to those he met.

---

[76] I use the masculine pronoun here because virtually all subjects of police discipline in such cases are male.

[Fieldnotes] Joni is the son of an Indonesian Brigadier General and a Dutch woman. His elder brother is a Major heading up East Surabaya's military police. Joni was born in 1968. When he was young his father used to insist that he arrive home right on time. If he was even a few minutes late he had to do pushups. His father was said to have some powerful *ilmu*. His mother told how when his father was fighting against the Dutch he could run across water. When his father died some years ago his teacher in *ilmu* started taking care of Joni. Joni and the rest of his family are from Surabaya but the teacher was from Banten. Now his mother lives in Bandung.

Joni went to the Military Academy. At the Academy they were given really tough training, like making their way through ditches filled with shit. He graduated from the Academy in 1987 and probably soon after went to East Timor, later returning for a second tour of duty. In Timor he held the komando (i.e. was commander) of a battalion that wore long hair and tore its signs of identification from its uniforms because the Timorese would kill them if they knew what unit they were from. He twice led battalions into ambushes, with most of the men being killed. In one of these cases the Timorese were waiting up in trees at night and shot them with bows and arrows. Some got it through the head, some through the throat. Joni then told his men to be quiet and not to move. They waited until they could see where the attackers were and then shot them out of the trees with their AK's. Joni got the leader of these men who was the *kepala suku* [tribal chief] and cut off his head. He still has a photo of himself holding the man's head. He says that the Timorese have powerful *ilmu* and that they can even shoot through bullet-proof helmets. Joni was given a tiny Al Quran by his father's *guru*. Because he has a Dutch mother he never really believed in it. But he brought it to Timor anyway. There were others who said that when he slept they could see two tigers watching over him. He never saw them but once he pretended to be asleep and he could smell them.

When he returned to Surabaya he was given a komando and he and his underlings did some tough things like swimming to Madura from East Java. This is an area known for sharks so he was pretty worried. Having returned from Timor he says he knew nothing about *ampun* [mercy], feeling like he was still back in Timor (which he attributed to "trauma"). Thus, for example, one night he was walking along and a man came up behind him and held a knife to his throat saying that if he moved he would kill him. He wanted money. But he didn't make Joni put his hands up so Joni was able to grab his gun. He then held the gun to the man's head and told him that if he moved he would be shot. Joni then tortured him, beating him and then shooting his kneecap. He always had extra bullets so he could refill his gun, pretending none had been fired.

While in Surabaya he also got at least one special order to kill a dangerous criminal. One of these was a man of whom the police were afraid because he was *kebal* [invulnerable] to being shot. Joni's order was to shoot him and put him in a rice bag (*dikarungin*). The man had tattoos all over. When he did it Joni still had long hair and a beard because he had just come back from Timor. He was wearing a long grey jacket. His relatives had told him to make sure to say a prayer before shooting so that the bullet would go through (*menembus*). Before going he made sure to *mengisi* [fill] the bullet by saying the *ayatkorsi* [a prayer to exorcise spirits]. The man was in a market when Joni ran up and shot him in the head saying "wismillah . . . ". And the bullet went through. Everyone around ran away and he put the *mayat* [corpse] in a bag and dumped it.

He is glad not to be in Surabaya now because during the trial of that case the family of the dead man said, "Oh, this is the man who killed my brother. No matter where he goes in the world we will find him and kill him, and if not us then our children will do it." And indeed a younger brother did appear once and stabbed him in the stomach, and Joni then pulled out his gun and shot him. If he hadn't been helped by some bystanders right away he probably would have died. (He lifts his shirt and shows the scar). [...]

Recently Joni got an order here in Bandung to kill a *penjahat kelas kakap* [big-fish criminal] named Rudi. Supposedly Rudi has robbed a bank in Bogor and got away with it, and has raped. He is now in Bandung. The other people in Joni's team are all *bapak-bapak* [older men] who are in their forties, so they don't want to do it. They passed it on to Joni. Joni is not sure he wants to do it though because he now has a wife and kid. It's been a week since the order came down and he hasn't done anything yet but he probably will have to soon. He is worried that there will be a *balas dendam* [revenge] and his family will get it. This happened to his elder brother after he had killed a criminal. They came and killed his family, chopping off his wife's legs. Now his brother is known for his toughness. Every criminal who is caught in the area he controls leaves with his legs broken or maimed.

Even more than Prasetyo's account, Joni's stories emphasize the incredible power of his adversaries, be they independence fighters in East Timor or *preman* in Surabaya. Attributed to all of them is a magical power that makes doing battle with them an almost supernatural affair. In this case, however, Joni is quite clearly using the power of his adversaries to demonstrate his own power: the *ilmu* passed down from his father that allows him to sleep safely in East Timor and to kill someone in Surabaya who had, until then, been considered invulnerable. Unlike Prasetyo, the authority to which he lays claim has nothing to do with the recognition he receives from his superior officers.[77] (In fact, he was ambivalent about the military hierarchy since he had been court-martialled for striking a superior and thus had lost prospects for much advancement). It has to do, rather, with his survival and killing skills, and the *ilmu* he inherited from his father. It is especially the latter—his use of a *dukun* (shaman), his being guarded by tigers, his "filling" of the bullet, and his reciting of the *ayatkorsi*—that gives him power over death. It is also this that distinguishes him from others in the state (his comrades in East Timor or the Police in Surabaya) who do not have such power.

In sum, the appropriated phallic or magical power of *preman* is not always given an undifferentiated locus in the "government" or the "state". Rather, individuals and fraternities within the state, through their actions and stories, may seek to control the circulation of this power for themselves.

---

[77] As Joni talked about his orders, I got the sense that he did not really know where exactly they came from, only that he must obey them. And at no time during our discussions did he mention any of the ideological reasons behind the war in East Timor or the operations against *preman*. For him the "reasons" for these wars never even entered the picture; he was concerned merely with the power and danger associated with his own role in them.

4. The Threat of Revenge

Joni's story also shows, however, that there is an inherent danger in the mimicry of "criminals," for it can lead to a cycle of revenge. The phenomenon of revenge, in which "criminals," kin groups, or territorial communities seek to recuperate the power they lose when the state—or persons or fraternities within it—kill, beat, or imprison people, is a common one in post-Petrus Indonesia. It is evident, for example, in the numerous cases in which communities reassert their own power to *main hakim sendiri* against the power of the Police in cases of sorcery, theft, sex outside of marriage, and extortion. In cases such as these the Police usually do not risk charging suspects for fear that they themselves will become objects of the community's wrath. When the Police do overstep this line, the usual response is not actual killing but the spectacular destruction of Police precincts by crowds of upset people. The most explosive of these cases occur when the Police are said to *main hakim sendiri* against someone who is respected locally.[78] However, even in these cases, it is extremely rare that the communities will actually avenge the crime directly and proportionally, and so genuinely reassert their power over death. Rather, they will restrict their violence to property so as not to challenge state authority too directly. Nonetheless their actions are a powerful reminder to representatives of the state that there are other sources of power that count.

In other cases, the revenge against the government is more direct but remains in the realm of fantasy. As one man in Bandung's prison who claimed to be doing time for fraud explained:

> [Fieldnotes] All you have to do is a bit of arithmetic. In the time of the PKI, how many people were killed? A million? Now, if all those people had children, how many people is that? Two million? Remember, all those kids grew up without their parents and cannot get jobs because they are stamped PKI. Now add the hundred thousand [sic] people killed during Petrus. All their kids grew up without their fathers and they know who it was who killed them. They ask: why don't I have a father? And they blame the government. That's why the government here is so scared. They know that there are so many millions of people who want to seek revenge.

The man who expressed this fantasy of revenge was an unusual character. He could perform magic to make money disappear and told fascinating stories about his criminal history that stretched the limits of credibility without ever breaking them.

---

[78] This might trigger full-scale riots, as happened in Tasikmalaya in 1996. In that case, according to one of the rumors circulating right after it occurred, a police commander had sent his son to a *pesantrèn* (Islamic boarding school) for disciplining as he had been caught stealing. At the *pesantrèn* he was caught stealing again and received punishment from the *pesantrèn* head. The boy was angry and reported to his father that he had been tortured. Upon hearing this the commander sent some his "boys" to bring in those who were said to have done the beating and revenged the beating by beating them (some rumors said to death). Word of this got out to *pesantrèn* students and in the riot that ensued almost all the Police stations in the city, as well as shops, churches, etc. were burned and destroyed.

Other interpretations of the same event suggested that the riot was in fact instigated so as to make it look like the people were angry with the Police. These analyses claim that a faction in the Army was the inciter, implying that the real source of such violence is fraternities rather than the masses.

Among other things, he claimed to have been a counterfeiter, a *dukun*, and a fraud artist. But one thing about him was clear: when he spoke, people listened. Whereas the prison's canteen was usually filled with multiple conversations, when he was there everyone else fell silent. And when he spoke about the inevitability of revenge, one almost started to believe it. The revenge he had in mind was not the personal or local forms feared by Joni and local police precincts, however. It was collective, implicating not just *preman* but all those who had been criminalized by the New Order's repressive regime.

*   *   *

In sum, the process of mimicry that was evident among inmates who desired the power associated with tattoos was also evident in Petrus and its aftermath. As Siegel has shown, the overall function of this mimicry was to identify the state with the power that criminality represented: magical power, the power of unlimited expression, excessive violence. Through this identification, Petrus insured that anyone who took an interest in such power would come to associate it with the state. We have also suggested that "criminality" might not have been the only figure that was being mimicked; the actions of the state could also have been identified with—or perhaps even modeled upon—the most potent moment in the expression of collective territorial power: *main hakim sendiri*. With regards to the consequences of these forms of mimicry we have made two observations. First, the power that is appropriated to the state may itself be subject to claims by individuals, or function as a currency within fraternities, so that it is not always the state as such that becomes the new locus for this power. Second, both "criminals" and territorial communities, through their threats and fantasies of revenge, offer reminders that they are still forces to be reckoned with. While we will not investigate the implications of these possibilities here, it is important to keep them in mind.

Tattoos And Preman After Deterritorialization

When the power attributed to tattoos and *preman* is appropriated by the state, it creates a whole new type of *preman* and even a new type of tattoo. Consider the following newspaper story:

> The Malang court last Tuesday sentenced S (29 years old) to seven months in prison for having committed fraud by claiming to be a commander of Pomal [Navy Military Police] working as a *petrus* (mysterious murderer) and extorting [money] from a person who sells games . . . Evidence included a TNI-AL [Navy] membership card, a Kodam 0802 [Army] membership card, and a number of threatening letters and lists of names of people who were going to be *petrus*-ed
> . . .
> On Friday October 28 [the victim] was visited by S, an unknown man who claimed to be the commander of Pomal and working as an agent of Petrus. S showed him a list of names who he was going to *petrus*, among them two of the victim's younger brothers.
> Because he was worried and afraid, the victim did what S asked and gave him Rp.17,000. On Tuesday November 1 the victim received a letter from S the

contents of which demanded Rp.35,000 in order to have the names of his two younger brothers erased from the list of people who were going to be *petrus*-ed. [After that the victim reported it to the police who arrested S].[79]

In this story an extortionist claims power to intimidate not by showing tattoos but by showing lists and identity cards. He mimics Petrus mimicking "criminals" like himself. The difference, of course, is that the identity cards and lists this man has derive their power not from a territorial inscription but from state language and its power over death. This language has a source in the state and a claim to referentiality. The importance of this fact became apparent at the man's trial, when the judges asked him about the Army identity card and he told them he found it on the street. Knowing that there was no such thing as a Kodam with a four-digit number "0802" in the world "out there," and therefore that the man's identity cards were counterfeit and his claims false, the judges were able to laugh, secure in their own possession of the truth.[80]

Not all such identity cards and lists are so easily dismissed, however. Certainly in the mid-1990s, in the press and on the streets one was always hearing about *surat sakti* (magically powerful letters) that would clear a business project through any bureaucratic office, people who were *kebal hukum* (invulnerable to the law), and others who were not true white-collar criminals but rather *preman berdasi* (*preman* with neckties, i.e. impersonating officials or businessmen). Ordinary people, moreover, were always going out of their way to show anyone who was interested their own special signs which, without exception, traced their power back either to an institution like the military or to a fraternity. Stickers on cars that said Kopassus (the Special Forces) or Pom (Military Police), name cards from important officials, identity cards and paraphernalia from the Harley Davidson club (which was known to be headed by a General and fraternity leader) were all examples of the new type of tattoos. They could all be used to intimidate villagers, avoid fines and exactions if one was stopped by the traffic police, and simply to impress one's friends. Periodically the institutions would try and exert their control over the circulation in order to distinguish the "originals" from the "false" ones; for example, by conducting operations to remove ABRI stickers from cars driven by people who could not produce an ABRI membership card. But while the circulation of these special signs or tokens might extend beyond the particular groups of people who could legitimately hold them, this was ultimately a minor point. The important thing was that they derived their invulnerability and magical power from their connection to the state's institutions and fraternities rather than their connection to some other source of power (like territorial gangs, illegal political parties, outlawed religious sects, etc.). In this respect, Petrus might be called a watershed as it marked the point at which territorial power became deterritorialized from the figure of the *jawara* and reterritorialized within the state and its fraternities. That is, it marked the point at which the power that at one time would have been associated with tattoos became

---

[79] *Surabaya Post*, January 25, 1984, p. 5.

[80] Other cases of these Petrus impostors: "Wanita Pemeras yang Mengaku Penembak Misterius Ditangkap" (Female Extortionist Claiming to be a Mysterious Shooter Arrested), *Surabaya Post*, January 14, 1984, p. 3. "Memeras dengan Dalih 'Petrus'" (Extortion Under Cloak of Petrus), *Surabaya Post*, June 2, 1984.

subject to a whole new set of disciplines that were rooted in surveillance and fraternities rather than in bodies and localities.

LOCAL SECURITY AND THE STATE AFTER PETRUS AND SISKAMLING

Taken together, Petrus and Siskamling changed the face of local security. On a strictly institutional and demographic level, this change was evident in the explosion in the numbers of Satpam and Hansip. With *preman* killed or intimidated, businesses, bus terminals, markets, malls, and so on all came to hire Satpam; and many neighborhoods hired Hansip. By the end of 1995, there were about 200,000 Satpam members across Indonesia, making them more numerous than the Police.[81] That every member of Satpam and Hansip had a particular overseer among the Police, and that the Police co-ordinated with the guards themselves, not just their bosses, meant that this expansion of Satpam provided a relatively powerful means for disciplining local security practices.[82] In this respect, Siskamling provided for the extension of Police surveillance into the local sphere. Much of the time, this additional surveillance also acted as the premise for a far greater involvement of the Police in local protection rackets than had previously been possible when such rackets were either under the control of gangs, heads of RT/RW, or the Army.[83] While there is always a tendency for the type of petty criminals that Petrus targeted to return, the Police deal with this by launching operations much like the ones that preceded Petrus. In these operations, everyone on the streets is rounded up and fingerprinted, some are charged, some are "developed" by the Police, and some are sent off to *pesantrèn* (Islamic boarding schools) or foundations for reform.[84] In this way the Police maintain their local domination (except in relation to gangs with *bekking*[85] from the Army) despite their extremely low numbers. None of this would have been possible without Petrus.

Petrus, however, was about far more than just demographic and institutional changes; it was about the deterritorialization of the power associated with

---

[81] *Media Indonesia*, December 27, 1995. This was approximately one Satpam member per nine hundred people, while the ratio of police to inhabitants was one officer to 1,200 inhabitants. In urban areas the ratio was far greater. According to Police data, in 1996 in Bandung, there was about one Satpam or Hansip member for every two hundred inhabitants and only one police officer for every 733 inhabitants. The total number of Satpam in 1996 was 6,345, up from 336 in 1984 and none before 1980.

[82] At the same time, Bimmas provided a rubric for expanded Police oversight not just of security guards but of youth groups, *pesantrèn*, *ojèk* (motorcycle taxis) drivers, and "informal" local leaders. Many of these received training and coordination from the Police and became what the Police referred to as their "long arms" (*perpanjangan tangan*).

[83] Some gangs continued to operate with *bekking* (backing) from fraternities in the Army or the Police.

[84] Those that are sent-off for reform outside are sent to collaborating *pesantrèn* or to ex-convict organizations that escaped Petrus through connections to the right powers in Jakarta. These latter groups, sometimes trained by the military, are useful for political purposes like instigating riots since their members can always be threatened with being killed or imprisoned if they do not cooperate. For example, one such group was used in the bloody take-over of the PDI (Indonesian Democratic Party) headquarters in July 1996.

[85] *Bekking* means that a gang is "backed" by people in the military. Such *bekking* protects the gang from the law and allows the military to be involved in protection rackets without appearing to be so.

"criminals," *jago*, and territorial communities, and its reterritorialization within the state. Such deterritorialization proceeded by means of mimicry coupled with surveillance. Mimicry allowed the state to identify itself with the said power, releasing it from its locus in "criminals," *jago*, and territorial communities. Surveillance, through its ultimatum forcing "criminals" either to recognize themselves as the state would or to die, and through its control over what "true" identities are, insured that the circulation of this power would lead back to one source: the state. The process was the same as that used for *kentonganisasi*: a copy of the *kentongan* in villages around the country is created at the center, one that is bigger than any of the rest, and then all the other *kentongan* are counted and subjected to regulations that oblige them to derive their significance from the one at the center. The difference, however, was that nobody was killed in the process of *kentonganisasi*, and *kentongan* were not themselves associated with the type of power that the specter of crime evoked, so *kentonganisasi* did not attract the same attention as Petrus. With Petrus, the people who were killed were invested with a "suprabiological force" that should resist death (their tattoos, invulnerability, force of expression that knows no bounds); and yet, it seemed, the state could control even this force.[86]

---

[86] I borrow the phrase "suprabiological force" from a paper by James T. Siegel. See Siegel, "A New Criminal Type in Jakarta: Counter Revolution Today." Paper presented at the conference, Crime and Punishment: Criminality in Southeast Asia, sponsored by the Center for Asian Studies. Amsterdam, March 20-22, 1997.

MILITARY IDEOLOGY IN RESPONSE TO DEMOCRATIC PRESSURE DURING THE LATE SUHARTO ERA: POLITICAL AND INSTITUTIONAL CONTEXTS

Jun Honna

INTRODUCTION[1]

For the last decade, democratization figured as a core theme of public discourse under the authoritarian New Order polity. Political society insisted on the need for improving human rights accountability, eliminating ABRI's (Angkatan Bersenjata Republik Indonesia, Armed Forces of the Republic of Indonesia) praetorian political intervention, and—more generally—for broadening space for political participation. In this process the mass media and political figures introduced such concepts as globalization (*globalisasi*) and civil society (*masyarakat madani*) into New Order political discourse, thus identifying their own demands as historically inevitable and, once accomplished, irreversible.[2] Citing the concept of globalism, generally accepted

---

[1] This work is based on my doctoral field research carried out between May 1996 and May 1997 and between October and November 1998 in Jakarta. I am grateful to Dr. Harold Crouch, Professor Benedict Kerkvliet, Professor Benedict Anderson, and Grayson Lloyd for their valuable comments and criticism on an earlier version of this article. I also thank Professor Jeff Kingston and Marcus Mietzner for commenting on parts of the article.

[2] Although it is hard to trace exactly when the popular usage of these terms started in Indonesia, we suspect that, as elsewhere, the end of the Cold War and the dissolution of the Soviet Union were the most significant events that generated the proliferation of these concepts emphasizing the expansion of universal values beyond national boundaries. One of the earliest discussions in Indonesia can be found in late 1990. A leading evening newspaper

as an irresistible world trend, democratic advocates both within the regime and in society strengthened pressure for the elimination of authoritarian practices long adopted by Suharto and ABRI.

The purpose of this chapter is to examine the way in which ABRI countered these democratic challenges by reshaping its ideological framework in a manner that identified such dissent as a national "threat"—a legitimate target of security operations. The concept of *globalisasi* has played a decisive role in this ideological reformulation and been used to rationalize the hardline military approach to democratic movements. Our investigation focuses on the how and why of such developments.

DEVELOPMENTALISM AS THE CORE IDEOLOGICAL BASIS OF THE NEW ORDER MILITARY

Since the birth of the New Order in 1966, military ideology has celebrated the pursuit of economic development as a means to save the nation from the politico-economic catastrophe that took place under President Sukarno. Developmentalism, or modernization ideology, provided the military with a rationale that identified political stability as the precondition for development. "Long-term" military control of politics was justifiable since modernization was a decades-long national project. The dream of catch-up industrialization strengthened two earlier perceptions regarding international-domestic interactions. First, the perceived need for a massive infusion of foreign capital from the West reinforced the idea that ongoing political stability was crucial to attract foreign investments. Second, the geopolitical concern that communist infiltration during the Cold War would escalate domestic subversion also convinced officers to insist on the prominent role of the defense forces in maintaining national integrity; that integrity would be achieved by military surveillance in all fields of national life.[3] Having packed this development theory into its arsenal, ABRI no longer felt the need to insist that its intervention in politics was temporary in nature or undesirable in principle. The doctrine of the dual function, or .*dwifungsi*, which was officially adopted at the beginning of the New Order, claimed for the army a "permanent" role in the defense and sociopolitical fields.

However, this ideological framework had to be frequently reasserted and revised to insure that the military's intervention in politics was perpetually required by new evidence of national instability. In this ideological reproduction, the military claimed

---

demanded that ABRI adjust its role to face and accommodate globalization. See "Tugas ABRI dan Era Globalisasi" (ABRI's Mission and the Era of Globalization), *Suara Pembaruan*, October 5, 1990. ABRI, in its own newspaper, reacted to this challenge by insisting that ABRI's efforts to safeguard the national ideology were necessary to prevent the sort of national disintegration that took place in the Soviet Union and Eastern Europe. See "Dalam Era Globalisasi, Ideologi Tetap Diperlukan" (In the Era of Globalization, Ideology is Still Needed), *Angkatan Bersenjata*, November 12, 1990.

[3] For an early attempt to formulate these ideas, see Ali Moertopo, *Some Basic Thoughts on the Acceleration and Modernization of 25 Years' Development* (Jakarta: Centre for Strategic and International Studies, 1973). Ali Moertopo was Suharto's protégé from the 1950s until early in the 1970s. To a large extent, it was US-trained economists at the Army Staff and Command College (Seskoad) who indoctrinated the anti-Sukarno officers with the developmentalist ideology described above. On the military's conception of economic development, see also Harold Crouch, *Army and Politics in Indonesia* (Ithaca: Cornell University Press, 1978), p. 273.

that it had the ability to maintain a stable nation, but at the same time regularly insisted that it had not achieved complete stability. Thus, since the launching of the regime, continuous efforts were made to construct an image of national instability. After 1978 this effort was formally programmed and routinized within ABRI on the initiative of the National Defense Institute (Lembaga Pertahanan Nasional—Lemhannas). This military education institute established a program, the so-called National Vigilance Refresher Course (Penataran Kewaspadaan Nasional—Tarpadnas), for the indoctrination of both officers and civilians, who were taught about the widespread "potential" political threats to national stability. According to Lemhannas, this organizational effort for vigilance (*kewaspadaan*) indoctrination was almost completed by February 1988.[4] Assessing the content and development of this program during the period 1978-1988 helps clarify the standard images ABRI used to represent "threats" prior to the emergence of the social movement demanding democratic *keterbukaan* (openness).

TARPADNAS AND THE IDEOLOGICAL SETTING OF MILITARY *KEWASPADAAN*

Tarpadnas, a joint project of Lemhannas and the state security apparatus, the Operational Command for the Restoration of Security and Order (Kopkamtib), was begun in June 1978, and it was open to ABRI members and staff of other Departments.[5] It was not a coincidence that the program was initiated in June 1978, following the regime's crackdown on the 1977-1978 student movement opposing Suharto's presidential re-election.[6] One document prepared for the Tarpadnas in 1979 asserted that the "New Left" had mobilized students and intellectuals to take over leadership of communist activities after the Indonesian Communist Party (PKI) was banned in 1966. According to the document, the New Left in the campuses had used labor and land disputes to attract supporters, and also infiltrated various mass

---

[4] "Surat Keputusan Gubernur Lemhannas No: SKEP/07/II/1988, Tanggal 24-2-1988, Tentang Penggunaan Buku Materi Penataran Kewaspadaan Nasional dan Kegiatan Semacamnya" (Decision of the Governor of Lemhannas, No. SKEP/07/II/1988, Dated 24-2-1988, on the Use of Source Books for Refresher Courses for National Vigilance and Similar Activities), in *Materi Balatkom* (Materials on the Latent Communist Danger) (Jakarta: Lemhannas, Mabes ABRI, 1988). In the mid-1990s, the National Defense Institute was renamed the National Resilience Institute, but its Indonesian acronym remained unchanged.

[5] The program was launched following a change of leadership within the military in June 1978. Lemhannas had been headed by Lt. Gen. Sayidiman, who was widely believed to be critical of the officers who had dominated ABRI's intelligence sector, all close Suharto allies, such as Admiral R. Sudomo, Gen. Yoga Sugomo, and Maj. Gen. Benny Murdani. In the 1978 reshuffle, which placed General Mohammad Yusuf as the new ABRI Commander, Sudomo became Kopkamtib Commander while he concurrently held the post of Deputy Commander of ABRI. Sugomo, Head of BAKIN (State Intelligence Coordination Board), who was directly responsible to the President, was posted as the Chief of Kopkamtib in October without sacrificing his BAKIN position. Similarly Murdani held the posts of Assistant for Intelligence in the Defense Ministry, Head of the Strategic Intelligence Center (Pusintelstrat) in the Defense Ministry, Assistant for Intelligence at Kopkamtib, and since 1978 the post of Deputy Head of BAKIN. Soon after the implementation of Tarpadnas, Sayidiman was transferred to an ambassadorship (Japan), in October 1978. The new governor of Lemhannas was Lt. Gen. Sutopo Juwono, former Head of BAKIN. Thus, the Tarpadnas project reflected the ongoing dominance of the intelligence sector within ABRI.

[6] On nationwide student demonstrations, see The Editors, "White Book of the 1978 Students' Struggle," *Indonesia* 25 (April 1978): 151-182.

organizations and government institutions.[7] Regarding the "extreme right"—Islamic fundamentalists—the document claimed that it had become fanatic and militant because it lacked the sort of attractive propaganda that would help expand its organization and so was forced to rely on religious messages.[8]

One year later, in 1980, the Tarpadnas course published a statement claiming that, in order to alleviate the latent danger represented by the New Left and the fundamentalists, it was urgently necessary to reduce the increasing economic gap between the rich minority and the poor majority and to minimize government manipulation of power and authority.[9] With this statement, Tarpadnas acknowledged that the regime's and ABRI's own failures had been factors encouraging extremism. However, the military was not consistently in favor of easing government controls. In response to the government's decision gradually to release PKI political prisoners, Lemhannas warned that about 105 of these prisoners were still "diehards" unwilling to renounce communist ideology, and it named as examples the authors Pramoedya Ananta Toer and Rivai Apin. Therefore, the paper concluded, ABRI should not relax its *kewaspadaan* against these people.[10] This logic was reinforced by the notion that communist activities could be maintained through networks of cell members which were not formally organized: "organization without organization" (*organisasi tak terbentuk*). Lemhannas insisted that PKI supporters under the New Order used this strategy and tried to undermine national unity based on the Pancasila by attempting to infiltrate the "floating-mass" and looking for opportunities among the labor, agrarian, student, women's, legal, and cultural movements which had emerged in the process of national development (*pembangunan*).[11] Such a *kewaspadaan* perspective, which perceived the latent danger of communist resurgence in a changing society, reflected the legacy of military attitudes cultivated during 1966-7, when the PKI was eliminated. These attitudes were formally standardized for officer indoctrination during the first few years of the Tarpadnas program.

Once the program had been established and indoctrination routinized within ABRI, the target audience was expanded in 1985 to include lower-level governmental

---

[7] *Naskah Induk Tentang Subversi dan Penanggulangannya* (Basic Text on Subversion and How to Tackle It) (Jakarta: Lemhannas, Dephankam, 1979), pp. 23-27. The definition of the New Left is not provided in this document, but it should be noted that, as Benedict Anderson argues, people who had been with the Left before the New Order were rarely university-educated. Benedict Anderson, *The Spectre of Comparisons: Nationalism, Southeast Asia and the World* (New York: Verso, 1998), p. 290. Thus, perhaps ABRI identified the increasing role of universities as a new development for the Left.

[8] *Naskah Induk Tentang Subversi dan Penanggulangannya*, p. 26.

[9] *Pengamanan Ideologi Pancasila Terhadap Pengaruh Ideologi-Ideologi Besar di Dunia* (Safeguarding the Pancasila Ideology Against the Influence of Major World Ideologies) (Jakarta: Lemhannas, Dephankam, 1980), n.p.

[10] *Perkembangan Bahaya Laten Ex-Partai Komunis Indonesia (PKI)* (The Development of the Latent Danger of the Former Communist Party of Indonesia) (Jakarta: Lemhannas, Dephankam, 1980), pp. 23-24. This document was also among the Tarpadnas materials. There is, however, no explanation of how "105" people could pose a threat to national security.

[11] *Taktik-Taktik Komunisme* (Communism's Tactics) (Jakarta: Lemhannas, Dephankam, 1981), pp. 1-2, 5. The concept of the "floating-mass" was introduced in the early New Order period. It proposed that the mass of the people should express their political preferences only in general elections held every five years, so that their daily activities could be fully dedicated to economic development. The major advocate of this theory was Maj. Gen. Ali Moertopo.

bodies and official organizations such as the National Journalists' Association (PWI), the Indonesian National Youth Council (KNPI), the Chamber of Commerce and Industry (Kadin), and so on. At the regional level, Kopkamtib's Inter-regional Special Operations (Laksuswil) conducted the program for members of the regional branches of the organizations listed above and also for provincial parliamentarians. Moreover, at the lowest level, Kopkamtib's Regional Special Operations (Laksusda), in cooperation with Military Resort Commands (Korem), coordinated meetings of Tarpadnas alumni to maintain the *kewaspadaan* indoctrination for those who had already been introduced to it.[12] The extension of this indoctrination program was directed in August 1984 by General Benny Murdani who had become ABRI Commander and Kopkamtib Commander approximately one year earlier, in March 1983.[13] As Suharto's right-hand man and as the New Order's intelligence czar, Murdani endeavored to expand the military's ideological surveillance of society to further enhance New Order political control.[14] Murdani's effort was fully assisted by Maj. Gen. Soebiyakto—another intelligence officer and an aide to Murdani—who was installed as the Lemhannas Governor two months after Murdani's promotion to Pangab.[15] The *kewaspadaan* project, which was first intended to standardize the military's (and the government's) portrait of a nation threatened by subversive forces, was now transformed into ABRI's security-intelligence project, a project that aimed to shape and control political ideas in society. This move resonated perfectly with the Suharto regime's program to require all social organizations to adopt Pancasila as their sole philosophical foundation.[16]

The *kewaspadaan* formula discussed above provides interesting insights into the development of New Order military ideology. Earlier, certain regime concepts, such as *pembangunan* and the floating-mass, were presented as antithetical to the communist-influenced Old Order led by President Sukarno and therefore as basically in accord with the New Order. By the late 1970s, however, *pembangunan* and the floating-mass were being identified as elements in a vulnerable social space that

---

[12] For details, see *Pengarahan Aster Kasum ABRI Pada Rakerter ABRI Tahun 1985 Tanggal 1 Agustus 1985 Tentang Kebijaksanaan Pembinaan Teritorial* (The Territorial Assistant to ABRI's Chief of the General Staff's Directive to ABRI's 1985 Territorial Working Session, dated August 1, 1985, on Policy for Territorial Training) (Jakarta: Staf Teritorial, Mabes ABRI, 1985), pp. 25-32.

[13] "Surat Telegram Pangkopkamtib No: STR. 61/Kopkam/1984 Tanggal 18 Agustus 1984 Tentang Pelaksanaan Tarpadnas dan Kegiatan Semacamnya" (Telegram of the Kopkamtib Commander No. STR. 61/Kopkam/1984, dated August 18, 1984 on the Implementation of Tarpadnas and Similar Activities).

[14] About Murdani's intelligence power, see the Editors, "Current Data on the Indonesian Military Elite (Continued)," *Indonesia* 37 (April 1984): 149-152.

[15] Significantly, Soebiyakto was a former military attaché to Moscow (1977) and was regarded as a "communist expert" within ABRI.

[16] Since his Independence Day speech of August 1982, Suharto had hinted about this plan, and in 1985 the legislation was formally adopted. The plan was widely perceived as Suharto's attempt to undermine the influence of political Islam. A month after Murdani's instruction noted above, violent riots broke out in Tanjung Priok, North Jakarta, where hundreds of angered Muslims were shot to death by security forces. This event encouraged a growing perception among Muslim groups that Gen. Murdani, a Catholic, had been operating to de-Islamize Indonesia. Regarding this series of developments, see, for example, John Bresnan, *Managing Indonesia: The Modern Political Economy* (New York: Columbia University Press, 1993), pp. 218-244.

could provide the stage for underground extremist activities. This new assessment reflected the process by which ABRI's original "threat theory" had been broadened to identify a greater number of informal organizations as potentially subversive, a process that then justified military efforts to oversee the "consequences" of *pembangunan* after the first decade of New Order administration. Since ABRI's developmentalist ideology had rationalized long-term military control of politics by insisting that the military must safeguard national development, the established *kewaspadaan* doctrine—that identified incorrect or contaminated *pembangunan* as a source of threat—enhanced the ideological justification for the military's continued control.

In ABRI's internal study of the latent communist danger (*Bahaya Laten Komunisme*—Balatkom), contradictions appear whenever Pancasila is identified as the ultimate basis for the national philosophy. In a February 1988 document that was formulated by Maj. Gen. Soebiyakto as a standard text for the subsequent Tarpadnas project, the history, thought, and activities of the PKI were described in detail, followed by the conclusion that Marxist ideology—whether it was implemented by communist or other groups—was opposed to and destructive of Pancasila society. However, this one-hundred-page paper simultaneously adopted a neo-Marxist perspective to critique international capitalism. It argued that capitalism had made the rich richer and the poor poorer because the rich were the owners of capital. The paper asserted that the recent rise of multi-national corporations also resulted in the accumulation of capital in industrial countries, and this had strengthened the structural dependency of the poor countries.[17] The document's criticisms of both communism and capitalism are not necessarily contradictory or inconsistent, since conceivably both could undermine the ideological basis of Pancasila.[18] But it should be noted that in this document, Lemhannas officers made use of neo-Marxist language while at the same time warning against *bahaya laten komunisme*, and these arguments together were intended to consolidate the *kewaspadaan* ideology. Soebiyakto—the communist expert—seemed to know the utility of Marxist ideas.

More interestingly, all Lemhannas papers examined above implied that in order to construct this Pancasila dialectic, both communism and capitalism-liberalism were "needed" as the thesis and antithesis. ABRI's standard assessment is expressed in the following comment.

> When we adopted our political system, there were two mainstreams in the world, i.e. Western democracy based on individualism and the Communist regime based on class. However, they were not suitable for Indonesia where the sense of togetherness [*kebersamaan*] in society transcended both individual and class [interests]. This was the foundation of our Pancasila democratic system.[19]

---

[17] *Materi Balatkom*, pp. 3-5.

[18] As Weinstein's vivid study illustrated in 1976, one feeling shared among political elites since the time of the Revolution was the fear of dependence on the capitalist countries, which were defined as inherently imperialistic. Thus the officers' distrust of capitalism was not new. See Franklin B. Weinstein, *Indonesian Foreign Policy and the Dilemma of Dependence: From Sukarno to Soeharto* (Ithaca: Cornell University Press, 1976).

[19] Interview with Gen. (ret) Edi Sudradjat, Minister of Defense and Security, February 19, 1997.

It was against this background that, with or without real evidence, the Balatkom campaign gradually attained its position as a ritualized element in the hypernationalist agenda that upheld Pancasila as the absolute value.[20] In the history of New Order anti-communist thinking, this was a major development, as the ritualized warnings against subversive forces no longer required "real" threats, since the maintenance of the ritual itself became the end of organizational activity. This development enabled ABRI to adopt Balatkom as a weapon against any societal element which did not follow this rite established by Suharto and the military.

It was notable that the completion of Lemhannas's Balatkom study was soon followed by Suharto's decision to abolish Kopkamtib—ABRI's major tool for social control—in September 1988. The loss of Kopkamtib was unlikely to undermine ABRI's established Balatkom thinking, and it did not interrupt the Tarpadnas project. Nevertheless, in the political context, the disbanding of Kopkamtib and the completion of Balatkom were significant indications of growing intra-regime contestation. It was widely believed that the liquidation of Kopkamtib was primarily intended to diminish the power of Murdani, who was unhappy with Suharto's choice of Lt. Gen. (ret) Sudharmono (the head of the state secretariat, or Sekneg, and the chairman of Golkar—the government party—since 1983) as vice president for 1988-1993.[21] Murdani was eased out of his command of ABRI and transferred to the Department of Defense as Minister just before the presidential (and vice-presidential) elections at the People's Consultative Assembly (MPR, Majelis Permuyawaratan Rakyat) in March 1988. The growing disenchantment of Murdani's officers with the President became evident when Brig. Gen. Ibrahim Saleh of the ABRI fraction (F-ABRI) in the parliament (DPR) interrupted a session in the MPR by openly objecting to the nomination of Sudharmono as vice-president. Ibrahim's unprecedented show

---

[20] Maj. Gen. Soebiyakto, Lemhannas Governor, at the opening of Tarpadnas meeting in 1988, explained that the PKI had revolted three times, so a fourth attempt might well be likely. But he said PKI activities were difficult to detect. See "Mewaspadai yang Keempat" (Vigilance Against a Fourth), *Tempo*, November 5, 1988. For an acount that examines the ritualization of the anti-communist campaign, see Rob Goodfellow, *Api Dalam Sekam: The New Order and the Ideology of Anti-Communism* (Clayton: Centre of Southeast Asian Studies, Monash University, Working Paper 95, 1995). It should be noted that the first of the three revolts mentioned by Soebiyakto was the famous 1926-27 uprising against the Dutch colonial government. This suggests that the New Order (and ABRI) identify themselves as a late reincarnation of Dutch colonial rule. For an account that expands on this point, see Benedict Anderson, "Old State, New Society: Indonesia's New Order in Comparative Historical Perspective," *Journal of Asian Studies* XLII (May 1983): 447-495, especially pp. 492-493.

[21] On the Murdani-Sudharmono antagonism, see for example, The Editors, "Current Data on the Indonesian Military Elite," *Indonesia* 45 (April 1988), pp. 142-145. Suharto began to find that he had become too dependent on ABRI and started to widen his power base by relying less on Murdani's ABRI in non-security affairs. It was under such circumstances that Sudharmono (a retired officer, but not a man regarded as representing the military community) increasingly gained the president's trust. As Sekneg, he had authority over budget allocations and allocated much of it to support the business activities of indigenous Indonesians, *pribumi*, with a resulting decline in budget allocations to ABRI. Also, as the Golkar Chairman, Sudharmono attempted to make Golkar more independent from ABRI by recruiting new cadres from the ranks of business who might provide financial support for Golkar. ABRI leaders were hostile to such attempts by Suharmono even though his actions were approved by Suharto. For a detailed analysis of the rise of Sudharmono, see Robinson Pangaribuan, *The Indonesian State Secretariat 1945-1993* (Perth: Asia Research Centre on Social, Political and Economic Change, Murdoch University, 1995).

of resistance was unsuccessful, but not entirely isolated. Other ABRI officers had also raised questions about Suharto's policies.

Gen. Try Sutrisno, a close ally of Murdani, who had replaced the latter as ABRI Commander, spoke to his officers just after the MPR session:

> This time, the atmosphere [of the MPR] was different from the past. There was a tendency of a certain group to force its wishes in such a way as to endanger Pancasila democracy. We have to watch out for this. Recalling the MPR session that just ended, we are almost ready to conclude that ABRI's sociopolitical activities for securing the purity and consistency of Pancasila and the Constitution will be significantly difficult in the future.[22]

In July, Sutrisno again expressed his opinion at a meeting of officers who would be posted to non-military positions. This time, he stressed that:

> Indonesia should have a healthy and dynamic Pancasila democracy in which we can nominate more than two candidates for the vice-presidency and vote to decide on one of them at the MPR. This is important to improve the professionalism of all sociopolitical forces.[23]

These two statements by the new ABRI Commander reveal the ABRI leadership's objections to the appointment of Sudharmono by the president; they are rare examples of an ABRI Commander's open expression of dissatisfaction with Suharto's political projects. This was the first time that ABRI accepted the idea that there might be competition for the vice-presidency and, implicitly, for the presidency.

ABRI mobilized Kopkamtib to identify communist penetration in the Sudharmono-led Golkar. During the period between the March MPR session and the election of the Golkar chairman in October, Kopkamtib conducted an intensive campaign to discredit Sudharmono by claiming that he had been involved in communist activities in the early 1960s; this campaign was presumably part of Murdani's roll-back strategy against Suharto and Sudharmono.[24] Suharto's

---

[22] Try Sutrisno, "Amanat Panglima ABRI Pada Upacara Penutupan Susyawan ABRI Angkatan ke-XIV di Bandung Tanggal 14 March 1988" (The ABRI Commander's Address at the Closing Ceremony for the 14th Course for ABRI Seconded Officers, Bandung, March 14, 1988), *Mimbar Kekaryaan ABRI* 208 (April 1988): 47.

[23] Try Sutrisno, "Amanat Panglima ABRI Pada Acara Pertemuan Dengan Pakokar dan Karyawan ABRI Eselon-1 di Markas Besar ABRI Tanggal 15 Juli 1988" (The ABRI Commander's Address at the Meeting of Echelon-1 Seconded Officers at ABRI Headquarters, July 15, 1988), *Mimbar Kekaryaan ABRI* 211 (July 1988): 44.

[24] A few days before the Golkar Congress in October, Kopkamtib announced that a head of a Golkar branch in West Sumatra had been involved in PKI activities, thus effectively discrediting Sudharmono's management of Golkar. This Balatkom campaign was also pursued in April by retired Lt. Gen. Sarwo Edhie Wibowo, who announced his resignation from the DPR/MPR in protest against the alleged presence of ex-PKI figures in key governmental posts. Sarwo's action was widely seen as ABRI's attempt to tag Sudharmono as a communist. Then, for the rest of the year, the "latent danger" campaign was conducted under the name of *bersih diri* (clean-self) and *bersih lingkungan* (clean-environment) and mobilized to seek out those in the government (and their family members) who had any past association with PKI activities. Sudharmono finally decided not to run for the Golkar chairmanship. For details of this extraordinary campaign, see "The Latent Danger of the PKI," *Tapol Bulletin* 87 (June 1988);

September decision to abolish Kopkamtib was made under these circumstances. These events demonstrated how the intra-military program of ideological standardization had been transformed into a tool for security surveillance in society, and how it finally became a weapon used by ABRI to challenge Suharto's political plans. It is ironic that the project, which was intended to secure the stability of Suharto's regime based on Pancasila conformity, was transformed into a military doctrine capable of undermining the cohesion of the elite and threatening Suharto. The evolving *kewaspadaan* doctrine during the decade up to 1988 strongly reflected the pre-eminence of the intelligence sector within ABRI which had long been dominated by Murdani. It was remarkable, in this sense, that the completion of the Balatkom project was accompanied by the decline of Murdani's power.

However, the fall of Murdani did not mark the end of the *kewaspadaan* ideology within ABRI. It was the life-giver for the New Order military, which had to struggle continuously to maintain the legitimacy of its permanent political involvement in the state—as if pumping the heart to keep sending blood into the body of a living dinosaur. It was in this context that the growing democratic movements and their frequent appeals to the concept of "globalization" attracted the attention of ABRI's doctrine managers.

THE HARD-LINE MILITARY'S THINKING ON GLOBALIZATION

Globalization was a concept originally invoked by the media and democratic movements in their attempts to challenge the legitimacy of the military's control of politics and to expand democratic space in the country's political discourse. Advocates of democratization—including students, legal activists, NGOs, and elite critics, among them retired generals and civilian politicians—asserted that "regime opening," or *keterbukaan*, was irresistible and justified since the communist threat so often cited by ABRI had lost all credibility after the fall of the USSR and the dissolution of the Communist Bloc. This was an unprecedented challenge to ABRI's established *kewaspadaan* doctrine. However, ABRI discovered—or invented—an "opportunity" in this new debate to reassert the supremacy of *kewaspadaan* thinking and expand the political territory in which ABRI was free to project its ritual warnings against communism into the country's actual political program. This dynamic had nothing to do with the ongoing friction between Suharto and ABRI, but reflected ABRI's corporate interest in preserving its dominant political power. However, the changing Suharto-ABRI relationship influenced the "style" of the doctrinal application. We will look at these two spiraling developments and examine how the globalization discourse provided ABRI with a critical opportunity to synchronize its old ideological structure with the new social discourse in such a way as to strengthen ABRI's hardline approach to popular democratic movements.

ABRI's strategic plan, published in 1988, illuminates the military's attitudes in the early stage of the *keterbukaan* movement. It consisted of three pillars, i.e. long-term (twenty-five years), medium-term (five years), and short-term (annual) assessments. To synthesize with the Balatkom study produced by Lemhannas, the Defense Department headed by Murdani formulated a short-term strategic assessment in 1988 that expressed a number of *kewaspadaan* concerns. It stated that

---

"The 'Clean-Self' and 'Clean-Environment' Witch-Hunt," *Tapol Bulletin* 90 (December 1988); and Goodfellow, *Api Dalam Sekam*, pp. 15-28.

for the next few years into the 1990s, as international communication was becoming increasingly accessible and widespread, special vigilance would be needed to guard against the infiltration of foreign values—especially communism and liberalism—into Indonesia. The report warned that these alien values would penetrate in places where excessive economic development had widened the social gap between the rich and the poor.[25] Therefore, the internal security threat in the early 1990s, the document concluded, would be in the form of "new-style communism" (*komunisme gaya baru*—KGB) that might infiltrate the government and society. *Kewaspadaan* would be urgently required to monitor the activities of: (1) social organizations that had initially been hesitant to accept Pancasila principles as the sole foundation for all such organizations, but had later accepted Pancasila irresolutely; (2) the fourth-generation communist groups that employed "new-style" communist tactics, meaning that they used constitutional methods and intellectual networks in their efforts to "depoliticize ABRI"; (3) extreme groups that would try to use extra-constitutional means—instigation of mass riots, for instance—to further their political interests based on racial and separatist motivations; and (4) a certain group of people (*pihak tertentu*) who wanted to institute liberal democracy with unlimited freedom, and whose messages were broadcast through academic forums, discussions, and seminars as well as via the mass media.[26] In order to counter these "dangers threatening Pancasila, the Constitution, national integration, and development," this short-term strategic study advocated maintaining a strong *kewaspadaan* with the aim of eliminating any idea in society that might contradict Pancasila and the national interest.[27] Though the term "globalization" was not yet introduced, the paper identified expanding international relations as the key factor that would activate these threats.

ABRI's intermediate-term strategy for 1989-1993 paid special attention to security management during the 1992 election and the presidential election at the general session of the MPR in 1993. The policy guideline for the territorial apparatus stated that certain groups in Indonesia manipulated emotional issues to stir up conflicts, such as land disputes, and encouraged demonstrations and riots in response to racial-religious issues in order to further their political interests in both the general and the presidential elections.[28] In response to these threats, the territorial commands were instructed to sustain the *kewaspadaan* effort, scrutinize the activities of former political prisoners, manage political conditions for the election and the

---

[25] *Analisa Lingkungan Strategi Pertahanan Keamanan Negara 1988-1989* (Analysis of the Strategic Environment of the Defense of National Security 1988-1989) (Jakarta: Direktorat Jenderal, Perencanaan Umum dan Penganggaran, Dephankam, 1988), pp. 126-127.

[26] Ibid., pp. 128-130. The second category here shows how ABRI perceived public criticism of *dwifungsi*—namely criticism of ABRI's political repressive acts, its support for Golkar during the elections, its extensive control of seats in the parliament and civilian posts in the government—as an attempt to depoliticize ABRI. It interpreted such criticism as threatening to national stability and political life based on Pancasila, and consequently designated these critics as proper objects of security operations. The third category is relevant to the situation in Aceh and ABRI's response. In 1989 the government and ABRI decided to impose on Aceh the status of a Military Operations Area (Daerah Operasi Militer—DOM) in order to intensify the security operations against the separatist movements in that region. The two other areas designated as DOM were Irian Jaya and East Timor.

[27] Ibid., p. 66.

[28] *Pokok-Pokok Kebijaksanaan Pembinaan Teritorial Tahun 1989-1993* (Core Policies for Territorial Management, 1989-1993) [No: Kep/04/VII/1990] (Jakarta: Mabes ABRI, 1990), pp. 10-11.

MPR session, neutralize the negative impact of economic development and technological innovations, and combat any effort by certain groups to manipulate religion for political gain.[29] These directives showed that the concept of "vigilance against certain groups" was a core element in ABRI's territorial operations, now put into practice.

However, ABRI's harsh conduct of security during the election and its handling of the MPR gave legitimacy to those who demanded that the repressive security practices of previous years be relaxed.[30] ABRI responded to this demand on the twenty-eighth anniversary of the failed "communist" coup of 1965 (G30S/PKI) in September 1993, when Lemhannas published a thick document about *kewaspadaan* and Balatkom at the instruction of the Lemhannas Governor, Maj. Gen. Hartono. Hartono asserted that communist tactics had now been "borrowed and adapted" by "certain groups for certain political interests."[31] Distinguishing the method from the ideology, Hartono argued that non-communists also utilized communist methods in their attempts to topple the government. Needless to say, this interpretation was quite useful in those situations when ABRI wished to condemn certain popular movements but couldn't find even a whiff of communist ideology. Also, since the term "certain group" was open-ended, any political trouble-maker so identified by ABRI could be brought into this category if necessary. To support this approach, the document developed an argument which can be summarized as follows.

It first countered the claim that the communist threat had evaporated since the end of the Cold War and the collapse of the Soviet Union. The document explained that with the end of the Cold War the world had entered an era of globalization and free-flowing communications that affected Indonesia's development because the boundary between the domestic and international systems was rapidly becoming meaningless. This phenomenon introduced a new spectrum of threats into every sphere of national life. In politics, globalization encouraged the penetration of capitalism, liberal thought, and other foreign ideologies into Indonesia, all of which contradicted the Pancasila philosophy and jeopardized the Indonesian defense system based on Total People's Defense (Hankamrata).[32] In the economic field, the free-market economy threatened Indonesia's Pancasila economy based on *kemitraan* (partnership), while in religious life, globalization facilitated the influx of foreign values disturbing to religious groups. The document concluded that these threats would damage social harmony and national resilience (Ketahanan Nasional).[33] The *kewaspadaan* campaign was meant to repel these perceived threats. Significantly, this Lemhannas document repeatedly emphasized the campaign's synchronization with

---

[29] Ibid., pp. 20-23.

[30] I discuss the events at the 1993 MPR in the next section.

[31] *Sekitar Padnas, Bahaya Laten & Tapol G.30.S./PKI* (On National Vigilance, the Latent Danger, and the G30S/PKI Political Prisoners), p. III. As a logical consequence, Hartono insisted that such a new trend become the target of *kewaspadaan* in ideological, political, economic, sociocultural, and defense fields.

[32] These purported concerns about capitalism broadcast by ABRI in the early 1990s should be judged in context; in fact the Suharto regime had invited massive foreign investment by Western capitalists since the mid-1960s.

[33] Above explanations are from *Sekitar Padnas, Bahaya Laten & Tapol G.30.S./PKI*, pp. V, 1-10. Ketahanan Nasional is a national doctrine that encompasses security-political-social-economic-ideological barriers erected to maintain Indonesia's autonomy in international society. This concept was officially formulated in the 1978 Broad Outlines of State Policy (GBHN).

Ketahanan Nasional. Together these would constitute a total defense policy. This was the argument ABRI invented when it realized that the umbrella of Ketahanan Nasional—an indisputably national concept—could be useful to rejuvenate the ritual of Balatkom and *kewaspadaan*. By attaching the *kewaspadaan* project to Ketahanan Nasional, ABRI found a new way of rationalizing the project in the post-Cold War period.

Hartono, who was promoted to be the Armed Forces' Chief of Social and Political Staff with the rank of lieutenant-general in January 1994, expressed his views on the national threat more systematically in a Lemhannas journal.[34] This time, he emphasized the threat posed by capitalism-liberalism, which accompanied globalization, rather than emphasizing communism as he had done previously. According to Hartono, the rapid development of science and technology (IPTEK) in the era of globalization profoundly influenced the ideological-political-economic-sociocultural-military (*ipoleksosbudmil*) areas of national life, so it became necessary for "professional" ABRI officers to anticipate its negative influences. He argued that:

. . . the bipolar international system under the Cold War has ended and been replaced by a tendency to form a uni-polar system under Western capitalism-liberalism. [As a result], the global economy sped up the penetration of foreign culture through advanced information/communication technology and made Westerners think that their cultural values were universal. They then started to pressure other countries over the issues of human rights and environmental protection.[35]

Hartono's assessments were widely shared by state administrators. However, as seen in the Lemhannas document on national vigilance, this shared perception effectively opened discursive space for ABRI to assert the need for strengthening its own ideological-political control in order to resist "latent danger." Hartono's promotion to the position of Army Chief of Staff in February 1995 strengthened ABRI's inclination to adopt this approach in political practice. The starting point for this development should be sought in the context of Suharto-ABRI relations as they had evolved and changed since the 1988 MPR session. As discussed earlier, that session was colored by ABRI's overt frustration with Suharto's choice of Sudharmono as vice-president.

TRANSFORMATION OF SUHARTO-ABRI RELATIONS

The lingering antagonism between Suharto and the ABRI leadership had been reflected in events such as the dissolution of Kopkamtib and the creation of the

---

[34] R. Hartono (Letjen TNI), "Pengaruh Perkembangan IPTEK Terhadap Aktualisasi Pengabdian Generasi Penerus ABRI" (The Influence of the Development of Science and Technology on the Actualization of the Commitment of ABRI's Second Generation), *Majalah Ketahanan Nasional* 60 (1994): 43-56. As seen in the next section, Hartono's appointment to this position—which commands ABRI's political policies—reflected the rise in fortunes of Muslim officers typified by the promotion of Gen. Feisal Tanjung, who had replaced Try Sutrisno as ABRI Commander in March 1993.

[35] Ibid., pp. 43-45.

Indonesian Association of Muslim Intellectuals (ICMI).[36] For Suharto, both these moves undermined the influence of Murdani-linked officers and helped insure that ABRI was fully under his control. These attempts were accompanied by his move to limit the freedom of the current ABRI leaders to conduct their *dwifungsi* mission in politics. Suharto's intentions were apparent in a statement he made in November 1990. As he was receiving the visit of high-ranking officers following the ABRI Leadership Meeting (Rapim ABRI 1990), he emphasized that ABRI's role in society should be *tut wuri handayani*.[37] Since it was Suharto, as President and Supreme Commander of Armed Forces, who implied a need to shift ABRI's posture, this inevitably gave democratic advocates a new opportunity to question ABRI's *dwifungsi*. Suharto's statement thus resulted in the escalation of critical debate on ABRI's role in politics.

Suharto's interest in curtailing the influence of the military under the Murdani-Sutrisno leadership was also apparent in his handling of the so-called Dili incident, in which ABRI troops fired on thousands of demonstrators in Dili, East Timor, on November 12, 1991.[38] On the day after the incident, the ABRI Commander, Gen. Try Sutrisno, condemned the demonstrators for causing chaos and claimed that the troops were forced to shoot when the mob brutally attacked the soldiers. However, Suharto—as ABRI's Supreme Commander—quickly decided to dismiss two officers, Brig. Gen. Warouw and Maj. Gen. Sintong Panjaitan, both of whom were considered formally responsible for violations that took place within their areas of command even though they were not directly involved in the shooting. It was the first time in the New Order period that general-ranking officers were held responsible for the shooting of civilians by their troops. In addition, nineteen soldiers directly involved in the shooting were court-martialed. Suharto's measures were resented by many officers who believed that the shooting was proper. As a result, officers began to feel that Suharto was unwilling to protect ABRI's institutional interests. Powerful international pressure brought to bear on Indonesia after the Dili killing was the primary factor that pushed Suharto to set up the National Human Rights Commission (Komnas HAM) in December 1993. From the perspective of ABRI, now increasingly disenchanted with the president, this "government" body established to investigate ABRI's human rights abuses constituted another attempt by Suharto to publicize military problems for his own benefit.[39]

The military leadership under Murdani and Try Sutrisno did not stay silent. In the June 1992 general election, ABRI adopted a "neutral" attitude toward Golkar and also "tolerated" retired officers who supported the Democratic Party of Indonesia (PDI).[40] The implication was clear. This was ABRI's reminder to Suharto that the

---

[36] ICMI was launched in December 1990. This Suharto-sponsored body was chaired by his civilian protégé, Prof. B. J. Habibie (Minister of Research and Technology), and was widely seen as Suharto's tactical incorporation of Islam for the broadening of his political power base.

[37] A Javanese expression to describe how a father supports his young children from behind as they learn to walk.

[38] The Indonesian official account for the death toll was nearly fifty. But foreign human-rights organizations estimated it to be from one hundred to three hundred.

[39] For this account, see Human Rights Watch/Asia, *The Limits of Openness* (New York: Human Rights Watch, 1994), p. 126.

[40] Interview with Lt. Gen. (ret) Hasnan Habib, former Chief of Staff of the Defense Ministry (1973-75) and Ambassador to the United States, August 9, 1996. Although Golkar obtained the

established New Order political system could not be maintained without ABRI's active support. ABRI's response was highlighted in the vice-presidential election at the MPR session in March 1993. In February, Murdani's aide, Lt. Gen. Harsudiono Hartas, announced ABRI's nomination of the Pangab, Try Sutrisno, as the next vice-president. This was a clear challenge, for it had been the established New Order practice for ABRI to wait for Suharto to nominate his vice-presidential candidate before announcing its own preference. In facing such a high-profile challenge, Suharto—who is said to have favored Habibie—finally accepted the *fait accompli* and chose Sutrisno as his running mate for the Sixth Development Cabinet (1993-1998). As a final consequence of this Suharto-ABRI conflict, officers such as Murdani, Sutrisno, and Hartas were all removed from the military structure.[41]

This 1993 event was a turning point in Suharto-ABRI relations. It convinced Suharto to reconstruct the military so that it would be amenable to him. Dismantling the legacy of Murdani's ABRI and recruiting loyalist officers were his two major goals. Suharto's political survival depended on how well he could transform ABRI within the next five years, in preparation for the 1998 presidential election. Even if he himself did not ultimately choose to stay in office, establishing an amenable military was necessary for his management of the succession. A structural impediment encountered by Suharto in this effort was the generation gap. As a remnant of the revolutionary generation, Suharto seems to have been less capable of judging loyalist officers of the new generation—except for his military aides. Inevitably, Suharto started to accept the advice of trusted cronies in selecting officers who would occupy strategic positions. The role of his family, including Habibie, whom Suharto had known since Habibie was a child, became increasingly apparent in military promotion practices.[42]

The ABRI leadership under Feisal Tanjung, who replaced Edi Sudradjat in May 1993, further adapted itself to Suharto's shifting political preferences, as indicated by two events. First, at the Golkar Congress in October 1993, Feisal announced that ABRI would not nominate a candidate for Golkar Chairman, a decision that expedited an effort by the Suharto-Habibie group to promote the "civilianization" and ICMI-zation of Golkar by installing Harmoko (Information Minister and a member of ICMI's Advisory Board) in the position.

Second, in January 1994, ABRI's central intelligence agency, BAIS (Armed Forces' Strategic Intelligence Body), which had been developed by Murdani, was liquidated and replaced with the less powerful BIA (ABRI Intelligence Body). The dissolution of BAIS further dismantled the personal network of Murdani (a process dubbed "de-

---

majority of votes in the 1992 election, its share of the vote declined from 73 percent in 1987 to 68 percent.

[41] Murdani was replaced by Army Chief of Staff Gen. Edi Sudradjat. Edi—a secular-nationalist officer—enjoyed a wide range of support within the military, but the position of Defense Minister was less influential as a place from which to consolidate an independent power base. However, he was a close associate of Murdani and frequently made statements critical of the government and the new ABRI leadership under Gen. Feisal Tanjung, a devout Muslim and long-time friend of Habibie. Gen. Feisal became ABRI Commander in May 1993 with the strong recommendation from Habibie to Suharto. Feisal's Islamic orientation synchronized with Habibie's desire to cultivate military support for his ICMI.

[42] Feisal Tanjung's promotion was one such case. Also Wismoyo Arismunandar, who replaced Edi Sudradjat as Army Chief of Staff in May 1993, was a brother-in-law of Suharto's wife. In February 1995, Wismoyo was replaced by Hartono who had been close to Prabowo and to Siti Hardijanti Rukmana, Suharto's eldest daughter.

Murdani-zation"), while simultaneously diminishing the organizational basis of autonomous military power that could evolve beyond Suharto's control.

The transformation of ABRI's high command in the post-Murdani period was managed through such processes. Suharto's efforts to reconstruct presidential-ABRI relations on a new basis, and his search for loyalist officers to this end, were increasingly mediated by Habibie and Feisal and also by Brig. Gen. Prabowo—the ambitious son-in-law of Suharto. When Hartono was promoted to Army Chief of Staff in February 1995, his elevation was interpreted as the result of an initiative by Prabowo.[43] The renewed ABRI leadership led by Feisal and Hartono was pro-ICMI and amenable to the First Family. Suharto relied on this leadership to prepare for the smooth handling of both the 1997 general election—which was expected to face a serious opposition movement centered on Megawati, who chaired the PDI—and the 1998 presidential election, which must not be marred by disturbances of the sort that had erupted in recent memory, i.e. Ibrahim Saleh's interruption in the MPR and Harsudiono Hartas' premature nomination of a vice-president.

Against this political background, the new ABRI leadership sought a rationale to legitimize political repression against the widening popular criticism of the Suharto regime and the growing societal demands for democratic *keterbukaan*. Their decision to rely on the routinized *kewaspadaan* approach which had been institutionalized by the previous ABRI leadership was understandable, as it had long been regarded as a legitimate practice within the military. Perhaps it was perceived as a painful task, since these actions were certain to erode the people's trust in ABRI even further. But the new military leaders found a hope; they hoped their *kewaspadaan* approach might appeal to Muslims if it used the Islamic cause as a rallying point.

KEWASPADAAN POLITICAL PROGRAMS DURING THE FINAL YEARS

The Feisal-Hartono leadership therefore adapted the established *kewaspadaan* doctrine. As discussed earlier, the identification of *pembangunan* as potentially fertile ground for subversives was already a part of the standard interpretation of Balatkom. Under the new military leadership, the details of this doctrine were frequently adjusted to cultivate Islamic sympathy. Discussion of the problem of the widening social-economic gap, which was also cited by democratic advocates critiquing New Order developmentalism, came to be focused on Chinese-Indonesians. Reference to the gap was often a code for appealing to Islamic sentiments against rich Chinese. Although publicizing a stark dichotomy between the rich-Christian-minority-Chinese and the poor-Muslim-majority-Indonesians threatened to stir up ethnic disharmony, the political usefulness of the approach was still considerable. If this approach were coupled with hardline thinking on globalization, the missing link between the Islamic cause and support for the regime could be established. Gen. Hartono's close associate, Brig. Gen. Farid Zainuddin, for example, wrote in a Lemhannas journal as follows:

> The West is always antagonistic to Islam. This is not unrelated to the recent international campaign for political liberalization [by the West] . . . which has

---

[43] Hartono and Prabowo established a political think-tank, the Center for Policy and Development Studies (CPDS) in 1995, which had a strong Muslim and anti-Murdani orientation.

also been promoted in Indonesia as the revival of Islam becomes apparent. . . . It is globalization that facilitates this [campaign]. It [globalization] also strengthens the international network of non-*pribumi* business which has dominated the Indonesian economy since the beginning [of the New Order].[44]

This proposal that the West be perceived as a force threatening Islam evoked the concept of globalization in order to highlight the "Chinese problem" in economic life. It was expected to promote Islamic "nationalism" and demonstrate ABRI's sympathy. It also provided an opportunity to argue that the democratic movement— allegedly manipulated by Western anti-Islamicism—should be treated with suspicion by Muslims.

The military leadership also strove to invent a new logic to identify evolving democratic pressure from society as a reason for the need to sustain the Balatkom campaign. The opportunity arrived in July 1995, when Suharto decided to release some G30S-related political prisoners, including Soebandrio, Omar Dhani, and Soetarto.[45] When the Minister of Justice Oetojo Oesman announced Suharto's plan to grant amnesty to these figures, ABRI Commander Feisal Tanjung—who had claimed before that there were still more than three hundred PKI supporters at large— responded negatively, insisting that this issue had to be handled carefully and would take time.[46] The military leadership also reintroduced the latent danger theory to combat the idea that ABRI's vigilance was unnecessary in the current stable situation. Maj. Gen. Syarwan Hamid—who had been promoted to Assistant for Sociopolitical Affairs to the Chief of the Sociopolitical Staff in March—stated that:

> . . . communism has in fact become bankrupt, but its "teaching" is still alive today. For example, when we listen to the music, ABRI does not see the singer but listens to the song, and tries to recognize whether or not the melody comes from the old song even though the musical instrument is different from in the past.[47]

Having insisted that the communist song could be played on new instruments, Syarwan asserted that current political issues such as *keterbukaan* and human rights provided excellent opportunities for singing the song.

Now, in the age of the post-Soviet world order, the "outside threat" evolved from communist doctrines to communist-type activities fomented by the infiltration of universal values. The target of repression was no longer limited to communist

---

[44] Brig. Gen. Farid Zainuddin, "Reaktualisasi Peran Sospol ABRI Dalam Rangka Memantapkan Kemandirian Bangsa" (Reactualization of ABRI's Sociopolitical Role in the Framework of Consolidating National Autonomy), *Majalah Ketahanan Nasional* 63 (1995): 109. Non-*pribumi* refers to ethnic Chinese Indonesians. Zainuddin was Hartono's assistant for political-security affairs and was promoted to become the Head of BIA in August 1997.

[45] Soebandrio was the former deputy prime minister and foreign minister, and Omar Dhani was the former Air Force Commander, while Soetarto was a high police intelligence officer during the Sukarno era. None of the three was a PKI member.

[46] "Silang Pandangan Mengampuni PKI" (Conflicting Views on Pardoning the PKI), *Gatra*, July 22, 1995.

[47] See Syarwan's interview in "Dengar Lagu, Bukan Orangnya" (Listen to the Song, Not the Singer), *Gatra*, July 22, 1995.

supporters, but was expanded to include popular movements conducting anti-regime activities.

Then late in 1995, the issue of "formless [communist] organizations" (*Organisasi Tanpa Bentuk*, or OTB) was raised by ABRI's Chief of the General Staff, Lt. Gen. Soeyono, who identified fifteen government critics as OTB figures. He explained that there were two groups of communists—one consisting of former PKI supporters and the other of those who had been influenced by the first group and now tried to discredit the government by using the issues of human rights, democratization, and environmental protection.[48] Furthermore, Soeyono insisted that as the PKI had used "agitation and propaganda" (*agitprop*) in the past, these same methods were now being used by these figures to attack the government. Linking the OTB issue and the alleged impact of globalization, his theory attacked both the Internet and NGOs, asserting that current evidence of communist emergence was almost the same as in 1965, except that the method of the contemporary subversives was different, as they could infiltrate the nation via the Internet.[49] Regarding the NGOs, which had already become important political actors through their efforts to expose ABRI's frequent human rights abuses, he warned that "we now know their color and will scrutinize them to reveal many of their gray activities."[50]

---

[48] See "ABRI Names Faces Behind Incidents," *Jakarta Post*, October 17, 1995; and "Letjen TNI Soeyono: Cara-Cara PKI Sudah Dilakukan Terang-Terangan" (Lt. Gen. Soeyono: PKI Methods Blatantly Used), *Forum Keadilan*, October 23, 1995. Soeyono was a former Presidential adjutant. The group of fifteen alleged critics consisted of: five academics, including George Adicondro, Arief Budiman, Kuwat Triyanto, Harsono, and Lie Sing Tew—all had links with the Christian University of Satya Wacana; a labor activist, Mochtar Pakpahan; an anti-regime novelist, Pramoedya Ananta Toer, who received the Ramon Magsaysay Award in 1995; a vocal Muslim parliamentarian, Sri Bintang Pamungkas, who was kicked out of parliament; human-right lawyers Mulyana Kusumah and H. J. C. Princen; a former Minister during the Sukarno period and long-time political prisoner, Oei Tjoe Tat; a Chinese student living in Canada and active on the Internet, Paul Salim; a hugely popular public speaker and supporter of Megawati, Permadi; a retired general purged after 1965 for his links with Moscow and his leftist past, Soehario Padmodiwirio; and an undergraduate student, Petrus Hariyanto. Many of them were prominent democratic-reform advocates.

[49] Ibid. ABRI's concern about the Internet—which was beyond the state's control—led to the establishment of a special Internet unit in ABRI headquarters. This was announced a few days after Soeyono's OTB statement on October 16. See "Perangi Info Sampah ABRI Masuk Internet" (Fighting Garbage Information: ABRI Joins the Internet), *Republika*, October 20, 1995. On the political impact of the Internet "revolution," see David T. Hill and Krishna Sen, "Wiring the *Warung* to Global Gateways: The Internet in Indonesia," *Indonesia* 64 (October 1997): 67-89. It was thought that the main objective of this unit was the collection of information about anti-government activities and—as described by an officer involved in this project—"counter-information" on the Internet. Interview, October 1996.

[50] Quotations are from Soeyono's interview cited above, published in *Forum Keadilan*, October 23, 1995. According to Syarwan, ABRI had already identified thirteen NGOs which exploited the issues of human rights and democratization. See his interview in "Assospol ABRI Syarwan Hamid: PKI Kini Sedang Bermetamorfosa" (ABRI's Assistant for Sociopolitical Affairs Lt. Gen. Syarwan Hamid: Today the PKI is Metamorphizing), *Forum Keadilan*, November 6, 1995. The prominence of NGOs in late New Order politics was paralleled by the growing wave of strikes that started about 1990. These strikes had been supported and encouraged by many human rights NGOs. Details are analyzed, for example, in Vedi R. Hadiz, "Workers and Working Class Politics in the 1990s," in *Indonesia Assessment 1993: Labour—Sharing in the Benefits of Growth?*, ed. Chris Manning and Joan Hardjono (Canberra: Department of Political and Social Change, Research School of Pacific and Asian Studies, Australian National University, 1993), pp. 186-200. ABRI's hostility to these NGOs might have been intensified by

Several critics responded to ABRI's witch-hunt by arguing that this was all merely a repetition of old rhetoric meant to enhance ABRI's political bargaining power vis-à-vis the emerging democratic forces.[51] It is interesting to note that former vice-president Sudharmono, who had earlier been the target of rumors branding him as communist, responded negatively to the OTB campaign by warning against "instantly labeling certain people as OTB or having an 'unclean [family] environment' [*tidak bersih lingkungan*]."[52] The father of the Tarpadnas project, Lt. Gen. (ret) Soebiyakto, asserted in 1997 that: " . . . today's ABRI insists on the latent danger of PKI, or formless [communist] organizations (OTB), and always claims that there is a PKI-ghost behind democratic movements. But they are talking nonsense, there is no threat from the PKI any more."[53]

In facing these criticisms, the military leadership responded in two ways. First, it reiterated the established interpretation of Balatkom. Lt. Gen. Moetojib, who had replaced Hartono as Lemhannas Governor, wrote in his house journal that the issues of democratization, human rights, and *keterbukaan* had all been shaped by foreign advocates, and that discussion of these issues encouraged the formation of critical public opinion—including criticism of ABRI's political role—which posed a threat to national stability.[54] Here civil society concepts were all automatically identified as threats to stability and the object of *kewaspadaan*. The consolidation of ABRI's interpretation of Balatkom was more evident in a report issued by the territorial staff section in ABRI Headquarters.[55] After describing the chronological events leading to the emergence of public debate over the OTB in the previous year, the report claimed that OTB members believed in communist techniques as their most effective tool. The alleged techniques relied on the "theory of contradiction" [*sic*] to encourage conflict between groups, for instance between the rich and the poor, between religious groups, between ABRI and laborers, and between old and young people. By using these methods, the report continued, OTB elements created antagonistic conditions

---

the fact that military personnel were often hired by private enterprises as security guards, i.e. strikebreakers.

[51] Many critics also saw that the campaign had political goals. A human rights activist, H. J. C. Princen, argued that the campaign was ABRI's effort to emasculate government critics before the 1997 general elections. Paul Salim, an Internet commentator, argued that the government needed the campaign to legitimize its theory that stability was endangered. Both Princen and Salim were included in Soeyono's list of fifteen OTB members, cited above. For their responses to the campaign, see "Curiga Lima Belas Dalam OTB" (Fifteen Suspicions in the OTB), *Forum Keadilan*, November 6, 1995.

[52] The comments of Sudharmono and Sarwono are from "Mewaspadai Lawan Baru: Tanpa Bentuk" (Vigilance Toward a New Enemy: Without Form), *Forum Keadilan*, November 6, 1995.

[53] Interview, January 8, 1997. Soebiyakto's rejection of OTB seemed to be derived largely from his antipathy—strongly shared by former Murdani allies—to Suharto and the new ABRI leadership.

[54] Moetojib (Letjen TNI), "Stabilitas Nasional Sebagai Landasan Kokoh Bagi Pembangunan Politik dan Ekonomi" (National Stability as a Sound Foundation for Political and Economic Development), *Telstra* 38 (January-February 1996): 10. Since March 1996, Moetojib served as the head of BAKIN until replaced by Lt. Gen. (ret) Zein A. Maulani in September 1998.

[55] Staf Teritorial ABRI, *Tinjauan Teritorial* (Territorial Considerations) (Jakarta: Mabes ABRI, No. Triwulan I 1996/1997). *Tinjauan Teritorial* is the quarterly report of ABRI Headquarters' Territorial Section (Ster ABRI).

and conflicts of interests in society, which would eventually lead to rioting and political instability.[56]

The military's second response to criticism was a search for evidence to help construct the reality of Balatkom in the current situation. First, academics became the target. In October 1995, Brig. Gen. Djoko Subroto, Chief of Staff of the Central Java Military Command, announced that the Command's investigation found proof that three academics at the Protestant University of Satya Wacana had been involved in communist activities in the distant past. Asked about possible action to be taken against these three, Djoko suggested that the University Rector had the power to act, thus placing the case beyond ABRI's direct responsibility.[57] The pressure on campus activists continued as Lt. Gen. Soeyono in November warned that he could bring military tanks to any university if necessary, even if there had been no formal request for tanks.[58] His threat was a response to the growing number of student demonstrations in recent years. This high-profile warning to students was followed in December by the arrest of Petrus Hariyanto, a prominent student activist and Secretary General of SMID (Students in Solidarity for Democracy in Indonesia) who was included in Soeyono's list of fifteen OTB figures and was suspected of leading a recent petition movement to the Dutch Embassy.

Together with academics, NGO activists were also targeted. In May 1996, the book *Bayang-Bayang PKI*, or "Shadows of the PKI," was banned by a Supreme Court decision. The Publications Investigation Team of Bakorstanas (the Coordinating Agency for the Maintenance of National Stability) concluded that, despite the stated purpose of the book as a general reference for young people studying the G30S/PKI, its content was marred by historical distortions, notably distortions meant to discredit ABRI and the national leadership.[59] After this, ABRI's surveillance of NGOs via the territorial apparatus from Provincial Military Commands down to the Koramil (Military Subdistrict Commands) was tightened. It was in the midst of such tension between NGOs and ABRI that Megawati was toppled as head of the PDI, and a physical clash between the two sides triggered a riot on July 27, 1996. The riot was immediately followed by ABRI's purge of NGO activists that especially targeted the People's Democratic Party (PRD, Partai Rakyat Demokratik)—a student NGO which had recently declared itself to be a political party. Let us examine this development.

---

[56] Above references are from ibid., p. 3. The "theory of contradictions" is Mao's contribution to modern political language.

[57] See "Kodam IV Teliti Dugaan Tiga Dosen UKSW Sebagai Eks PKI" (Fourth Military Command is Studying the Suspicion that Three Faculty Members of the Satyawacana Christian University are ex-PKI), *Suara Merdeka*, October 26, 1995. The three faculty members were Kuwat Triyanto, Harsono, and Lie Sing Tew. They faced this accusation in October 1994 when the faculty conducted a "democratic" strike against the dismissal of Dr. Arief Budiman—a sociologist and long-term New Order critic—who had protested against the improper procedures used in the selection of the University's new rector.

[58] "Saya Bisa Bawa Tank ke Kampus" (I Can Bring Tanks to Campus), *Kompas*, November 28, 1995.

[59] Bakorstanas was established to replace Kopkamtib in 1988. The assessment by Bakorstanas is in Staf Teritorial ABRI, *Tinjauan Teritorial*, pp. 5-12, with the title, "Hasil Penelitian Tim Karya Tulis Bakorstanas Terhadap Buku 'Bayang-Bayang PKI'" (Research Results of Bakorstanas' Publications Investigation Unit with Regard to the Book 'Shadows of the PKI'). The report demanded that the Supreme Court immediately ban the book and also asked ABRI's territorial apparatus to watch out (*mewaspadai*) for the circulation of this book in society.

At the July 1993 PDI congress in Medan, ABRI Headquarters had received an order from Suharto to intervene and overthrow the chairman, Soerjadi. Three years later, the ABRI Commander, Feisal Tanjung, claimed that the PDI leadership conflict was still unresolved and, acting again under instructions from Suharto, he called for another PDI congress in June 1996. This time the goal was to topple Megawati—the only politician with a chance to loosen Suharto's stranglehold on Indonesian politics—and reinstate Soerjadi. The rebel congress elected Soerjadi to replace Megawati and soon received government endorsement. Megawati then filed legal suits against senior government and military officials, including Feisal, alleging that they manipulated the congress in order to divide the party. She also launched a daily "free speech forum" (*mimbar bebas*) at party headquarters in central Jakarta. The forum was joined not only by Megawati's PDI supporters, but also by student groups and NGOs demanding democratization.

As the free speech forum expanded from an intra-party protest to an anti-Suharto grassroots movement, ABRI Headquarters started to view the forum as a security threat and warned Megawati supporters to stop it. The Jakarta Military Commander, Maj. Gen. Sutiyoso, announced on July 25 that any political action that disturbed law and order would be repressed. The following day, Lt. Gen. Syarwan Hamid warned that the forum was being manipulated by an anti-government movement.[60] The next morning around eight hundred government-supported Soerjadi cadres and other unidentified men, with the help of security forces (possibly including Brig. Gen. Prabowo's Special Forces personnel in mufti), took over the PDI building, sparking a two-day mass riot and clashes with military troops. Nearly two hundred people were arrested during the first day of the riot, and many of these remain missing.[61] A few days later, Maj. Gen. Sutiyoso issued a "shoot-on-sight" order to his soldiers.

It was in ABRI's interest to shift public attention from the Suharto-manipulated Medan Congress to the alleged *dhalang* (masterminds) of the riot. The PRD—an active participant in the *mimbar bebas*—was identified by both Suharto and ABRI as the organization that had planned the riot. The military leadership mobilized its resources to label the PRD as communist and threatened to investigate any individuals or groups that had a previous relationship with the PRD, an investigation that threatened to net many prominent democratic activists.

To conduct this campaign effectively, sustain high pressure on the anti-regime political movement, and thus insure smooth implementation of the general election in May 1997, the Feisal-Hartono leadership needed ABRI to show solidarity in accepting this interpretation of the PRD, and it needed the support of the Islamic sector. In one attempt to strengthen internal solidarity, ABRI spokesman, Brig. Gen.

---

[60] "Pangdam Jaya: Ganggu Kamtibnas, Aksi Politik akan Dihentikan" (Jakarta Military Commander: If They Disturb National Security and Order, Political Activities Will Be Stopped), *Kompas*, July 26, 1996; "Kassospol ABRI: Aksi-aksi Akhir-akhir ini Merupakan Gerakan" (ABRI's Chief of the Sociopolitical Staff: Recent Actions Have Become a Political Movement), *Suara Pembaruan*, July 26, 1996.

[61] "Pangab: 176 Ditangkap" (The ABRI Commander: 176 Have Been Arrested), *Harian Terbit*, extra-edition, July 28, 1996. According to the final report of Komnas HAM, the riot resulted in five deaths, 149 injured, and 23 missing. For the full Komnas document, entitled "Pernyataan Komnas Mengenai Peristiwa 27 Juli" (The National Human Rights Commission's Statement on the July 27 Affair), see Santoso (coordinator), *Peristiwa 27 Juli* (The July 27 Affair) (Jakarta: Institut Studi Arus Informasi and Aliansi Jurnalis Independen, 1997), pp. 59-65. The government banned this book in February 1997.

Amir Syarifuddin, appealed to the elite Green Berets (the Army Strategic Reserve Command, or Kostrad) whose participation was significant for any political-security project conducted by ABRI.[62] He stated that communists had seen an opportunity to revive their activities after the liquidation of Kopkamtib, and the PRD was the final product. The PRD should be seen as a communist group because: (1) its manifesto was clearly anti-Pancasila, and its behavior recalled the PKI attempt to stage a coup in Madiun in 1948; (2) its organization was formed in communist style, by uniting many labor, peasant, artist, student, and intellectual organizations which were often led by ex-PKI figures; and (3) its tactics were communist-oriented because the PRD had organized labor-agrarian strikes and mass demonstrations in Irian Jaya, West Kalimantan, Ujung Pandang, Bogor, Surabaya, Solo, and Semarang during 1996 with posters demanding "remove *dwifungsi*." Syarifuddin's clarification was circulated to all the territorial commands, who were instructed to tighten regional security surveillance in anticipation of counter-actions by the underground members of the ultra-left PRD.[63]

As this campaign was being conducted, ABRI attempted to mobilize Islamic support by warning against still-active "atheist" communism. Officers involved expected that this "theory of contradiction" would be accepted by the current military leadership, which included top-ranking officers with strong Muslim backgrounds. Among them, Lt. Gen. Syarwan Hamid seemed to be the most active.

A week before the July 27 riot, Syarwan held a meeting with sixty-one pro-government youth organizations, including many Islam-oriented ones such as MDI (Majelis Dakwah Indonesia) and Pemuda Muslim Indonesia, urging them to watch out for OTB activities and condemning the free-speech forum held by Megawati's wing of the PDI as illegal. These organizations publicly announced their support for the proposal that ABRI take action against the PRD and PDI-Mega.[64] Also on July 30, Syarwan held a meeting with a delegation of Islamic youth groups, such as Pemuda Ansor, AMII (Angkatan Muda Islam Indonesia), and Pemuda Tarbiyah. On the next day, they declared their willingness to fight against communism and condemned the PRD as a dangerous element that had instigated the riot. Other Muslim organizations, such as Pemuda Muhammadiyah, HMI (Himpunan Mahasiswa Islam), and the government-sponsored MUI (Majelis Ulama Indonesia) also released statements endorsing ABRI's red-purge campaign after the riot.[65] Furthermore, on August 6, Syarwan had a three-hour talk with key figures in the United Development Party (PPP). This was his first meeting with a political party after the riot, indicating the significance of Muslim organizations in ABRI's PRD-bashing campaign. The Head of PPP, Ismail Hasan Metareum, expressed his full support of

---

[62] See Amir Syarifuddin (Brigjen: Kapuspen), "Mewaspadai Bangkitnya Kembali Gerakan Komunis di Indonesia" (Watch Out for the Resurgence of the Communist Movement in Indonesia), *Darma Putra* 37 (1996): 24-29. *Darma Putra* is Kostrad's internal organ.

[63] Staf Teritorial ABRI, *Tinjauan Teritorial* (No. Triwulan II, T.A. 1996/1997): 11-19.

[64] "Kassospol ABRI: ABRI Minta PDI Hentikan Mimbar Bebas" (ABRI's Chief of the Sociopolitical Staff: ABRI Asks the PDI to Stop its Free Speech Forum), *Kompas*, July 21, 1996.

[65] For details, see "Terlalu Naif, Kalau Anggap ABRI Jadikan PRD Sebagai Kambing Hitam" (It's Too Naïve to Think that ABRI is Scapegoating the PRD), *Kompas*, August 1, 1996; "Pernyataan Bersama dan Trauma Ormas Islam" (Joint Statement and the Trauma of the Islamic Mass Organizations), *Forum Keadilan*, August 26, 1996.

ABRI's effort.[66] Finally on August 11, more than ten thousand people from major pro-government mass organizations gathered in Jakarta to release an official declaration of support for the government and urged ABRI to ban the PRD as communist. Syarwan-led ABRI delegates at the meeting insisted that the declaration was spontaneous, while at the same time it emphasized the danger of the communist PRD and the need for promoting close cooperation between ABRI and Islam.[67] The "contradiction theory" adopted by ABRI was aimed at redefining the nature of this political event so that it did not appear to be an authoritarian crackdown against a popular movement, but, rather, an integral part of the Islamic struggle against the communist remnants.

In this way, the "Crush the PRD-Mega" campaign, which was carried out by Feisal's ABRI, heavily relied on the *kewaspadaan* approach established under the previous military empire of Gen. Murdani, with some curious adjustments of its definition of the threat and the target population for counter-mobilization.

THE LOSS OF MILITARY COHESION AND THE RISE OF DISSENT

Although the promulgation and evolution of *kewaspadaan* ideology was an element in the "corporate" interests of the military as a whole, this did not mean that implementation measures were unquestioned and always welcomed by the officer corps at large. As discussed earlier, the transformation of Suharto-ABRI relations after the fall of Murdani produced issues that threatened to accentuate cleavages within the military. The question of ABRI's autonomy vis-à-vis Suharto, the rise of Prabowo, ABRI's links to ICMI, the use of Islamic rhetoric in pursuing military policies, and dogmatization of the military response to popular movements all had the potential to ignite internal criticism. Indeed, the emergence of intra-military cleavages contributed to the rise of reform-minded officers concerned about the direction of the Feisal-Hartono leadership. Since military organizations are fundamentally based upon discipline and chain of command, it is difficult to find public statements by active duty officers about internal problems. But dissenters were represented by retired generals who had become openly critical as they perceived the military leadership's failure to address the dissatisfaction of many officers. Such developments during the final years of the Suharto regime facilitated the perception that reshaping the role of the military in political life—reconsidering President-ABRI relations, Golkar-ABRI relations, and, more generally, society-ABRI relations—was crucial to prevent ABRI's further loss of trust.

The ABRI-Golkar-ICMI Axis: Nationalism and Neutrality in Question

The first major event was ABRI's rapprochement with Golkar in mid-1995. As mentioned above, Feisal Tanjung had cooperated with Suharto and Habibie in appointing a civilian for the first time as Golkar chairman in 1993. In September 1995, as preparations for the 1997 general election got underway, Maj. Gen. Syarwan

---

66 "Syarwan: Kita Sudah Ingatkan Tetapi Dituduh Mengada-ada" (Syarwan: We Gave a Warning But Are Accused of Fabrication), *Suara Pembaruan*, August 7, 1996.

67 "Apel Kebulatan Tekad Dukung Orde Baru" (Roll Call for Unreserved Support for the New Order), *Suara Pembaruan*, August 12, 1996, and personal communication with an anonymous journalist who attended the meeting, August 1996.

Hamid insisted that ABRI could not be politically neutral since, as a sociopolitical force, it needed to choose a partner in order to promote national well-being. This stance invited intense public criticism on the grounds that it contradicted ABRI's role as "national guardian."[68] As the critical mood spread through society, Feisal Tanjung asserted that there was no political activity without partnership; thus the "ABRI-Golkar" alliance was reasonable.[69]

The escalation of public debate concerning ABRI's overt rapprochement with Golkar was followed by the establishment of a group that declared its concern about the sectarian tendencies in national politics, which were being increasingly influenced by ICMI. On October 23, Lt. Gen. Bambang Triantoro, former Chief of the Sociopolitical Staff (1985-7) under Murdani, announced the creation of a new political association, the Foundation for National Brotherhood Harmony (YKPK); in his capacity as its general chairman, he explained at a press conference that his actions were motivated by growing concerns about national unity and integration. This sixty-eight-member group attracted considerable attention, partly because it was perceived to have been set up in opposition to the "sectarian" ICMI and partly because of its high-profile membership.[70] The establishment of YKPK was, of course, welcomed by secular-minded military officers. It was publicly endorsed by the Speaker of Parliament, Lt. Gen. (ret) Wahono, the Minister of Transmigration Siswono, and the Minister of the Environment Sarwono, the latter two commonly regarded as being in the Cabinet's "nationalist" camp. Equally interesting was the emerging prominence of retired generals who had been associated with the military leadership under Murdani and grown more critical of Suharto and the ABRI leaders. The presence of these discontented officers, such as Lt. Gen. (ret) Bambang Triantoro, Lt. Gen. (ret) Kharis Suhud, and Maj. Gen. (ret) Samsuddin, significantly enhanced the public political role of recently retired officers.

Moreover, three times during the preceding three months, Edi Sudradjat had stressed the need for strengthening nationalism within ABRI, thus demonstrating his

---

[68] For example, Subagyo from the PDI stated in Parliament that Syarwan's comment would not only confuse people, but also invite social unrest ("Aspirasi Politik Keluarga Besar ABRI Tetap ke Golkar" [The Political Hopes of ABRI's Big Family Are Still With Golkar], *Suara Merdeka*, October 4, 1995). Matori Abdul Djalil, the former secretary-general of the PPP, insisted that ABRI would lose its credibility if it sided with Golkar. Since all political parties had already accepted Pancasila as their sole principle in the mid-1980s, there was no reason for ABRI to choose a partner ("Langkah Mundur Jika ABRI Tetap Memihak Golkar" [A Step Backward if ABRI Continues to Side with Golkar], *Bernas*, October 1, 1995). Retired Lt. Gen. Kemal Idris, former Commander of the Army Strategic Reserve Command, who was widely regarded as one of the founders of the New Order in the mid-1960s, argued that Syarwan's comment illustrated the arrogance of power that made power-holders believe "I can do no wrong." ("Kemal Idris: ABRI Terlalu Terlibat di Segala Bidang" [Kemal Idris: ABRI is Too Much Involved in Every Sphere], *Forum Keadilan*, October 23, 1995).

[69] "Feisal Tanjung: Dwifungsi Lestari Sepanjang Masa" (Feisal Tanjung: Dwifungsi Is Eternal), *Forum Keadilan*, October 23, 1995.

[70] They included, for example, Lt. Gen. (ret) Kharis Suhud (former Chair of MPR/DPR 1988-1993), Maj. Gen. (ret) Samsuddin (former Head of F-ABRI), Gaffar Rachman (former Secretary General of Nahdatul Ulama, or NU, the biggest Islamic organization in Indonesia), Hasjim Wahid (brother of Abdurrahman Wahid, the NU Chairman, who had criticized ICMI as a sectarian group), Marzuki Darusman (former Golkar politician now Deputy Chairman of the National Human Rights Commission), and Kwik Kian Gie (prominent Chinese economist affiliated with the PDI). Because of the various backgrounds of its members, the group was called the "rainbow alliance" (*aliansi pelangi*).

concerns about the sectarian tendencies within the military and its overt alliance with one particular political party. In July and again in August 1995, Edi warned that ABRI was now thought of as a "tool of the rich," given the reality that some ABRI members had close ties with business tycoons.[71] On September 8, addressing an ABRI Seminar in the Armed Forces' Staff and Command College (Sesko ABRI), Bandung, Edi reiterated his argument that ABRI must be reformed.[72] In public, YKPK Chairman Bambang Triantoro denied that he intended to try and curb the runaway influence of Habibie and ICMI, but in an interview he admitted that his sixty-eight-member group shared the thinking of Gen. (ret) Murdani, a leading anti-ICMI figure, though the latter was not directly involved in the establishment of YKPK.[73]

Bambang's movement, endorsed by Edi and "shared" by Murdani, met with a negative response from Syarwan Hamid. When asked about ABRI's perception of ICMI, he said that many in ABRI hoped that ICMI could bring Muslims—who comprised 88 percent of the Indonesian population—into the mainstream of national development. He warned that if the YKPK did not contribute to the national interest, the system would ostracize it and cause it to fade away before it could develop.[74] At the First National YKPK Discussion held in Surabaya on January 8-9 in 1996, Maj. Gen. Iman Utomo, a close ally of Hartono, who had earlier headed the East Java Military Command, appealed to his soldiers, veterans, and Golkar members to boycott the event.

In March 1996, while addressing a Golkar meeting in Central Java, at which Siti Hardijanti Rukmana, or Tutut, the President's oldest daughter and a Chairperson of Golkar's Central Leadership Council, was also present, Hartono told five thousand Golkar cadres that ". . . every ABRI member is a cadre of Golkar and there is no need for them to be dubious about stating their allegiance to Golkar." Showering praise on Tutut, he went on to say that: "as a Golkar cadre, my duty is to receive advice and instruction from Mbak [sister] Tutut."[75] On the next day, March 14, at the Sabilil Muttaqien Pesantren in Magetan, East Java, this former East Java Commander again expounded his theory of ABRI-Golkar relations. Wearing a yellow Golkar jacket, he declared in front of Golkar supporters that "Kodim [Military District Command] commanders and regional police chiefs are members of Golkar's regional advisory council, which means that all their staff are also Golkar members." Since not only

---

71 "Kredibilitas ABRI Tergantung Sikap ABRI Sendiri" (ABRI's Credibility Depends on ABRI's Own Stance), *Kompas*, July 21, 1995; "ABRI: Berjuang, Jangan Berdagang" (ABRI: Fight, Don't Do Business), *Forum Keadilan*, August 28, 1995. Golkar had been backed by many business tycoons, including members of the Suharto family.

72 "ABRI Harus Bersih dan Berwibawa" (ABRI Must Be Clean and Command Respect), *Bernas*, September 9, 1995.

73 "New Group to Counter Habibie Influence," *Reuters*, October 25, 1995. Bambang explained that both he and Murdani were concerned about some groups in the regime that put religious interests before national interests. Interview, December 16, 1996.

74 "Mayjen Syarwan Hamid: Yang tak Bermanfaat akan Layu Sebelum Berkembang" (Maj.-Gen. Syarwan Hamid: What's Useless Will Wilt Before Flowering), *Republika*, December 9, 1995.

75 "KSAD: Setiap Anggota Abri Kader Golkar" (Army Chief of Staff: Every ABRI Member is a Golkar Cadre), *Kompas*, March 14, 1995. Officially Tutut was only one of eight chairpersons under General Chairperson Harmoko. Thus Hartono's statement declaring the fusion of ABRI-Golkar could also be understood as an expression of his personal loyalty to Tutut, since in making that declaration independently Hartono bypassed Harmoko.

local commanders, but even Feisal Tanjung, were members of the Supervisors' Council, he concluded that all ABRI members were in fact Golkar cadres.[76]

Although ABRI leaders had often pointed out that ABRI had established Golkar, Hartono's remarkable statement was the first in which a high-ranking military officer described ABRI as subordinate to Golkar. This re-interpretation of Golkar-ABRI relations was quickly corrected by ABRI Headquarters in the following days; they argued that Hartono had mistakenly stated ABRI's standard theory of civil-military relations and also exceeded his capacity as Army Chief of Staff by speaking as if he represented all four armed services. The next day Feisal Tanjung explained that ABRI members who joined Golkar did so to "supervise" it, meaning he rejected Hartono's portrait of ABRI's subordination to the political party.[77] Syarwan Hamid too made an official announcement, saying that Hartono's statement was made in his personal capacity, not as Army Chief of Staff.[78]

This disagreement between the two ICMI-affiliated generals—Feisal and Hartono—was relatively insignificant for non-ICMI figures who now understood that the current military leadership did not hesitate to declare that ABRI, in its entirety, had overtly allied itself with a single political party. Edi Sudradjat, however, insisted that ABRI should work with other parties and not just Golkar, to help develop the nation.[79] Invoking Law No. 20, created in 1982, which stipulated that all parts of ABRI must work together with all sociopolitical forces to insure national development, he stressed the supremacy of the law over any other considerations.[80] Several retired generals and civilian leaders supported Edi's criticisms. For example, Lt. Gen. (ret) Hasnan Habib argued that, "if ABRI sides with one group, it does not need F-ABRI any more." "Law No. 20/1982," Hasnan continued, "neither allows civilian nor military supremacy, so ABRI can never be a cadre of the civilian Golkar."[81]

The ABRI leaders' move toward Golkar in 1995-6 reflected a determination to acquiesce in Suharto's political program involving Golkar-ABRI cooperation to insure that the coming general election would run smoothly and predictably and thereby secure his presidential re-election in 1998.

---

[76] "Hartono: Frivolous Questions About Golkar Allegiances Cause of Concern," *Kompas Online*, available <http://www.kompas.com/>, March 15, 1996.

[77] "Feisal Tanjung: ABRI Tetap ABRI" (Feisal Tanjung: ABRI is Forever ABRI), *Kompas*, March 16, 1996.

[78] "ABRI Sebagai Kekuatan Sospol dan Hankam" (ABRI as a Social and a National Defense Force), *Suara Pembaruan*, March 18, 1996.

[79] "ABRI tidak Hanya Berjuang dengan Golkar" (ABRI Doesn't Just Fight Alongside Golkar), *Suara Pembaruan*, March 25, 1996.

[80] Edi's comment, however, should be interpreted in the context of a power struggle with the pro-ICMI forces, rather than as a simple legal argument. Note that in 1993 he had suggested the nomination of ABRI candidates for the position of Golkar Chairman, who would work to secure ABRI's influence in Golkar.

[81] "Sekadar Menghebohkan Hubungan ABRI-Golkar" (Just Making an Issue of ABRI-Golkar Relations), *Forum Keadilan*, April 8, 1996.

Prominence of Retired Officers

The decline of cohesion within the military was further exacerbated in 1996, following the toppling of Megawati from the PDI and the launching of a security operation to crush the PRD, the *hantu PKI* (PKI ghost). A few days after the Medan congress, Defense Minister Edi Sudradjat claimed that national stability could never be built on authoritarianism. A day after the three-day riot in Jakarta, the Speaker of Parliament, Lt. Gen. (ret) Wahono, asserted that ABRI should limit its reliance on repressive measures because it could only succeed in its political role when it had public support. Former Army Chief Gen. (ret) Rudini insisted that the time had passed when ABRI could invoke the specter of communism to justify repressive measures, and ABRI had to show strong evidence to support its accusations. Otherwise, he said, ABRI and the government would lose the people's trust.[82]

However, Lt. Gen. (ret) Soesilo Sudarman, the Coordinating Minister for Political and Security Affairs, who also headed Pepabri (the Association of Retired Officers), maintained that some retired officers were behaving inconsistently. Admiral (ret) Sudomo also displayed his annoyance, saying, ". . . if retired generals want to correct the nation and its development, they should direct their views to the President rather than advertise problems in the mass media." ABRI Commander Feisal Tanjung went much further. Recalling the July 27 riot, he claimed that the problem arose from the ideological distortions generated by the so-called "rainbow alliance" (*aliansi pelangi*), with the communist PRD as its rising star. He branded the PRD as radical and anti-New Order/ABRI and charged that the "rainbow alliance" was trying to replace Pancasila and the Constitution. Some officers, he concluded, had deviated from military discipline and acted disloyally.[83]

Feisal's remarks stirred up strong reactions from retired officers, who criticized ABRI's political role more assertively, not only in the media but particularly at ABRI's internal meetings. In early September, the 1996 ABRI Seminar was held to solicit advice from several experts regarding ABRI's policy preparations for the Seventh Development Cabinet starting from 1998. Lt. Gen. (ret) Hasnan Habib objected to a statement in ABRI's draft paper for the Broad Outlines of the Nation's Direction (GBHN). Pointing to the original statement, which said that the emerging criticism of ABRI's political role stemmed from an erroneous assumption that civilian and military responsibilities were somehow opposed to one another, he argued that the crucial issue was not this dichotomy between civilian and military, but rather ABRI's obvious domination of national life, which restricted people's political

---

[82] Above comments are from "Menhankam: Stabilitas Nasional tak Dibangun di Atas Kekuasan yang Otoriter" (Defense Minister: National Stability Can Not Be Built on the Basis of Authoritarian Power), *Kompas*, July 6, 1996; "Ketua DPR/MPR: ABRI Harus Kurangi Reaksi-reaksi Represif" (Speaker of Parliament/MPR: ABRI Must Reduce its Repressive Reactions), *Kompas*, August 1, 1996; and "Rudini: Semua Pihak Harus Menahan Diri" (Rudini: All Sides Must Restrain Themselves), *Kompas*, August 2, 1996.

[83] Quotations are from "Di Depan Presiden Soeharto, Soesilo Akui Ada Purnawirawan Kurang Konsisten" (In the Presence of President Suharto Susilo Admits Some Retired Officers are Inconsistent), *Republika*, September 26, 1996; "Ketua DPR Sudomo: Bila Ingin Melakukan Koreksi, Lebih Baik Langsung ke Presiden" (Speaker Sudomo: If They Want to Carry Out Corrections, They Should Go Directly to the President), *Kompas*, September 26, 1996; "Pangab, Soal Purnawirawan tak Konsisten: Mereka Ekstradisiplin dan kontraloyalitas" (The ABRI Commander: Retirees are Inconsistent: They Have Broken Discipline and Are Disloyal), *Republika*, September 27, 1996. Feisal, however, did not identify the retired officers.

participation. He also objected to a section that claimed that Pancasila ideology was now threatened by communism, contending that the threat came from the government's arbitrary interpretation of Pancasila.[84]

Two months later, ABRI's Staff and Command College held a seminar entitled "Actualization of ABRI's Sociopolitical Role," to which noted retired officers and civilian intellectuals were invited. On this occasion, Gen. (ret) Rudini argued that the concept of ABRI's political role should be revised to accommodate new social developments.[85] Lt. Gen. (ret) Harsudiono Hartas also argued that ABRI had now deviated from its ideals. If such deviations continued, he concluded, it might undermine ABRI's traditional, valued role as a force of "freedom-fighters."[86]

On the same day as this seminar, the Army Staff and Command College (Seskoad) in Bandung also held a panel discussion on ABRI's political role. One of the panelists, Maj. Gen. (ret) Zein A. Maulani, argued that ABRI's political role should be redefined because the task of protecting national stability could no longer be monopolized by the military under currently stable social conditions. He went on to criticize the influence of business-capitalist groups in ABRI, noting many occasions when, in conflicts over land and industrial relations, ABRI had sided with capitalist groups. He warned that the coalition between ABRI and various business interests had brought the army far from its original ideals and undermined popular acceptance of ABRI's political involvement.[87]

Judging from the patterns of previous debates, one can guess that if these arguments by Hasnan, Rudini, Hartas, and Maulani had been offered by civilian critics and NGOs rather than by officers, the ABRI leaders might well have accused them of being too Westernized, of ignoring history, or possibly of being anti-*dwifungsi* and thus anti-Pancasila and subversive. But in responding to the intensive

---

[84] Hasnan Habib, "Pembangunan Nasional Bidang Hankam Pada Pelita-VII (Tanggapan)" (Response to National Development in the Defense Sector in the Seventh Development Plan), paper prepared for Naskah Makalah Awal "Pokok-Pokok Pikiran ABRI Tentang Pembangunan Nasional Pada Pelita-VII" (First Drafts for 'Essentials of ABRI's Thinking About National Development in the Seventh Development Plan'), Seminar ABRI, Mabes ABRI, Jakarta, September 3, 1996.

[85] Rudini, "Legitimasi Sosial Peran Sospol ABRI" (Social Legitimation of ABRI's Sociopolitical Role), paper presented at Sarasehan Sesko ABRI Tentang Aktualisasi Peranan Sospol ABRI, Sesko ABRI, Bandung, November 4-5, 1996.

[86] "Penerapan Dwifungsi ABRI Masih Sering Menyimpang" (The Application of ABRI's Dual Functions Still Often Deviates), *Kompas*, November 5, 1996. The term "freedom-fighter" refers to the role played by the military during the independence war. It is a symbol of ABRI's nationalist orientation.

[87] See Z. A. Maulani, "Implementasi Fungsi Sospol ABRI pada Masa Kini dan Masa yang Akan Datang" (Implementation of ABRI's Sociopolitical Function, Today and in the Future), paper presented at the panel discussion, Forum Kajian Dwifungsi ABRI, Seskoad, Bandung, November 5, 1996. Maulani was Habibie's adviser for military affairs at that time. He was a classmate and friend of Feisal Tanjung, and commanded the Kalimantan Kodam during the period of 1988 to April 1991. He was one of the most successful officers to emerge from the class of 1961 at the military academy, but his career was stopped by Defense Minister Murdani in 1991, allegedly due to Murdani's unhappiness with Maulani's Islamic orientation. He then became Secretary General of the Department of Transmigration and was later recruited by Habibie as his advisor. His criticism, cited above, represented a common perception in society and did not coincide very well with the interests of Habibie who owned many big businesses.

criticism at ABRI-sponsored seminars, Feisal Tanjung merely claimed that it was an irony of *dwifungsi* that its success invited criticism.[88]

Concerns of Serving Officers

In private, a serving brigadier-general at ABRI Headquarters complained that, "many of us are concerned about the political role of ABRI today, which is being used only to support Pak Harto [Suharto]. Who will pay the price of being unpopular among the *rakyat* [people]? It is the next generation of officers who will inherit the leadership in the near future."[89] In intra-military communication, however, criticism was muted, since open criticism would jeopardize an officer's career.

Personnel management was also becoming a concern. Syarwan's assistant, Maj. Gen. Suwarno Adiwijoyo, expressed his worry about the officers' growing uncertainty regarding their tours-of-duty, especially at the top level of the army. "After getting a new position, a general needs at least one year to settle into the position and should not be replaced in a haphazard way, at least during the five-year cycle of one ABRI Commander." He believed that this pattern had been distorted by promotional decisions that were influenced by politics and favoritism, and had led to increased dissatisfaction among ordinary officers. Suwarno stressed that the job criteria should be codified more clearly and personnel data should be computerized in order to avoid subjective promotions.[90] The fact that Suwarno had a strong Islamic orientation indicated that the concern was shared by officers on both sides of the cleavage along religious lines; the more significant division on this issue was the one

---

[88] "Pangab Tentang Dwifungsi: ABRI Dipaksa Tanggung Beban dari Keberhasilannya Sendiri" (The ABRI Commander on the Dual Function: ABRI is Forced to Bear the Burden of Its Own Success), *Kompas*, November 23, 1996.

[89] Confidential interview, December 1996.

[90] Mayjen Suwarno Adiwidjoyo, "Pemandu Bakat Kepemimpinan Perwira TNI-AD Yang Handal di Era Globalisasi" (Guiding Leadership Qualities Fitting the Era of Globalization Among Army Officers), *Yudhagama* 59 (July 1996): 61. After the July 27 riots, personnel transfers were conducted in August 1996 which affected more than a hundred officers and contradicted Feisal's announcement in February that there would be no major reshuffles until the general election in 1997. A series of big rotations in the last few years had generated concern about the growing instability of career paths. Maj. Gen. (ret) Z. A. Maulani claimed that the pace of transfer was abnormal. See his "Regenerasi ABRI 1995-1996" (The Regeneration of ABRI, 1995-1996), *Profile Indonesia* (Jurnal Tahunan CIDES, No. 2, 1996): 139. Maj. Gen. Theo Syafei of F-ABRI openly addressed this issue. At a parliamentary session in March, he pointed out a growing distortion in current personnel management caused by political influence (he was referring to Suharto's political maneuverings, which had placed officers loyal to the regime in top military posts). Although politics had always influenced promotions, Theo Syafei insisted that the recent reshuffling led to a notable "inflation of generals" (*inflasi jenderal*) and a shortage in the number of posts available for general-ranking officers. Edi Sudradjat responded to Theo Syafei by saying that the question now was whether or not the pace of transfer was too fast, acknowledging the problem in personnel management. See "Bila Gerbong Mutasi Macet di Atas" (If the [Railway] Coach of Transfers Gets Stuck at the Top), *Forum Keadilan*, March 25, 1996 and "Pangab Mengenai Tiga Letjen tak Punya Jabatan" (The ABRI Commander on Three Lieutenant-Generals Without Postings), *Kompas*, March 6, 1996.

separating officers close to the Presidential Palace from those who were not.[91] Finally, the army seminar of 1996 should be noted. It was held on June 18-19—a day before the Medan Congress of the PDI—to prepare for the army's final input to the GBHN for 1998-2003.[92] The seminar criticized the state apparatus generally as inconsistent in policies, lacking discipline, corrupt, feudalistic, egoistic, and contaminated by nepotism.[93] It also criticized the intervention of the executive branch in problems concerning the nation's political infrastructure—made up in part of sociopolitical organizations—and called on the former to reduce its dominance through open democratic communication.[94] Along the same lines, the seminar stated that recent governmental interventions in Golkar and political parties had been too overt and urged that the government use more opaque methods (*jangan terlalu transparan*) if it really had to (*terpaksa*) intervene in order to avoid arousing social opposition.[95]

These suggestions, which issued from the final army seminar to be held under the Suharto regime, were, however, quickly buried by the government's and army's repressive campaign to oust the popular pro-Megawati forces from the formal political arena before the 1997 elections. But within the military, calls for reform intensified throughout the next two years until Suharto's last day on May 21 in 1998. Disenchanted officers were motivated to be "reformists" either by: (1) their deepening concern about the eroding credibility of the military in society; or (2) their power struggle with rival officers in Suharto's patrimonial structure; or by both considerations.[96]

---

[91] An interesting remark was made by Feisal Tanjung in August 1998 when he said that during his term as ABRI Commander, no one—not even he himself, a four-star general—could freely visit the Special Forces sites controlled by Prabowo, a major-general. See "Feisal: Saya Tidak Terlibat Kasus Penculikan Para Aktivis" (Feisal: I Wasn't Involved in the Kidnapping of Activists), *Media Indonesia*, July 25, 1998. This showed how ABRI's command structure had been distorted by the special preference Suharto gave his son-in-law.

[92] GBHN is the "Broad Outlines of the Nation's Direction," which the new Cabinet produces every five years. The seminar was held at the Army Staff and Command College, and its Steering Team was headed by Brig. Gen. Bambang Yudhoyono (Chief of Staff, Jakarta Military Command), while the discussion team was led by Brig. Gen. Agus Wirahadikusumah (Deputy Assistant for General Planning to the ABRI Commander). Both were widely respected as intellectuals in uniform. Wirahadikusumah, a classmate of Bambang, is a son-in-law of former vice-president Umar Wirahadikusumah and the first officer to receive a Master of Public Administration degree from Harvard University. After the transition of ABRI leadership from Feisal to Wiranto in March 1998, both played key roles in formulating ABRI's internal reform plans.

[93] Quotations are from seminar documents. *Perspektif Pembangunan dan Pengembangan Bidang Politik pada Pelita VII* (Perspectives on Development in the Political Arena during the Seventh Development Plan) (Hasil Seminar TNI-AD, Bandung, 18-19 Juli 1996), pp. 50-52. *Suplemen Substansi Materi Dalam Perspektif Pembangunan dan Pengembangan Bidang Politik pada Pelita VII* (Supplement of Materials for Perspectives on Development in the Political Arena during the Seventh Development Plan) (Hasil Seminar TNI-AD, Bandung, 18-19 Juli 1996), p. 38.

[94] *Perspektif Pembangunan dan Pengembangan Bidang Politik pada Pelita VII*, p. 18.

[95] *Suplemen Substansi Materi Dalam Perspektif Pembangunan dan Pengembangan Bidang Politik pada Pelita VII*, p. 11. If we consider the timing of the PDI Congress in Medan, we might conclude that the seminar's assessment reflected concerns about the way the government—and implicitly the ABRI leadership—handled the Megawati case.

[96] For convenience, I use the term "reformists" to refer to the officers who were concerned about the direction being taken by the military leadership at that time. However, their views were not necessarily similar to the visions of reform held by civilian democratic activists,

WORLD VIEW, DOMESTIC THREAT PERCEPTIONS AND SELF-ROLE BELIEFS

As we have observed, the *kewaspadaan* doctrine applied since the early 1990s consisted of three main components—i.e. a defined world view, a defined domestic threat, and the military's perception of its own role—which were linked by hardliners to construct a discursive technique for neutralizing democratic pressures. We have discussed the elements in the hardliners' approach. But there were two other approaches developed within the military which deserve attention.

One approach emphasized the emergence of political threats resulting from globalization and insisted on the need for ABRI to expand the scope of its political activity without, however, evoking any Balatkom connotations. Maj. Gen. Budi Harsono, for example, explained that:

> [T]he gap between the OKB [*orang kaya baru*: the new rich] and the OMB [*orang miskin baru*: the new poor] in big cities is becoming serious. The OMB are far poorer than the people in the village . . . and globalization encourages this phenomenon. ABRI needs to watch out for this tendency carefully and promote professionalism in order to overcome this impact of globalization.[97]

Another intellectual officer, Col. Syarifudin Tippe, perceived a similar challenge in the global and domestic political arena and described ABRI's increasingly important role as democratizer. He wrote:

> Globalization . . . facilitates the linkage between democratization in foreign countries and the demands for political opening [*keterbukaan*] in our society. One obvious dimension [of this phenomenon] is the increase in accusations against the military's dominant role. This happens everywhere in the world, including Indonesia. Coupled with the wave of democratization, demands for improving human rights and civil rights in politics have become stronger. All these demands ask ABRI to share power with other [non-ABRI] parties. . . and to play the *demokratisator* (democratizer) role.[98]

---

especially in the cases of officers preoccupied by internal power struggles with Suharto favorites.

[97] Interview, January 31, 1997. Maj. Gen. Budi Harsono was Assistant for Sociopolitical Affairs at that time, serving the hardline Syarwan Hamid.

[98] Syarifudin Tippe, *Peran Sosial Politik ABRI Dalam Meningkatkan Kualitas Pengamalan Wawasan Kebangsaan di Tengah kecenderungan "Global Paradox"* (ABRI's Sociopolitical Role in Upgrading the Quality of the Implementation of the National Idea in the Midst of the Trend toward the 'Global Paradox') (Narasi) (Bandung: Forum Pengkajian Seskoad, Orasi Ilmiah Pada Ulang Tahun Seskoad Ke-44, 25 May 1995), p. 6. Tippe at that time served Gen. Feisal Tanjung as Personal Staff Coordinator, and was also a devout Muslim. Reflecting the anti-Murdani posture of many ICMI-linked officers, this Feisal follower (graduate of the ABRI Academy in 1975) criticized the old intelligence policy of the 1980s that compelled officers to obtain ABRI permission before publishing any statement in the mass media. Tippe argued that this restriction had killed the officers' intellectual creativity. See his interview in "Syarifudin Tippe: Banyak Perwira yang Pinter" (Syarifudin Tippe: There Are Many Intelligent Officers), *Forum Keadilan*, July 3, 1995.

Tippe would solve problems resulting from globalization by absorbing social demands, rather than rejecting them, and by transforming ABRI into a "democratizing" force. But democracy here, in common ABRI language, meant a democracy based on Pancasila—the state ideology of anti-liberalism. ABRI's proposed responsibility as the promoter of democracy, therefore, did not reduce its role in politics. The emphasis in these soldiers' view was different from the hardline approach of asserting the resurgence of the old threat—communism—in order to justify the military repression of popular movements. It was less dogmatic, but still conformed with ABRI's traditional paternalistic self-image.

A third school of thought recognized that the social space ABRI required to carry out its political role was shrinking. Maj. Gen. (ret) Maulani observed:

> In the past, until the 1980s, the main threat was ideological conflicts, physical insurgencies, and political party conflicts. . . . Reflecting these, ABRI's management of stability was oriented by political and military approaches. However, the current threat is colored by the economic gap between the rich and poor and social injustice as represented by land disputes. It is globalization that has brought these issues to the surface. In order to respond to these threats to stability, ABRI's previous politico-military approaches are useless. What is required is the improvement of distributive economic policy and a strong judicial system to implement consistent and impartial decisions, which result in a reduced role for ABRI and broader participation of social sectors.[99]

A similar opinion was expressed by a serving two-star general who emphasized the multi-dimensional impact of globalization and insisted on the need for a rational division of labor, arguing that:

> [T]he current wave of globalization pushes social values in one [universal] direction . . . and Indonesia is not an exception. This invites the question of the military's place in a modern society. . . . ABRI should not believe that it can solve all problems. That would be counter-productive. Rather, non-ABRI sectors should be empowered and, in this process, the political center will move to the Interior Ministry [from ABRI], while security matters, especially in the big cities like Jakarta, should be handled by the Police. Thus, ABRI has to change its way of thinking . . . but the problem now is: who wants to lose power? There are still many conservatives within ABRI.[100]

The emphases in these two statements differ in that Maulani saw the main threat to Indonesian society shifting from the political to the economic, while the active-duty officer above insisted on the convergence of global values. However, both minimized the need to defend the country from globalization and recognized the necessity of

---

[99] Interview with Maj. Gen. (ret) Zein Maulani, Adviser for Military Affairs to B. J. Habibie, Minister of Research and Technology, November 28, 1996. Maulani became Chief of Staff of the Vice-Presidential Office when Habibie was elected vice-president in March 1998. In September, he was appointed as the head of BAKIN—a body directly responsible to President Habibie. His willingness to assign ABRI a lesser role in politics may reflect his support for the civilian Habibie.

[100] Confidential interview, January 1997. The term "conservatives" here may be identical to "hardliners."

reducing the army's role as a self-appointed guard against global-domestic pressures for change.

IDEOLOGICAL REPOSITIONING AND THE INSTITUTIONAL LEGACY OF THE *KEWASPADAAN* MIND-SET

The transfer of military leadership took place when Army Chief of Staff Gen. Wiranto was appointed ABRI Commander at the end of February 1998, a welcome change for those concerned about the political ambitions of Prabowo. Though he had served as a former presidential adjutant (1988-93), Wiranto was regarded as a professionally oriented officer.[101] Feisal Tanjung was transferred to the post of the Coordinating Minister for Political and Security Affairs and played a watchdog role in insuring that the March MPR session endorsed Suharto and Habibie as president and vice-president for the next five years. Immediately thereafter, however, there was a large escalation of student demonstrations demanding that Suharto resign. The new ABRI leadership—under Wiranto (who was also appointed as Defense Minister in the new Cabinet) with the support of the new Army Chief of Staff, Gen. Soebagyo, and the new Chief of the Sociopolitical Staff, Lt. Gen. Bambang Yudhoyono—showed a "responsive" attitude toward the anti-Suharto movements, offering several occasions for dialogue rather than resorting to Balatkom propaganda.[102] The escalating street demonstrations led by students finally resulted in Suharto's resignation and the announcement that he would hand over his presidency to Habibie on May 21. This happened six days after the Jakarta riot that terrified the country and highlighted Prabowo's influence.[103]

The political reform campaign that followed the collapse of the Suharto regime inevitably found a target in ABRI. The military's past human rights abuses—including the abduction of political activists, a practice dating back to the July 27 riot

---

[101] Wiranto graduated from the Military Academy in 1968, and served as the Commander of the Jakarta Military Command in 1994-96, as the Commander of the Army's Strategic Reserve from April 1996 to June 1997, and as Army Chief of Staff after Hartono. Bambang Yudhoyono was his main supporter in the intra-military struggle with the Prabowo circle. Suharto, master of the "divide-and-rule" strategy, let their competition go on in order to create the power balance which would make both sides dependent on him.

[102] Four days before Suharto's resignation Bambang Yudhoyono was invited to the Salemba campus of the University of Indonesia, where he conversed with several critical retired officers, academics, and religious leaders. They adopted the "Salemba Declaration" calling for Suharto to step down. Bambang said that the meeting expressed the people's aspirations, and he characterized the demand for Suharto's ouster as an expression of their love for the nation, a demand which should be heard by ABRI and the government. See "Jenderal Purnawirawan dan Guru Besar ke DPR, Mendesak Segera Digelar Sidang Istimewa" (Retired Generals and Professors Go to Parliament, Urging Immediate Special Session), *Jawa Pos*, May 18, 1998.

[103] It was only five months after the riot that the government-established Joint Fact-Finding Team (TGPF) for the May riot submitted its final report. The Team was formed in July and consisted of military officers, bureaucrats, lawyers, and NGO activists under the leadership of Marzuki Darusman. The estimated death toll during the riots of May 13-15 ranged from four hundred to 1,200; the Team avoided providing its own count. The report, however, recommended that the government court-martial Prabowo and investigate his role in provoking the riots. See *Laporan Akhir Tim Gabungan Pencari Fakta Peristiwa Tinggal 13-15 Mei 1998* [Ringkasan Eksekutif] (Final Report of the Fact-Finding Team on the Events of May 13-15, 1998 [Executive Summary]) (Jakarta: Tim Gabungan Pencari Fakta, October 23, 1998), chapters IV.3.2 and VII.2.

in 1996—were openly discussed and its withdrawal from politics widely demanded. In the first few months since Suharto's departure, Wiranto's response to these pressures was generally accommodating. The new military leadership decided to withdraw some troops from East Timor, Irian Jaya, and Aceh, all regions where ABRI had previously conducted intensive security missions after designating them as Military Operation Areas (DOM), a designation that freed the army to try to crush separatist rebellions with methods often *virtually* outside the law.[104] In Aceh, past accounts of military repression were widely publicized by the NGOs when a number of mass graves of the victims were identified. Every day, further horrors in these regions were exposed by the media—newly "empowered" by Habibie's decision to end press censorship in late May. Facing such a public mood, Wiranto publicly apologized to the people of Aceh—the first time in Indonesian history that a general had offered such an apology—and he abolished the DOM designation in August. However, the apology was not enough to halt the acceleration of separatist movements in these regions. Continuing resistance was evidence of the New Order's failure to integrate the nation through military repression, which had indeed intensified since the late 1980s. Wiranto also accepted the proposal to reduce the number of ABRI's appointed seats in Parliament from 75 to 55, while at the same time deciding to separate the police from the military structure. "Reformist" officers like Bambang Yudhoyono openly admitted that ABRI had made many errors in the past and that it planned to reduce its political involvement in the current era of political reform.

We must consider this chain of developments, including, notably, the end to press censorship, when assessing the direction of ABRI's ideological shift under the new military leadership. In the previous section, I attempted to identify ABRI's ideological orientation based on three components—namely world-view, domestic threat perception, and its definition of its own role—and posited three types of doctrinal approaches: hardline, moderate, progressive. The military leadership during the first three months of the Habibie government seemed to have taken the "moderate" approach, which recognized the need for an adjustment of ABRI's role in order to guide the regime's transition in the changing domestic and international environment. This view was strongly reflected in the first proposal formulated by ABRI's reform team, which was led by Bambang Yudhoyono. Their report, submitted to Habibie, asserted ABRI's commitment to democratic reforms and acknowledged its responsibility for protecting citizens' human rights—a significant move, since "human rights" had long been represented by hardliners as a dangerous foreign concept. The report also called for Indonesia's ratification of international human rights conventions, including the Vienna Declaration and Program of Action adopted by the UN World Conference on Human Rights in June 1993.[105]

---

[104] Withdrawal of one thousand troops from East Timor was announced in August. But it was later discovered that ABRI had covertly increased the forces in East Timor during 1998.

[105] *ABRI dan Reformasi: Pokok-Pokok Pikiran ABRI Tentang Reformasi Menuju Pencapaian Cita-Cita Nasional* (ABRI and Reform: Core ABRI Thinking on Reform Aimed at Achieving National Ideals) (Jakarta: Mabes ABRI, June 1998), p. 21. The Vienna Declaration and Program of Action said that "the promotion and protection of human rights and fundamental freedoms at the national and international levels should be universal and conducted without conditions attached" (Article 8). Accepting this clause required ABRI to abandon its long-standing "cultural relativism" in the human rights debate.

Elements of the "progressive" approach can also be discerned in this general discourse. One of Wiranto's advisors, Lt. Gen. Agus Widjojo, had written in 1992: ". . . ABRI's ideology has to be guided by rational, open and discussable methods rather than dogmatic indoctrination." Moreover, with regard to *dwifungsi*, he insisted that "we should be brave enough to decide the priority between defense and political roles, because ABRI does not have enough time to produce personnel who are competent for the two roles simultaneously."[106] ABRI's priority, of course, should be in the defense field. Evidence that Widjojo's "progressive" attitude influenced events can be seen in the decision to separate the Police from ABRI, a measure which Widjojo himself handled in his role as Assistant for General Planning. Those officers who subscribe to this third "progressive" approach explain ABRI's gradual retreat from non-military fields as an inevitable consequence of domestic and global changes. In line with this, Bambang Yudhoyono insisted at an ABRI seminar—held in September 1998—that he would even support the idea of liquidating ABRI's sociopolitical section if the people believed its function was irrelevant.[107]

Under Wiranto, however, a new ideological doctrine for ABRI was not institutionally established. A day after the ABRI seminar, Balatkom language re-emerged in ABRI's political discourse. The escalating student demonstrations—participants now demanded Habibie's resignation and the abolition of *dwifungsi*—finally pushed the new president to instruct ABRI to use severe methods to stop street activities dangerous to the government. Following these instructions, Wiranto made a *kewaspadaan*-type public statement in which he said that the "style" of recent demonstrations resembled that of the communists, and he identified the Forkot (*Forum Kota*, or City Forum), an organization consisting of students from thirty-seven universities, as communist-oriented.[108] Not only in Jakarta, but also in West Java,

---

[106] Col. Agus Widjojo, "Upaya Peningkatan Kualitas Personil ABRI Sejalan Dengan Upaya Peningkatan Kualitas Sumber Daya Manusia" (Efforts to Improve the Quality of ABRI Personnel (to be) In Line with Efforts to Improve the Quality of Human Resources), *Widya Dharma (Majalah Sesko ABRI)* 18 (1992): 71, 85. This article was originally written during his training at ABRI's Staff and Command College and was selected as the best working paper for the regular course of 1991-1992. Widjojo, a graduate of ABRI's Military Academy in 1970, was regarded as one of the key intellectual officers—together with Bambang Yudhoyono and Agus Wirahadikusumah—helping Wiranto shape ABRI's new paradigm. He is a son of Maj. Gen. Sutojo, one of six generals killed in the abortive coup of September 30, 1965, and a holder of Master's degrees from Georgetown and Manchester Universities. Under the Wiranto leadership, he served as Assistant for General Planning (Asrenum Pangab) until January 1999, then became the Commandant of ABRI's Staff and Command College.

[107] "Berubah Sebelum Ditinggalkan Sejarah" (Change Before Being Left Behind By History), *Tajuk*, October 1, 1998. This seminar, held at the ABRI Staff and Command College (September 22-24), produced the second official paper—following the June paper prepared by the Bambang team—concerning the future political role of ABRI. The liquidation of ABRI's sociopolitical section was Bambang's own idea, as it was not mentioned in the final seminar paper—*Peran ABRI Abad XXI: Redefinisi, Reposisi dan Reaktualisasi Peran ABRI dalam Kehidupan Bangsa* (The Role of ABRI in the 21st Century: Redefinition, Repositioning, and Reactualization of ABRI's Role in National Life) [Makalah Awal Seminar ABRI] (Bandung: Sesko ABRI, September 1998). In November, however, the idea was officially adopted and the sociopolitical section was replaced by the territorial section. It is doubtful that this reorganization actually reduced ABRI's political commitment, however, as ABRI's territorial operation was essentially aimed at maintaining its political authority.

[108] "ABRI Waspadai Gerakan 30-S Forkot" (ABRI is Watching the 30th of September Movement – Forkot), *Republika*, September 25, 1998. Forkot had been one of the most active

East Java, and Sumatra, student groups were suddenly identified as left-wing elements who should be kept under observation.[109] Wiranto's initiation of a ghost-hunting campaign reasserted the Balatkom doctrine developed by the Feisal-led ABRI in the mid-1990s. Thanks largely to the earlier efforts of Hartono, Syarwan, and Soeyono, Wiranto was able to tag popular movements as communist, claiming that they had used *agitprop*—and other communist-type methods—in conducting demonstrations. His initiative ran counter to the Bandung Seminar's proposal that all dogmatic doctrines and operations should be eliminated from ABRI.[110] It is in this context that the continuity of ABRI's ideological orientation should be considered.

In the late New Order state, Suharto was the center of political power, and the military leadership was shaped by officers loyal to him. The development of a hardline approach could not be separated from this political context. The situation under Habibie was very different. Under Habibie, state power seemed to have no single center, and the military leadership was not recruited primarily based on the officers' loyalty to the new president. However, the post-Suharto regime did inherit two legacies intact from its predecessor. The first was the structural nature of the Presidential-military relationship, and the second was the New Order military's traditional *dwifungsi* characterization of its own role in the nation. As discussed in the previous section, "reform-minded" officers were concerned about the subordination of the military to the political interests of Suharto and its consequent loss of public trust. It was against this background that key officers in Wiranto's circle arose to call for limiting the power of the president and rejuvenating ABRI's autonomy in political life.[111] Because the president of Indonesia acts as ABRI's Supreme Commander, he has the power to "order" the Commander to provide support in conducting his political projects. In post-Suharto civil-military relations, this structural legacy remained untouched, and Wiranto's adoption of the hardline approach was, to some extent, a direct reflection of this.[112] He did not have the power to institute reforms independent of Habibie.

---

groups demanding Habibie's resignation, the establishment of a transitional government led by a presidium, and the elimination of *dwifungsi*.

[109] For a discussion of the campaign, see "'Hantu' PKI di Era Reformasi" (The `Ghost' of the PKI in the Reform Era), *Tajuk*, October 1, 1998.

[110] *Peran ABRI Abad XXI*, p. 30.

[111] This point was reflected in the assessment of the Bambang team in June. See *ABRI dan Reformasi*, pp. 13, 15. Also at the Bandung Seminar in September, Widjojo argued that during the Suharto era the President expanded the role of the military in order to use it to further his own interests. Mayjen TNI Agus Widjojo, "Peran ABRI pada Abad XXI: Redefinisi, Reposisi dan Reaktualisasi Peran ABRI dalam Kehidupan Bangsa dengan Obyek Bahasan pada Paradigma Baru," working paper presented at Seminar ABRI tentang Peran ABRI Abad XXI, Bandung, Sesko ABRI, September 23, 1998, p. 5.

[112] Two major-generals close to Wiranto both insisted that Wiranto's gradual subordination to Habibie and his reluctance to say "no" had resulted in the postponement of ABRI's implementation of its internal reform programs. Interviews, October 1998. Harold Crouch also argues that Wiranto's personal support within ABRI was not sufficient to prevent Habibie from appointing another senior officer in his place. Habibie could replace Wiranto at any time, but Wiranto could not unseat Habibie. See Harold Crouch, "Wiranto and Habibie: Military-Civilian Relations since May 1998," paper presented at the conference entitled "Democracy in Indonesia?: The Crisis and Beyond," Monash and Melbourne Universities, December 11-12, 1998, p. 8.

On the other hand, Wiranto's partial adoption of the Balatkom approach also illustrated the durability of the *kewaspadaan* doctrine that had been repeatedly invoked under the New Order, regardless of the characteristics of the military leadership. As discussed previously, the core institutional incentive for this doctrine was ABRI's permanent need to reproduce the legitimacy of its role as national guardian, a need that has prompted ABRI to conjure up imagined threats to national stability. As it has faced seemingly endless public criticism since the very beginning of the Habibie government, ABRI has found that popular movements have ignored its declared willingness to carry out politico-military reforms gradually. It is not surprising that military figures began to perceive this escalating anti-military pressure as a serious threat to its established self-image as the defender of the nation. In fact, as ABRI's past human-rights abuses increasingly occupied the country's political debates, Wiranto started to argue that ABRI's in-house reform should not be on the public agenda, and claimed that "certain groups" were now attempting to discredit ABRI.[113] The military's perception that civilians who intervene in the military's professional affairs may try to discredit ABRI does not harmonize very well with ABRI's declared commitment to democratization. A reactive, combative, self-defensive discursive legacy apparently still influences civil-military communication. We note that a two-star general in ABRI's education sector recently insisted on the need for strengthening *kewaspadaan* against the extreme left, right, and others. As a response to these threats, he argued, the Tarpadnas project ought to be upgraded.[114]

The *kewaspadaan* mind-set, therefore, reasserts itself in ABRI's institutional efforts to defend its established perception of its own role and to declare that growing popular demands for the elimination of *dwifungsi* and for military reform threaten national stability. From this perspective, the manipulation of world-view—involving the evocation of concepts like globalization—continues to enable ABRI to interpret such demands as dangerous "foreign" ideologies that must be extirpated.

---

[113] "ABRI's Internal Affairs 'Are Not A Public Issue,'" *Jakarta Post*, September 5, 1998 and "Wiranto Tak Setuju Nama Kopassus Diganti" (Wiranto Does Not Agree that the Name of the Special Forces be Changed), *Jawa Pos*, September 5, 1998.

[114] Interview, October 1998.

THOUGHTS ON THE VIOLENCE OF MAY 13 AND 14, 1998, IN JAKARTA[*]

James T. Siegel

> While Suharto was in power there was practically no one who accused him of corruptly using up the people's money. Were they to have done so, their fate was evident: it is certain they would end up in jail.
> Haruskah (daripada) Soeharto diadili? [Must Suharto be brought to trial? Rather than that?] *Ummat,* June 8, 1998, p. 14.

The artless confession in this news magazine, speaking to and about the middle class, helps in understanding the course of events that led to the resignation of President Suharto. By May 1998, Indonesia had shared in the economic difficulties of East Asia for ten months, and though a great many people were feeling its effects and there was much political discontent, no one seemed to have anticipated Suharto's resignation. After it took place, however, people in Jakarta, though initially surprised, thought it was easily explicable. Suharto left office after two violent incidents. Students, who had originally demonstrated against the rise in prices that accompanied the fall in value of the rupiah, had begun to demand *Reformasi* (reform), sometimes in effect taking up the vocabulary of the IMF when they asked for "transparency" which, for a while, was an important item of political rhetoric.[1]

[*] I want to thank Budi Susanto, Henri Chambert-Loir, Benny Subianto, Rudolf Mrázek, Joshua Barker, Arndt Graf, and most especially Benedict R. O'G. Anderson for their comments on this piece and their contributions of material. I am responsible for the errors and they are responsible for much the reader may find accurate and well conceived.

[1] "Transparency" of course was used to indicate the possibility of knowing the true state of financial institutions and also public access to the awarding of contracts, etc. It soon was used to describe the desirability of political events also being open to view. It had no antonym except perhaps in KKN, *Kolusi, korupsi, nepotisme* in Indonesian (collusion, corruption and nepotism), the assumption being that what was hidden from view was corrupt and that corruption in the New Order took these three forms. The use of visual metaphors throughout the period deserves attention. Here I only note that the demands for *reformasi* were not

Students at the private Trisakti University in Jakarta, known by the term "mamas' children," because they often came from privileged families, had been late to join the demonstrations. However they too began protests. On May 12, in the course of a rally, four Trisakti students were shot dead. At first, it was presumed that the killers were from the Police, who were then accused of using real rather than rubber bullets; soon after it was widely thought that elements from the army had done the shooting. In the afternoon of the next day, May 13, rioting broke out against Indonesian Chinese in many parts of Jakarta, and continued the following two days. Students from Jakarta and elsewhere occupied the grounds and the roof of the National Assembly, the military mysteriously allowing them to do so. On May 17, Harmoko, Speaker of the Assembly, a long-time servile follower of Suharto, called for his resignation. Subsequently fourteen of Suharto's ministers resigned, and he could not find people to serve on a new Commission for Reform. A major demonstration was called off on May 20 when Amien Rais, the head of the Muslim organization Muhammadiyah, announced that a certain general, later rumored to be Lt. General Prabowo, the son-in-law of President Suharto, had said that it would lead to bloodshed. On May 21, President Suharto resigned. The train of events seemed to the many people with whom I spoke in June 1998 to be self-evident. But if so, it is because events which were at first surprising were set within the workings of Indonesian political discourse and made to seem natural.

The last years of the New Order saw political protest of various sorts. The strongest was no doubt the long struggle of the inhabitants of East Timor resisting their forced inclusion in Indonesia after the invasion of that former Portuguese colony in 1975. Student demands, however, made no mention of East Timor. Crowds gathered outside Cipinang Prison when President Habibie released the labor leader Mochtar Pakpahan and other political prisoners, but no student delegations were present.[2] That the students failed to include in their demands the causes of labor or of the Timorese or of other groups, such as the Aceh Independence Movement, for instance, partly reflects their own newness on the political scene. Their appearance was, in fact, so recent that one is hard put to say who their leaders were and what it is that they concretely wanted. Interviewed after the National Assembly sit-in, one student, a "supply coordinator" for his comrades, formulated their demands this way: "[We want] to change the regime now in power for a new bureaucratic elite

---

demands for popular representation but insistence that the political system be open to view. It is truly "reform" and not, of course, "revolution." Exposure, one can say, became a political idea first with "transparency" and then with rape.

[2] So at least go the news reports of the event which sometimes list groups present to greet the released prisoners but make no mention of students. See for example, "Tapol/Napol: Bebas Semua atau Tidak?" (Political/Criminal Prisoners: Will All Be Freed or Not?), *D&R*, June 6, 1998, pp. 24-25; and see "Merdeka! Atau Bebas" (Freedom! Or Freed), *Ummat*, June 8, 1998, p. 29. *Ummat* was close to ICMI (Indonesian Association of Muslim Intellectuals), the group of reformist Muslim leaders formed by Habibie when he was vice-president. The newsweekly *D&R* was then perhaps the most influential of the weeklies, meaning the most au courant with political gossip; it largely took the place of the banned weekly *Tempo*.

I should point out that this text concerns only Jakarta. In other areas, students united or tried to unite with other groups. Jakarta is, of course, the city where the middle class is most developed. Army policy was to keep students separated from other groups; in Jakarta it easily succeeded. There were youth groups in Jakarta who, during the late New Order, were interested in coalitions but their influence was not apparent during the events of May.

more favorable to the people."[3] One notes the lack of space left for the seething masses.

The protesters' failure to offer much in the way of a political program, along with their failure to take up the demands of labor and regional groups, cannot, however, simply be explained by the recent appearance of students on the political scene nor, as the magazine *Ummat* suggests, by the fact that until recently political protest meant jail. There were those such as Mochtar Pakpahan, or inhabitants of Timor Timur and Aceh, who made their demands felt knowing that they would be jailed or killed. If students did not act earlier it is because, despite occasional discontent, most of them tacitly supported a regime which did so much to establish the class to which they belonged. Only when the *krismon* (the acronym for *krisis moneter* or "monetary crisis") became acute, did they act. An explanation based on interests alone however will not entirely explain the inflections of political discourse in the aftermath of the events of May. These events brought up questions of the relations between classes and the place of race and sex in national identity.

Let us start with the students. President Habibie, the successor to President Suharto, proclaimed the four murdered Trisakti students "Heroes of Reform." They were, one journal said, "inscribed as makers of a new history."[4] To be a hero of reform seems almost an oxymoron, reform being usually gradual and peaceful in contrast to revolution. If the predicate "hero" seemed appropriate for the victims, however, it was not only because they were shot dead, but also because the word implicitly referred to earlier moments when, during the Revolution of 1945-49 and again at the beginning of the New Order, youths moved events forward in violent circumstances. As usual in Indonesia, forward movement was put in terms of generations. Furthermore, students borrowed much of the iconography of the Revolution. Yet they were quite different from their nationalist forebears. In the 1930s, parents of young nationalists were often thought to belong to a world of custom and hence were considered incapable of understanding their children; during the Revolution, youth acted without much reference to parents. But in May 1998 there was an understanding between parents and children (if not between generations as such, which is a wider political term). Parents of students and alumni of Jakartan universities brought the protesters provisions as they occupied the National Assembly. Students are reported to have acted with the consent of their parents, not merely seeking their approval afterwards. The usual norms of familial behavior were still in force. The days of heroic reform were not a period of license but of normal relations between the sexes. Female students often continued to make themselves up on the grounds of the National Assembly—that is, to look at once attractive and proper—and there was the same sort of flirting that took place on the campuses.[5] There was scarcely anything rebellious about their actions. In demanding Suharto's resignation, they were merely asking for what their parents also wanted. By comparison, the youngsters who in August 1945 abducted Sukarno to force him to proclaim national independence were ahead of their elders.

---

[3] "Saya Kurang Ngerti Politik, tapi . . ." (I don't understand politics, but . . .), *Panji Masjarakat*, June 10, 1998, pp. 47ff. *Panji Masjarakat* is an Islamic reformist journal of long standing and is connected with the Muslim organization Muhammadiyah. This interesting article has much about the students' behavior during their occupation of the National Assembly grounds.

[4] Ibid.

[5] Conversations with various students; also "Saya Kurang Ngerti Politik, tapi . . . ," pp. 47ff.

My interest is in the popular political assumptions of the middle class as they were refracted in explanations of the events. Before the burning and pillaging began, it was not only the middle class that was interested in a change of regime; the lower classes as well felt the pressure of the sudden regression of the economy. There was a high rate of unemployment while some of those still with jobs found their salaries inadequate to feed their children. Thus at the moment that the riots of May 13 and 14 began, a student, speaking for "the people" (*rakyat*), could assume that they, "the people," were behind him. Students, however, quickly refused an alliance with those on the street. In retrospect, it was widely thought that the actions of "*massa*," as such people were called, were instigated from above. But it took time for this opinion to be generated. The students' refusal of an alliance when one seemed possible had other causes as well.

Here is the experience of one student at Trisakti University where the four student demonstrators were shot. It was reported in a woman's weekly.[6] Alya Rohali is a television actress as well as a student.[7] She went to the Trisakti campus, three kilometers from her house, on Wednesday, May 13, the day after the four students were killed and the day the riots broke out, in her own car. Various speeches, called by the term, scarcely used until recently, "*orasi*," were given by various "*orator*" (Indonesian) including Adnan Buyung Nasution, a famous lawyer and civil rights activist. Some students went on to the burial ceremonies for two of their slain comrades. Others stayed at the university. The latter were still on the university grounds when the riots broke out. The military had allowed student demonstrations on the condition that they be confined to university campuses. In her statement Alya says that the people on the street asked the students to join them.

> "I really remember how at the time some people wanted us to gather outside the campus. But we refused. Because of that they ["they" here refers to the rioters, referred to as *massa* meaning "mass" or "masses"] started to throw things toward the campus," related Alya. "Fortunately the *massa* actions didn't get any of us," she added.

Alya was worried when she saw that the atmosphere around the campus was tinged with the clash between the *massa* and the security apparatus. To control the brutal *massa* actions, the [security] apparatus, indeed, used tear gas.[8]

---

[6] "Hadapi Gas Air Mata Pakai Softlens: Pengalaman Jadi Demonstran Trisakti" (Facing Teargas with Contact Lenses: The Experience of a Trisakti Demonstrator), *Nyata*, June 11, 1998, p. 2.

[7] Alya Rohali was involved in a controversy when, elected Miss Indonesia, she was attacked by certain Muslim groups for partipating in immoral activities, i.e., this beauty contest. She was also rumored to be a candidate for marriage with Tommy Suharto, the president's youngest son, who, however, married someone else. The references to the "favorite" Cakra car, the car made by Tommy's company, probably allude to that piece of history.

[8] I am told by Benny Subianto that it is unusual for the Jakarta security forces to use tear gas. That they did so was no doubt an effect of the situation aroused by the killing of the students. As we will see, it was unusual for the police to act at all on May 13. They were notable for their nearly complete absence. That they were present at Trisakti was no doubt because of the student killings and not in response to the street demonstrations. That the police acted against the people on the streets around Trisakti indicates that, if the security apparatus was in collusion with street demonstrators elsewhere, it was not the case there.

Indeed, Alya panicked when she was hit by the gas. "In all my whole life, this was the first time I was hit by tear gas," Alya said. "Fortunately, I had on *softlens*," [italicized in original] she said with a smile.

The activist students, some of whom had come to Jakarta from various regions to participate in the political events, were shocked to see action begin on the street and were often quick to disavow it. In this case, Alya was already afraid to join with the people who, at this point, had yet to begin the looting, arson, and rape which marked the next two days. So far as she was concerned, to go on to the street was to defy the army and acknowledge a common cause with people she mistrusted. "...On the street it's difficult to know our friends from our enemies and hard also to anticipate people who slip in with different goals," she says. She is afraid of who she will be with. Those who "slip in with different goals" might perhaps be looters, out to get what they can; thus, in her mind, they deviate from the ends of the students and are perhaps misled by other protesters with indistinct, but different, aims. Or more likely they could be elements from the army or police who hope to incite students to violence, thus setting the stage for violent reprisals. Both students and those on the street have political goals. In Alya's judgment, the differences are that her comrades, while not exactly on the side of the law, at least act with the understanding of military authorities who, for instance, allowed them into the grounds of the National Assembly and permitted them to demonstrate within the confines of their campuses. The other difference between her and the *massa* concerns property. She and her friends do not want what does not belong to them. The rioters' relation to goods was much more ambiguous. On the one hand, the general events were commonly said to involve "looting" (*penjarahan*); on the other hand, the agents of this activity were rarely said to "loot" (*menjarah*) or to "steal" (*curi*), but were said merely to "take" (*ambil*) what they felt was theirs by a right whose nature we will ask about later. To anticipate for a moment, the difference comes when one chooses whether to think of these people as either "*massa*" or as "*rakyat*"; "the people" take out of need; the *massa* loot.

When they see the events on the street, Alya and her friends are afraid to stay on the campus and afraid also to leave. Finally, they climb the wall dividing their campus from that of a neighboring university, Tarumanegara, and from there enter the narrow side streets in back of campus, where it is calm. They are still afraid to enter the major avenues; they stay with a friend who lives nearby until, at nine in the evening, her father comes to get her. "'I was relieved to have Papa meet me,' says the girl born in Jakarta on December 1, 1975."

Despite her fear, she goes out again the next day. The situation has calmed, and she goes back to the campus.

Alya rushed to get her favorite Cakra sedan and move it to her grandmother's house in Kampung Melayu, Jakarta Timur. It was a good thing Alya's car was safe from the brutal actions of the *massa*. [In fact, 1,119 cars were reported burned.] "Boy, if it were burned I would have been really upset. The price of cars these days is out of sight and there are fewer and fewer jobs," she said with a smile.[9]

The reporter adds that the events of May 13 and 14 were "menacing" [*menyeramkan*] and "scarily tense" [*mencekam*]. Alya adds, "It was just like war. But I hope that nothing like that happens again. It really was terrifying . . . " The reporter points out in the course of his article that Alya has had an experience which university students who want to be active demonstrators could keep in mind, particularly those who wear glasses for nearsightedness.

> "During the demo on the campus, I was lucky to be wearing *softlens*. The tear gas could not get into my eyes. It's different with my friends; their eyes stung and watered. So my experience can be a lesson. Whoever wants to join a demo, wear *softlens* to protect against tear gas," said the student from the Law School in her eighth semester with a smile when she met Zulkarnaen from *Nyata*.

She, like many other students, is not afraid of the police but is "terrified" of the *massa*. The police (it was rumored later to be the army) killed four of her fellow students. But Alya is perfectly safe from them; she wears *softlens*. Nothing the police do harms her. What protects her is a cosmetic device which she presumably wears in the attractive photo which accompanies the article. We clearly see, no matter what lens we are wearing at the moment, the division of her sentiments. Alya is for *Reformasi* and herself gives a speech advocating reform of the economy. She is for a change of government and says that she wants President Habibie to have the chance to prove himself. She thinks the army chief, General Wiranto, would be an excellent president. She is against corruption, upset about the way the government has been run, and concerned about the economy. But what "terrorizes" her is the "*massa*" who, in her own discourse, acted by themselves, without direction from above, as was widely reported later. One should keep in mind too that her statement was made before stories of rape began to circulate. She has seen two kinds of violence. One is the arson and looting of the "masses." The other, which she did not see herself but which affected her enough to bring her back to the university after the shooting, was the killing of four of her comrades by the police. Only one of these events "terrified" her; the first. The second moved her but left her perfectly safe. This division of sentiments was widespread if not universal and is so much a part of Jakartan assumptions that it seems to go unremarked.

The police shot her comrades, but she fears "the *massa*." It is a question of the *softlens*. It is not that she sees better with it. Rather, protecting her from the tear gas the police used against the "*massa*," it renders her fearless of them. Perhaps it is the way she looks. Her contact lenses are an element in the construction of her appearance, like her Cakra sedan, that assure her she is recognized for what she is: a member of the class the police usually protect. If, exceptionally, they shot her comrades, it does not change her essential position either toward them or toward those of the lower classes who for a moment seemed to share her interests. Her political vision, at least, is safe with her *softlens*.

---

[9] The number of cars burned is based on a figure from the National Commission on Human Rights as reported in *Gatra*, "Cerita Lain dari Kerusuhan" (Another Story from the Riots), June 13, 1998, p. 37.

THE MASSA

The "*massa*," it is agreed, were "brutal" and worse. Who exactly were they? In the first stories of the riots that were widespread in Jakarta, the "*massa*" were largely represented as local people. In Glodok, the old "Chinese" section of the city, a major shopping center was burned and looted and at least seventy homes destroyed as the flames from the market spread. The five-story market, a center for the sale of electronics, clothing, and so on, faced onto an older row of shops in front of which ran an arcade. On the sidewalk under the arcade, merchants, for the most part "*pribumi*" ("natives"), i.e., not "Chinese," sell various items. These merchants told us that when the *massa* approached, they recognized them because they too were *pribumi* and because they too lived in the vicinity, so they told them not to touch their shops; to destroy them would mean that the livelihood of their neighbors also would be jeopardized. The shops in fact were not touched.[10] Across the street, a group of merchants standing in front of the burned-out shopping center where they formerly traded repeated the same story. From Pantai Indah Kapok, a new housing complex located in Pluit in the north of the city and occupied largely by "Chinese," there came a similar story. Here sixty-four houses were burned out and over four hundred, which means most of them, were looted.[11] People there told us that the looters were from the neighboring area, a part of the city crowded with rows of shacks. The victims were furious; they felt betrayed by the police, the army, and the government who had failed to protect them and who, indeed, they were sure, instigated the riots. Yet to say "the government" instigated the riots would be too broad. Elements within the army, they were certain, had done it. "They came in trucks and some had on [military] boots." I heard this sentence more than once in just these words in several sections of the city. As in Glodok, we heard that before the local people arrived, others were already there, also arriving in trucks. In Glodok these early visitors had large crowbars they used to pry up the metal shutters of the shops. They then told the locals, mainly male youths, to help themselves to the goods. These military types then themselves spread gasoline and set the place afire. Of the about 1,100 people reported killed during the events of May 13 and 14, most of them are said to have been looters who died in these fires; but at the time of this writing, there seems to be no way to confirm how many actually died.

In East Jakarta, where again shopping centers were burned down, I was told by a friend that the first people to arrive came in trucks, again wearing military boots. They set alight tires from whatever cars were nearby to attract locals. They then, he said, pried open the shop shutters, took out goods, and showed the locals that they could do the same. After that they left. My friend, a retired official of the Ministry of Religion, told me that local mosques used their loudspeakers to dissuade the looters from their work, but their efforts were only sometimes successful.

A secretary in her twenties told of leaving work at noon and crossing Jakarta to get home. There was only one bus running, and it went only part of the way. She walked for six hours before reaching home, by necessity often walking through

---

[10] I am indebted to Benny Subianto who accompanied me on this occasion.

[11] According to Sudarno Tasmin, "Chinese," director of an insurance company and the Neighborhood Association leader (*kepala* R.T.). I spoke with him on June 7, 1998 accompanied by Henri Chambert-Loir.

looters at work. She remembered thinking as she watched them, "These are not human beings. They are animals." She heard the *azan* from the mosque chanting the call to prayer, without, in this case, any special message for the looters and thought, "What a contrast." She traversed a place where women and children, among others, were carrying sacks of rice and cartons of Indo Mie (packaged noodles) out of a shop. Another woman said to them, "'What you are doing is shameful. It's not human." The woman who was busy with her stolen cartons answered in one word: "Chinese." The first one persisted, arguing "Chinese" too were human. But to no avail.

The secretary, let us call her Rahmah, went on to say

> Some people think the looting was maneuvered by someone or other, but I don't think so. At the big malls, maybe, but not at these small shops. The trouble is that for so long these people have seen on TV, on the news, in the soap operas, how much luxury some people have. Now with the economy the way it is, they have nothing. There is such a gap and they have been patient for so long.

These sentiments and even the phrases about the enticement of television, particularly the soap operas, which are often about wealthy families and about the "gap" between rich and poor, have for a long time been heard in the press and in the speech of Jakartans who consider themselves middle class.

Rahmah is typical in sympathizing with the plight of the rioters but condemning their rioting. The suffering of "the people" is a common theme in the middle-class press. Rahmah does not want to deny it; quite the contrary. But she sees the actions of the looters as "inhuman." One does not excuse the other. She simply does not put the two attitudes in conjunction with one another to arrive at a consolidated conclusion.

Rahmah's thinking is similar to that of Alya's, who on the one hand advocates reform of the economy to help "the people" (*rakyat*) and at the same time perceives the looters (*massa*), through her *softlens*, as the chief danger to her safety. The difference between these two women, perhaps, is that Rahmah, never having taken a political position, was not forced to decide between the security forces and the *massa*. I asked Rahmah if she was not afraid on her travels home. She said no, that she was with many others, all forced to pass through looters at work. She, like the woman who chided the rioters, did not feel that she herself was in danger. She was not worried, for instance, at being thought "Chinese." The only time she was frightened, she said, was when soldiers fired into the air as she passed a shopping mall. Then, like everyone else, she ran. When I told her, "then you were afraid of ABRI," she was surprised to find it was the case. In my opinion, however, she was not afraid of ABRI at all; she was afraid of guns.

That this young woman felt safe walking among the rioters shows the depths of her identification with them. She understands very well their need, and she understands as well the attraction that the goods in these stores have for them. On the other hand, she finds their actions deplorable. I do not doubt the sincerity of her conviction on either score. To say that she understands them is to say not only that she sympathizes with them in their situation, but also that she feels, with them, the lure of the enormous wealth displayed on television. The difference between her and the looters is that she would not give in to this attraction. It is just here that a question of class arises. The *massa* are, as looters, uncivilized. Their looting is an indication of how much further they need to develop. She is as certain of what separates them from her as she is of what links them to her.

The Indonesian middle class is not merely wealthier than the underclass; it is almost comfortable with its wealth; it does not feel it will be devoured by it. The lower classes, by contrast, are often suspicious of the effects of ownership of wealth while still finding it attractive. Those who can refrain from taking easily available market goods merit the title "middle class." Those who cannot may or may not still live in a traditional ambiance; either way, in Indonesia today they are sometimes identified as the *massa* and sometimes as "the people," and there is no need, as we have seen, to make a definitive judgment. In Europe, conflict between classes shaped class identity; in Indonesia, by contrast, class is largely the result of undesired distinctions within the body of the nation. Conflict has not played a large part in developing class identities. Rather attitudes toward wealth are a central point of differentiation.

If Rahmah feels safe during riots, it is not only because of the complicated quality of her identification with "the people." It is also because she is certain that she is not "Chinese" and that she will not be taken for "Chinese." Moreover, her understanding of the term "Chinese" matches the rioters' understanding, at least in part. She sees "Chinese" as having what the poor lack, and she ranges herself with those who have little. The "we"/*pribumi* and "they"/"Chinese" divide is a question of wealth expressed as a question of race and appearance. For Rahmah, as for most members of the *"pribumi"* or "indigenous" middle class, the word "Chinese" distinguishes those so designated as rich relative to the comparatively poor *pribumi*, and this distinction continues to be accepted as true even when it doesn't fit the facts.

"Chinese" as used for certain inhabitants of Indonesia is a racial category, one that marks identity through inheritance of physical traits and moral characteristics. It supposedly designates those whose ancestors (or sometimes themselves) were born in China. "Chinese" are likely to be born in Indonesia, not to speak "Chinese," and to have ancestors who may have intermarried with *"pribumi"*; they are not likely to have Chinese names.[12] An inborn quality keeps them "Chinese," or so it is thought; this quality is the state of being wealthy, even when they are in fact poor. Rahmah is not anti-"Chinese" in her sentiments. But she is confident she is not "Chinese" not only because she does not look "Chinese" (many "Chinese" are indistinguishable from other Indonesians and some *pribumi* look "Chinese") but also because she knows she is not made of wealth, whereas "Chinese" are somehow inherently so fabricated. Exactly the same confusion of appearance and property arose in other *pribumi* I spoke with who were afraid that they did, in fact, "look Chinese," that is, look wealthy, and that therefore they might be subject to looting, as though wealth were a physical and therefore a racial trait.

But Rahmah also identifies herself with the victims of the riot. It is again a question of class. She is not rich, but neither are most "Chinese." Certainly the owners of the small shops she watched being robbed were not wealthy. But it is not because she is realistic about the actual wealth of "Chinese" that she is able to find

---

[12] Chinese from China, I am told, find those called "Chinese" in Indonesia indistinguishable from other Indonesians and lacking, therefore, in whatever characteristics make one Chinese according to Chinese. "Chinese," then, the term for those so called in Indonesia, is not a matter of inherent characterisitics but, particularly given their long history in the archipelago and consequent intermarriage, an arbitrary linguistic practice. For this reason I put the term in quotation marks.

something in common with them. She is not threatened by their wealth because she knows that she can guard herself against wanting it. She said of the looters that they were "spontaneous" in their actions once given the example of other looters; that, in view of their restraint for so long, once it was all "free" (*gratis*) they could not resist. She grants to the "Chinese" what she grants to herself; the ability to resist the lure of (imagined) wealth. This leaves the word "Chinese" or "*Cina*" in her parlance, ambiguous. They are other than she insofar as they are wealthy. They are the same as she insofar as they are "human beings," that is, trained, educated, able to resist the immediate availability of wealth, real or imagined; both are, in fact, middle class.

Some looters were not very different from her. Here is a letter to a columnist in an Islamic magazine which publishes advice to its readers:

> On May 14th I nearly joined the looters. Maybe because of the influence of the masses, I lifted a twenty-inch television set in an electronics store. As a matter of fact, for a long time I had wanted to change my fourteen-inch television [for a bigger one]. But suddenly, both hands and feet started to tremble. I thought of God. "Ya, Allah, how can I take the responsibility for this?" Then I set the thing down again and asked God's forgiveness. *Ustadz*, is what I did a sin? Can this sin be forgiven by asking forgiveness? Do I have to ask forgiveness from the store owner? ARH (Bekasi).[13]

The writer of this letter acknowledges thinking that he too can do what the people around him are doing: take goods. He is influenced by their example. But that is not enough. He thinks of what it is that he has wanted "for a long time." The writer recalls that "for a long time" he wanted a bigger television set; his own is merely "fourteen-inch." There in the shop broken open just in front of him he recognizes what he has long thought about, a twenty-inch set. There is, here, no question of need, as there is in the usual discourse of why looters looted or "the people" acted. It is simply a question of finding what he has long awaited. Even were he not poor (there is nothing to say that he is, in fact) he would still loot, at least to the extent that he did so on May 14. What we see is that Rahman's description implicitly fitted the looters, at least if this man is typical; they were perhaps in need, but certainly desirous. They had seen what "others" had. The others on television were not "Chinese." But magically transported by the synapses in operation in times of anti-"Chinese" riots, the television that had once been seen, perhaps, on a soap opera, appears now in the possession of "Chinese," which means it is available; available with them and not with others.

The widespread statement of the need of the poor conceals the opening of desire as it is fostered in the market: on television and, as it were, through the television set. The defense against this desire, the ability to keep it in control, is the ability to consume moderately. To think of God as one lifts someone else's property, to set

---

13 "Nyaris Berdosa" (Almost Sinned), *Panji Masyarakat*, July 1, 1998, p. 52

their property down again, is to put desire in touch with a source of restraint.[14] By contrast to say "Chinese" as the woman lifting a sack of rice did in defense of her actions is to make "Chinese" the mere equivalent of "riches." It is a word that for some at a certain moment blotted out other thoughts; but, in the next days as in the previous ones, fell back into its everyday sense.

Something snaps into place in the immediate present, a wish that until then, "for a long time," had been realized only by someone else some place else. We are not sure that this man or others "for a long time" wanted what they at least attempted to take. It may be that when seeing the television set, in the way of ordinary shoppers in a mall, this man looked at something he'd never thought of wanting at all, but, somehow, in the moment of seeing it, he thought he'd always wanted and even needed it. Viewed in the soap operas on television, the twenty-inch set is a theatrical prop rather than private property. In the context of the riot, the twenty-inch set stood out amongst the goods visible through the open facade of a shop. It was—according to his testimony—his wish about to come true. The abrupt realization that he could have his wish comes with the word "*Cina.*" The word was the means by which an element of scenery changed its setting, moving out of the theater but not out of a theatrical or imaginary realm. Its new setting was "Chinese" meaning at that instant: "what I have been wishing for," "wealth," and "here waiting for me."

It is quite likely that the woman carrying off the sack of rice buys her daily rice from the same merchant. She is likely also to have had cordial relations with him and to have such again in the future when her present supply of rice runs out. What distinguishes her from Rahmah and the middle-class people who refuse to loot is not only respect for property or its lack. It is her inability to put the word "*Cina*"—"Chink" might be its English equivalent—in its pejorative and magical sense in touch with the person with whom they deal daily.

The condition for her thinking and of those like her is precisely unlike the condition of the trembling letter writer. They do not see catastrophe looming before them should they give in to what the word "*Cina*" means: "what I now know I wanted for a long time, which is available in front of me at this moment." No disaster threatens. They are not transformed in their identity, suddenly becoming criminals or sinners, contaminating their sense of being good Indonesians. And the next day or the next month the store and its owner will be there again. Catastrophe, they feel, threatens neither them nor their victims.

Indonesian culture at present is racist, but Indonesians are not racist in the same manner as Europeans. The ease with which Indonesians ward off catastrophe distinguishes them from the latter. European racists find the presence of Arabs or Jews or Africans or Turks intolerable because, it seems, they embody elements of themselves they cannot bear and which threaten disaster. This intolerable other seems constantly present; it becomes necessary to expel it or, I should say, "them." Those Indonesians bothered by "Chinese" have a different complaint. It is not that "Chinese" should leave Indonesia, but that they should become better Indonesians.

---

[14] The restraint here is religious but that is only one of its modes. In this case, the religious expert to whom he addressed his letter advised him he need not ask pardon of the Chinese and he need make no further religious efforts to be free of sin since, by putting the set down, he had stopped before he had transgressed. In the light of the diverse roles Islam took in the riots, it is interesting to see the legalistic emphasis on property rather than an ethical response to people of other religions, to violence, and so forth, in this answer. It makes no mention of "Chinese" whatsoever.

The current form of this idea is that "Chinese" should *introspeksi*, that is, meditate on their failure to mix with *pribumi*, meditate on their own intolerance, which takes the form of promoting their own kind in their banks and big enterprises over worthy *pribumi*.[15]

Until Habibie became president, non-Javanese often remarked that only a Javanese could be president and that Javanese are favored in the government bureaucracy. Indeed, Indonesian firms are sometimes segregated, with certain taxi companies employing almost none but Javanese, others no Javanese. Such segregation is not thought comparable to the kind of segregation practiced by the "Chinese." When the *pribumi* favor one ethnic group over another this does not raise fears or charges of separatism. The same behavior by "Chinese" makes *pribumi* sometimes feel that "Chinese" will not or cannot or do not want to become "true" Indonesians.

Of course, anti-Semites claim Jews are clannish and keep to themselves. But a racism that not only levels charges of exclusivism but that claims to want to remedy it by inclusion requires another kind of thinking than that we apply to the European variety.[16] It means that "Chinese" are not in the place of the consolidated, insupportable other, constant bearer of all that threatens lethal contamination, tolerated at best and then only provisionally. In other words, though they may be stolen from, murdered, raped and be the victims of arson from time to time, they are not hated. But they remain outside the capacity of many *pribumi* to accept them comfortably and from time to time they snap into the place of the intolerable, this intolerable being uncontrollable desire.

There is a relation between class, race, and national identity in Jakarta that keeps racism under control, albeit imperfectly. In the stories of the riots, the "Chinese," as I have said, are sometimes blamed for starting the riots simply by being who they are in Indonesian society. But the real danger in these stories is, indeed, not the "Chinese" at all but those who are unable to keep themselves from looting. The anti-"Chinese" riots I am familiar with from Java usually begin abruptly and end the same way.[17] As they go on, they evoke uneasiness in many who are not "Chinese," in part out of fear that they themselves will be next should the riots exceed their original targets. It is usually at that point that the riots cease. The danger of disorder arising from below, the danger of the *massa*, is greater than that of "Chinese" who are only the lure that attracts the *massa* and sets them on their riotous path. Catastrophe might come from the underclass, but the double view of them—as *massa*, therefore a source of catastrophe and as *rakyat*, the people, part of the nation—keeps catastrophe out of mind most of the time.

It is a question of how the relation between the two terms is managed. The assumption, as we will see, is that "the people" need to be educated, an idea perhaps as old as Indonesian nationalism. It is the job of the government and the enlightened class as a whole to do so. In this notion there is already the idea of a "gap." Following

---

[15] For an example in English of this commonly expressed attitude, see the letter to the editor of the *Jakarta Post* by S. Sastrowardojo of May 30, 1998.

[16] Further analysis of the assertion that "Chinese" fail to mix with their neighbors can be found in my "*Kiblat* and the Mediatic Jew," *Indonesia* 69 (April 2000): 9-40.

[17] On the trajectory of such riots see my *Solo in the New Order: Language and Hierarchy in an Indonesian City* (Princeton: Princeton University Press, 1986). The 1980 riots in Solo were different from the 1998 riots in Jakarta in that the rioters were not the *massa* but students. However, underlying assumptions about wealth and "Chinese" were the same.

Benedict Anderson, I believe there was already a fear of the underclass during the Revolution with the stifling of a social revolution.[18] This fear was identified as a "gap" (*kesenjangan*) between the people and the well-to-do during the New Order, when not merely "Chinese" but other Indonesians began to grow wealthier. The use of the word "gap" is practically coterminous with the existence of a middle class on a large scale. It is usually spoken of as a difference between "Chinese," who are wealthy, and the underclass, who are poor. If there is disorder, it is in the first place said to be because the underclass is tempted by the wealth of "Chinese," as we have seen. The wealth of the non-"Chinese" middle class is thus obscured or denied.

The difference between classes can be managed when desire for wealth can be controlled. The insistence that "Chinese" are wealthy and therefore we, the rest of the middle class, are not, shows the ambiguity of middle-class identifications. They too feel the threat of their own impulses, and they know as well that from the point of view of the underclass they are a target. They need not have a lot to feel vulnerable; they need only have somewhere within them the same notion of riches, a notion which, of course, the New Order fostered in both official policies of Development and in allowing the enormous development of consumerism. To fear the *massa* is to displace their own interior menace.

One recourse is to blame the government for allowing such a gap to develop, thereby giving "Chinese" too great a place in the economy, and to hope also that the government will keep order. If disruption does occur, there is another source of reassurance. Not long after an outbreak public disorder, rumors and speculations about the instigators of the events often circulate among people, particularly in Jakarta. Always someone in the government, particularly in the military, is thought to have provoked the actions. The reasons adduced for the riots include allowing the *massa* to attack Chinese as a diversion from political difficulties. But the major effect is to show the need for government control. Thus it is widely believed that Suharto, in Egypt on May 13, ordered the actions of that day and the next in order to demonstrate the need for his own presence and perhaps to justify instituting military law. The other person widely accused was Suharto's son-in-law, Lt. General Prabowo, who was said either to have acted on behalf of Suharto or, in another version, in his own behalf in an attempt to gain power. Neither story has been confirmed at the moment I write this. In June, however, as I have mentioned, there were many rumors of men with military bearing, wearing boots, arriving in trucks on the scene where riots were to take place, then summoning the crowd and inciting them to looting. These rumors emerged in the press by the end of June and early July.

The educated classes found the question of who exactly ordered the riots to be a matter of much interest. The tone of these conversations was likely to be similar no matter who engaged in them. The events were shocking. It was a serious matter but, at the same time, discussion of "who was behind it" generated a degree of satisfaction that initially seemed inappropriate, given the shocking quality of the events. The general conversation in the press about the place of the "Chinese" had the same quality. One felt that the writers, shocked though they were, were pleased to be able to deal with a matter of such importance. The satisfied tone is not incompatible with an appreciation of the brutality of the events. Once the events are

---

[18] Benedict R. O'G. Anderson, *Java in a Time of Revolution* (Ithaca: Cornell University Press, 1972).

thought to have been manipulated by high authorities, people understand that, in fact, the situation, no matter how violent, is under control. There is no need to fear that the *massa* are out of control. Furthermore to know, if that is the correct verb in this instance, who behind the scenes was responsible is to feel connected with that political backstage. The satisfaction comes, ultimately, from feeling that one shares in the workings of power. One knows someone who knows someone who knows who did it. The assumption, of course, is that those in power demonstrate their position by control of those otherwise dangerously violent, namely, the *massa*.[19]

Moving down the social scale, one encounters less interest in and less gossip about who did it. But people with whom I spoke still held to the conviction that the events were manipulated. Such people may or may not claim that "Chinese" are at fault because they refuse to integrate themselves, that "Chinese" are overly concerned with money, and so on. But they often say that the riots were a mistake since the result was to put more people out of work. In the end, though many such persons told me how they were barely managing to earn enough to feed themselves, they showed little uneasiness. In their case too, the sense that, ultimately, things were under control even if mistakes had been made remained strong—strong enough to assuage fears that the economy was out of control and that they would be its victims.[20]

By far the most common opinion was that the events were manipulated, hence controlled. The other possibility, that the *massa* acted "spontaneously," however, could also lead to a similar feeling of personal safety, even, as we have seen, for a young woman walking home in the midst of looting. The "Chinese" with whom I spoke also believed the events to have been manipulated. I met sixteen people who had lost everything or nearly everything. Their houses had been looted and sometimes burned. Their real estate was worth nothing. In some cases, they had also lost shops and cars. They were living with relatives. They were, in fact, internal refugees. Many of these people were understandably angry. They were angry, however, not so much with the rioters themselves as with the authorities. Some told me of having given large amounts of food to people in the neighboring slums to help them through the crisis before the rioting. Then, as one said, "Just look what they did." But this person spoke not so much in anger as with irony and patience. He pointed to the anti-Chinese slogans painted on his house. He certainly was not pleased with them. There were some people squatting on the curb a little way off as he spoke. I asked him if they were likely to have been amongst the looters. He said he thought so, but he seemed quite neutral. Then he went on to tell me something often heard: how when the riots began he and others first called the police and then

---

[19] On the structure of Indonesian political gossip, see my "'I Wasn't There But...': Gossip and Politics in Jakarta," *Archipel* 46 (1993): 46-59.

[20] The same logic governs the question of bringing Suharto to trial. The authoritative exposure of the Suharto family wealth in journals such as *Forbes*, which listed him amongst the richest people in the world, convinced people of what they already knew. Most people I spoke with think Suharto is a crook, but the sense that, even in the midst of disorder, in fact particularly in the midst of disorder, there is control makes them patient. They do not want to risk the disorder they feel would eventuate if there were strong calls to bring Suharto to justice. Even Suharto's brutality becomes an asset to him because it indicates his strength, determination, and control, which people are not certain has been permanently contained. The reluctance, surprising to me, to hang him by his heels, shows his murderous qualities to be a valued part of Indonesian political life in the past; and these qualities are now perceived as a menacing force in the present and therefore not to be disturbed.

various army officers. No one, however, came to help them. They were left to flee
with their families and servants to a nearby golf course where they were safe. In his
view, his impoverished *pribumi* neighbors were not at all admirable. But his anger
was largely reserved for the police, the army, and for those he was convinced had
allowed these people to act. He had no doubt at all that the riot was instigated. He
felt entitled to government protection (and he had given money to the police for that
purpose). It was unjust that he had been robbed. He worked hard for his money; he
got up daily at five o'clock, he returned home from work after dark, he worked
weekends. He deserved what he had. But his fury was reserved not, as I have said,
for those who left his house absolutely empty but for the authorities who should
have stopped them and who were in fact themselves responsible for the disorder.
They should have acted differently and, he assumed, they would act properly at
some other time in the future. His anger, in other words, was based on an
assumption that he had and has a right to protection, and that he was not only
justified in asserting that right but that he would prevail, at least sometimes.

The man just cited was the angriest "Chinese" I met. Others, who had lost as
much, were certainly perturbed, but less upset. At Pasar Glodok, men who had lost
their entire businesses told me that their creditors would understand and not
demand payment for the goods they had on loan. It was understood that later, when
the market was rebuilt and they reopened their businesses, they would get more
goods on credit. Their standing protected them. These men also blamed the
government for lack of protection. Like the others, they too had no doubt that they
merited protection, not merely on human grounds but because they had been born in
Indonesia, they were citizens, they lived honestly. Not to have the protection of the
government was outrageous. Such an attitude implies that their rights and the
possibility of invoking them have not evaporated entirely. They too felt a connection
to the government; they too had their own access to it. They told me that they indeed
paid elements in the police and the army to ensure they were protected.[21] The fact
that the people they had paid failed to respond when they were needed and
summoned increased their anger. But at the same time, they knew that they had the
right to protection, and they retained the expectation that they would be protected
again. In the end, one has to say that they were exasperated. Some, families with rape
victims or members afraid of suffering sexual violence indeed left the country. They
were like refugees during World War II, certain they were the constant target of
hatred, their lives in unceasing danger, simply because of who they were by birth;
but most did not feel this way. These "Chinese" could make themselves known to
political authorities and certainly planned to do so again. They too believed it was a
good thing for "Chinese" to integrate into the nation and the local community and
felt that integration was already the overriding reality.

The assumption behind the logic just outlined is that Indonesian society can
always contain its elements. None of them are by nature a source of irreparable
rupture, neither "Chinese" nor the underclass. In this view, society may be composed
of groups or individuals, each with its own characteristics, but in addition there is a
correct way to behave, "custom" or *adat*, right manners, which is common to all and,

---

[21] The police sometimes responded. Jakarta is the site of the world's largest *vihara* (Buddhist
monastery). Henri Chambert-Loir and I were told that during the riots it was filled with
people taking refuge there, and that it was safe. The local police post had been called and sent
men; they were paid for their efforts.

as the idea has evolved out of assumptions originating in the regions, national in its scope and definition. No matter who someone is, there is a proper way of speaking that allows one to include that person. Social discourse in that sense is perfect; its breakdown can only come from those who are as yet ignorant of its rules. These people, the *rakyat*, are in the process of development; the educated classes will see to it that they learn; in the meantime they will be controlled, one hopes, by those in power. Thus "Chinese," though they might offer too tempting a target for those who do not understand how to control themselves, are not an inherent threat to national society because those who have not yet learned control are controlled by others. The foundation of social order is ideas of right behavior applicable to all; in case of their failure, there is governmental authority.

I have never heard an Indonesian admit that his or her national society is inherently flawed by racism and that certain groups or individuals are intolerable. The experience of the former Communist political prisoners and their descendants still surveyed and discriminated against not withstanding, Indonesians continue to hold on to their assumption that all peoples of the nation belong there. In the case of "Chinese" this assumption is put into doubt, but not given up. There is an unresolved contradiction. On the one hand, proper behavior forbids exclusion; on the other, "Chinese" are sometimes improper not by behavior but by identity.

The result is embarrassment. At the beginning of the New Order, *"Cina"* (Chinese) was a word of contempt which the government forced into use. The respectful term till recently rarely heard was *"Tionghwa."* The embarrassment caused by *"Cina"* for Indonesians is indicated by the series of euphemisms that followed, including "WNI," meaning "Indonesian citizen," used only for "Chinese," and most recently *"keturunan,"* meaning *WNI keturunan Cina,* "Indonesian citizens of 'Chinese' descent," as though one indicates one's delicacy by pointing to "Chinese" as (also?) citizens or people with ancestors. Many "Chinese" are likely to evade the problem by using the English term "Chinese," while retaining, for instance, the term *"Tiongkok"* for "China." These linguistic vagaries show that the subject of these terms figures as something Indonesians want to turn away from. But there is also linguistic evidence to the contrary in the use of *"Cina."* After decades of use, for some, particularly younger people, both Indonesian and "Chinese," the word is no longer pejorative. The necessity to include everyone in discourse and long usage have neutralized the term for certain people.

There is a more sinister version of the same theme. "Chinese" have a special code on their identity cards, thus exposing them even if, as most have, they no longer use Chinese names. It is as though assimilation must be denied. The fact is that "Chinese" have been assimilated in every way except that they are not fully accepted. The embarrassment the terms for "Chinese" evoke is not caused by anything inherent to "Chinese" themselves but by the prejudice against them rubbing against Indonesians' characteristic refusal to think that people who behave well can be excluded.

Indonesians make trouble for themselves. When they point to the preferred place of "Chinese" in colonial times, or charge that not all "Chinese" took part in the Revolution, or complain about "Chinese" pay-offs of government officials, they act in bad faith. Other Indonesian groups also enjoyed preferred status under the Dutch and even fought alongside them, yet they are not targeted. And probably most Indonesians pay bribes when they find it necessary to get official permits. The tendency to associate "Chinese" with wealth, as we have seen, is at the heart of

Indonesian difficulties. One might argue that in peasant societies there is somehow a necessary friction between those who deal in money and those who think in other terms. If there is, it applies in societies where money exchange is limited. Life in Jakarta, even for its large number of immigrants from the countryside, involves money transactions with a range of people, not merely "Chinese." It is not only "Chinese" who should be the target if actual money dealings were the cause of resentment. Furthermore many non-"Chinese" Indonesians are extremely wealthy. Many are traders, some are hugely wealthy, but none have their nationality discounted. Thus to point to an historic association of "Chinese" with wealth as the source of prejudice or to the character of a society clinging to peasant qualities without asking why such prejudice is limited to one segment of the population is to glide over the fact of prejudice. This becomes evident when one notices the call for "Chinese" to return from abroad after the riots because, amongst other reasons no doubt, their money is needed; or the commonly expressed idea, held even by those who resent "Chinese," that the riots were a mistake because the destruction of businesses meant loss of jobs. Real wealth gives "Chinese" a place; figurative wealth leads to riots.

One can reasonably say that New Order Indonesia has been invaded by the market in many forms and that this has caused difficulties. But the problem is more general. It is not commodity exchange as opposed to other forms of circulation that gives rise to the difficulty. The assumptions of Indonesian national society are pinched not necessarily by their traditionalist residue but by the terms of emancipation from tradition and colonialism which guaranteed that modern Indonesian society would always be moral, in contrast to both the backwardness of older prenationalist generations and the immorality of Europeans.[22] This left no place for the autonomous workings of desire, which is to say, no place for the disruptions internal to the person, so easily aroused in a society where the market dominates; in other places such dislocations are simply expected. Indonesian discrimination springs from energies interior to the nation which it cannot account for and which it attributes to "Chinese." Had Indonesian thinking about desire evolved during the New Order, the fears that came with heightened desire might have been alleviated. Perhaps anxiety of this sort can never be stilled. But it is a grave fault of Indonesian culture and intellectual life that it is expressed through violence and prejudice.[23]

RAPE

The balance between racist and assimilationist thinking, and the paradoxical reassurance or perhaps denial which followed the riots was shaken, however, when stories of rape began to circulate a few weeks after the events. Reports first circulated in the "Chinese" community, so far as I can tell, and then spread throughout Jakarta. They then emerged in the press; first and most extensively in the English language *Jakarta Post*, and then in the major papers and magazines. These were stories both of

---

[22] On this topic, see my *A New Criminal Type in Jakarta: Counter-Revolution Today* (Durham: Duke University Press, 1998); and *Fetish, Recognition, Revolution* (Princeton: Princeton University Press, 1997).

[23] On the relation between violence and identity see Hent de Vries and Samuel Weber, eds., *Violence, Identity and Self-Determination* (Stanford: Stanford University Press, 1997), particularly the articles by de Vries, Weber, and Derrida.

rape and molestation of women. The second concerned "Chinese" women trying to return home, being stopped, dragged out of their cars or off their motorbikes, forced to undress in front of a gang of men and ridiculed, but not always raped. Often in these stories an older man from the neighborhood or a taxi driver showed up and led the woman away. In other stories, which came to predominate, women were gang raped. These stories emerged gradually. It also turned out that some women were burned to death as their apartments were set afire after they were raped, that some later committed suicide, and many fled to Singapore or Australia.

There is no doubt about the depth of feeling these stories evoked. Anti-"Chinese" activities have occurred since the beginning of the Republic and, in fact, long before.[24] But anti-"Chinese" sentiment has evolved in recent decades and stories of rape were new. In June 1998, these stories evoked genuine outrage and shame in every person with whom I spoke, no matter from what class or religion or sex.[25] When Indonesians, "Chinese" or not, told me the stories, there was invariably a break from whatever we had been speaking of earlier. The somewhat pious tone of disapproval in which stories of looting were usually told gave way to uncertainty not about the facts but about what to say about them or, I felt, how to speak at all.

Press accounts varied in tone. Rarely were these written in the first-person. Most were taken from the meetings of the Human Rights Commission at which family members testified to the experience of their wives and daughters. Some stories were told over the telephone by victims who had fled the country. Many accounts came from the victims via the women's groups which counseled them after their terrible experiences.

The reports show that the reporters were shaken. Here is an example:

A young woman, call her Joana, twenty-five-years old. The young mother of an eight-month-old child never imagined that the place she lived, Cinere, South Jakarta, would be the target of rioters, much less that she would be the victim of rape by savage human beings.

In the blink of an eye her house, neatly arranged and cleaned, was in complete disorder. The glass was smashed. Her things were all taken out. Joana and her husband were in a panic [*panik*]. They screamed for help. Useless. Their voices were lost in the tumult of the *massa*.

Carrying their little one, her husband tried to save himself and looked for a safe place. Unfortunately for Joana, she was not allowed to get away. Someone

---

[24] On the connection between anti-Sinicism and Indonesian nationalism, see Takashi Shiraishi, "Anti-Sinicism in Java's New Order," in *Essential Outsiders: Chinese and Jews in the Modern Transformation of Southeast Asia and Central Europe*, ed. Daniel Chirot and Anthony Reid (Seattle and London: University of Washington Press, 1997).

[25] By the end of June these stories too were taken up into the discourse of manipulative, therefore ultimately reassuring, power. It was said that the rapes too were instigated. In the meantime, the police said that they had no report of rapes; General Wiranto, Minister of Defense and head of the armed forces, was rumored to have told women's groups that the rapes may not have occurred. The Minister for Women's Affairs first said she could do nothing since there had been no official reports of rapes; then, under pressure from women's groups, she set up a hot line for complaints which, gossip had it, were mainly directed against her lack of action. The entanglement of the stories in questions of administration did not lead to the abatement of descriptions in the press, however. These reports were in no way prurient; they demonstrated the widespread feeling of shame and of identification with the victims of these attacks.

grabbed her arm and pulled her out of the room. Joana's husband was not able to help. While others were busy looting, someone unknown tried to let loose his cruelty by staining Joana. Joana was pushed outside by several people before she was raped by one after the other. Her screams of pain went unnoticed.

At that moment the light of Joana's life went out. There is not a drop of happiness left in her life. She is in trauma. *Shock* [in italics and English] has flooded her life. . . . Though the doctor has allowed her to go home, her friends testify that Joana is still gloomy and abstracted. Occasionally her face will show the depths of her sadness. In fact, she once wept and wept, lamenting her fate. Actually Joana is reluctant to see her husband. There are only a few people she will see. . . .

For Joana what she experienced is a stain, a shame [*aib*] which cannot be forgiven, but has to be obliterated. So that her descendants after her will not be ashamed.

The bitterness Joana is going through is not only the bitterness of Chinese women, but of women in general.[26]

The language of this piece might make the reader of English suspect a certain lack of directness of feeling. It is, indeed, the case that not all rape accounts have this tone. The use of such language, particularly in a magazine whose reporting is usually far more direct and even "hard-hitting," indicates the difficulty of knowing how to speak of rape or perhaps of sexuality. Indeed, the only time rape was likely to be reported at all before the riots was in the popular newspaper *Pos Kota*, generally looked down upon by the middle class as sensationalist.

To speak of the "light going out from Joana's life," for instance, recalls the language of the Malay classics. It indicates respectfulness and the need to have recourse to language quite different than the spoken language or the usual lexicon of reporting. To begin the description of what happened to her by calling the agent "someone unknown" might reproduce what Joana saw as her attacker approached. To continue by saying "someone unknown tried to let loose his cruelty by staining Joana" is to veer away from the event into a standardized language of euphemism and moral condemnation. It is also to apply an Arabic word, *aib* (stain) to the "Chinese" woman. With rape, a certain universalism applies. But whether it is because the theological term comprises all women, Muslim or not, or, because the rapists were Muslim, the stain itself becoming a mark of a corrupted Islam, I cannot say.

At the moment of rape the word I have here translated as "savage," *biadab*, occurs. This word moves the account away from the woman's experience toward an understanding of the place of savagery in a general explanation of Indonesian culture. The standard dictionary of Indonesian translates "*biadab*" this way:

1. *belum beradab; belum maju kebudayaan*. Not yet civilized; not yet culturally developed.
2. *tidak tahu adat (sopan santun); kurang ajar; anak itu benar, tidak segan mengucupakan kata kata kotor di hadapan umum*. Without knowledge of custom

---

26 "Kisah getir amoy-amoy korban perkosaan" (The Bitter Story of Chinese Beauties who were Victims of Rape), *Aksi*, June 16-22, 1998, pp. 4-5.

(politeness); uneducated; that child really doesn't hesitate at all to say dirty words in public.
3. *tidak beradab; kejam; pemerkosan anak di bawah umur adalah perbuatan yg biadab.*
Uncivilized; cruel; the rape of minors is savage.

I had no choice in English but to use the word "savage" because it combines the sense of "cruel" and "uncivilized." Weak in American, that connection is strongly apparent in Indonesian. Not to be courteous, not to know how to behave with manners, means also, in Indonesian, to behave "savagely" in the sense that one is not yet civilized and, often, that one acts violently and belongs to a different class of beings. The almost invariable use of the word *biadab* to describe rape contains the implication that the rapist is savage in these senses. This, indeed, is close to the use of the word "*bodoh*," usually translated as "ignorant," to describe "the people" (*rakyat*). It is up to the leaders and those already cultured to help "the people" become courteous, that is, no longer ignorant, loutish, and unaware of civilized behavior. Such usage is not always contemptuous, merely condescending in the older sense of that term.

There is another implication of this word which is contained in the second meaning. The television commentator Wimar Witoelar, for instance, said in a written article:

> I think the biggest tragedy, greater than the ruin of the economy and the political disorder is our lack of morals [*budi pekerti*] as a people who clearly allowed savage [*biadab*] behavior toward those equally human. The issue of rape and looting is much bigger than the obvious fact we have the same citizenship and are far removed from the racial friction of the Dutch East Indies and Indonesia. How could we act toward other human beings in that way? How could we allow torture, rape, and murder of other human beings?
>
> In part the lack of civilized behavior is a product of corrupt and unbalanced political and economic development; in part it comes from the low morals and ignorance [*kebodohan*] of people who still harbor very primitive racial instincts.[27]

As I have said, the term *biadab* usually modified the word "rape." Looters here are *biadab* because they are first of all rapists. Racism apparently may be excused on historical grounds. But the morals of the rapist-looter, according to Wimar Witoelar, are inhuman; the issue is one of common humanity. Culture here, the opposite of savagery and of impoliteness, is general to humankind. On the other hand, the "we" is not "all human beings" but "Indonesians." The culture involved, though it is implied to be general, is Indonesian, the national culture. The source of knowledge of proper behavior is here national. Its failure appears in the lower-class people who raped and also in the upper-class elements of the political class who allowed them to do it. "Savagery" is a characteristic of the undeveloped lower classes; the upper classes should have fostered their development and thus supervised the eradication of their savagery, or, if such has not yet been accomplished, at least kept them in place.

In effect, the writer spells out the assumptions of the word *biadab* "impolite/savage." In doing so he indicates the connection between the moral

---

27 "Tragedi yang Jauh Lebih Besar" (A Much Bigger Tragedy), *Kontan*, June 29, 1998, p. 16.

condition of the rapists and the political class. Wimar Witoelar, known as a critic of Suharto, is clearly amongst the majority who thinks that the regime itself was responsible for the rapes, at the very least in the general sense of creating the conditions for it. Here, however, rather than there being a certain satisfaction in naming the upper-class instigator, there is outrage at both the rapists and those who allowed them to act. A reversal in attitudes has taken place; those who express their opinions no longer feel any reassurance that "we" are safe because violence is controlled by elements of the government, but rather fear that "we" are endangered because the regime, or elements of it, is itself violent. In the meantime, however, Suharto had resigned leaving the question of power ambiguous; at least some of those responsible had left office. But people suspected that they were, nonetheless, still at work.[28]

At stake here is not merely who started the riot but the failure of sociality itself in important segments of the population, including elements of the government and military. The assumption underlying stories about disruption was that violence was always possible, but that violence was limited to the lower class or, in the worst case, to elements in the government who borrowed their ferocity from elements they then controlled, as happened, for instance, in the murders of presumed criminals in the 1980s.[29] In that instance, Suharto ordered killings without trials, carried out by soldiers in mufti. Corpses were distributed on city streets. The government thus appropriated the power of criminality for itself. Most Indonesians seemed grateful for the suppression of these supposed criminals. In the violence of 1998 in Jakarta, however, the government, or at least the army, appears tinged with a criminality which is of no use to it. Orchestrated appearances of men with crowbars in hand did not aid in keeping order. When Wimar Witoelar uses "we," he generalizes condemnation to the point where "we Indonesians" are culpable and thus puts in doubt the very foundation of social behavior.

There is another feature of these stories of rape. The victims were described as members of families. It would be possible to tell the stories differently. Reporters describing women traveling alone who were stopped on the highway and pulled from their cars, could have finished their portraits without mention of the victims' husbands, fathers, children, and mothers. The feelings of wonder and revulsion the rape stories elicited were linked to seeing these victims as daughters and mothers. The paths of identification thus led to them and not to their violators.

These stories, told for the first time and told as they were, were impossible or at least difficult to recuperate for the usual political purposes. For that to happen, disruption has to be thought of as controlled from above and there has to be

---

[28] No doubt partly because it is now safe to do so, the press has brought up incidents from the New Order's past, such as the shooting of rioters in Tandjung Priok, in 1984, asking for the truth about the numbers killed. It was partly also out of fear that the sections in the Armed Forces thought responsible for the recent riots were still at work even if the same individuals were not involved. The rioters of Tandjung Priok were Muslims, and it was Muslim groups who asked that the case be reopened. It is not interest in this case alone which has been revived. See, for example, the cases reported under the title "Saat Kita Berterus-terang" (Time to Come Out with It), *D&R*, June 27, 1998, pp. 15-30; and "Gerakan Politik Jenderal Benny" (General Benny's Political Activity), *Panji Masyarakat*, June 17, 1998, pp. 15-22. As of the time of writing, it is also clear that the Habibie regime and some Islamic groups want to deny the rapes, the former to protect whoever was responsible and the latter to avoid taking the blame for the *massa* being Muslim.

[29] On this topic, see my *A New Criminal Type in Jakarta*.

confidence in such control. But the conditions that would allow the usual cycles of aggression and accommodation to take place—so that "Chinese" would become targets, then anti-"Chinese" sentiment would evaporate and everyday business would continue without much trouble later—did not pertain in the cases of rape. The word used time after time was "trauma," from the English, to mean that the effects of rape would not disappear. The "stain," (*aib*) in the old-fashioned Arabic vocabulary used to speak of the act, was just that. It was a mark of the *massa* which would not go away. Stories followed of disease, suicide, pregnancy, depression, and broken family lives. Given this new public understanding, the reconversion of "*massa*" into "the people" (*rakyat*) must become more difficult. The notion of *rakyat* implies its complement, "leaders." When the unconscious sliding between *massa* and *rakyat* is more difficult, leadership is also put in doubt. The idea that later, and not much later, normality will restore itself was thus also put in question. The lack of confidence in Habibie, Suharto's successor, was due to this as well as many other reasons.

If the rapists were not defined as people controlled from the top, but as autonomous actors, then their acts, widely shared in, witnessed, and transmitted from mouth to mouth, would be an assertion of the power of the *massa*, a power used to upset basic tenets of behavior. Rape could then be a revolutionary deed whose target would be the middle class. The state itself along with middle-class society would be threatened. This possibility remains latent. Rape reinflected political discourse, but as an element in the call for "*reformasi*." Indonesia's only successful revolution was anti-colonial, not social; the potential for a social revolution remained inherent in the events of May. Whether such a revolt might be incited from the top or not becomes less important at this point, since a vision of widespread civil unrest prompts people to realize that no one can insure control from the top will always work, and since the need to control the *massa* of course implies that they are always a threat. But in the end, the idea that the rapes were instigated by the government meant that they were really under control. That control, terrible as it was in its exercise, and even thought to be directed against "us," the middle class, was preferable to the "spontaneous" act of the savage—and therefore potentially revolutionary—*massa*. The *rakyat* has only the aims of its leaders; the *massa* have their own impulses and these can only be feared.

Rape was placed in a political discourse centering on the question of its control but with a second dimension, "trauma," which further reinflected this discourse.[30] The idea of an unforgettable experience with effects which, we will see, transcend those of the sufferer, comes with descriptions of victims' experiences (as opposed to mere use of the word "rape"). These were rarely written in the first-person since the victims cannot or are reluctant to speak. Here is an exception published in a woman's tabloid:

> Really I don't want to tell anyone about this shame. Life has no meaning for me all the more so since my boyfriend no longer sees me. He seems to be disgusted.

---

[30] The word "trauma" in English, or as an English word adopted by Indonesian, was used to describe the suffering of the rape victims. "Trauma" is a fairly new term in Indonesia, used commonly only well after the commencement of the New Order. On the introduction and use of this term see my *A New Criminal Type in Jakarta*, Chapter 4.

But, okay, I will start this story on the 6th floor of my office building at 10:30 a.m. (Thursday, May 14) when I saw Jakarta thick with smoke.

Many nearby buildings were on fire. I quickly got my things together and phoned home. My servant told me that in Pluit where I live it was still quiet.

As soon as I got out of the office in the area of M. H. Thamrin [Street; a major place of international business], I raced my car north heading for the toll road in front of the Metropolitan Police [Headquarters]. It turned out there were no toll collectors so I didn't pay anything. I kept racing on north and got out at Jembatan Tiga [in one of the major older Chinese quarters] because I saw smoke coming from Pluit. I turned onto Bandengan Utara Street.

But from behind the steering wheel I saw the *massa* hurling things at the buildings. The glass was shattered and along the street you could see many groups of people carrying all sorts of goods. It felt like customers could suddenly buy everything cheap.

Without my being aware of it, all of a sudden my car was near this swarm. Some of them saw me and yelled out, "*Cina!* Get Out!" I was scared to death and couldn't drive the car because in front the *massa* blocked it with wood and metal.

I stopped the car. This *massa* then threw things at it and struck it with metal and wood. The glass in front and back shattered. Feeling really afraid I then got out and asked them for mercy.

As soon as I started to move, several people pushed me. Someone took my purse with a *handphone* in it and about Rp. 2,000,000. The *massa* then got at the accessories in the car like the tape recorder, a doll, and so on. I said to them, "Take it all, just don't burn the car."

Because I gave an order, someone hit me. Others of the *massa* did the same. Then they took my jacket off. Then a whole lot of them pulled off the rest of my clothes.

I was forced to stay on the side [of the road] in front of the car by the *massa*. At the time I was only wearing a bra and underpants. A group of them pulled off my red blouse and short blue skirt and the office uniform jacket. I cried and asked for mercy but they paid no attention and they savagely attacked me.

While I was still conscious, several big men pulled me by the legs and one after the other they raped me. After that I lost consciousness.

I only regained consciousness when an ambulance came and several attendants lifted me up from the side of the street. My body was without clothes and covered with paint. I had a chance to see the carcass of the office car. Burned and shapeless.

The attendants brought me to the hospital. My body was weak and my private parts hurt.

I was treated for a week in the private hospital on Pangeran Jayakarta Street. I was really traumatized and even now I see it in front of me.

My boyfriend who knows what happened wept several times. On the day it happened he called me several times on the *handphone* but a man answered. Then he hung up. I am sure that the guy was the one who looted my telephone.

I had been going with my boyfriend for six months. We even planned to marry next December. Really, and I swear it, up till now I never had any physical contact. In the sense that my *status* [in English] before I was raped was I was still a virgin.

Now I don't ask what my relationship will be. Its clear though that for a week, since I have been out of the hospital, my boyfriend hasn't gotten in touch with me or come to the house. In the meantime every day I have to take medicine and get antibiotic shots because the doctor said there are patients who went through what I did and then died of infections of the womb and reproductive system.

Fortunately my boss is paying for the medicine. He and his wife are the ones who visit me most often in the hospital.

And he is trying not to say anything about this to the other employees. And my brothers, afraid to leave the house, send their wives or servants to look after me.

In fact I don't want to be interviewed and have it in the paper. What for, what good does it do me? It's just one more burden for me. I am ashamed in front of people, especially my friends.

I also refused when some people from a Jakarta foundation said they wanted to help. Help how? I know that that foundation will get a *fee* [English] from the donors just as soon as I register with them.

I know that nothing can clear this up. I don't know the ones who did it; there were a lot of them. If I go to the authorities even before I make a charge my face will be on TV.

So far as I am concerned, that isn't important. Let the Almighty God act against them for what they did. They're religious people, right? They have a God. Their God surely didn't want to see this happen. The law of karma will always work. Whoever sows the seeds, he will reap the fruit. I know that's the most just law.

I still have lots ahead of me. As a girl of twenty-six I still have lots of chances to find a better life. But not in this land where I was born.

After I get well I plan to go to Australia via New Zealand. As someone who is wrapped up in the business world, I think that for the next ten years our economy won't be stable.

But I love Indonesia, the land of my ancestors [*tumpah darah saya*]. My mother is of Chinese descent but my grandparents were born and raised in Bengkalis, Riau.

You have to put down that I never felt China was my land, all the more so since my grandparents were *pribumi*. Its true we still use *ghe* [Khek] but only sometimes.

In Sungai Pakning, Bengkalis Regency in Riau, our house is surrounded by *pribumi* immigrants. We all know each other and on certain occasions we work cooperatively outside the house.[31]

---

[31] She concludes by saying she understands Riau Malay and has studied Mandarin and English. She graduated from high school in 1991, works as a secretary with a salary of Rp. 1.5 million a month and goes to university, paid for by her employer, who is in the export-import business. She lives in an apartment with a servant. "Sekarang, Pacar Saya pun Merasa Jijik: Jeritan Hati Korban Pelecehan Seks Tragedi Jakarta" (Now My Boyfriend Feels Revolted: The Cry from the Heart of a Victim of Sexual Humiliation in Jakarta), *Nyata*, June 4, 1998, pp. 6-7.

Compared with the video tapes of testimony before the Human Rights Commission, in which the facts come out rawly and with unrestrained emotion, without forming much of a story, this newspaper account is already formulated. Shortly after it was published, a story, "Clara" by Seno Gumira Ajidarma, was published by the Islamic newspaper *Republika* [Online edition, June 26, 1998; translation by Michael Bodden published in *Indonesia* 68 (October 1999):

Stories such as this one are distinguished from the earlier stories of looting and destruction that I noted by being said to be unforgettable and by the irreparability of the damage done to the victims and their families. "Chinese" merchants may have lost everything including their homes. They or their families may even have died in the fires. But few insist that their loss is irreplaceable. It is assumed, as I have said, that shortly the world, including "Chinese," will return to its normal state. Rape stories, at least as published, seem always to include the word "trauma." As used in other Indonesian contexts, sometimes this word simply means "extreme effects." But here, it further suggests that something has been irretrievably lost or irreparably wounded which cannot be put out of mind. Loss of a woman's honor means profound shame, shame so deep that it prevents almost all social intercourse. "Actually Joana is reluctant to see her husband. There are only a few people she will see." There is not merely a rift between the woman and her violators or between "Chinese" and *massa*. The woman is excluded from her own family. There is nowhere to turn to repair her exclusion. What, for instance, could she do if her rapist asked forgiveness? And when the government denies or minimizes the rapes and refuses to search for their perpetrators justice is not possible. The physical consequences of rape, though sometimes severe, are usually said to be nothing

---

157-163] with a similar plot. The narrator, however, is a policeman who hears the complaint of a woman telling an experience which matches the one in the report above. She tells her story in the first-person, he takes it down, but, he says, "I have to be suspicious" to be sure there is not some other purpose to her story. With this justification he forces her to describe the rape, even though she sometimes falls unconscious doing so. "I have to know what happened after your underpants were ripped off; if you don't say, what will I write in my report?" he tells her. She claims she fell unconscious when that happened and he tells her "How then can you know that you were gang raped?" and warns her not to spread the word of the rape: "Rape is hard to prove. If you are wrong you will be considered to have spread slander." As he writes, he is attracted to the woman. He starts his story saying, "Maybe I am a dog. Maybe I am pig—but I wear a uniform. You will never know who I really am." In the end, he implies he has raped her himself. He ends his story saying, "Of course I do not need to report to my superiors. Its only to myself that I tell the truth, but taken down in notes—all that is secret. So don't tell anyone."

Here one sees the ambiguous reaction that developed in some Islamic groups. Like the government, they denied, or at least implicitly denied, that the rapes took place, on the grounds that there was no proof. In the case of *Republika*, this stance was partly in defense of Habibie, partly because the rioters were considered Muslim. On the other hand, the ambiguous revulsion about rape also, in my opinion, is a cause of the denial. In this story, taking the action down in notes, making a record, which is precisely what the police and the government refuse to do, is a source of arousal, thus a further excuse for denial. As though, the doubtlessly unintended implication goes, were the government to make a record of the events, they, the police, would rape some more women.

Given the government's attempt to claim there were no rapes and that stories to the contrary were mere attempts to discredit Indonesia, one has to be cautious in assuming newspaper accounts are authentic. I caution the reader not of course because I am uncertain whether rapes occurred or not—they did and on a wide scale—but because there have been attempts, perhaps by the government, to plant false stories in order to say that all stories are false. What we have in the case above, it seems to me, is an actual event put into a framework suitable for the papers and for the elaboration of stories. In other words, we have the beginning of a discourse on rape; what remains doubtful is not the sentiments expressed but the possibility that these are not the actual words of the victim. The direction in which this discourse can progress and be discredited is shown in the shrewd story published in *Republika* Online.

compared to the lasting social and psychological wounds whose import is estrangement: estrangement from the larger society, estrangement of the woman from her own family. The wound is passed down: her children are infected and so also risk estrangement. Nothing is available to cure this wound since its locus is as much in Indonesian society, in its inability to reclaim the raped woman. Forgetting, it is said, is impossible. One would have to do away with shame itself to allow the violated woman and her children to return to society. The cure itself suggests the victory of the *biadab*, though that is not the only possible solution. Hence the national trauma.

The fact that the woman who dared to give the story of her rape to the newspaper thinks of emigrating shows the limit of the word "trauma." Her suffering continues through the memory of the aggression against her; she cannot live any longer in Indonesian society. But she might be able to live somewhere else. This woman assesses her chances and the economic prospects of Indonesia. She will emigrate because, as she says, she still has "lots ahead" of her. "As a girl of twenty-six I still have lots of chances to find a better life." She will find her chances, "But not in this land where I was born." Rape has damaged her, but the damage is irreparable only in Indonesia.

Enough people felt as she did for there to appear advertisements in the Jakarta papers for houses in Perth, Australia. Given the absence of a tradition of exile in Indonesian culture, one sees how great a modification these riots, and in particular these rapes, have made in Indonesian culture. Indonesian national society has been shown to be unable to contain its own citizens, both the *massa* and those it has impressed with the mark of itself.

The sense of catastrophe, largely missing in stories of previous anti-"Chinese" riots, appears in the stories of rape. We have seen this passage:

> For Joana what she experienced is a shame and a stain (*aib*) which cannot be forgiven, but has to be obliterated. So that her descendants after her will not be ashamed.

Shame that must be obliterated (but how?) and that nonetheless will not be forgiven is a difficult notion. The woman raped will never forgive, therefore never forget, her violator. The mark of the violation, the shame itself, which is also a stain, will be passed down to her descendants if it is not obliterated. Even when this woman has children by her husband, her children will be marked as shameful. Rape in that sense harms not only women but threatens legitimacy of descent. Even when her children know their parents and can prove they are born in wedlock, they will be shamed in the way of the illegitimate.

This dimension of trauma, the ineradicable stain, disrupting descent, making even legitimate descent shameful, returns Indonesia to an earlier era. In the formation of Indonesian nationalism, it was thought that modern ways would lead to the formation of the nation. Liberated from the constraints of parental traditionalism, Indonesians found love (*cinta*) linking young men and women across the hundreds of different ethnicities of the archipelago. This liberation was also a new morality, family centered, which by implicit contrast made the old ways immoral. Presidents Sukarno and Suharto's fear of being thought illegitimate reflects this effect of the formation of the nation. The menace of the ineradicable stain of rape which again refuses legitimacy to descent is the eruption of a prenational element, lodged in the fears of national culture. The trauma of rape is latent in the disintegration of the *rakyat* into the *massa*, which itself brings a return to a state feared to be that before Indonesian nationalism.

There is yet another element in explaining why the rape of "Chinese" women shocked the non-"Chinese" middle class. The "gap" so often referred to between the middle class and the *massa*, leaving the latter at best on the margin of the nation, also threatened the identity of those who profited from the country's new wealth. From the standpoint of the New Order's theory of Development, wealth should not create conflicts of identity. The economic development from which the middle class profited and expanded should be thought of as part of national development. But in the context of these new events, a context marked by the end of populist policies, a new question arises: who is the new member of the Indonesian middle class? Certainly I never heard of anyone complaining that owning a new house, a new car, or fashionable clothes, was in anyway undesirable. Wealth was, at least consciously, thought to enhance those who possessed it. And yet, if one looks, for instance, at the photographs in magazines, and perhaps especially women's magazines where fashion is the subject, one sees how a problem developed. On the one hand, fashionable clothes are also considered correct, continuing a long-held assumption in Indonesian culture which stressed the propriety of expensive dress. The person of wealth was entitled to it because wealth had the ability to create propriety; this idea runs contrary to the prejudiced notions implicating "Chinese" wealth. This propriety in the days of the development of Indonesian nationalism in the 1920s and 1930s was nationalist. One sees pictures of young Indonesian men, either in Holland or in the Indies, dressed in suits and ties. Dress itself, which was costly, distinguished them from the traditionalist world. To dress up was to enter a world governed by nationalist assumptions. To put on a suit and tie was to dream of Indonesia. Now, of course, though dress is still expensive, a suit and tie suggests "business" and "*bisnis*," the Indonesian version, has a shady reputation.

There are other scenarios implicit in the photographs of women's fashions. Once again, fashionable dress means propriety; it means an enviable domestic life. But there is also the murkier implication of sexuality always inherent in women's fashion. So long as this meant "love" in the Indonesian sense, "*cinta*," in which desire always led to marriage, there is no difficulty. But in the climate of the raising of desire in the market, the incessant gossip about the mistresses of important men, the scandals about the drug Ecstasy, discotheques, expensive hotels and so on, this is no longer an assumption easy to hold on to.

If one looks at Indonesian fashion photographs, like fashion photography in other places, it often lacks background. One cannot tell where the beautifully dressed woman is to be found. The setting is, finally, the camera or the film itself. This removal from the social scene that goes with proper dress, the implication that fancy dress places the wearer elsewhere—with that place unspecified—suggests another dimension to the "gap" of Indonesian society created by the unequal distribution of wealth. It is not only the *massa* who are placed at the edge of the nation, it is also the middle class. Wealth, instead of establishing social place, leads to an indistinct fantasy of affluence, the mirror of the imaginary wealth of "Chinese" in the minds of looters.

If one asks why it is that the non-"Chinese" middle class was shocked by the rapes of "Chinese" women, why they, men and women, seemed to imagine themselves in the position of these victims, one might guess that, already fearing the *massa*, they imagined themselves as having something shameful and desirable and improper. Unable to lean on the weakened notion of Development, the national unconscious found wealth to be as shameful and as coveted as it was an instrument of propriety. This facilitated their identification with "Chinese." Their uncertainty of ownership, of having the right to what they possessed, and yet the wish to protect it against the *massa* completed that identification.

THE *MASSA* AGAIN

It is rare to hear anyone identify himself as part of the *massa*. It is a category created by the middle class, the projection of their own shamelessness onto the underclass, added to the fear of losing what they have. The *massa* are only realized when the middle class finds its fears about to come true. Here is an anecdote from everyday life. I once rode in the car of a middle-level bureaucrat, a conscientious man mindful of the plight of the poor and a pious Muslim. This man was driven to work in his own car each day. We had a flat tire. As usual in Jakarta several people appeared to fix it for us. Because of the anxiety he showed when he had to step out of the closed, air-conditioned car, I could not tell whether he was paying for a service or paying for protection when he took out his money. Inasmuch as it was the latter, these men off the street were candidates for the *massa* and not part of the people. My friend himself, I am sure, could not tell. When violence breaks out, however, there is no doubt.

The *massa* embody the projections of middle-class fears. They are activated at certain moments. Had there been even the suggestion of menace when my friend had a flat tire, the men off the street would have been bad types, but they would not yet constitute the *massa* since the *massa* are always numerous. The *massa* in May 1998 was formed, if one can believe the accounts one hears, from above. Local men and boys had to be instructed to break into shops and they had to be taught how to rape. Later, after the major incidents were over, the following document was distributed in various Indonesian cities and over the internet. Though it dates from after the events, it gives us an idea of how the riots might have been incited. It takes the form of an official document, one emanating from an organization:

Return of Ancestral Goods Stolen by Various Chinese
Goals:
 1. Enjoy this life
  a. Visit the places of your friends and relatives
  b. Do whatever you have wanted to do (which you have not yet done)
  c. Ask pardon of *PRIBUMI* [non-"Chinese" Indonesians] you have injured.

Plans:
 2. We have already decided that within a short time we will take back OUR ANCESTRAL WEALTH, by these means:
  a. Burning Chinese HOUSES and WEALTH
  b. Cutting off men's PENISES
  c. Stripping naked men and women
  d. Raping Chinese GIRLS

Desirable:

>   Making Chinese males our chauffeurs
>   Making Chinese women our servants

There is no other way to wipe out Chinese ARROGANCE, so long as [your] WEALTH and lives still exist, it cannot be done, [therefore] we have planned this as carefully as possible and now wait for the right moment [to carry it out]. We wish you peace in using well what life remains to you.

NB: Photocopy this for other Chinese

For Miss Pretty Chinese we will use a curtain rod as a LAMP WICK (we do not want to dirty our own goods).

>   Respectfully,
>
>   Pribumi Fighters

This document is widely called false. It is not believed to be the product of an organization called "Freedom Fighters" at all but rather to have been disseminated by elements from the army, perhaps the same elements thought to have been responsible for the riots of May. In any case, it displays some of the same structure as those riots. The document, distributed to "Chinese," is also in the hands of members of the underclass. It is not, however, likely to have been conceived by the latter. If, after seeing this document, they find it congenial, it is because the makers say what they, the recipients, think. But, one remembers, rape is new on the political scene and an invention, probably, of the army. The idea comes from somewhere else; the agreement of some of the underclass is not an accord between what they knew and wanted before May 13, 1998. Nonetheless, after being heard, the document comes to speak for certain of the underclass. It is not in the first place a representation of their wishes; only after the fact does it say what they want and what they think. This is similar to the workings of desire in the modern market. In the shopping mall, one finds things one never thought of before. But seeing them, somehow one knows that one has always wanted this particular jacket, that particular cap; one even feels one has needed them for a long time. If this is the way the events of May were stirred up, it means that the *massa*, in May 1998, materialized when someone spoke for it. First came a voice, the voice of a man in boots who descended from a truck, and then came a mass of people who learned that he said what they wanted to do. This incoherent group of people became the *massa*. When the booted man left, or when the *massa* were told the event was over, the *massa* disappeared, to be replaced with the inhabitants of the area who wanted the "Chinese" to reopen their shops.

The goods taken from "Chinese" will be burned, not appropriated by looters. The enjoyment of wealth is postponed until society is restored through a reversal of conditions, "Chinese" being reduced to servants, *pribumi* becoming masters. This reversal is the conclusion of the banishment of desire in the present. If "we" want wealth back it is not in order to become wealthy, but to cease being bothered by what others have. When we have back what is rightfully ours, we can stop wanting; which is to say, we can get rid of desire itself. At that point, the weaknesses of both national identity and kinship identity will be rectified.

Wealth in this document takes the form "our" goods in the possession of "Chinese" ("we will take back OUR ANCESTRAL WEALTH"); and wealth is ancestral, the ancestors being "ours," not theirs. There is a double implication here. It may be that the "ancestors" are "Indonesians" as a whole or as type, and that national wealth has been stolen. Indeed, this charge is sometimes made against "Chinese." But the charge is usually made without the word "ancestral." By adding that word, one implies that transmission through descent has been somehow perverted; what should have been passed down has taken a devious path and fallen into the hands of "Chinese." The strange recourse against "Chinese," castration and rape, makes descent impossible for them. "Chinese," I have noted, are often called *"keturunan,"* "descendants," short for "of 'Chinese' descent," as though only "Chinese" had ancestors. Rape and castration suggest that in the thinking of these rioters-to-be, the end of descent for "Chinese" is the rectification of descent for *pribumi.*

Indonesia, in the conception of its founders, was based on its power to absorb the different ethnic groups of the archipelago and in so doing to form a new, single, national identity. This power was fundamental to the formation of a unified nation. When "Chinese" are accused of being "arrogant," as they frequently are by their enemies, it means that they do not consort with "us," other Indonesians, whereas they ought to. They are blamed for refusing to do so, but one could just as well see in the accusation the implication of the failure of the power of the nation to assimilate its peoples. In its place, another hierarchy is set up, one where "we" are the drivers and the domestic servants of "Chinese." In this view, it is "Chinese," and not the Indonesian nation, who have the ability to relate people to one another.

They do so, it is charged, in an unfair manner. They steal "ancestral" goods, which are distributed by their own rules among themselves. This vision of the "Chinese" as thieves is racist, but it is not based on a concept of racial purity; rather its opposite. "Chinese" in the view of anti-Sinites are not like Jews in the view of anti-Semites: they do not threaten genetic contamination. Rather the threat is their power to build a structure within the nation that exists by its own energies and has its own regulations. In the absence of the ability of Indonesia to absorb "Chinese," they, "Chinese," pull those who might form part of the *massa* into another structure, rather as though they had built a foreign state inside Indonesia. Rape, arson, looting at once destroy "Chinese" power and restore it to those who had lost it.[32]

Finally, we have this observation about the *massa.* They are thought to be Islamic. As Benedict Anderson pointed out to me, when the Christian Batak riot, they are not thought of as *massa* but as "Batak," defined by their ethnicity and not by their religion. The *massa* are a category of the nation and not of the regions. As a transformation of "the people," they have much in common with Indonesians of the class above them. As should be apparent by now, the Indonesian middle class feels remiss about ignoring them because it partially identifies with them and fears them at the same time. In the minds of the middle class, the underclass is savage but it is also Islamic. The *massa, biadab* as they are, embody the potential subjects of a

---

[32] If the events of May had not occurred, it would be difficult to take this document seriously, not so much for what it says, as for the strange form of its expression. Its offical format and its impoverished prose does not lead one to feel the wish of someone to say something. But the whole of the events of May were expressed in a nonserious prose, from the commercial rhetoric naming the *softlens* to this throwsheet. The seriousness of the event and the lack of seriousness of its languages are not in conflict. The ability to shift registers, to treat "Chinese" as valued acquaintainces one day and as ogres the next, depends on a certain lack of investment in language, one which, nonetheless, leads to grave consequences.

religious reformation in which rationality guided by religion learns to constrain cravings, wishes, and erotic energy.[33] Such views were incompatible with consumerist New Order Indonesia during its prosperity and no doubt produced guilt at the moment of the economic crisis. The middle class cannot afford these ideas, but has never revised them. The violence of May 1998 constituted a perverse return of such religious thinking against those who believe. The Islam of the *massa* reflects the beliefs of the middle class about itself, showing it its own possibilities, while at the same time aggravating its guilt for having neglected the *rakyat*.[34]

The use of Islamic rhetoric and the attribution of Islam to the rioters, as when, for instance, "Allahu Akbar [Allah is Great]" was written on buildings in Arabic script to save them from destruction and or when the Arabic word *aib* was used to describe the stain of rape, indicate a projection of Islam onto the *massa*. At the same time, almost every important Muslim leader on the national scene condemned the riots even though some are not known for friendliness toward "Chinese." One cannot see these rioters as led by the figures of national Islam. Indeed, the difficulty for many is, as I have said, that they were not led at all or that they were misled. It seems to me an implicit assumption of much of the discussion of the riots that the lack of Islamic leadership aggravated the expression of unmediated desire.

The *massa*, a transformation or perhaps a remnant of the *rakyat*, are the product of the imagination of the middle class; they are the menace left once the body of the nation has divided in two and identity, in both its national and kinship forms, is thought uncertain. It remains only to bring the *massa* into existence. With the collapse of credit not merely in the economy but in the government, certain elements not from the underclass did bring the *massa* into existence. The result was rapid swerves in the sympathies and identifications of the middle class: with the looters and against them, sometimes against "Chinese" but now with "Chinese" women and against rapists, once with the government and now against it. All these motions are predicated on a fear of the revolutionary tendencies of the underclass, a fear cultivated by the government in different forms during the New Order: fear of Communism, fear of criminality, and fear of the *massa*. Now, only apparently paradoxically, the latest form of this fear is the government itself.

Many Indonesians seem to feel that poverty is shameful and that the remedy for poverty is wealth.[35] At the same time, many of the same people feel that "Chinese," even poor ones, are inherently and shamefully wealthy. The doubt cast on descent and therefore on morality by wealth and by poverty were manageable when everyone was doing better economically. Such contradictions are perhaps common in every culture and do not matter except in times of crisis. The Indonesian nation

---

[33] See my *The Rope of God* (Berkeley: University of California Press, 1969) for an explication of Islamic ideas of desire.

[34] Here one can include the response to the rapes by the segment of the Islamic community that refused to condemn the riots. Rapes, in their view, have not been proven to have taken place. The issue of rape is an attempt to blame Muslims. For them the rivalry between "Chinese" employers and Muslims is central: "Really, pity the poor Islamic community. So many facts about Muslim domestic servants raped by non-*pribumi* bosses and it's as though they are wiped out by the cases of rape from the middle of last May whose proof is not yet clear." One notes that in the press the rape of domestic servants was not charged solely against "Chinese bosses." Nuha, "Kecerobohan Majalah 'Jakarta-Jakarta'" (The Hastiness of the Magazine Jakarta-Jakarta), *Media Dakwah*, August 1998, p. 14.

[35] On this topic see my *A New Criminal Type in Jakarta*.

during the New Order (I do not speak of its victims) could afford a racism which was only intermittently violent, one which gave a privileged place in the economy to certain "Chinese" but kept all of them out of public office and governmental bureaucracy as though they were shameful, and allowed them occasionally to be the victims of riots. There was an oscillation between shameful wealth (theirs) and wealth which covered shame (ours) that was tolerated even, perhaps, by some of its victims. Racism, though it originated well before the New Order, was a component of its chief policy, Development. But when the economic crisis, the *"krismon,"* arrived, the balance of political and economic life was lost.

When the world economy affected the nation most immediately, not merely the workings of the national economy, but the very notions of ownership and circulation were placed in doubt. Rape means that one's most precious possessions are not one's own. To "own" becomes a dubious idea when there are people who can take anything. They caused irreparable loss, and not only to those raped, as the values of *adab*—culture, politeness—which Indonesians relied on to keep things to themselves depreciated with the rupiah. Not only commodities but the most valuable private possessions shamelessly whirled into circulation.

It took rape to make clear that the violence inherent in the Indonesian political system was permanently harmful and that notions of culture and shame could not limit violence, the latter now as much a property of the political class as of the *massa*. The relations of wealth and shame are scarcely new to Indonesian culture. The economic modernization of the New Order, the invasion of the market, assumed them but left them little chance to develop in a manner that would safely accommodate the desires raised in a society of consumers. The events of May revealed their inadequacy in the face of economic crisis.

"Chinese," I have said, was a word that permitted massive theft. But Indonesians assumed there would be a limit to such activities. Once the word "Chinese" permitted rape, the limits of Indonesian racism were surpassed. Rape threatened legitimate descent and the founding myths of Indonesia. It showed that the savagery out of which the nation arose could always return. The evolution of the nation was proven to have been driven by a growing economy unmatched by concomitant cultural evolution. A culture of the market had developed rapidly. Desire was generalized while little was devoted to its mediation. One can ask, does the New Order have cultural achievements? None that were not banned and few even of those. A nation that relied on shame rather than sublimation to brake desire, to extend and transform it, and that conceived of sexuality in premodern forms left itself open to the events of May.

I admire the Indonesian women and men who are so bravely insisting that rape be made a public issue, its perpetrators punished, its victims understood, and that women be granted security. But it remains to be seen whether the continuing fear of the underclass and the impoverished cultural legacy of the New Order offers room for the important changes in the lives of women and men and for the true democratization Indonesia so painfully needs to prevent rape from being a permanent addition to the savage habits of Indonesian political life.[36]

---

[36] As noted earlier, what I have written above concerns only Jakarta. What happens next depends not only on Jakarta and the other great cities of the country, but what will occur as well in the provinces and the countryside. There is no space here for me to take up the question of how fear of the underclass is related, historically, to the idea of the emancipated Indonesian woman as a (mere) household manager. See my *Fetish, Recognition, Revolution.*

Appendix

I do not want to understate the strength of feeling of "Chinese" who were so savagely attacked. Here are excerpts from one of the strongest statements of a merchant. It appeared in the weekly newsmagazine *Forum* seven weeks after the events. It was made by Hadi Wijaya, 47, owner of the optical store "Sinar" on the second story of the Glodok market as well as another shop:

> At the time of the crisis [*krisis*; meaning the economic crisis] I gave basic goods [*sembako*] to the poor. But now it's me that gets donations of basic goods from the Buddhist monastery. That's the fate of my family since these riots.
>
> Now, where the shop which used to be so busy there is nothing but the stench of smoke and stifling, stinging ashes. The passageways are deep in darkness. In the corners the only thing to see are pellets of debris which used to be merchandise. There are sacks of the remains of contact lenses, all ruined, and contact lens bottles heaped up in what used to be a kiosk.
>
> What can I say to my three children who are nearly adult now about this tragedy [*tragedi*]? Thirty years of work gone in a day. I never felt exclusive [*eksklusif*] and better than others. That I worked hard and got to be what I am today is only the result of never-ending struggle. From the time I was ten I was selling on the street corners. Often enough I was picked up by the police, beaten, and lifted into a truck [to be brought to jail for selling without a license, presumably]. Even while selling on the street, I kept going to school till I had finished junior high school. I mixed with the other street sellers who were mainly *pribumi*.

"I began with nothing," Hadi Wijaya said, and then gave his mercantile history; how he cleaned other people's stores, saved his money till he had some capital, traded dishes, then recordings, and finally opened two optical stores.

> How is it my business prospered? It's because I really worked. Not only that, I didn't fool around. Once in a while, a friend would say we should go somewhere but I always refused. It's better to save your money. Even eating, I always ate at home. With what I saved I opened an optical store in the shop house near where we live in Taman Harapan Indah. It's run by my brother-in-law.
>
> At the time of the riots, on the thirteenth and fourteenth of May, both optical shops which took me decades to build were gone in a second. Our store in Harapan Indah was smashed and looted on the thirteenth of May. I saw with my

own eyes, with my wife and children, how the *massa* smashed and ruined all our wealth. My child who is now at the university can't even get up from seeing this brutal, brutal looting . . .

At the time of the events, I tried not to weep in front of my wife and kids. But after I sent them off to the house of my relatives in Angke, I wept till I had no more tears. Speaking of being afraid, we are still in the grip of fear. It's true, in the day time we dare to go out, but as soon as it gets dark, no one thinks of leaving the house. Trauma [English] isn't easy to get rid of. And what's more, the government still hasn't guaranteed our security, us the descendants [*keturunan*].[37]

Stories collected from "Chinese" men tend to have the same elements. They are stories about the injustice of the events. About the victims' entitlement to their possessions because they worked hard for them. Stories too about helping the poor who then robbed them and, not to be slighted, stories of the brutality of the rioters. There is sometimes too, as in this moving example, the pathos of having lost so much and of feeling oneself a victim in front of one's children and one's wife. The sense of personal diminishment is matched by anger at the government for its lack of protection and, as in this example, for not, even weeks later, promising to guarantee the victims' safety. This man is angry; the government should listen. He has, then, recuperated himself, and he expects that eventually he will be heard by, amongst others, "the government." The story moves from one of loss and humiliation to anger and to possible connection with the government. It ends on a tone of reassurance as it gives the foundation for the rebuilding of his life.

Among other effects, these stories lead to questions of the position of the "Chinese," widely discussed in the press, and questions also of "Reform," "*Reformasi*," the slogan under which the change of regime was carried out. These stories, in other words, lead to discourses already in place. The voices of those looted are recorded and the expectation is that readers hear them. Discourse, if it was broken, is restored, aiding in the rebuilding of assurance.

Ithaca, New York, October 25, 1998

---

[37] "Suara Hati: Kucuran Keringat Yang Mengering Sekejap" (Voice from the Heart: Torrents of Sweat Which Dried Up in a Flash), *Forum Keadilan*, July 13, 1998, p. 44.

PEMUDA PANCASILA: THE LAST LOYALIST FREE MEN OF SUHARTO'S ORDER?[1]

Loren Ryter

"Since the Beginning Pemuda Pancasila has always Supported *Reformasi* carried out Constitutionally. The Coverage by the Print Media and the Electronic Media of Pemuda Pancasila's presence at the DPR RI [Parliament] on May 19, 1998 is Mistaken and Without a Clear Source." So read the banner which hung in "strategic locations" in each of Jakarta's five boroughs within two days of Suharto's resignation. However, on May 21, two days before the banners went up and the evening after Suharto delivered his short statement of abdication, the confusion at Pemuda Pancasila (PP) headquarters had yet to be so institutionalized. "There's been a bad misunderstanding," pleaded a shaken Alwi, in lieu of a salutation. He went on in defense of his organization, insisting it wasn't members of PP who brought the sign reading "The President of Indonesia Remains Haji M. Suharto" to Parliament, but rather it was FKPPI.[2] FKPPI had left its banner behind and some Pemuda Pancasila members just happened to pick it up. If they were caught before the cameras holding the banner, that was only because some of the members are under-educated and didn't think to read the sign first, explained Alwi, a Pemuda Pancasila member who once staffed the cigarette stand outside the youth group's HQ in front of the Tebet train station in South Jakarta.

---

[1] This essay represents an overview of some main aspects of a dissertation project currently in progress.

[2] FKPPI (Communication Forum for Sons and Daughters of ABRI Pensioners) is headed by Bambang Trihatmodjo Suharto, Suharto's eldest son and a personal friend and hunting partner of Pemuda Pancasila Presidium Chief Yapto Soerjosoemarno and therefore PP's most likely point-man with the Cendana, Suharto's residence. ABRI: Angkatan Bersenjata Republik Indonesia, the Armed Forces of the Republic of Indonesia.

How is it that Pemuda Pancasila has been so routinely "misunderstood"? "Prodem" activists charge them with mobilizing the masses for counter-demonstrations, raiding NGO offices and party headquarters, expediting land clearing on behalf of developers chiefly by pressuring land-owners to sell at low prices, acting as private bodyguards for the Suharto family, and intimidating students and activists, especially in the months leading up to national elections. They had campaigned for Golkar (Suharto's electoral machine) since 1982.[3] Various police commanders have periodically tried to bring in their most prominent leaders—Yapto Soerjosoemarno SH and Yorrys Raweyai—on gambling, assault, or gun charges.[4] Office managers who have been hit up for large contributions tend to regard them, to quote one colorful comment, as "bandits, rotten, motherfuckers, gangsters, basically everything bad."[5] Society broadly is "under the impression" that they are an

---

[3] This essay assumes some familiarity with actions Pemuda Pancasila has participated in (or has been suspected of participating in) since the 1980s. Some worthy of mention are the violent disruptions of the PPP (Partai Persatuan Pembangunan, the Unity Development Party) campaign at Banteng Square, Jakarta during the 1982 elections; the burning of the Legal Aid Institute's offices in Medan; attacks on the Garut Student-Youth Forum (FPPMG), SMID (Solidaritas Mahasiswa Indonesia untuk Demokrasi, Indonesian Students' Solidarity for Democracy) activists in Surabaya, and Megawati's PDI (Partai Demokrasi Indonesia, the Indonesian Democratic Party) headquarters during 1996; counter-demonstrations against East Timor's Bishop Belo, recalled parliamentarian turned regime opponent Sri Bintang Pamungkas, and East Timorese refugees seeking asylum in Jakarta embassies, also in 1996. Rather than attempting to detail or demonstrate these cases (which would involve the notion of *bukti*, or proof, which both PP and the phenomenon of *preman* [see below] generally has contributed to problematizing), my intent is rather to discuss the conditions of the emergence of Pemuda Pancasila, both as available agents and as the usual suspects, in the context of youth during the Suharto period.

"Prodem," short for pro-democracy, a term frequently used by activists, especially in the 1990s, to refer to themselves. SMID is the People's Democratic Party's (PRD) student wing. PDI and PPP had been the sanctioned New Order political parties since 1973.

[4] Yapto was detained for gun possession in 1981, and Yorrys has been held in relation to two gambling cases, one in 1994 and the other in 1998, as well as having been accused of involvement in the fatal torture of the houseboy of PP's secretary-general in 1994. None of these cases has been tried, let alone resulted in a conviction. (The latter case started when the houseboy, routinely taunted by PP members who called him a queer, kidnapped the secretary-general's young son, whom he had to baby-sit. After his arrest, PP members "borrowed" him from the police, tortured him, slicing off his ear, then returned him to the police. He later died of his wounds in detention.) Yorrys was arrested in April 2000 in connection with the 1996 raid on Megawati's PDI. After some weeks in police detention, he was released. At the time of these revisions, no trial date has been set.

Yorrys, a half-Chinese, half-Irianese crocodile hunter and Phillips Petroleum manager from Serui, Irian Jaya, became involved in the Jakarta chapter of Pemuda Pancasila after Yapto took over in 1980. Before becoming head of the Jakarta chapter, he was entrusted with fundraising activities because of his connections with Chinese entrepreneurs and gambling. He is currently the "daily executive" chief of the national organization.

Yapto, an avid international hunter and adventure enthusiast, is the son of a Javanese General and a Dutch Jew. Yapto's background is further discussed below. Both Yapto and Yorrys are from mixed ethnic backgrounds, which is significant since the prominence of Indos (Eurasians) in thuggery and gangsterism has a history that goes back to the colonial era. See Pramoedya Ananta Toer, *House of Glass*, trans. Max Lane (New York: Penguin Books, 1992).

[5] Interview with a Jalan Sudirman bank officer who complained that PP comes around periodically asking her bank to buy invitations to social functions at several million rupiah each.

organization of *preman* (street hoodlums) working as extortionists, debt-collectors, parking attendants, and nightclub security guards—when not outright violating the law.[6]

Yet Pemuda Pancasila devotes considerable effort to correcting this impression. It claims to be a principled, disciplined, and militant organization of more than six million current members that vows to defend Pancasila and the 1945 Constitution, as it has done consistently since 1959, when other youth groups were still defending NASAKOM.[7] According to its own spokesmen, Pemuda Pancasila is an independent organization not affiliated with any political party, and it just happens to decide every five years through a regular congress to channel its members' aspirations to Golkar. It is the only youth organization brave enough to stand up for the youth of the informal sector. It "embraces" *(merangkul) preman* not for criminal purposes, but to raise their nationalist consciousness and return them to society. Some of its members do work as nightclub security guards and as parking attendants, but in their private capacity, not as members of the organization.[8] If a member is caught in a criminal act, he is only an *oknum*, so the good name of the organization should not be besmirched.[9] If he doesn't clearly possess a membership card, moreover, he is not necessarily a member at all.

Through this combination of contradictory appearances, which show Pemuda Pancasila members visibly upholding the highest national ideals and, alternately, appearing as the usual suspects of criminality, a prevailing logic of the Suharto period is clearly revealed. I wish to argue here that the emergence and rise to prominence of Pemuda Pancasila during the late Suharto era is a consequence of the need (and the effort since the early New Order) to transform a revolutionary nationalism of *pemuda* (youth) of the post-independence period into a nationalism expressed through loyalty to the (personalized) state itself, without, however, sacrificing the *semangat* (spirit) for which *pemuda* are renowned.[10] As such, *perjuangan*

---

[6] *Preman*, in contemporary usage, is a street hoodlum, but the etymology and ambiguous connotations of the term will be discussed below.

[7] NASAKOM, Nationalism-Religion-Communism, the trilogy formulated by Sukarno circa 1961 to express his idea of national unity, was at the time resented by some for its inclusion of communism. After Suharto's rise to power, this became one of the justifications for tying Sukarno to the fate of the PKI, the Indonesian Communist Party.

[8] In 1994, Yapto threatened to sue the weekly *Sinar* for calling Pemuda Pancasila an organization of debt collectors. The editors defended themselves on the grounds that they were quoting Jakarta Police Chief Major General Moch Hindarto's remarks at a seminar on debt collectors. *Prospek*, September 3, 1994; and *Jakarta-Jakarta*, September 3-9, 1994.

[9] *Oknum*, literally an "element" or an "individual" within a group, has come to mean any member of a group who acts outside of the mandate of the group, almost exclusively criminally. An approximate English equivalent might be "rogue." The term is used regularly in the press to refer to members of ABRI involved in robberies, shootings, gambling dens, and prostitution, and the like. According to journalists, its use to refer to the misdeeds of ABRI members has been an informal press regulation since at least the mid-1970s under the orders of Sudomo as Commander of Kopkamtib (Command for the Restoration of Security and Order). In addition to *oknum* ABRI and *oknum* of youth organizations, references are occasionally made to *oknum* students, *oknum* journalists, and so forth. The term seems to be so reflexive that even "*oknum preman*" has appeared in print, reinforcing the idea that *preman* has come to acquire a quasi-official status.

[10] I do not wish to argue for a total transformation of *pemuda* values. *Pemuda* always carried this potential. *Pemuda* is used throughout not to refer to any specific age group, but in the expansive way it is used in Indonesia. See Benedict Anderson, *Java in a Time of Revolution:*

(heroic struggle) had to take on a character that rewarded private material gain, which ultimately turned youth into privateers, or *preman*. As *perjuangan* increasingly became identified with *perebutan lahan* (turf wars), the categories of *pemuda* and *preman* became intermeshed. The importance of the terms *preman, pemuda,* and *oknum* to an understanding of these changes, in light of the expansion of Pemuda Pancasila, will be explained below.

PREMAN

The significance of the epithet *"preman"* as applied to Pemuda Pancasila is best appreciated in reference to its sudden salience in the last years of the Suharto period. The often noted ambiguity between criminality and authority in the archipelago, whose lineage begins with the robber-king Ken Arok and runs through the figure of the *jago* in colonial Java, found clear popular expression in the boom of *premanism* in the national press. *Preman,* in the sense of extortionists and hoodlums said to "prey on informal traders" and to "put society ill at-ease," began its phenomenal appearance on the national scene only after the fatal stabbing of First Lieutenant Budi Prasetyo at Blok M, Kebayoran in March 1995.[11] That a mere *preman* had the insolence to slay an army officer in broad daylight was sensational, and the story took off, *"premanism"* appearing as the cover story of several major weeklies. *Gatra* illustrated the "War against Preman" with a skull-tattooed, muscle-bound arm gripping a serrated knife against an urban nightscape. Although local "rowdy youths" *(pemuda berandalan),* as they were described at the time of his murder, had also attacked and killed former BAIS Brigadier-General Tampubolon a year previously, the blame for that attack was only assigned explicitly to *preman* in retrospect, after the Prasetyo slaying, as part of the same discourse announcing a phenomenal rise in lawlessness and social unrest.[12] Though the targets of *preman*

Occupation and Resistance, 1944-1946 (Ithaca: Cornell University Press, 1972). Generally, it refers to members of an entire generation that has not yet come of age or into official position. Thus the length of the Suharto era produced some rather aged *pemuda*.

[11] Prasetyo, a Police Science student, was killed on March 6, 1995 near Melawai Plaza. Blok M traders say that Prasetyo was a womanizing drunkard who hit them up for too much money, and that local *preman*, in defense of the interests of the traders, approved his murder in advance, bringing in killers from outside. (Confidential interview.) Prasetyo's partner, Captain Arman Depari, who got away with stab wounds, told the press that the killers taunted him with, "Aw, you're just a captain. My dad's a general. Whatcha gonna do?" An Ambonese youth accused of the murder was shot dead in police custody three days later. See *Gatra*, March 18, 1995; and *Forum Keadilan*, March 30, 1995.

[12] BAIS (Badan Intelijen Strategis) was ABRI's Strategic Intelligence Body. Tampubolon, killed on April 4, 1994, was a shady figure from the intelligence world and a classmate of Eddie Nalapraya from the Bandung Infantry Center in 1963. [Eddie Nalapraya was one of the first commanders of President Suharto's private security detail, held high staff positions in the Jakarta District Military Command during the 1970s, and served as Vice-Governor of Jakarta in the 1980s. See Tempo Weekly, *Apa & Siapa: sejumlah orang Indonesia 1985-86* (Jakarta: PT Pustaka Grafitipers, 1986). A long-time martial arts enthusiast, Eddie has served since 1994 as head of the Indonesian Pencak Silat (Martial Arts) Association, with Suharto's son-in-law Prabowo Subianto as one of his functionaries.] Tampubolon's death did not generate the press sensation that Prasetyo's did a year later. The impression that his death was a politically motivated hit was strengthened by the fact that coverage was limited. See *Editor*, April 21, 1994, pp. 19-30. One rumor circulating among journalists links the Tampubolon hit to the Eddy Tanzil corruption case, suggesting that Tampubolon had a list of names of generals and high officials receiving hush money or other pay-offs from Bapindo, the bank involved in the

subsequently tended to be described in the media as traders or as society in general, it is significant that *preman* only earned a place in the national vocabulary through direct assaults on the authorities.

The press outcry prompted many to come to the defense of *preman*. As much as *preman* represent the underworld, they also stand for the underclass. Like the small-time entrepreneurs they are accused of intimidating, *preman* are understood to originate from the least privileged sectors of society, to have been forced by circumstance to forego an education, and to be among the swelling ranks of city-dwellers who stand no chance of obtaining formal sector employment. Sympathizers argue that *preman*, having nothing to sell but their own muscles, have a right to be cut in on the take given the lack of economic alternatives. Extortion is, in effect, their line of work.[13]

More significant than the recurring debate about what to do about crime, however, was what *preman* implied about criminality and authority that a term like *gali-gali* did not. *Gali-gali (gabungan anak-anak liar)* were the "gangs of wild kids" finished off violently during the "Mysterious Shootings" (Petrus) operations of 1982-83.[14] Though such an operation could never be complete, *gali-gali* could be said to have disappeared, since use of the term ceased after Petrus; thereafter to mention *gali-gali* became somewhat akin to pronouncing a death sentence. In recent years, the term *preman* has acquired a connotation comparable to that of *gali-gali* before Petrus, with two important differences. First, *gali-gali* was a collective phenomenon: the threat was that of roving gangs. A *preman*, though also implicitly drawing strength from his gang, could stand as a lone figure. Second, and more significantly, in contrast with the term *gali-gali*, which connotes an unruly and unauthorized group, the term *preman* has retained a quasi-official ring.

Before the 1990s, *preman* more commonly referred to a policeman or a soldier who was not on duty, or to his civilian dress: *berpakaian preman* or *baju preman*, meaning "in civvies." Often it also meant an undercover cop. It could even refer to something held in private possession, something not owned by the state, such as a private car *(mobil preman)*. These were arguably the only meanings of *preman* in the national vocabulary at the beginning of the New Order, after which a slippage slowly began to occur.[15] The productive play between these meanings contributed to

---

scandal. The rumor is supported mostly by the timing of his death, as witnesses began to be called by the prosecutor around April 1994.

[13] Those who hold such views include reform lawyers and social researchers. Ruddy Agusyanto, for example, argues that *preman* is a profession, serving such socially necessary functions as debt collecting in a country where "the law cannot satisfactorily reach and manage the problem." Ruddy Agusyanto, "Preman adalah Profesi" (Preman is a Profession), *Gatra*, March 25, 1995, p. 20.

[14] See also John Pemberton, *On the Subject of "Java"* (Ithaca: Cornell University Press, 1994); Justus M. van der Kroef, "'PETRUS': Patterns of Prophylactic Murder in Indonesia," *Asian Survey* 25,7 (1985): 745-759.

[15] Early in the New Order, *preman* was used to refer to undercover agents or off-duty soldiers even in contexts where their suspects would today be called *preman*. See for example the (subsequently banned) satire *Langit Makin Mendung*, in *Sastra* 6:8 (1968), quoted from "Langit Makin Mendung," Bacaan 22, *Indonesian Readings*, ed. John U. Wolff (Ithaca: Cornell Southeast Asia Program, 1978), pp. 299-309: "*Si copet banyak menghajarnya ramai2. Si copet jatuh bangun minta ampun, meski hati geli menertawakan kebodohannya sendiri: hari naas, ia keliru njambret dompet kosong milik kopral sedang preman* [The pickpocket was pummeled by the crowd. The

the sensational response to the Prasetyo stabbing in 1995, since after all Prasetyo was killed while wearing *baju preman*, or plainclothes. Without making the connection explicit, *Tiras* ran its March 23 cover story under the headline "Preman and Preman." After the subsequent round-up of five hundred *preman* graduated from a two-week Express Skills Military Training Course, *Tiras* marveled at the transformation:

> Who wouldn't fail to recognize the *preman*? Uniformed in green, crew-cut, and lined up in neat rows, they not only didn't look spooky [*sangar*]. At first glance, they even resembled honest-to-god soldiers [*tentara beneran*].[16]

The ambiguity of the term is best understood by thinking of *preman* as a kind of privateer, an interpretation true to the colonial roots of the term *vrijman*, or free man. In fact, the lineages of *preman* can be understood in terms of its connotations in seventeenth-century Batavia and early twentieth-century Deli. To gain a perspective on *preman* in colonial Deli, it is useful first to consider briefly its folk etymology in North Sumatra today. By all accounts, the newly popularized meaning of *preman* as borderline-criminal, marginal youths first circulated in post-colonial Medan, though some Batak today would like to see the term cleansed of its criminal associations. Sociologist Usman Pelly explained that the term *preman* "derives from youths who don't want to be bound to any dependencies, including a job or a contract." In a similar vein, Mangara Siahaan has written that *preman* in Medan were just youths whose "hobby it was to hang out, wear cool clothes, and look for a wife or girlfriend. If they find a wife, they relinquish their *preman* status."[17] To be *preman* is a matter of pride, they point out, because a *vrijman* was a freed plantation slave.

Early twentieth-century usage in Deli, however, indicates that a *vrijman* was not a freed slave, but rather a non-contract overseer or a coolie day-laborer, thus still in the employ of the company, though not legally bound to it. A 1926 criminal case involving the torture of insubordinate coolies referred to one of the plantation overseers (*mandor*), who forced coolies to eat human and horse feces, as a *vrijman*. (The judge exonerated him, ruling he was only following orders of the chief *mandor*, a Japanese national, who was sentenced.) A *Kompas* article drawing on this case and other contemporary sources suggests that *vrijman* were involved in physical clashes between agents of plantation owners and Javanese and Chinese contract coolies. Although the article concludes that *vrijman* defended contract coolies against

---

pickpocket rose and fell asking for mercy, but he had to laugh to himself at his own stupidity: bad luck, he made the mistake of snatching the empty wallet of a corporal in his civvies]."

It should be noted here that perhaps the first appearance in the national press of *preman* in the contemporary sense came around June 1980, when the local government in Medan vowed to take firm action against "Si Preman," two months after Pemuda Pancasila clashed with another youth group, a story which also made the national press in April. See *Tempo*, April 19, 1980; see also *Kompas*, June 13, 1980.

[16] See Cahyo Sukartiko, "Pembinaan Pasca-'Perang'" (Post-'War' Training), *Tiras*, April 6, 1995, p. 55. In this course, the *preman* were nominally taught skills in machinery, sewing, and automobile repair. They learned military discipline and pledged to be good citizens in front of then Jakarta commander Wiranto.

[17] *Sinar*, March 18, 1995 and March 25, 1995.

plantation thugs, the actual evidence quoted is ambiguous, stating only that they often "caused trouble."[18]

A *vrijman* of early seventeenth-century Batavia was similarly semi-employed. *Vrijman* meant someone "who is not in the service of the [Dutch] East India Company [VOC, Vereenigde Oost-Indische Compagnie], but has permission to be in the Indies, and carries out trade for the sake of the [VOC]."[19] In other words, he was a trader not listed on the company payroll. A *vrijman* was literally a free agent, with one stipulation: that his agency was directed toward the requirements of VOC commerce. Not incidentally, in order to go about his business he required a permit from the company, to whose jurisdiction he therefore deferred. In Batavia, the *vrijman* was neither exactly a company man nor precisely *not* a company man.

The logic of this notion of freedom is nicely expressed by Pemuda Pancasila head Yapto Soerjosoemarno, who, as the Jakarta head of an organization that first truly prospered in Medan, is well-placed to bridge the Batavia-Deli divide:

> *Preman* means a free person, exactly *free-man*. I am one of these. A *preman* is a person who is free, not tied by any knot, free to determine his own life and death, as long as he fulfills the requirements and the laws of this country. But I am free to choose, to carry out the permitted or the not permitted, with all of its risks. For example, if you're a thief, you take the risks of being a thief, meaning if you're caught, you're finished. If you aren't caught, you're no thief, right? Legally that's the way it is; we hold to the principle of the presumption of innocence.[20]

Yapto is bound by the very limitations he establishes, expressing a thematic ambivalence to the law. On the one hand, the law establishes the outer limits of freedom, as the trade permit did for the VOC *vrijman*, but with more complicated stipulations and a wider territorial reach. Yet the law is such a strict creature of orthodoxy that, ironically, one of its tenets (the presumption of innocence) provides the possibility of freedom from law itself. In a legal system where the proof *(bukti)* required to pronounce guilt is itself a commodity or an object easily wished into absence by those close to power such as Yapto, the presumption of innocence provides a gateway beyond the law. Freedom lies precisely in the ability to violate the law without being exposed.

The ability of Pemuda Pancasila to accomplish this goal has rested on shedding its members' *preman* status by putting on the camouflaged uniforms of a youth organization. I mean something more than the charge that Pemuda Pancasila "hides behind the jacket of a youth organization." The nature of the jacket, the camouflage orange-and-black uniform, affects a resemblance to and expresses an affinity with exactly those forces that would have the power to limit PP members' freedom by calling them to account for their transgressions—transgressions which, however, are

---

[18] *Kompas*, February 6, 1994. The Poelau Mandi case, published in full in the daily *Benih Timoer* between October 19-30, 1926, is reprinted as an appendix in H. Mohammad Said, *Koeli Kontrak Tempo Doeloe: Dengan Derita dan Kemarahannya* (Medan: Harian Waspada, 1990), pp. 203-248. Note that although ungrammatical in Dutch, *vrijman* in Malay (like *preman*, a word used interchangeably with *vrijman* as early as the 1920s) is used as both singular and plural.

[19] M. de Vries, L. A. de Winkel et al., eds., *Woordenboek der Nederlandsche Taal*, vol. 23, VR-VUUSTER ('s-Gravenhage: M. Nijhoff, 1987).

[20] Interview, *Matra*, January 1993.

frequently of service to those very authorities. That these authorities themselves always reserve the ability to transform themselves into *preman* by taking off their uniform only makes the distinction between *preman* and *preman* a matter of a thin, reversible skin. This reversibility, as I will argue, is what made Pemuda Pancasila both needed and ultimately outworn.

ORIGIN STORIES

The roots of the symbiosis between the military, gangs, and formal youth organizations go back to the Revolution. However, before the existence of a regular army, these entities were hardly discrete. During the Revolution, *pemuda* groups were or became irregular militias which fought in tandem with personnel trained by the Royal Dutch Army (the KNIL) and people recruited as military auxiliaries during the Japanese Occupation. At a time of revolutionary flux, and in the absence of a recognized legal system, the distinction between youth militias and roving gangs was difficult to draw, as Ann Stoler has shown with the *laskyar* militias. Robert Cribb's study of the role of gangs in the Indonesian Revolution assumes a prior distinction between younger nationalist politicians (read: *pemuda*) and rural gangsters, interested for their own reasons, whom the nationalists chose to recruit to achieve nobler ends.[21] However, it is probably more accurate to imagine a clear distinction between the army, youth groups, and gangs emerging only after the consolidation of the Republic and the regularization of the army.

The appearance of Pemuda Pancasila can be seen in the context of efforts by former fighters (*pejuang*), and by the army itself, to find an appropriate political format during the party-dominated parliamentary order of the 1950s, following the end of the Revolution and the 1949 transfer of sovereignty to the Republic. Although there is reason to doubt that Pemuda Pancasila as reorganized by Yapto Soerjosoemarno beginning in 1980 bears significant resemblance in terms of personnel to the organization as it existed before 1965, there are institutional and a few personal threads that connect the organization across the Sukarno and Suharto regimes. (As explained below, a few of the founding Pemuda Pancasila leaders from North Sumatra were instrumental in recruiting Yapto in order to create a genuinely national organization.) The importance of the connection is also expressed in PP's sense of its own lineage. When recalling its history, Pemuda Pancasila's literature unfailingly notes, in the vaguest of terms, that Pemuda Pancasila was founded as an *onderbouw* (subordinate wing) of the IPKI party (Ikatan Pendukung Kemerdekaan Indonesia, or League of the Supporters of Indonesian Independence). Pemuda Pancasila was born on October 28, 1959, the literature says, as part of the effort to "back-up" the Presidential Decree of July 5, 1959.[22]

---

[21] Anderson, *Java in a Time of Revolution*; Robert Cribb, *Gangsters and Revolutionaries: The Jakarta People's Militia and the Indonesian Revolution 1945-1949* (Honolulu: University of Hawaii Press, 1991); Ann Laura Stoler, "Working the Revolution: Plantation Laborers and the People's Militia in North Sumatra," *The Journal of Asian Studies* 47,2 (1988): 231-232.

[22] The decree, which dissolved the Constituent Assembly and returned the country to the 1945 Constitution (UUD 45), marks the beginning of Guided Democracy. PP writes its founding story consistently if vaguely. See for example, *Pancasila Abadi*, June 1996, p. 25. *Pancasila Abadi* is PP's internal magazine, published irregularly in the late 1980s and relatively regularly beginning in December 1990.

Most likely the only accurate part of that statement is that Pemuda Pancasila was indeed born of General A. H. Nasution's IPKI, as a youth wing of the sort also possessed by the other political parties. Two years after his removal as Army Chief of Staff in 1952, Nasution formed IPKI in an effort to advance the army's agenda in a civilian political format. Members of IPKI were recruited from both active military men and former *pejuang* who had returned to civilian professions, as well as their families and friends. Through IPKI, Nasution was influential in pressing Sukarno to dissolve the Constituent Assembly and return to the 1945 Constitution, which gave space for non-elected functional representatives (such as members of the army) to sit in parliament. IPKI stood against political parties and "-isms" in general and adopted Pancasila as a symbol of what it conceived to be its neutral, even transcendent, stance.[23] It considered itself a movement rather than a party, though it competed in the 1955 elections with poor results—winning only four seats. In any case, it was army representatives, including Nasution in person, who successfully lobbied Sukarno into agreeing to return to the 1945 Constitution. By all accounts the founding of Pemuda Pancasila followed the Presidential decree.

The specific reasons for, and circumstances of, the formation of Pemuda Pancasila are not clear, and differing opinions on the matter reflect a complete split within IPKI over the organization's willingness to embrace Sukarno and his doctrine of Manipol-USDEK.[24] At its third congress in Surabaya in July 1961, Ratu Aminah Hidayat, the wife of General Hidayat and a confessed admirer of Sukarno, became general chair of IPKI, occupying the IPKI offices at Menteng Raya. Her appointment was not accepted by Soegirman, IPKI's former chair, who regarded Ratu Hidayat as a person close to Moscow by virtue of her position on the Indonesian-Russian Peace Committee. Soegirman later retreated with his camp to his personal residence at Kebon Sirih. Soegirman's group had its own youth organization, Pemuda Patriotik (Patriotic Youth), but its chronology and relation to Pemuda Pancasila are matters of dispute.

All versions agree that Pemuda Pancasila was first inaugurated formally as an *onderbouw* of IPKI at the Surabaya congress, but there is no consensus on how Pemuda Pancasila came into existence or on what became of Pemuda Patriotik. Members of Hidayat's group say that something called Pemuda Patriotik existed previously, then in 1959 dissolved itself to become part of Pemuda Pancasila, whose existence, in turn, wasn't formalized by IPKI until the 1961 congress.[25] The founders

---

[23] David Bourchier, "Lineages of Organicist Political Thought in Indonesia" (PhD dissertation, Department of Politics, Monash University, 1996), p. 122. It is beyond the scope of this article to detail the social and ideological underpinnings of IPKI, though its efforts were clearly important in the rise of a corporatist state. On Nasution and IPKI, see ibid., pp. 119-130. On Nasution and the transition to Guided Democracy, see Daniel S. Lev, *The Transition to Guided Democracy: Indonesian Politics, 1957-1959* (Ithaca: Cornell Southeast Asia Program, 1966). In its own literature, IPKI tended to hyphenate its abbreviation as IP-KI, perhaps in an effort to separate itself from the PKI.

[24] The Political Manifesto of August 17, 1959 was Sukarno's official explanation of the July 5, 1959 decree and represented an attempt to fashion an interpretation of the 1945 Constitution in his own (sloganistic) terms, abbreviated as USDEK: the 1945 Constitution, Indonesian Socialism, Guided Democracy, Guided Economy, and the Indonesian Character.

[25] Based on several interviews with IPKI members from the period, including Ponke Princen, M. Noeh, J. L. L. Taulu, and Victor S., and on a document prepared by M. Supangat entitled "Hubungan Ideologis dan Historis IP-KI dengan Ormas Karyawan Pancasila" (IPKI's

of Pemuda Patriotik say they only came together in 1960 at the request of Nasution, and that Pemuda Pancasila never existed before they agreed to the name change at the Surabaya congress.[26] After these Soegirman supporters realized that they had been trumped by Sukarno and Hidayat, Pemuda Patriotik continued to maintain a separate existence, never in practice fusing with Pemuda Pancasila under the orbit of Hidayat's IPKI until after September 1965, when General Suharto's spin on G30S made the PKI available as the new common national enemy.[27]

For an organization that now boasts of its militant anti-communism, it is ironic that today's Pemuda Pancasila has adopted the history as recalled by Hidayat's camp, a history that illustrates PP's tradition to have been grounded in loyalty to Sukarno (and, like the New Order itself, with roots in Guided Democracy). It also reflects PP's concern with form. Indeed, its founding day appears to have been chosen retrospectively mostly for its symbolic significance as the anniversary of the 1928 nationalist Youth Pledge. Spego Goni, who calls himself the founder of PP and was chairman of Hidayat's Pemuda Pancasila from 1961, writes "[October 28, 1959] is the date that I gave to Mr. Yapto Soerjosoemarno SH, in Menado, as the birth date of Pemuda Pancasila. The date since has been made into the historical 'birthday' of Pemuda Pancasila." His activities on that day, he admits, consisted of writing his name as a representative of "Pemuda Pancasila" (rather than as secretary of Jakarta's IPKI branch, which he then was) in a guest book at a ceremony celebrating the anniversary of the Youth Pledge. At the time, there was no organization, but he soon prepared a letterhead and a stamp.[28]

Oddly enough, the impulse to create a militant, mass-based youth organization arose from a beauty contest. It was also a demonstration of loyalty. At the end of December 1961, in the midst of Sukarno's call for mass mobilization to "liberate" West Irian from the Dutch, Spego Goni was busy organizing the first Miss Indonesia contest. After Sukarno publicly denounced the contest on the grounds that it was not in keeping with the national character, Pemuda Rakyat (People's Youth, the youth wing of the PKI) members throughout Jakarta tore down publicity posters and banners. Crushed by the Great Leader of the Revolution's rejection, Spego "wanted to prove that his ideas weren't limited to the Catwalk, but also [could be applied] on the battlefield."[29] Spego then put forward the idea of forming Pemuda Pancasila combat-ready troops and offering to send them to West Irian. On January 4, 1962, he led a group to the National Front HQ, where they presented a letter announcing their

---

Ideological and Historical Connection with Pancasilaist Function Mass Organizations) prepared in June 1998 at the request of M. Noeh.

[26] The reason given at the congress for the name change was that the name "Patriotik" smelled of communism. Interview with J. L. L. Taulu and Victor S., August 24, 1998.

[27] G30S—short for the September 30th Movement—is used as a shorthand reference to the beginning of the regime transition and does not imply any particular claim about who were its instigators.

[28] See Spego Goni, in *Sejarah Singkat Lahirnya "Pemuda Pancasila"* (Brief History of the Birth of "Pemuda Pancasila"), ed. YAPPKI (Jakarta: Yayasan Amal Pembangunan Pejuang Kemerdekaan Indonesia, 1993), pp. 40-42. The book is not distributed—or authorized—by Pemuda Pancasila's central board of directors.

[29] Phill M. Sulu in *Sejarah Singkat Lahirnya "Pemuda Pancasila,"* pp. 28-37. According to Princen, another IPKI figure who worked with Spego on the beauty contest, Spego was not much of a politician, "but knew what people liked." Conversation with Princen, August 20, 1998.

support of Trikora[30] and the existence of one thousand trained members and forty thousand other members standing by throughout Indonesia, awaiting the command to be sent to the front lines. The problem was that PP did not have a complete secretariat, let alone a mass base. To make the bluff credible, Spego instructed a fellow Menadonese, Phill Sulu, whom he had just made a secretary, to come up with a list of ten thousand names. As one of several thousand former Permesta rebels who were at the time being re-indoctrinated in East and Central Java, Sulu had access to the rolls of Permesta battalions being rehabilitated.[31] He copied these names directly into the fictive ranks of Pemuda Pancasila, adding some names from Jakarta supplied by Spego. This bluff resembles a tactic that PP eventually adopted during the New Order, when, in order to make itself visible to Golkar, it sent busloads of members along the campaign trail in advance to "greet" campaigners like Harmoko as they rolled into towns where PP as yet had no members.[32]

Pemuda Patriotik, however, went about building a mass base in Jakarta by recruiting urban marginals for construction work, a method later to become standard for PP. Pemuda Patriotik realized that *pemuda* were necessary to create a mass base for IPKI, and if nothing else they constituted a good work-force able to perform tasks such as putting up campaign posters. In order to "accumulate masses" (*menghimpun massa*), the organizers gathered "vagrants and the unemployed" from the Pasar Senen area and trucked them to the Senayan sports complex to perform "service work" under the IPKI flag. IPKI had been granted the contract for the development of Senayan because there were a number of IPKI ministers in Sukarno's Working Cabinets, including Minister of Trade Arifin Harahap. The new recruits were given a wage, and thereafter became members of Pemuda Patriotik.[33]

Yet in the early 1960s, Pemuda Pancasila took on its character mostly outside Jakarta, particularly in Medan. Close to the time of the Surabaya IPKI congress, a boxer named Effendi Nasution, known as Effendi Keling as well as "the Lion of Sumatra," was recruited as Pemuda Pancasila chair.[34] He was acquainted with the North Sumatra IPKI chief because he controlled black market sales of movie tickets at the Medan Theater, located directly across the street from the IPKI offices. Before he joined Pemuda Pancasila, Effendi already led his own youth organization, P2KM (Persatuan Pemuda Kota Medan, Medan City Youth Union), which may have set a precedent in that it was a formal organization not attached to any party or political organization and appeared mainly as a means to build a personal power base for the charismatic figure of Effendi himself. P2KM, like PP-Medan which it became, was primarily an enterprise employing street youth in extortion and private security as night guards, particularly for ethnic Chinese. In 1967, Effendi became a parliamentary delegate representing the youth element of IPKI, and he brought a

---

[30] Trikora (Tri Komando Rakyat) was the instruction announced by Soekarno on December 19, 1961, calling for crushing the Dutch puppet state of Papua, raising the Indonesian flag in West Irian, and preparing for popular mobilization of volunteers to be sent there.

[31] Permesta, the so-called Semesta (Total) Struggle, was an armed movement based in Sulawesi put down in 1958 by the central government. See Barbara S. Harvey, *Permesta: Half a Rebellion* (Ithaca: Cornell Modern Indonesia Project, 1977).

[32] Interview with Adil Meliala, July 24, 1998.

[33] Interview with J. L. L. Taulu and Victor S.

[34] Effendi was not a *keling* (of Indian descent), but a Mandailing Batak. There is a common agreement that he was called Effendi Keling because he was "black," as *keling* and black are thought to be synonymous by most residents of Medan who are not ethnic Indians.

number of his boys (*anak buah*) with him to Jakarta.[35] Although he returned after a year, many of these boys stayed behind. He remained a mobilizer of Pemuda Pancasila until his death in 1997 and was Medan's main point man for Jakarta.

After September 1965, Pemuda Pancasila in Medan and Aceh were particularly active in slaughtering suspected communists, arguably taking the leading role in North Sumatra as Pemuda Ansor of NU (Nahdatul Ulama) did in parts of Java and PNI (Partai Nasionali Indonesia, Indonesian Nationalist Party) did in Bali.[36] Having sliced off the ears of communists is still a matter of pride for PP elders from North Sumatra and Aceh. (Effendi himself is rumored to have presented Sukarno, to the president's displeasure, with a bundle of dried ears of ethnic Chinese he obtained during a large-scale anti-Chinese riot he and his boys provoked in December 1965.) Their targets included not only the PKI youth wing, Pemuda Rakyat, but also organizations considered close to the PKI, including the Indonesian Farmers' Front (BTI) and Baperki, the largely Indonesian-Chinese citizenship association. PP's conflict with Pemuda Rakyat started before G30S, as early as 1964, when acting as security for HMI and SOKSI functions, Pemuda Rakyat leveled at them such insults as "bandits, devils, and urban bourgeois."[37] Pemuda Pancasila literature boasts that the PP in Medan "took revenge" on the BTI for killing an army lieutenant working as private security at the Bandar Betsy plantation in May 1965. The literature emphasizes PP's bravery in the face of the BTI, but gives no specifics about the lieutenant's death (he was obstructing local farmers from planting on property claimed by the company) nor about Pemuda Pancasila's response (apparently there was no actual counter-attack on the BTI until army ascendancy after G30S made it safe, or encouraged them, to act). Early in November 1965, after Pemuda Pancasila attacked the village of Kampung Kolam, said to be a BTI base where PKI refugees were taking shelter, the bodies of two members of PP were discovered at a spot in the middle of a rice field where an obelisk monument has since been erected in their memory. Surviving residents say they know nothing of the bodies, only that on the night of the attack, all the men were taken in trucks to the regional military command post for a week-long interrogation. For four months thereafter people from Medan in *"preman"* clothes terrorized them, periodically yelling "Pancasila!" and stealing their clothing and chickens.

---

[35] J. L. L. Taulu and Victor S., cited above.

[36] On the part that youth groups played in the killings, see Robert Cribb, ed., *The Indonesian Killings of 1965-1966: Studies from Java and Bali*, Monash Papers on Southeast Asia (Clayton, Victoria: Centre for Southeast Asian Studies, Monash University, 1990); Harold Crouch, *The Army and Politics in Indonesia* (Ithaca: Cornell University Press, 1988), chapter 5; and Geoffrey Robinson, *The Dark Side of Paradise: Political Violence in Bali* (Ithaca: Cornell University Press, 1995). Note that despite the well-documented role of party youth wings in the killings, it is precisely *not* as rampaging mass-murderers that *pemuda* have become established during the New Order.

[37] Bonar Harahap, "Persepsi Pemuda Pancasila Terhadap Perjuangan Orde Baru" (Perceptions of the Pemuda Pancasila Toward the New Order's Struggle) (Skripsi, Fakultas Ilmu Sosial & Ilmu Politik, Universitas 17 Agustus 1945, Jakarta, 1992), pp. 32-35. Activists from HMI, the Islamic Students' Association, later tended to become prominent figures in the pro-New Order Student Action Commando (KAMI), and were subsequently rewarded with high positions. SOKSI (Sentral Organisasi Karyawan Sosialis Indonesia) was a federation of "functional workers" formed by the army to counter the PKI-affiliated labor federation, SOBSI (Sentral Organisasi Buruh Seluruh Indonesia). SOKSI later became one of the three founding organizations of Golkar.

Pemuda Pancasila members in Jakarta, like a number of other youth groups and gangs, were more interested in property theft than corporeal dismemberment. Although PP in Jakarta was relatively small by the standards of the capital, numbering at most five thousand, members took part in raids on PKI and Baperki properties, including the PKI Central Committee's Peace Committee office on Raden Saleh Street, where they made off with typewriters and stencil machines. (Later this property was used as offices for General Ali Moertopo's "Special Operations" intelligence unit, Opsus.) When they could, they would hang onto control of the properties, as they did with the Baperki office on Wahid Hashim Street. This became the Mapancas (IPKI's Pancasila Students) HQ for several years before being sold by a Mapancas chair for private gain, the eventual fate of many of the properties seized at the time. Although PP members in Jakarta asked for and were given thirty or forty short-term licensed pistols by the army, they never had to use them, as all the "communists" had already fled to the regions by the time they showed up at their homes in the "fence of legs" encirclement campaigns in the *kampungs*.[38]

After these youth actions at the advent of the New Order, Pemuda Pancasila as a national organization entered a period of quiescence. PP's literature invariably describes the entire 1970s, before the entry of Yapto as chairman, as a period when the organization was "fast asleep." However, Pemuda Pancasila continued to maintain a visible presence in North Sumatra. The difference between Medan and Jakarta can be attributed mostly to their respective patterns of recruitment and access to resources. Pemuda Pancasila in Medan deliberately recruited a majority of the city's *preman*, and into the 1970s they continued to control virtually all of Medan's movie theaters, and later expanded into entertainment complexes and small-scale gambling as sources of revenue. The license granted to their members during 1965-66 (PP members were allowed to go anywhere and defy night curfews in the hunt for suspected communists) won them substantial political clout and attracted new members, many of whom—especially members of the PNI's youth wing, Pemuda Marhaen—joined for self-protection.[39]

Pemuda Pancasila in Jakarta, on the other hand, had far fewer members, particularly relative to other youth organizations. Members of Pemuda Pancasila tended to be the children or relatives of IPKI party members and may have thus been more oriented to elite party politics, the "excesses" of 1965-66 notwithstanding. However, the claim that Jakarta's PP was "fast asleep" is not entirely accurate. It seems that during this period of quiescence in the 1970s, members of Pemuda Pancasila were active and instrumental in cleaning out the Sukarno loyalists in the PDI when, during the 1973 party fusion, IPKI and the PNI were both made to join PDI. With IPKI and the PNI now fused into a single party, Marhaenist elements (supporters of Sukarno's populist ideology in the PNI) could be easily undermined from within. Although PP declared itself independent from IPKI at the time of the party fusion, in practice many of its members continued to provoke and discredit Marhaenists at party and youth-wing meetings and congresses.[40]

---

[38] Interview with M. L. Tobing, August 13, 1998.

[39] PNI, the Indonesian Nationalist Party, was briefly banned in North Sumatra by General Sarwo Edhie after he became Commander of Military Region 2 in 1967. According to one Pemuda Marhaen activist, virtually all the Marhaenist Youths in his *kampung* joined Pemuda Pancasila.

[40] Interview with Endy Syafruddin, August 14, 1998.

THE ESTABLISHMENT OF THE HISTORIC ROLE OF PEMUDA

The vigorous participation of youth groups in the army's effort to eradicate its enemies, later to be enshrined as an "historic partnership," both cemented a nationalist logic of the "historic role of *pemuda*" and presented certain intractable problems during the consolidation of the New Order. The *pemuda* had already long been hailed as the driving force of Indonesian nationalism. Having been considered as the authors of the nascent notion of "Indonesia" by 1928 (as a result of the "Youth Pledge") and also as shapers of the character of the nationalist revolution against the Dutch (1945-49), *pemuda* were now available to be credited with ushering in the New Order regime (1965-66).[41] On the one hand, the role of *pemuda* provided an ideal way to legitimate the new regime within the teleology of the nationalist struggle. On the other hand, too much emphasis on the role of *pemuda* left open a possibility of an undesirable repeat performance. If youth had been designated as the embodiment of radical change, and change was now to be stalled in favor of stability and regime consolidation, the question became how to contain the excess of youth. Having established the historic role of *pemuda*, the task for the New Order, somewhat ironically, was to establish youth's role as merely historic.

This entailed refashioning the meaning of *pemuda* itself, so that it evolved from a term describing those in the vanguard of change to a term describing something like the bodyguard of "change." "Change" was presented as ongoing (the "renewal" of the New Order would be perpetual) but the word actually referred to a static and increasingly distant moment: the replacement of Sukarno and his regime. Thus by the mid-1970s, three "historic events"—the Youth Pledge in 1928, the Independence Proclamation in 1945, and the "coalition" of the students and the army that led to the establishment of the New Order—began to appear not as examples which represented something permanently and irrepressibly characteristic of youth, but instead as the defining events which, through their routinized recollection, pronounced any future outbursts of youthful energy to be superfluous. At the culmination of a progression of "radical" (and clearly delineated) changes, the youth appeared to have fulfilled their third and *final* obligation in their participation with the army in the establishment of the New Order regime.

This shift was accomplished through a realignment of the term *pemuda* itself, relegating it both institutionally and discursively to a position of relative stability (and backward signification) while producing different designations to delimit the young. University students, *mahasiswa*, were increasingly regarded as a separate category from *pemuda* and were themselves eventually cut off from active politics with the "campus normalization" policy of 1978. Meanwhile, young people as demographic and social beings found their definition in the newly popularized term *remaja*—or teens—and were thus transformed from political actors into passive consumers.[42] This left *"pemuda"* to be reserved as a term for historical actors, as well

---

[41] Anderson, *Java in a Time of Revolution*; Yozar Anwar, *Angkatan 66: Sebuah Catatan Harian Mahasiswa* (The Generation of '66: A Student's Daily Jottings) (Jakarta: Sinar Harapan, 1980); and B. Sularto, *Dari Kongres Pemuda Indonesia Pertama ke Sumpah Pemuda* (From the First Indonesian Youth Congress to the Youth Pledge) (Jakarta: Balai Pustaka, 1986).

[42] Although important to this discussion, detailing these linguistic changes is beyond the scope of this article. One might note that taking refuge in *remaja* may also have been a way for some young people to bow out of the political demands of *pemuda*. For more on *remaja*, see

as youths willing to wear the uniform jackets of the New Order, who could conceive of themselves as living agents of history within the bounds of modernist development. Institutionally, this meant cooperating with an expanding bureaucracy of Youth and Sports and participating within the framework of KNPI, the Indonesian National Youth Council, created in 1973 under circumstances described below.

These shifts did not happen all at once and were reflected on the streets of Jakarta by the changing dynamics of activism and youth gangs during the first few years of the Suharto period. The most notorious "gangs" were those centered in the various military complexes in the capital. Thus, Berlan, a complex of enlisted men and lower officers in the Matraman area which in colonial times was known as *Berenlaan*, gave birth to the Bearland Boys. Similarly, sons of the middle officers housed at the dormitory on Siliwangi Street near Banteng Square went by the name Siliwangi Boys Club. Several figures leading the reincarnation of Pemuda Pancasila in 1980, including Yapto, came out of the Siliwangi Boys. Their advantage over other gangs was their "facilities": they could always borrow their fathers' guns.[43] In the Kebayoran area, the Radio Dalam Club (RDC) was based in the navy complex. The elite areas of Menteng and Kebayoran Baru also had their own gangs, notably Legos (the "Nudge Rocker Boys") of Blok M.[44] Since the late 1950s, Menteng especially had known vaguely-defined "cross-boys," admirers of James Dean and Elvis Presley who liked to stay up all night and hold parties which the authorities considered to violate Indonesian values or even to be products of foreign intervention.[45] Various other groups were based on regional affiliation, such as Ams, Ambonese housed in the old colonial medical school building, Pamors (Padang-Manado Organization), and Sartana, mainly Menadonese who controlled the Sarinah-Tanah Abang retail districts. These latter groups were not necessarily "ethnically" based, because many of the leading figures were the sons of ABRI officers stationed in the "regions," who consequently grew up identifying with them.[46]

James T. Siegel, *Solo in the New Order: Language and Hierarchy in an Indonesian City* (Princeton: Princeton University Press, 1986).

[43] Interview with Tagor Lumbanraja, Secretary General of Pemuda Pancasila in 1981-1991 and once a Siliwangi Boys member, August 18, 1998. Though most of their fathers were colonels, Soerjosoemarno, Yapto's father, was a general. The Siliwangi complex was leveled in 1984 on the orders of Jakarta Commander Try Sutrisno, for the purpose of getting rid of the gangs.

[44] Members of Legos (Lelaki Goyang Senggol) openly entered politics. Its members included Mangara Siahaan, currently a leader of Megawati's PDI, and Leo Tomasoa, who was to become one of Ali Moertopo's agitators circa Malari through his position in the "Group of 10" at University of Indonesia, which also included erstwhile KNPI activists-cum-Golkar leaders Aulia Rahman and Freddy Latumahina. The nominally anti-Japanese and anti-foreign capital rioting in Jakarta in January 1974, subsequently called the Fifteenth of January Disaster, or Malari, has since been commonly interpreted as an outcome of conflict between Ali Moertopo and General Soemitro. The Group of 10 was a core of University of Indonesia students cultivated by Ali Moertopo. See *Sinar*, March 18, 1995; and Heru Cahyono, *Peranan Ulama Dalam Golkar 1971-1980: Dari Pemilu Sampai Malari* (The Role of Ulama in Golkar 1971-1980: From the Elections to Malari) (Jakarta: Pustaka Sinar Harapan, 1992), p. 161.

[45] One police speech given on the problem quoted a private driver's opinion that cross-boys are "enemies of the state." This speech questioned the perception that cross-boys were mainly an elite phenomenon. A. Soebroto Soedewo, "Cross-Boys Sebagai Masaalah Sosial" (Cross-Boys as a Social Question), *Bhayangkara* 9,2 (1959): 6.

[46] Confidential interview, July 18, 1998.

Many of these local gangs became part of the mass of protesters who, in 1965-66, became collectively known as KAMI and KAPPI.[47] Demonstrating was a "hobby," and a lucrative one too, since it justified the collection of "struggle funds" *(dana perjuangan)* from the Chinese, a tradition resurrected from the Revolution in the new context. After the years of demonstrations of 1965 and 1966 (which involved seizing properties and chasing suspected communists and other enemies), mass demobilization meant returning to respective neighborhood gangs. "With the end of the struggle at that time, all activities which channeled the spirit of teens and youth began to lose focus," writes Legos member Leo Tomasoa about his own gang.

> The demonstrators returned to their original function, where highschool students went back to the school bench, university students went back to campus, but not a few of them continued their habit of hanging out and goofing off which often meant hassling people who happened to pass by, asking for money from them, and picking fights.[48]

Thus these demobilized youths of the early New Order presented a problem to the state similar to that presented by the *pejuang* who had not been "regularized" after the Revolution, save that for the most part regularization of the *pemuda* did not so much require the provision of uniforms or the granting of ranks, as it required creating additional opportunities to provide certain services and, in some cases, integrating them into the bureaucracy or parliament.

I want to highlight a single turning-point which was to separate "new-style" *pemuda* from the lingering rabble-rousing student demonstrators of 1965-66 and set the stage both for the institutionalization of youth and for the various and varyingly successful efforts to integrate gangs into the state apparatus which culminated in Petrus (1982-83) and thereafter in the rise of Pemuda Pancasila. I refer to the "resolution" of student opposition to Mrs. Tien Suharto's fantasy "Beautiful Indonesia"-in-Miniature Park project at the end of 1971. In the years before the "historic generation" of 1966 succeeded in establishing itself as the "final generation," some youth and student groups continued to press for change in their characteristic manner, failing to realize that their mission was already considered to be accomplished. Nor did they heed the large no-trespassing sign on Cendana Street, where the Suharto family lived: to challenge the interests of the First Family directly was strictly off-limits. Criticism of the proposed land evictions required for the construction of the Mini Park and of wasteful extravagance only made Tien "all the more perfect in tackling the issue." Growing protests prompted the president to vow: "Quite frankly, I'll deal with them! No matter who they are! Anyone who refuses to understand this warning, frankly I'll deal with them!"[49] In a book published in 1971

---

[47] KAMI (Kesatuan Aksi Mahasiswa Indonesia, Indonesian Students' Action Unit); KAPPI (Kesatuan Aksi Pemuda Pelajar Indonesia, Indonesian Highschool Students' Action Unit).

[48] See Leonard Tomasoa, "Kepemimpinan Dalam Gang-X (Suatu Studi Terhadap Kehidupan Gang Di Daerah Kebayoran Baru)" (Leadership in Gang-X [A Study of Gang Life in Kebayoran Baru]), Skripsi, Fakultas Ilmu-Ilmu Sosial, University of Indonesia, Jakarta, p. 25. See also *Sinar*, March 18, 1995.

[49] Tien Suharto quoted in *Kompas*, December 16, 1971. On Taman Mini "Indonesia Indah," see John Pemberton, *On the Subject of "Java,"* pp. 152-161. Suharto's angry remark, quoted on page 153, was originally translated by Benedict Anderson in his "Notes on Contemporary Indonesian Political Communication," *Indonesia* 16 (October 1973): 65.

on the history of the youth movement, it was still possible to include youth protests against Tien's project as a new element in the historical line delineated by Budi Utomo (the first nationalist organization, founded in 1908), the Youth Pledge, the Revolution, and the ousting of Sukarno. This error was, in the spirit of the president's warning, almost immediately to be erased.[50]

Tien's "perfection" in tackling the problem found expression in the assault on demonstrators by members of the Berlan gang. On December 23, 1971 a group of long-haired boys confronted a number of youth demonstrators at the Miniature Park Project secretariat, which shared offices with Tien's Our Hope Foundation. When challenged, one said, "*Wah*, here's a cross-boy wants to make trouble, *nih*," pulling out a machete. Shots were fired, glass was broken, two demonstrators were stabbed and one shot in the thigh with a .45. "At the time, *we* were the long-hairs," recalled Asmara Nababan, one of the demonstrators, but added that the physical difference between the demonstrators and the attackers was "insignificant." Contemporary witnesses observed that the attackers were well-trained and that their long hair appeared to be wigs. The Berlan boys involved later defended themselves in court by claiming that they mistook the demonstrators for rivals from other gangs like Sartana, Casanova, or Siliwangi.[51] Thus army brats who happened to be gangsters passed as long-haired rowdy youths picking fights with "cross-boys" who turned out to be demonstrators yet resembled rivals from another barracks. In this confused quasi-failure of recognition, the transformation of gangsters into youth and youth into delinquents was effected.

The "clash" between these "rival youths" precipitated efforts to regularize and authorize youth, refiguring opposition as wild elements and subordinating gangsters (already informally linked to the army through their parents or other patrons) to the intelligence apparatus by "dissolving them." On January 15, 1972, Deputy Kopkamtib Commander General Soemitro issued an instruction dissolving and outlawing "groups and gangs of teen-youths" with the following considerations:

> 1) Recently especially in the large cities there have emerged groups of teen-youths calling themselves, *inter alia*, BERENLAAN GANG, GANG IC STRAAT, GANG SARTANA and so forth whose activities tend toward criminal acts, *inter alia*, fighting/battery/murder/rape/extortion/illegal Narcotic Drug use and robbery, and improper behavior.
>
> 2) Other than that it has been proven . . . that these GANGS were used by the Anti-"Beautiful Indonesia"-in-Miniature Movements to incite riots, which resulted in many people being wounded in inter-GANG fighting and then these victims were used as martyrs by the Anti-"Beautiful Indonesia"-in-Miniature Movements to stir up emotions and mass movements.
>
> 3) With this in mind, the growth and development of the lives of our teen-youths must be saved.[52]

---

[50] Peter Tomasoa, *Sedjarah Pergerakan Pemuda Indonesia. Koleksi Foto/dokumentasi: Leo J. Tanud* (The History of the Indonesian Pemuda Movement. A Photo-Documentary Collection: Leo J. Tanud) (Djakarta: n.p., 1972).

[51] *Tempo*, January 1, 1972; *Kompas*, December 24, 1971-January 5, 1972; *Kompas*, May 9, 1972. Conversation with Asmara Nababan, July 28, 1998.

[52] Bappenkar Jatim, "Perang Total Melawan Narkotika demi Keselamatan Generasi Remaja Kita Sebagai Harapan Cita-Cita Bangsa" (Total War Against Narcotics for the Salvation of Our Teen Generation as the Hope of Our National Ideals), East Java, 1972.

Although Tien had mobilized the Berlan gang to attack opponents,[53] the instruction faults the demonstrators for organizing their own attack with the intent of making themselves into martyrs, enunciating a procedure later to become standard: speak of your own infiltrators as your target's agitators. The instruction also reveals that the language of juvenility (here: *pemuda-remaja*) had yet to settle on a standard form. At the time, youth occupied a liminal space of semi-*remaja*, semi-*pemuda*.

"Dissolution" of the gangs proceeded apace with the formation of various units to tackle the newly defined youth problem. The approach tended to focus on turning youth on the one hand into teens and, on the other, into "human natural resources" (SDM, *Sumber Daya Manusia*), including resources available as—one might say— "mine-able" assistants of the authorities. Not to be outshone by Kopkamtib, Bakin expanded Bakolak Inpres 6/1971, a body established to control smuggling, creating a sub-unit known as Bappenkar, or Executive Body to Tackle Narcotics and Child-Teen Delinquency.[54] In February 1972, a solemn ceremony took place at the Jakarta Provincial Council, where some two thousand *pemuda* surrendered their "gang logos" and other parts of their "gang outfits" to District Police Chief Widodo and were given a chance to speak their minds. A representative of one gang blamed their parents: " . . . we are like new-born babies and are hurting because our parents don't give us milk." Another "demanded" that they be given jobs. By May 1973, the Bakin sub-team finally obliged, assembling the "former" heads of gangs for industrial training as mechanics, establishing a pattern followed by various army leaders. Taking their cue or their orders from Soemitro, local commanders throughout Indonesia began to increase their access to gangs by establishing various Teen Clubs, with an emphasis on sports. The Knighthood Teen Association (Ireka) formed in the Berlan complex played volleyball and sponsored dances. In Ujung Pandang, the local Kopkamtib commander unified a number of local gangs into a Nature Lovers' Teen Clubs Cooperative Body, organizing hikes, motor racing, and publishing a newsletter called "New Spirit" (*Semangat Baru*), and thus necessarily channeling funds to the teenified gangsters. This period also witnessed the consolidation and expansion of Special Anti-Bandit Teams (Tekab) under the Jakarta district police, which recruited members of gangs, including Sartana and Legos, to "secure their individual *kampungs*."[55]

The effort to make the better-educated and more formally organized youth (such as those belonging to the extra-campus student organizations) the object of family planning (literally) can also be seen as a consequence of the Mini Park affair. In March 1972, Ali Moertopo intervened in a dispute between extra-campus youth organizations over the right to control World Assembly of Youth funds meant for family planning, securing navy Captain Abdul Gafur a position on the National Youth Committee for the Family Planning Program. From this embryo, KNPI (Komite Nasional Pemuda Indonesia, Indonesian National Youth Committee) was born when it claimed in July 1973 the right to represent Indonesian youth in all international fora. Signatories of this "Youth Declaration" included Pemuda

---

[53] Several sources confirm that Tien Suharto ordered the attack.

[54] Bappenkar, Badan Pelaksana Penanggulangan Narkotika & Kenakalan Anak-Anak Remaja. Its first publication, cited above in note 52, was, in addition to being an outline of the Juvenile Delinquency problem, a frame for the dissemination of Soemitro's instruction.

[55] See *Tempo*, January 15, 1972, February 17, 1973, July 14, 1973, and January 26, 1972.

Pancasila chair M. L. Tobing, and David Napitupulu, erstwhile Presidium Chair of KAMI and representative of Pancasila Students (Mapancas), another IPKI *onderbouw* and therefore associated with Pemuda Pancasila. Though met with significant resistance, KNPI eventually became the "sole forum" for youth organizations in Indonesia, with all youth organizations being required to belong to it. KNPI pioneered a new mode of youth action fitting for the New Order *pemuda*, turning demonstrations into delegations supporting government programs or criticizing easy foreign targets.[56] Acting as the government's "partner," in close coordination with a new Ministry of Youth and Sports in which Gafur became the first minister, KNPI helped to make "building-up [*pembinaan*] the young generation" the defining approach to youth during the New Order.

HE WHO SHOUTS THE LOUDEST: THE RISE AND REIGN OF PEMUDA PANCASILA

Pemuda Pancasila's genius was in recognizing the opportunity to enact the "role of *pemuda*" as it became more clearly defined. If it could defend the nation against foreign and internal enemies and support the government's efforts in various fields, it could create the space for itself not only to "participate in the development process," but also to guarantee that its other activities would remain relatively undisturbed. Youth represented a vast and relatively untapped "potential" *(potensi)*, and as long as the majority could never be incorporated into the formal economy, a successful youth organization could manage marginal urban youth, providing members access to the formal labor market and the local administration when appropriate, and organizing them to lend some degree of order and "protection" to the streets when not. It is no coincidence that this strategy resembles the pattern of labor control in informal labor markets that gives rise to semi-criminal "underworlds" in other locations and periods.[57] However, Pemuda Pancasila's novelty rested in the expansion of this labor principle to include employment in political projects in the context of a new nationalism centered around the personal requirements of a single, national (president) boss.

The re-emergence of Pemuda Pancasila under the leadership of Yapto Soerjosoemarno beginning in 1980 took place in an environment where sporadic efforts to organize the urban "underworld" were being met with limited success. Perhaps in an effort to make local bosses and their followers visible and (financially) responsible to the authorities, groups of so-called "recidivists" were encouraged to consolidate themselves into formal organizations. The most prominent of such organizations, Prems, founded in 1979 (some say with the patronage of Admiral Sudomo), was organized into departments, including a legal aid division, and

---

[56] *Tempo*, November 2, 1974. In reaction to a University of Indonesia petition criticizing development strategy, in December 1973, KNPI led a "delegation" to the National Planning Board in order not to criticize, but to relay "the essentials of our thoughts for the perfection of the second five-year plan." *Tempo*, December 15, 1973. In 1975, KNPI protested the burning of the Indonesian flag in Holland by "remnants" of the RMS, the South Moluccan Republic secession movement. A week after the East Timor invasion, KNPI protested against Australia for its failure to perceive the matter in the Indonesian way. *Kompas*, January 15, 1975, and December 16, 1975.

[57] For a good description of this in late colonial Batavia, see Robert Cribb, *Gangsters and Revolutionaries*.

boasted fifty thousand members by the time it was broken up during the Petrus killings in 1983. Perhaps one of the failings of Prems was its public image as a purely (ex-)criminal association. Although Prems denied that the name was an abbreviation for "Aware Preman" *(Preman Sadar)*, it made no attempt to conceal the fact that its members were ex-cons and that its main function was to give them work, mainly in the security business.[58] Various local groups such as Greater Bandung Youngsters—which, like Pemuda Pancasila, claimed to guide youngsters so they would not get involved in criminal acts, yet in practice extracted money from "donors" *(donator)*—did not survive long, even though they had the "blessing of the authorities." Their strong sense of local identity (Greater Bandung Youngsters had a flag with the name of a Bandung street below a skull and crossbones) obstructed their chances for the kind of national recognition Pemuda Pancasila was able to gain.[59]

Pemuda Pancasila's competition not only organized ex-cons or local toughs, but also youth groups supporting Golkar, although the lines between the two, as I have been arguing, are indistinct. Its rivalry with Golkar's youth wing, AMPI (Angkatan Muda Pembaharuan Indonesia, Indonesian Renewal Young Generation), can be seen in the context of the effort to weaken Ali Moertopo's influence, which, as one theory has it, was also a chief purpose of the Petrus killings. Although it is beyond the scope of this article to discuss the various interpretations of Petrus, it is widely assumed that Suharto feared the ambitions of Ali Moertopo, especially his power-base in the *gali*, and that Benny Murdani was under orders to wipe out his underworld forces. Many of them, especially through formal youth constellations such as AMS (Siliwangi Youths), had supported Golkar (by way of both campaigns and the kidnapping and intimidation of opponents) during the 1982 elections.[60]

The "re-awakening" of Pemuda Pancasila followed on the heels of the 1978 formation of AMPI by Abdul Gafur (and hence, by extension, Moertopo). Yapto Soerjosoemarno began his efforts to assume control of PP after January 1980 by setting up branches, led by his personal friends and hunting partners, in several provinces, precisely one year after David Napitupulu toured the regions consolidating AMPI's regional base.[61] Gafur evidently saw Yapto as a challenge to AMPI, which he envisioned as unifying under the Golkar banner local youth groups

---

[58] In a letter to the editor in *Kompas* on February 17, 1982, Prems clarified that it was founded on November 10, 1979, as Yayasan Proyek Rehabilitasi Ex Naripidana Menuju Sejahtera (Project for Rehabilitation of Ex-Cons Aiming for Prosperity Foundation), abbreviated Yayasan Prems & Associates. Since the Jakarta District Police Chief had objected to the use of the term "Ex-Con," on August 31, 1981 it changed its name to Yayasan Proyek Rehabilitasi Material dan Spiritual (Project Material and Spiritual Rehabilitation Foundation), or Yayasan Prems. Despite this correction, in popular parlance the tag Preman Sadar stuck, carrying with it an ambivalence between the state of being "aware" in the sense of repentance arising from an awakened national consciousness and the state of being "aware" of their own collective power as *preman*.

[59] Greater Bandung Youngsters (Muda-Mudi Bandung Raya) tried to join KNPI, but were told that "there is no forum that can accommodate activities like yours." *Tempo*, September 3, 1983.

[60] This view is supported by the circumstances of Prems leader Agus TGW's disappearance. He was kidnapped by armed men immediately after a meeting with leaders of AMS. *Tempo*, June 25 1983. For more on Ali Moertopo and Petrus, see for example David Bourchier, "Crime, Law, and State Authority in Indonesia," in *State and Civil Society in Indonesia*, ed. Arief Budiman, Monash Papers on Southeast Asia (Clayton, Victoria: Monash University, 1990), pp. 193-195, which deals briefly with Pemuda Pancasila.

[61] *Warta Berita*, April 7, 1980; *Antara* reports, January 1979.

in Moertopo's orbit such as AMS, a goal not fully accomplished until the completion of the 1982 elections. David Bourchier suggests that Pemuda Pancasila was granted a national franchise on the underworld after the elections and the Petrus operations, thereby replacing Moertopo's network.[62] However, the fact that Yapto became chair of PP well before Petrus (and was building his base more than two years before the 1982 elections) suggests a more protracted and complicated conflict over control of local "human resources." This conflict brings into focus the fact that in order to win influence during the New Order, one had to do so in the context of being Golkar's most enthusiastic defenders.

Yapto's rise represented something of an internal coup against Pemuda Pancasila's then nominal leader, ML Tobing, who had cooperated closely with Gafur in the creation of KNPI. Yapto's imminent installment as chair of PP was strongly opposed by Gafur, on the grounds that Yapto himself was a *preman*, but more probably for the reason that Yapto was not *his preman*. Just before the March 1981 PP congress, Yapto was brought up on gun possession charges in an effort to obstruct him, though he was quickly released. Tobing himself was detained for three days by the Jakarta Military Command (then under Norman Sasono) in an effort to convince him to remain as chair, and only released after he signed a statement that Pemuda Pancasila's "aspirations" would be channeled to Golkar. Yapto, however, was determined, having already staged a convincing show of force by trucking in more than a thousand supporters from the regional branches he had established within the previous year. With Yapto's boys chanting things like "Viva Yapto!" during the congress, Yapto became sole candidate and then general chairman. Though he came accompanied by a thousand followers, it would be difficult to imagine that Yapto could have prevailed against the wishes of Gafur and Norman Sasono unless he had other support. Though Tobing was unaware of this at the time, he later concluded that the Suhartos needed their own "force."[63] If the Suhartos saw a need for a *preman* base, Yapto was a likely candidate for the job. Yapto and Tien were distant cousins from Solo, and his father, General Soerjosoemarno, was also a personal friend of the family. His eagerness to settle conflicts violently may have been a factor; during the 1970s he had already established a reputation in Jakarta for machismo *(kejagoan)* as a leader of the Siliwangi boys.

Yet it would be too simple to conclude that the whole organization was set up by Suharto or that it was designed to become the "sole vehicle" for nationalizing gangs. The impetus to revive Pemuda Pancasila appears to have come not from Yapto but from PP old-timers in Medan led by Effendi Nasution, mentioned above. Effendi originally approached Yapto about holding a reunion in Jakarta, which eventually took place at Ancol in January 1980. The "grassroots" membership had come to realize that in order to maximize profits, coordination and unimpeachable legality were crucial. Siliwangi figures like Yapto and Tagor "had names, but they didn't have any papers." With legality, one could deal with the authorities.[64] In the estimation of Pemuda Pancasila revivers, it took several years for PP to win the recognition and cooperation of the authorities. The turning point did not come until 1987, after a meeting with the Assistant for Sociopolitical Affairs to ABRI's Chief of Staff for Sociopolitical Affairs, General Harsudiyono Hartas, in which they convinced

---

[62] Bourchier, "Crime, Law, and State Authority in Indonesia," pp. 194-195.

[63] Based on several interviews.

[64] Interview with Tagor Lumbanraja, July 18, 1998.

him that, as fellow sons of ABRI, their interests were compatible. After that, Pemuda Pancasila branches and the respective Regional Military Commands (Kodam) immediately "matched."

In its "struggle" for recognition, PP's affinity with the *jago* is revealed. On the one hand, inasmuch as the *jago* has been perceived as a defender of the *wong cilik* (the little guy), the effort to assert the existence of the organization itself was a way to push for the interests of its expanding, largely disenfranchised, member base and to demand that it be taken seriously. In practice, this entailed the distribution of local turf concessions. On the flip side, insofar as the *jago* has been seen as a figure on whom authorities relied to maintain order in the face of potentially restless masses, PP's increasing success in expanding its influence promised that this threat could be curtailed. One of the most intriguing contradictions of Pemuda Pancasila is that it perceives itself to be fighting for the welfare of its grassroots members, while at the same time maintaining a hierarchical organizational structure that mirrors the administrative units of the state, from the center down through to the RT level. *Preman*, inasmuch as they conceive of themselves as free men, are also said to value group solidarity. Within Pemuda Pancasila, group solidarity takes the form of obedience to the chain of command. Thus, Pemuda Pancasila can be seen to have successfully translated the logic of the *jago* into a formally "modern" organizational framework, organizing what might be said to be a nested system of *jagos*, where local bosses would be formally subordinate to the higher level "manager" of the branch or district office, yet expect to retain significant local autonomy over revenues.

The way in which Pemuda Pancasila made itself, to quote a popular phrase in the organization, "disliked but needed," also mirrors the style of the *jago*, though PP is strengthened by the bureaucratic reinforcement a formal organization can provide. The source of the *jago's* power, to paraphrase Blok on the Sicilian Mafia, comes through maintaining or encouraging social tensions that he is strategically placed to resolve. As Siliwangi Boys member-cum-former PP Secretary General Tagor indicated, it is only through an "incident" that a gang exists. In order to grow strong, it must create conflicts to demonstrate its "existence." Indeed, the primary concern in the early years of PP's rebirth was the question of *eksistensi*, not questions of purpose. Pemuda Pancasila operationalized this logic beginning in local discos and, arguably, extending the pattern nationwide. To gain control over night club security, for example, PP would send in obnoxious drunkards who would make their association with PP known. Thereafter, in response to a request from the owner, PP members would be sent in to insure that this would be the last such incident. When PP members busted up billiard parlors in Grogol in the name of "wiping out gambling," they at once punished owners for not paying enough protection money and made sure that their services would continue to be needed. Yapto boasted that local army commanders often asked for the assistance of Pemuda Pancasila in putting a stop to rioting in the regions, adding as an afterthought, with some delight, that "it is also our guys who are doing it." Yorrys Raweyai's post-*reformasi* support of independence for West Papua, followed by his switch to support for local autonomy, can also be seen as conforming to this pattern. Within weeks, Yorrys was able to mobilize independence protests in Jayapura, then position himself as uniquely capable of convincing the "Irianese" to consider expanded autonomy instead.[65]

---

[65] Interviews with Tagor, cited above; Yapto Soerjosoemarno, August 25, 1998; Anton Medan, March 18-21, 1998. On PP Grogol Petamburan's efforts to eradicate gambling, see for example *Gatra*, April 12, 1997. On Yorrys and Irian, see *Panji Masyarakat*, July 15, 1998; *Sinar Pagi*,

Among the advantages the organization holds over the *jago* are an ability to rotate personnel and the "impersonality" of the organization itself. The *jago's* mischievousness is limited by the fact that his personality is unmistakable. If he makes a pest of himself in an effort to increase his own value, it is likely to be more in displays of his prowess than in wanton destruction. A *jago* is unable to disavow himself. However, the organization, inasmuch as it is itself embodied in law, is infinitely able to reorder or to disavow its constituent parts. With a tight enough structure of command, it is possible to bring in bodies from other regions or locales to create necessary incidents and then allow the local representatives to step in and save the day. Thus the perpetrators are unrecognized while the saviors are familiar. It can also insist on a division between the embodied organizational form and the fallible members who comprise it. The rational-legal organization itself thus takes on a divine, and ultimately vacant, form.[66] Pemuda Pancasila has perfected this understanding of modernity by enacting by-laws and organizational regulations, to which all members must pledge their loyalty, which specify important matters such as terms of office, formal organizational structure, the measurements and layout of branch sign posts and letter seals, and the styles of uniforms appropriate for various functions. Local-level organization leaders implore members to understand the by-laws while lamenting that the majority of members have never read them. For their part, members frequently complain that they have "not yet received" the regulations and perpetually wait for the branch offices to make photocopies available. It is as if a Platonic Form of the organization exists out there somewhere, always a step beyond perfect comprehension. Violators of this organizational form are nevertheless always *oknum*.

In Pemuda Pancasila's perfection of disavowal, it made itself needed by the regime. Its members are always available as *oknum* of an organization that is already, in terms of the state, an *oknum*. Pemuda Pancasila, as an organization, has no formal connection to Golkar, let alone the bureaucracy. It is an independent, idealistic, militant youth organization oriented towards "prestige and concrete service" in accordance with Pancasila Morals. Marching in this direction, at each congress Pemuda Pancasila releases a "political statement" resolving to channel its political aspirations to a "social-political force oriented toward constructive work and concrete service [*karya dan kekaryaan*], that is Golongan Karya."[67] Thus any

---

September 2, 1998; *Gatra*, September 19, 1998. Since *reformasi*, Yorrys has continued to position himself as a leading Irianese figure. Meanwhile, several Pemuda Pancasila leaders (especially provincial heads) have taken this "treasonous position" as reason to push for Yorrys's dismissal from the organization, although many of them admit that their actual motivation is to name a fall guy for Pemuda Pancasila's support for Suharto in May—and they realize this will not be Yapto.

[66] Daniel Dhakidae commented in a not unrelated context, "ABRI is a very good thing, so holy that there has never been a flaw in the body of ABRI. If there is a flaw, it is certainly an *oknum*. Even if 99 percent of ABRI members committed crimes . . . ABRI itself is holy." *Oknum* was originally a term in Indonesian Catholic theology referring to the three persons of God (the Father, the Son, and the Holy Spirit) in the Trinity. According to Dhakidae, this usage appeared in older Indonesian Catholic catechisms. Interview, July 10, 1998. This is the first definition of "*oknum*" in *Kamus Besar Bahasa Indonesia*. See Depdikbud, *Kamus Besar Bahasa Indonesia* (Large Indonesian Dictionary) (Jakarta: Balai Pustaka, 1988). On "*oknum*," see also note 9 above.

[67] See *Anggaran Dasar*, article 2 and "Pemuda Pancasila Political Statement" in *Hasil Keputusan Musyawarah Besar V, Pemuda Pancasila* (Resolutions of Pemuda Pancasila's Fifth National Conference), or the report from any congress after 1981, as the language is nearly identical.

"excessive" actions in support of Pancasila and the 1945 Constitution, such as shouting down treasonous activists, are no more than the result of the organizations' idealistic zeal or the spontaneous actions of its members, and not the responsibility of any government officials or institutions. In turn, if enthusiasm sometimes gets too zealous and turns into "excesses" such as assault or ransacking, Pemuda Pancasila can "regret" the actions of a few irresponsible *oknum*. A third stage of disavowal is the non-recognition of membership based on the non-possession of a membership card. Since Pemuda Pancasila "attributes" are available for purchase to anyone on the open market, a troublemaker wearing their trademark orange and black striped camouflage t-shirt is not necessarily a member.[68] This is doubly true for someone wearing *"baju preman"* (a preman outfit). Drawing on the state's identification of proof of citizenship and identity (to be in possession of one's KTP, the state-issued ID card, means to "have an identity"), one's PP-ship is not provable if one is caught in the act without a membership card. Thus local youths defending-the-state or wiping-out-gambling are not-necessarily-PP or already-dismissed-ex-PP, and PP, in turn, is not under the command of the ruling party, let alone the army, but only expresses its spontaneous support for them.

This reputation suggests another way PP has been of service to the state. With such all-but-unfulfillable requirements for proving PP's institutional involvement in these excesses of enforcement, Pemuda Pancasila has become the quintessential usual suspect, especially in a string of actions that took place immediately after President Suharto—with considerable fanfare—opened its sixth national congress in June 1996. Prodem activists routinely finger PP, even when repressive actions are spearheaded by other organizations such as FKPPI or involve the mobilization of hired *"preman"* (read: the desperate poor) off the streets. For instance, when a group of youths backed by the military raided Megawati Sukarnoputri's PDI (Indonesian Democratic Party) HQ in July 1996, many groups immediately suspected that those passing as supporters of Soerjadi, Megawati's government-installed rival, were chiefly Pemuda Pancasila members. This assumption, relayed through human rights groups from Jakarta to New York, was quickly adopted by several members of the US congress who, in a letter to the Indonesian Foreign Minister, called PP a "paramilitary group which was the vanguard of the attack on the PDI offices" and demanded Pemuda Pancasila's dissolution.[69] With PP taking the heat in this way,

---

Golkar must meet four conditions that are already part of Golkar's program to win the support of Pemuda Pancasila. *Kekaryaan* has been understood to include work beyond normal duties, such as a military officer assigned to a civilian post. For definition, see John M. Echols and Hassan Shadily, *Kamus Indonesia-Inggris* (Indonesian-English Dictionary), 3rd ed. rev. by John J. Wolff and James T. Collins (Jakarta: Gramedia, 1989). Thus it would include a "civilian" performing voluntary military duties as well.

[68] For example, during the early May 1998 rioting in Deli Serdang on the outskirts of Medan, seventy looters wearing PP t-shirts were later publicly disavowed by PP North Sumatra officials, who insisted the t-shirts were distributed by a "big thief" bent on discrediting the organization and taking advantage of the situation. This announcement was made at a press conference given on November 9, 1998, in which they threatened to sue the government-established Joint Fact Finding Team (TGPF) for slander. TGPF's report on the May riots included a statement that: provocateurs are "generally difficult to recognize, although in a number of cases [provocation] was carried out by groups from youth organizations (for example in Medan the direct involvement of Pemuda Pancasila was discovered)." TGPF, Executive Summary, Final Report, May 13-15, 1998 Incident, October 23, 1998.

[69] Letter to Foreign Minister Ali Alatas, dated August 6, 1996, signed by Patrick J. Kennedy, Barney Frank, Christopher Smith, and Nita Lowey. Although a known PP member named

ABRI commanders are freer to coordinate such actions using manpower tapped from other sources, including *preman* from the various military units themselves, as we have seen with a vengeance in Prabowo's mobilization of Special Forces and Jakarta Military Command *preman* during the May 1998 rioting.[70] This in turn has tended to undercut PP's necessity as an actual force, while shoring up its importance as a symbol.

In exchange for "concrete service," PP expects concrete concessions in order to fulfill its mission to "raise the welfare" of its members. Members expect to be allowed to control revenues generated in the informal economy, especially parking and the "management" of informal traders, management that includes the collection of money for the provision of such services as security, cleaning, electricity, and water. They expect to be compensated with transportation money for mobilizing masses for rallies and events in support of local and national officials. They expect the assistance of local officials in employing their boys (and sometimes girls) in district and village level offices. They also expect preferential access in channeling their members into other private and government positions. To facilitate this process, PP leaders have occupied positions controlling manpower. Yorrys has served as Jakarta head of the sole government-authorized workers' union SPSI, and Yapto served a period as "care-taker" of the Indonesian Manpower Service Association (IMSA, now APJATI), which coordinates labor export. Their control over security at night clubs, likewise, must be tolerated. Yorrys shored up PP's position in the nightclubs in the mid-1990s when he served as head of the Jakarta Tourist Industry Association, whose mandate includes entertainment complexes.

Pemuda Pancasila's control over these sources of "welfare" have come under challenge by another "Youth Social Organization," the Pemuda Panca Marga (PPM). PPM is headed in Jakarta by Harianto Badjoeri, an official in the Tourism Office, who has the authority to license pubs and discos, one thing Yorrys can not do. As the youth wing of the Veterans' League, PPM is also an undying supporter of Golkar and the army. In practice, PPM has not limited its membership to the children of veterans and has taken other "sympathizers" under its wing. Its position on the streets has been strengthened by figures such as Hercules, an East Timorese who made a name for himself as a private assistant of Prabowo Subianto in East Timor. Some of his followers were brought from Dili, promised jobs by Suharto's eldest

---

Cornelis was identified by cons in Salemba prison during the raid on Megawati's PDI on July 27, 1996, credible evidence also points to involvement by poor residents of Kapuk, North Jakarta, who on several prior occasions were gathered by the army under the pretext of preparing for a parade or *gotong-royong* (mutual help activity), and then given cash and sent home. On July 27, they found themselves wearing the PP's Medan congress t-shirts and being ordered to attack the PDI HQ. This suggests that raiders, pre-tested for obedience, were pulled from several locales. On Cornelis, see Tri Agus, "Bagaimana ABRI Menggunakan Preman: (Komandan Preman Penyerbu DPP PDI Itu Bernama Cornelis)" (How ABRI Uses Preman: [The Commander of the Preman Who Attacked the Central Executive Board of the PDI is named Cornelis]), *Apakabar-L*, October 3, 1996. On Kapuk, see *Adil*, October 16-22, 1996. To confess to participation in the raid also became a profit-making venture for one *preman*, Bella Seno, who hoped to sue Soerjadi for payment. He lost in court. See "Political Gangsters" in *Inside Indonesia*, January-March, 1998.

[70] See, for example, *Tajuk*, September 3, 1998. The Jakarta Military Command has threatened to sue *Tajuk* for publishing this testimony of someone who heard the confession of one of the deployed Special Forces personnel.

daughter, Tutut, then left to fend for themselves in Jakarta.[71] He and his boys, through the time-worn method of making and quelling trouble, sometimes wearing their camouflage PPM jackets and sometimes not, had in recent years assumed control of Tanah Abang and parts of Kota. Hercules has also "outbid" Pemuda Pancasila for Jakarta contracts to organize activities in support of East Timorese integration, such as some of the counter-demonstrations staged outside embassies during the asylum bids by resistance youths. This trend has created a rift between Prabowo and Yapto which is expressed in the latter's stated resentment of the government in general. "The government is putting in these other guys [from PPM] who don't even know what they are doing. . . . The discos where PP works as security are always safe and professional. The others are only collecting money and letting their friends drink for free."[72]

Fighting for national development (*memperjuangkan pembangunan nasional)* has, for the disenfranchised youth, come to mean dividing its blessings (*pembagian rezeki)* through seizing turf (*perebutan lahan)*. If one considers that a large number of Pemuda Pancasila district and local managers run construction companies or are involved in demolition for developers, it is reasonable for them to join in the fight for this "building-up" *(pembangunan)* known as national development. Even explicitly political actions in its defense—such as counter-demonstrations, or an appearance in support of Suharto at the DPR in May—tend to be expressed in terms of "projects" and winning tenders. It is also illustrative that these material conditions have generated, in the New Order generally, but within Pemuda Pancasila particularly, their own idealist philosophies of materialism and the concrete. Both Yapto and Yorrys have published collections of short essays on such subjects as truth, human resources, national awakening, and the new spirit, which quote Socrates, Emerson, John F. Kennedy, and Fukuyama, among others. To achieve the goal of "reaching a better future," writes Yorrys, a "new spirit" *(semangat baru)* is required. What is this new spirit? "Spirit, in terms of an automobile, is the fuel which moves and animates the working mechanism of the car. Without fuel, the car can't do anything, at most it can be pushed." Spirit will drive you, in your private vehicle, to the prosperous future. Along the road, however, the highest value is to fill one's stomach—alias to work—*ini yang kongkrit,* this is what is concrete.[73] Whatever else might be said about it, for many thousands of youths over the past decades, this philosophy worked. Given such prospects for youth struggle, it is easy to see how, to turn a phrase, the only way to be a spirited, patriotic *pemuda* during the New Order was to be a *preman.*

---

[71] An Asia Watch report details the role of Yayasan Tiara, a foundation controlled by Tutut, in recruiting and then abandoning East Timorese youth, in some cases forcing them to undergo military training at the Special Forces-run complex in Cijantung, West Java. See "Deception And Harassment Of East Timorese Workers," *Asia Watch,* May 15, 1992. According to one East Timorese living in Jakarta, some of these people became *preman* in Blok M and Tanah Abang. Some of the latter group joined forces with Hercules, while others became his rivals. Confidential interview, April 1998.

[72] Several confidential interviews, and interview with Yapto, August 25, 1998.

[73] Yorrys Raweyai Th, *Catatan Seorang Aktivis* (Notes of an Activist) (Jakarta: Shahnaz Swa Mandiri, 1994), p. 75; Yapto S. Soerjosoemarno, *Percikan Pemikiran Yapto S. Soerjosoemarno* (Scattered Thoughts of Yapto S. Soerjosoemarno) (Jakarta: Shahnaz Swa Mandiri, 1993); "Ini Yang Kongkrit" (This is What's Concrete), *Pancasila Abadi,* August 1996.

QUO VADIS, PANCASILA YOUTH?

In the days after Suharto's resignation, Pemuda Pancasila had reason to worry that their late appearance at the Parliament (in which at minimum they criticized Harmoko for speaking out of turn in calling on Suharto to resign) would damage their position.[74] There was even concern that their bases would be attacked. How did Pemuda Pancasila wind up being the last ones holding the fort, and what is likely to be their fate?

How one interprets their position depends on how one reads both PP's connections to Prabowo Subianto and Prabowo's game in relation to his father-in-law more broadly. For reasons suggested above, and for other reasons having to do with personal differences between Yapto and Prabowo, one can assume that by May 1998 Prabowo's reliance on Pemuda Pancasila as a source of his *preman* was minimal. In fact, if one reads the rise of Pemuda Pancasila partially in light of the decline of Ali Moertopo's "zoo" (a term referring to his collection of underworld agents), it is tempting to see Pemuda Pancasila's current limbo as the result of competition from Prabowo's own menagerie. Over the past several years, Prabowo cultivated militant supporters both in and outside military units like the Special Forces, focusing particularly on Islamic groups in West Java and on East Timorese and Irianese to whom he lent his patronage. One of the groups he cultivated most openly was Young Indonesian Knights (Satria Muda Indonesia), a *pencak silat* (martial arts) organization based in Banten for which he serves as Primary Advisor. He clearly played on anti-Chinese sentiments in various Islamic communities, particularly through sponsorship of the informal networks of Islamic congregations known as *majelis taklim*. One of the *taklim* pesantrèn (schools) for which Prabowo became a patron recruits repentant *preman* under the leadership of an ethnic Chinese former gangster from Medan-cum-Islamic proselytizer *(da'i)* named Anton Medan. Despite later evasions, Anton Medan did in fact take to the streets during the May rioting, privately boasting to several people shortly after the event that he burned down the home of Liem Sioe Liong, Suharto's legendary bagman.[75] The fact that he was briefly made into the leading scapegoat as the *dalang* (orchestrator) of the May rioting, but later was quietly dropped as a suspect, supports the idea that he has something to tell.[76] Prabowo also could mobilize more professional support, including operatives from the Special Forces and the Jakarta Military Command wearing basic black, or

---

[74] As mentioned in the introduction, Pemuda Pancasila disavowed openly supporting Suharto as president at the Parliament's meeting on May 19, 1998. They could not, however, deny that they were at the Parliament to criticize Harmoko, the Speaker, who the day before had called on Suharto to take the wise course and resign. PP was echoing General Wiranto's announcement that Harmoko's statement was not constitutional, that he had spoken out of turn without the agreement of all parliamentary factions. Ironically, PP brought a banner repeating a pun that regime critics had for years leveled against Harmoko when he was Minister of Information: *Harmoko, Hari-Hari Omong Kosong,* "Harmoko Bullshits Daily."

[75] See *Sinar*, July 14, 1998.

[76] He would most likely have things to tell about the involvement of then Jakarta Commander Sjafrie Sjamsudin. As an ethnic Chinese Muslim, Anton Medan appears to have been easily manipulated and was called on to demonstrate his loyalty to Islam, lest he himself become a target. This is the subject of another article, however. Anton was a rival of Yorrys in the gambling circles of Jakarta in the early 1980s. He bragged that he was driving a fancy sports car when Yorrys was driving around in a Honda Civic. Interview, March 18-21, 1998.

even uniforms from other units.[77] By any estimation, he had considerable resources outside of Pemuda Pancasila upon which to draw.

This is not to assert that Pemuda Pancasila took no part in the rioting, but only that if its members did take part, it was for rather different objectives. Assuming that Prabowo mobilized instigators of the destruction on May 13-14, 1998, there are at least two hypotheses about his motives. One is that he was making a personal bid for power, at the expense of "dad-in-law" (and as commander of Kostrad, following in dad-in-law's 1965 footsteps). The other was that he went overboard in an effort to create the pretext for maintaining Suharto in power, with a promotion to ABRI Commander as his bonus. Because of their closeness to Suharto's son Bambang Trihatmodjo and personal loyalty to the Suhartos, Pemuda Pancasila leaders would have cause not to support the former objective and to distrust the latter. At any rate, they appear to have only realized very late what was about to go down. On the evening of May 13, the day after the Trisakti shootings, and as fires were burning in several separate areas of Jakarta, Pemuda Pancasila leaders held a press conference at KNPI Headquarters. Their message was that they supported *reformasi*, but that they understood this to mean "reformation" in all sectors except presidential succession. "I've never heard the students demand a replacement of national leadership," Yapto explained. "This isn't their main demand. Pure [*murni*] students aren't doing that." Yapto offered Pemuda Pancasila's services in supporting the students' struggle for reformation by "disciplining" the demonstrations so that they would not turn to anarchy. Revealingly, he also offered to provide, if asked, PP's services in protecting "vital locations" such as companies, shops, or real estate, adding that PP operatives were highly professional.[78] These statements suggest two things. First, Yapto was reading developments in terms of conflicts between students and Suharto rather than in terms of larger power plays. Though it would be another several days before officials publicly jumped ship, scrambling to distance themselves from Suharto and climb aboard *Reformasi*, most players already assumed the endgame, unwilling to comment one way or the other about Suharto, but actively preparing for his fall. Yapto understood the power plays mainly as challenges to Suharto rather than as developments that had already shot far past Suharto, and this made him a relic. Second, his offer of protection suggests that, even given the fact that it was probably accompanied by a private agreement to riot, he had no conception of the *scale* of what was about to transpire. His offer was motivated by profit.

Events since May 1998 further indicate that contracts for Pemuda Pancasila in *preman* projects may be drying up, with the balance shifting in favor of ascendant Islamic-oriented *preman*. This no doubt reflects the tensions within ABRI between what has been termed Red & White and Green officers, or secular-nationalist versus Islamic factions within ABRI. The composition of the so-called Pam Swakarsa (roughly, Self-Security) "civilian" defenders of the November 1998 Special Session of the MPR dramatically illustrates this division. On November 11, the first day of the session, several Youth Social Organizations, including Pemuda Pancasila, Pemuda Panca Marga, and FKPPI, showed up in uniform to secure the MPR building from student demonstrators, who were challenging the legitimacy of the session. However, they were vastly outnumbered by thousands of plainclothes (*baju preman*)

---

[77] As one rumor had it, high police officials had complained that they were charged for a large number of uniforms they never ordered, which were in fact shipped to East Timor.

[78] Notes, May 14, 1998.

"volunteers," many armed with bamboo spears, brought in from Tanjung Priok, Banten, and elsewhere.[79] Shouting Islamic slogans, these groups were significantly more eager to confront the students physically. After the first day, Pemuda Pancasila and FKPPI withdrew their members, while Pemuda Panca Marga—which, though still considered "Red & White," is (in Jakarta, as explained above) more closely linked to Prabowo—stayed on. The Pam Swakarsa withdrew or were evacuated by the army only after physical challenges from students and the crowds led to fatalities; several of the Pam Swakarsa were beaten or hacked to death. I would suggest that despite its willingness to use violence, Pemuda Pancasila is not prepared to be on the defending side of a battle. During the New Order the main source of its strength was the visibility of a uniform that signified a united ABRI behind it. Yapto and company made the initial effort to return to time-worn patterns of backing-up the government's agenda at the MPR Special Session. They withdrew, however, when they realized that their involvement not only posed a genuine risk, but stood to diminish their popularity and, consequently, their marketability.

Given Pemuda Pancasila's current tarnished reputation and indecisive position, one could predict at least two, not necessarily compatible, futures for the organization. In one future, the organization will get out of the political game and return to its basis in protection. This option seemed likely to anyone who witnessed the bleak mood among members at PP HQ in the immediate aftermath of the May riots. Much of Kota had been burned, and thus a main source of PP livelihood destroyed. A field operative called "the ranger" gave a thumbs up to the news that Liem Sioe Liong's house had been burned down, but he followed it with a sigh. "We have to admit, whatever else, that PP lives from the Chinese," he said, returning to the phone, ringing up possible Chinese clients. In an alternate, or perhaps parallel, future, PP will enter the political scene in the context of *reformasi*, but it will do so by shedding its trademark orange and black camouflage outfit. Yapto notes that PP favors the district electoral system, because PP has members in villages throughout Indonesia, and the organization is sure to win one or two seats in parliament wherever it fields candidates. In this context, it is worth quoting a Bakin sub-team report on *preman*: "*Preman* don't always wear tattoos . . . During the last decade, *preman* used tattoos for group identity. However, because the authorities see tattoos as the mark of *preman*, they have tried to erase this mark. . . . *Preman* these days are more clever than the generation of *preman* before them, and make themselves appear as if they weren't *preman*, so that their operations run more smoothly."[80] True to its

---

[79] Unlike their style for describing such actions before the resignation of Suharto, the mass media widely reported that these Pam Swakarsa were well-organized and promised payment. An internet source *(Kabar dari Pijar,* or *KdP)* also revealed that the Indonesian Catering Entrepreneurs' Association (APJI) had been contracted to coordinate provisions for the Pam Swakarsa during the Special Session, but complained that many of their members were never paid. KdP advised APJI to pursue its complaint with the Indonesian Committee for World Islamic Solidarity (KISDI) chief Ahmad Sumargono and leaders of the Star-Moon Party (Partai Bulan Bintang); both these groups are commonly considered to be connected to Prabowo. *KdP Net*, "Pam Swakarsa mengemplang pengusaha catering Jakarta ratusan juta rupiah" (Pam Swakarsa slaps the faces of Jakarta's catering businessman to the tune of hundreds of millions of rupiah), November 21, 1998.

[80] Mintarsih A. Latief, *Strategi Penanggulangan Preman, Penggunaan Alkohol dan Zat Adiktif Lain* (Strategies for Dealing with *Preman*, Alcohol Abuse, and Other Addictive Substances) (Jakarta: Yayasan Bersama and the World Health Organization, 1997), p. 15. Yayasan Bersama, which released the report, is under Bakolak Inpres 6/1971, mentioned above.

roots in IPKI, Pemuda Pancasila would in this future become an integral part of the new democracy for a reformed Indonesia.

POSTSCRIPT

If political change during the New Order was accomplished more through back street turf wars than through institution building or open competition for office, in the two years following the ouster of Suharto, Indonesia witnessed relatively competitive elections, two new presidents, a parliament more active than it has been in more than a generation, and the birth or demise of all manner of institutions. Yet the period between the original publication of this essay in late 1998 and the time of these revisions in mid-2000 has given little reason to consign *premanism* to history. If anything, the continuing violence in Aceh, West Timor, Maluku, and elsewhere lends new urgency to understanding *premanism*. Though this postscript can offer no thorough discussion of the changing face of *preman* in general or of Pemuda Pancasila and other Youth Social Organizations in particular, a few observations are in order.

Premanism rose to a new level of public concern and acquired new significance with the widespread debate about provocateurs which began in earnest after the release in November 1998 of the Joint Fact-Finding Team's report on the May riots. The subject of provocateurs was further ignited by the rioting and clashes of December 1998 and January 1999 in the Ketapang district of Jakarta, then soon thereafter in Kupang, West Timor, and in Ambon. Everyone, from social commentators to the police, accepted that the initial violence in Ambon, at least, was sparked by clashes involving *preman*, after which it spread seemingly beyond control. Unlike May 1998, where rioting was meant to send a message about the consequences of allowing "the masses" to express rage against a regime, there was nothing obviously "political" about these incidents. The "communal violence" between Muslims and Christians that the incidents instigated appeared as "horizontal conflicts" between "elements of society" rather than as potentially insurrectionary violence.

And yet, the public discourse on provocateurs repeatedly brought the state back in. Whereas during the New Order commanders and officials succeeded in representing provocateurs—more typically then called "third parties" or "infiltrators"—as subversives, discussions of these new-style provocateurs generally concur that their sponsors are established political elites with a vested interest in opposing rapid political change. The object of promoting horizontal violence, as the theory has it, is to maintain the power of the military or to halt criminal investigations into corruption and past abuses perpetrated by the chief beneficiaries of the New Order—most notably "Suharto and his cronies." Such accusations have frequently appeared in the press, outing Suharto or top commanders like Wiranto as the puppetmasters of the violence. The Human Rights Abuse Investigation Commission's determination that Wiranto bore ultimate responsibility for failing to halt the militias' scorched earth campaign in East Timor which followed the referendum of August 1999—and the implication that he directed it—became a public pretext for his removal from office.

Military and elite involvement in provoking violence through *preman* proxies had thus graduated from public secret to a matter of open accusation. Yet such public exposure alone cannot halt the violence. Until judicial and other institutions are prepared to hold the sponsors of violence accountable, public accusation will only serve to advance the nominal objective of the violence itself insofar as it effectively demonstrates that these elites still have the power to promote extra-judicial violence and have no reservations about doing so when it advances their interests. The more they appear to be in control, the more in fact they are.

If an earlier logic of disavowal is nevertheless still in effect, contracts for violence are now more open for tender than they have been previously. Established groups like Pemuda Pancasila have been bypassed in favor of new talent less obviously connected to the old regime. Very few of the militia leaders in East Timor appear to have been members of New Order Youth Social Organizations or even the other various pro-Indonesia East Timorese organizations established during the last years of the regime. Nevertheless, expertise in the logistics of organizing chaos has not been discounted. Pemuda Pancasila's Yorrys Raweyai has been connected to Ambonese *preman* accused of sparking the violence in both Ketapang and Ambon. In his involvement in the Papuan independence movement, Yorrys has likewise preferred not to involve Pemuda Pancasila, choosing instead to mobilize a network of ethnic Papuans in his capacity as a leader of the Irian Jaya Society Familial Association.

Since the fall of Suharto, Pemuda Pancasila has, for the most part, managed to maintain a low profile and avoid open involvement in agitation.[81] PP has instead followed the dual routes suggested in the conclusion of this article: parliamentary politics combined with efforts to maintain or expand its hold of sectors of the informal and illegal economy. Although nationally visible parliamentarians like Yorrys were ousted, other Pemuda Pancasila leaders and politicians held or gained seats at national and local levels.[82] At its national congress in April 1999, PP decided to free each member to support his party of choice, which meant effective access to them all. Meanwhile, PP has in some cases been able to take advantage of institutional changes to shore up its position on the streets. The separation of the police from the rest of the armed forces enabled PP in Medan to encourage the police to crack down on IPK, its chief rival for control of gambling whose main backer has been the regional military command.[83]

For *preman*, multiparty politics produced new opportunities. Political parties, in the rush to produce the appearance of party militancy and grassroots support, recruited them *en masse* to augment their party youth wings and respective task forces (*satgas*). Many Pemuda Pancasila members traded in their orange and black camouflage for the basic black and red trim of PDI Perjuangan's *satgas*, helping to boost the impressive turnouts for the party's campaign rallies. Campaign season standoffs in Jakarta between PDI Perjuangan backers and Habibie supporters nearly

---

[81] There have been exceptions. In April 1999, several Pemuda Pancasila members dressed in PDI Perjuangan outfits violently disrupted a Golkar election campaign rally in Purbalingga, Central Java, evidently in an effort to replay the scheduled "chaos" at Golkar's rally at Banteng Square in 1982. See, for example, *Minggu*, April 11, 1999.

[82] The national secretary-general of PP retained his Golkar seat after the 1999 elections. Other leaders became influential figures in other political parties, such as one PP senior in Medan who now sits on PAN's advisory board. PAN, the National Mandate Party (Partai Amanat Nasional) is the political party of Amien Rais.

[83] In the midst of protracted street battles between IPK and PP in Medan in December 1999, the police mobile brigades took sides, shooting up the headquarters of IPK and the private residence of its chief, Olo Panggabean.

turned to open clashes, in part due to the participation of *preman* on both sides, including *preman* from Tanah Abang backing Habibie under banners such as that of PPP's (Partai Persatuan Pembangunan, the Unity Development Party) Ka'bah Youth Movement (GPK). Many *preman* who had thrown their support behind Habibie found themselves disenfranchised following his defeat. These days, however, some of them have found new employment fanning the flames of conflict in hot spots such as Maluku. Laskar Jihad, another group which had supported Habibie, deployed some three thousand members to Ambon in May 2000.

The longer these conflicts persist, the further President Abdurrahman Wahid's nascent government is destabilized. If Wahid cannot resolve them through formal institutions, he may yet elect to respond in kind. He was named the Commander-in-Chief of Banser, Nahdatul Ulama's own paramilitary force, at a mass rally involving hundreds of thousands of Banser personnel held in April 2000 at the East Java Regional Military Command's Headquarters. The Banser rally was widely read as a show of force in response to Laskar Jihad, which had only made public its plans to ship its own members to Ambon a few weeks before.

This shows that the new president does not in principle object to building his power in ways not altogether dissimilar from that of his long-reigning predecessor: through the mass mobilization of civilians in fatigues whose loyalty is beyond question yet whose actions are beyond the responsibility of the state.[84] To be an effective source of power, however, this juncture of the loyalty of the leader's supporters and the unaccountability of the leader for their actions must produce a space for positively encouraged criminal terror. To the extent that Wahid is incapable of or unwilling to encourage Banser in the way that Suharto encouraged Pemuda Pancasila, he will never succeed in fighting fire with fire, *preman* with *preman*. In this respect, the only way to cut the power of *premanism* is to devote all resources to supporting genuine legal accountability for anyone accused of employing provocateurs of violent conflict. Public accusation without accountability only succeeds in publicizing the effectiveness of terror as a lasting source of power.

---

[84] Already, Banser has shown itself willing to use extra-legal means to defend the president with tactics comparable to those of New Order organizations of the type of Pemuda Pancasila. Banser occupied the offices of the *Java Post* and threatened to shut it down after the daily published accusations of corruption and nepotism involving Wahid, his family, and associates.

THE TROUBLE WITH NORMAL: THE INDONESIAN MILITARY, PARAMILITARIES, AND THE FINAL SOLUTION IN EAST TIMOR

Douglas Kammen[1]

> The Indonesian military could not remain in power without the help of civilian "militias" composed of native East Timorese. Abolish the militias and Indonesian domination over East Timor will end.
>
> – Aniceto Gutterres[2]

On August 30, 1999, a United Nations-sponsored referendum was held in East Timor. Despite several months of organized terror by elements of the Indonesian military and the so-called "pro-autonomy" militias, there was enormous voter turnout (98.5 percent of the eligible electorate) and a strong vote in favor of independence (78.5 percent). The United Nations and foreign observers jubilantly declared the referendum a resounding success. Two days later this euphoria was shattered by the outbreak of massive violence. Armed gangs set about destroying cities, towns, and villages and attacking pro-independence supporters and Catholic clergy. Thousands of non-Timorese fled the territory, most returning to their native places in Indonesia. Hundreds of thousands of East Timorese were forcibly

[1] I would like to thank Ben Abel, Ben Anderson, Sidney Jones, Made Tony Supriatma, Sarah Maxim, and Jos Wibisono for their encouragement and valuable comments on this essay. I am grateful to Charles Petrin for exceptionally capable and knowledgeable assistance. The title of this essay is borrowed from a song by Canadian singer Bruce Cockburn.

[2] Interviewed by Made Tony Supriatma in Dili, April 25, 1998. Aniceto Gutteres is the director of Yayasan HAK, a Dili-based human rights organization.

evacuated across the border into Indonesian West Timor, while several hundred thousands more fled into the hills.[3]

With coverage of the violence and destruction broadcast around the world, United Nations officials and foreign governments reacted with shock and outrage to the devastation and depopulation. During the run-up to the referendum, the UN had repeatedly promised that it would protect the East Timorese from violence. In the days after the vote, UN Secretary-General Kofi Annan was quoted as saying "If any of us had an inkling that it was going to be this chaotic, I don't think anyone would have gone forward" with the referendum.[4] Two months later Ian Martin, the outgoing chief of the UN mission to East Timor, admitted that, despite knowledge that some elements in the Indonesian military favored a "scorched-earth policy," the UN had "miscalculated," counting on the Indonesian government and military to safeguard their international reputations by preventing atrocities.[5] Whether the UN was in the dark, as Annan claimed, or whether in fact it had taken a carefully calculated gamble, as suggested by Martin, the truth is that detailed reports had emerged early in 1999 revealing the nature of the Indonesian military's intentions and, more importantly, the contingency plans that lay behind the massive violence following the referendum.

Indonesia's invasion of its neighbor in December 1975 was poorly planned and met fierce resistance. Despite its insecure and only partial territorial control, in 1976 Indonesia declared that it had "integrated" East Timor as its twenty-seventh province. The real problem lay in securing international acceptance and recognition of the alleged act of integration. Although only a few countries showed any real concern about the Indonesian annexation (and a number actively abetted the invasion and military occupation), the legality of Indonesia's act remained in question in the international arena. Two weeks after the initial invasion, the United Nations Security Council condemned the Indonesian action and called for it to withdraw. In late 1976 the UN again condemned the occupation and refused to acknowledge Indonesia's claim to have integrated the territory as the Republic's twenty-seventh province. Votes and discussion in the UN, the European Community, and the US Congress against Indonesia were to become an annual exercise and, though lacking in enforcement mechanisms, their regular condemnations of Indonesia's occupation of East Timor were a constant reminder of the dilemma of annexation.[6]

Once a common tool of statecraft, since the Second World War territorial annexation has become increasingly rare. In 1960 India swallowed the tiny Portuguese colony of Goa, but did so by offering full participation in a democratic polity. In the early 1970s Morocco's annexation of Spanish Sahara was met with long-standing resistance and remains disputed. Argentina's grab for Britain's sheep paddocks in the Falkland Islands and Saddam Hussein's invasion of the Kuwaiti emirate and its oilfields both stand as failed attempts at annexation. In contrast to

---

[3] This is out of an estimated population of only 800,000.

[4] Quoted in "Diplomatic Gambles at the Highest Levels Failed Voters in East Timor," *The Wall Street Journal*, October 21, 1999.

[5] See "UN Official In E. Timor Says World Community Miscalculated," *Associated Press*, posted on Joyo@aol.com, November 18, 1999.

[6] The UN votes are listed in the chronology provided in Peter Carey and G. Carter Bentley, eds., *East Timor at the Crossroads: The Forging of a Nation* (London: Cassell, 1995), pp. 238-250.

this limited universe of cases, Indonesia's annexation and sham integration of the former Portuguese colony stands out and is notable both for the way it was implemented—the brutal occupation of the country, coupled with extensive efforts to "Indonesianize" the population—and for the way it was received—with *de facto* international acceptance belatedly followed by reversal under the UN-sponsored referendum.

If the interests and motivation behind the pre- and post-referendum violence are relatively clear, their origins lie further back in East Timor's tragic recent history. This chapter traces the lineages of military rule and paramilitary activity in East Timor over the past two decades. It argues that the recent devastation of East Timor and its population was the end product of an ongoing attempt to "normalize" the occupied territory. For Indonesia "normalization" meant demonstrating to the world that East Timor was not under military occupation, that it was not governed by a special administrative and legal status, and that it was being treated no differently from any other province. This process of normalization proceeded along two countervailing axes—demilitarization and remilitarization. While the former involved the withdrawal of troops and transformation of the East Timor military commands, the latter should be understood as both a necessary counterbalance to these efforts and an active strategy carried out by segments of the armed forces to maintain the military presence. Thus, over the course of two decades, efforts by the Suharto regime to demilitarize the administrative and legal rule in East Timor were offset by the further militarization of East Timorese society.

THE ORIGINS AND INSTITUTIONALIZATION OF PARAMILITARY "TEAMS"

One of Indonesia's first hesitant attempts to modify its occupation of East Timor came in March 1983. In the face of increasing rebel attacks, the Indonesian military elite instructed the commander of the Dili-based sub-regional Military Resort Command (Korem 164), Colonel Purwanto, to sign a secret cease-fire with the president of the Revolutionary Front for an Independent East Timor (Fretilin), José Alexandre "Xanana" Gusmaõ.[7] An admission of the military's inability to eliminate the resistance through combat operations alone, the cease-fire was intended to open a two-pronged approach in the occupied territory. On the one hand, Indonesian leaders hoped that the cessation of combat activities would enable Jakarta to begin to secure foreign recognition of the integrated territory. On the other hand, Indonesia believed that the appearance of a "softer" policy within the territory would reduce popular support for the resistance. Tentative though it was, the aim of the cease-fire was the nominal "normalization" of Indonesian rule.

The timing of the cease-fire initiative reflected the arc of Indonesia's national political cycle. In 1982 the New Order held national legislative elections, with

---

[7] The cease-fire is discussed in John G. Taylor, *Indonesia's Forgotten War: The Hidden History of East Timor* (London: Zed Books Ltd., 1991), pp. 135-137. Fretilin's armed front is the National Liberation Armed Forces of East Timor (Falintil). According to Arnold Kohen, in 1983 the Indonesian military also sent a team to East Timor to assess the possibilities of holding a referendum, but concluded that it would lose a genuinely free ballot. Arnold Kohen, *From the Place of the Dead: Bishop Belo and the Struggle for East Timor* (Oxford: Lion Publishing, 1999), p. 171.

the regime's electoral vehicle Golkar claiming 99.4 percent of the vote in East Timor.[8] In early 1983 the Indonesian People's Consultative Assembly (MPR, Majelis Permusyawaratan Rakyat) rubber-stamped Suharto's selection to a fourth term in office. As was customary during the New Order, Suharto used the occasion of a new cabinet to appoint a new military Armed Forces Commander, General Leonardus Benyamin Murdani. And in May, Major-General Dading Kalbuadi, the long-serving and brutal commander of the Military Region 16, which covered East Timor, was replaced.[9] With the completion of the national electoral charade, the Suharto regime became eager to extend its claims to legitimate rule so that they encompassed its troublesome twenty-seventh province. It did so by signing the secret cease-fire and turning to a political solution to the East Timor problem.

The cease-fire bore immediate results in terms of Indonesia's international relations. On July 28, 1983, an Australian Parliamentary delegation arrived in East Timor to assess conditions.[10] This visit paved the way for Indonesian-Australian talks and culminated in 1985 with "the Labour government's *de jure* recognition of Indonesian sovereignty" in East Timor.[11] With the Australian visit completed, the new Armed Forces Commander General Murdani and the Indonesian military (ABRI) quickly broke the peace. On August 8, one week after the Australian delegation departed from East Timor, ABRI opened a new offensive, and a month later President Suharto declared a state of emergency in East Timor and the initiation of Operation Unity (Operasi Persatuan).[12]

The renewal of combat operations was accompanied by new emphasis on the use of East Timorese combatants. Intent on employing East Timorese against East Timorese, ABRI had established two "organic" (i.e. locally-based) battalions attached to the Dili-based Korem 164 in the late 1970s.[13] During the heavy fighting in this period, ABRI combat units also relied on the use of locally-recruited paramilitary "teams" with knowledge of regional dialects and terrain. The size and role of these auxiliary "teams" was greatly expanded at the time of the 1983 cease-fire and subsequent offensives.[14]

The career of Juliaõ Fraga illustrates the development and role of these non-regular East Timorese "teams." In 1981, then Private Fraga, aged thirty, was appointed commander of the fifty-two-member Railakan I combat team attached to the Indonesian Special Forces. In 1982 Railakan I was involved in armed combat in January (capturing thirty-two rebels and five weapons) and February (killing

---

[8] Statistics from "Penegasan Diosis Dili" (Affirmation of the Diocese of Dili), *Suara Timor Timur* (*STT*), May 28, 1997. (Hereafter *Suara Timor Timur* will be abbreviated *STT*.) Based on interviews, Taylor provides slightly different figures and claims that more votes were cast than there were eligible voters. See *Indonesia's Forgotten War*, p. 133.

[9] Dading Kalbuadi played a major role in the initial invasion, was commander of the East Timor military command from 1975-1978, and then served an exceptionally long four and a half years as commander of Kodam 16, which includes East Timor. Cited in Editors, "Current Data on the Indonesian Military Elite," *Indonesia* 36 (October 1983): 122.

[10] John Taylor, *Indonesia's Forgotten War*, pp. 137-140.

[11] Michael E. Salla, "Australian Foreign Policy and East Timor," *Australian Journal of International Affairs* 49,2 (1995): 217.

[12] Taylor, *Indonesia's Forgotten War*, p. 206.

[13] See, for example, *Suara Merdeka*, July 29, 1978.

[14] See the extensive military documents in Carmel Budiardjo and Liem Soei Liong, *The War Against East Timor* (London: Zed Books, 1984).

eight and capturing two weapons), and in September it attacked Xanana's forces on Mount Tilon (killing nine and capturing two weapons). In the wake of the cease-fire, Railakan I nearly doubled in size to ninety members and was made part of Wanra (abbreviated from *Perlawanan Rakyat*), the People's Militia attached to the military structure. The change in status was a crude effort to accommodate these non-regular combat "teams" within Indonesia's outdated doctrine of "people's defense." Following these changes, in 1984 Juliaõ Fraga's Railakan I was involved in further combat, in March (capturing twelve rebels and two weapons), September, (killing fifteen and capturing one weapon), October (killing eight), and December (killing nine).[15]

The 1983 cease-fire was a tentative, indeed abortive, first attempt to place a new spin on Indonesian rule in East Timor. The cessation of armed combat was seen as a necessary step in securing foreign recognition of Indonesian sovereignty in East Timor. It was accompanied, however, by alternative forms of violence, as the Indonesian military placed renewed emphasis on the development and use of East Timorese combat "teams." Expanded and given more formal status alongside the military structure and ideology, these teams played a crucial role in Indonesian offensives against the East Timorese resistance. This process—national elections, policy shifts on East Timor, and heightened use of paramilitary squads—was to be repeated and deepened with striking regularity at five-year intervals.

FROM *APERTURA* TO MASSACRE

Indonesia's second attempt to "normalize" the status of East Timor was initiated in late 1988. Based on military intelligence assessments and its own propaganda about the success with which it had integrated the former Portuguese colony, Indonesia announced the "opening" of East Timor in December 1988. This involved removing travel restrictions for East Timorese within the territory, allowing Indonesian citizens to enter freely, easing press restrictions, and permitting foreign tourists to visit eight of the thirteen districts.[16]

This decision was motivated by two considerations. The first factor was the changing nature of the East Timorese resistance. While armed resistance continued throughout the 1980s, this in itself never posed a serious threat to Indonesian rule. Beginning in the mid-1980s, however, "Fretilin strengthened contacts with young Timorese in the cities, especially Dili, and encouraged a policy of non-violent resistance" to Indonesian rule.[17] This move away from armed resistance allowed Jakarta to pursue new political avenues.

The second factor contributing to a policy shift was the annoying question of international relations. In 1986, Portugal became a member of the European Union. Given the EU's rule requiring unanimity in deciding foreign policy, this effectively ruled out the possibility of European recognition of Indonesian rule. Throughout 1988 the European Union raised the East Timor issue with increasing frequency, culminating in September with the European Parliament calling for Indonesia to

---

[15] The information in this paragraph was obtained through personal communications.

[16] See "Timor Timur di Ujung Tahun" (East Timor at the Turn of the Year), *Tempo*, January 14, 1989.

[17] Adam Schwarz, *A Nation in Waiting: Indonesia in the 1990s* (Boulder, Co.: Westview Press, 1994), pp. 208-209.

withdraw troops and to allow the people to exercise their right to self-determination. Six weeks later 229 members of the US Congress sent a letter of concern about conditions in East Timor to Secretary of State George Schultz.[18] Despite objections by hard-liners in the military, Suharto "was swayed by diplomats who contended that Indonesia had to respond to international concerns over East Timor if it was to achieve a respectable international profile."[19]

Once again, the timing of the shift in East Timor policy corresponded to the completion of the national electoral cycle. In 1987 Indonesia held national legislative elections, with Golkar "winning" 73.1 percent nationally and an overwhelming 93.6 percent of the vote in East Timor.[20] In early 1988 the MPR selected Suharto to serve a fifth term as president. This time Suharto acted to preempt the influence of the powerful ABRI Commander General Murdani, replacing him before the MPR met and appointing the compliant General Try Sutrisno to lead the military.[21] Having fulfilled the formalities required by procedural democracy and reasserted his authority over the armed forces, Suharto agreed to calls from within the senior political elite for a new policy on East Timor.[22] Following a brief visit to Dili, on November 5, 1988, Suharto announced Presidential Decree No. 62/1988 granting East Timor "equal status" with Indonesia's twenty-six other provinces.[23]

The decision to open East Timor set in motion a series of changes in military personnel. In April 1989, Colonel Rudolf Warouw was appointed as commander of the Korem 164. Further personnel changes followed in both the territorial and

---

[18] Taylor, *Indonesia's Forgotten War*, pp. 209-210.

[19] Schwarz, *Nation in Waiting*, p. 210. According to Herb Feith, economists also played a role, arguing that greater openness in East Timor would lessen political abuses of power and economic distortions. Herb Feith, "East Timor: The Opening Up, the Crackdown and the Possibility of a Durable Settlement," in *Indonesia Assessment, 1992: Political Perspectives on the 1990s*, ed. Harold Crouch and Hal Hill (Canberra: Research School of Pacific Studies, 1992), p. 63.

[20] "Penegasan Diosis Dili," *STT*, May 28, 1997.

[21] Discussed in Editors, "Current Data on the Indonesian Military Elite," *Indonesia* 48 (October 1989): 65-96.

[22] This coincided roughly with the adoption of a more tolerant approach towards dissent and the press within Indonesia, known by the name *keterbukaan* (openness). No explicit links were made between *keterbukaan* and East Timor, however. See Sidney Jones, *The Limits of Openness: Human Rights in Indonesia and East Timor* (New York: Human Rights Watch, 1994).

[23] See "Keputusan Presiden Republik Indonesia, Nomor 62 Tahun 1988 Tentang Penyelenggaraan Pemerintahan dan Pembangunan di Propinsi Daerah Tingkat I Timor Timor" (Decision of the President of the Indonesian Republic No. 62/1988 on the Organization of Administration and Development in the Province of East Timor), published in *Himpunan Peraturan Negara* (Collected State Regulations), Triwulan IV, 1988 (Jakarta: Sekretariat Negara Republik Indonesia), pp. 1103-1105. This decree transfers administrative responsibility for East Timor from "central authority" (Tingkat Pusat) to the various state organs (Departemen dan Lembaga Pemerintah Non Departemen) responsible for provincial government affairs in Indonesia. Note that it does not mention the existence of a special military status for East Timor; contrary to popular belief both within and outside of Indonesia, no such special status existed. The only official reference I have ever found to East Timor being classified as a "Military Operations Area" (Daerah Operasi Militer, DOM) appeared in mid-1998, when the question of DOM status in Aceh was under public discussion. See, "Danrem Tono: Timtim tetap Daerah Operasi Militer" (Korem Commander Tono: East Timor Remains a Military Operations Area), *STT*, August 11, 1998.

combat commands. Warouw set out to implement the new soft-line Operation Smile (*Operasi Senyum*), allowing greater travel, releasing a number of political prisoners, and reducing the use of torture during interrogations. These changes were intended to assuage foreign concern about East Timor. During this period Indonesia also allowed a number of foreign dignitaries tightly supervised visits to the territory to see for themselves the success of integration. The most notable of these visits was that of Pope John Paul II in October 1989, who was greeted by huge crowds and was clearly sympathetic to the plight of the East Timorese people.

But the new policy of openness presented a dilemma: while soft-line policies were seen as being necessary to ease international concern and win recognition of Indonesian sovereignty, they also created greater political space for urban protest. This dilemma was particularly apparent on the occasion of foreign visits, and it led to the paradoxical situation in which greater openness was accompanied by the heightened use of covert operations and terror. In July 1989, for example, at precisely the time that the territorial Korem 164 under Colonel Warouw was implementing Operation Smile, the combat Security Operations Command (Komando Operasi Keamanan, Koopskam) conducted a new offensive against Fretilin, with the aim of capturing Xanana Gusmaõ. At the same time, new covert operations were unleashed in Dili and the urban centers. During this period hooded gangsters, referred to locally as *buffo* (clowns), terrorized Dili at night.[24] One Timorese student activist offered the following account of the period:

> In order to cow and intimidate the population in advance of the Pope's visit, numerous Timorese were rounded up, imprisoned and tortured. Lieutenant-Colonel Prabowo, President Suharto's son-in-law, at that time serving in East Timor, personally tortured [my friend] Idelfonso Araújo, breaking his leg and his teeth. This climate of terror, however, did not prevent the demonstration from taking place at the end of the papal mass on October 12.[25]

Further changes in the military structure in East Timor were introduced in May 1990, when the old Koopskam was replaced by the East Timor Operations Implementation Command (Komando Pelaksana Operasi, Kolakops).[26] The name change was not simply an attempt to place a kinder face on military rule; it was also intended as a warning to military personnel that new standards were to be enforced. In line with these moves, Warouw was appointed to command Kolakops and promoted in rank, replacing the hard-line Brigadier-General Mulyadi. Building on the policies begun the year before and in his new capacity as

---

[24] Editors, "Current Data on the Indonesian Military Elite: July 1, 1989-January 1, 1992," *Indonesia* 53 (April 1992): 99. They note that "these are likely to be successors of the notorious *nanggala* of the late 1970s and 1980s—East Timorese collaborators given special training by the Special Forces for intelligence, interrogation, and assassination work."

[25] Donaciano Gomes, "The East Timor Intifada: Testimony of a Student Activist," in *East Timor at the Crossroads*, ed. Carey and Bentley, p. 107. Gomes goes on to describe arrests and torture following the demonstration.

[26] See the detailed commemorative volume *Kolakops Timor Timur Dalam Gambar Dan Peristiwa Tahun 1992-93* (The East Timor Kolakops in Pictures and Events, 1992-93) (Dili: no publisher, 1993). It is worth noting that in 1989 a sister command was established in Aceh named the Red Net Kolakops (Kolakops Jaring Merah).

commander of the combat command, Warouw sought to deepen the soft policy on dissent and further normalize Indonesian rule.

Throughout this period Indonesian Foreign Minister Ali Alatas actively worked to bury the East Timor question by agreeing to hold UN-sponsored dialogues with Portugal. Against the wishes of military hard-liners, Alatas invited a Portuguese delegation to visit East Timor in 1990, and plans were made for a delegation to arrive in October. Fearing a repeat of the demonstrations that had accompanied the 1989 Papal visit and the 1990 visit by US ambassador to Indonesia John Monjo, military personnel on the ground in East Timor again stepped up the use of terror. As Adam Schwarz describes it:

> The military, more worried than it let on, began a campaign of intimidation and harassment to dissuade would-be protesters from demonstrating during the Portuguese visit. An important tool in this campaign was the use of Timorese as paid intelligence agents. As documented by Timorese refugees, priests, Governor Carrascalao, foreign aid workers, and human rights activists, the tactic had a highly disruptive effect on Timorese society, turned families against one another and greatly heightened the general level of distrust. Nightime raids of homes of suspected protesters became common and hundreds of Timorese were incarcerated without trial.[27]

The new policy soon exacerbated tensions within the Indonesian military command responsible for East Timor. The Editors of the journal *Indonesia* have written: "It is rather clear that one of the missions of the popular Menadonese Commander, Brig. Gen. Rudolf Samuel Warouw . . . was to clear up the conduct of the entrenched local military mafia." They go on to argue that the policy of disciplining hundreds of military personnel during this period "naturally made him [Warouw] unpopular with many of his subordinates and encouraged plotting against him."[28]

Additional tensions emerged in the restructuring of combat troops posted to East Timor.[29] The first of these involved adjusting the relationship between the combat and territorial commands. Heightened foreign scrutiny of Indonesian rule meant that expressly "combat" units would need to play a less conspicuous role. Similarly, attempts to encourage new investment required assuring the business community that the war was over, something best achieved by emphasizing the territorial administration over the combat command. The second, even more significant, dynamic at work in the early 1990s involved new central controls over combat units posted in East Timor. One of the units that played a regular role in the Timor campaign during the 1980s was the Army Strategic Reserves (Kostrad)'s Third Airborne Brigade (Brigif Linud 3) headquartered in Maros, South Sulawesi. The peculiar feature of this Brigade was that during the 1980s it operated

---

[27] Schwarz, *Nation in Waiting*, p. 211.

[28] Editors, "Current Data on the Indonesian Military Elite: July 1, 1989-January 1, 1992," *Indonesia* 53 (April 1992): 98.

[29] The following section is modified from Douglas Kammen, "Notes on the Transformation of the East Timor Military Command and Its Implications for Indonesia," *Indonesia* 67 (April 1999): 65-66.

independently of the two Java-based Kostrad Infantry Divisions, reporting directly to the Kostrad commander. This permitted it unusual freedom from immediate supervision. In April 1991, as part of the overall shift in administrative emphasis in East Timor from Kolakops to Korem 164, this Brigade was now put directly under the command of the West Java-based Kostrad First Infantry Division.[30] This reorganization was intended to provide greater coordination and control over combat units stationed in East Timor and to prevent officers and units from acting outside of the chain of command. Its consequences were the opposite.

These dynamics—foreign visits, structural change in the dual military commands, the increased use of covert action—came to a head in late 1991 as officers threatened by these developments sought to reverse the opening of East Timor and to discredit Brigadier-General Warouw.[31] In October the Portuguese visit was canceled, suggesting that the intimidation was working and providing military personnel with a partial respite from foreign scrutiny.[32] On October 28 a clash between pro-independence and pro-integration youths at the Motael church in Dili resulted in two deaths. On the morning of November 12, a funeral mass was held at the Motael church for one of the men killed two weeks earlier, after which several thousand mourners walked to the Santa Cruz cemetery to lay flowers. During the procession military personnel attempted to confiscate pro-independence banners and a scuffle broke out. A short time later, as the procession reached the cemetery, a column of soldiers opened fire with automatic weapons. Hundreds were gunned down, others bayoneted.[33] Thanks to the presence of foreign journalists, one of whom smuggled out video coverage, the Dili massacre was broadcast for the world to see.

In the face of fierce international condemnation, military officials and politicians in Jakarta resorted to denials, finger-pointing, and, finally, to the

---

[30] The history of the Brigade is worth noting. Special Forces Group 3 was established in 1963 from troops that had participated in the campaign to "liberate" West Irian from the Dutch. In 1985, as part of General Murdani's reorganization of the military structure, Group 3 became Special Forces Airborne Infantry Brigade 3 (Brigif Linud 3 Kopassus); the following year it was transferred from Special Forces to Kostrad. In a 1996 interview about Special Forces under his command, Brigadier-General Prabowo commented, "at the moment the dormitory [*asrama*] in Ujung Pandang [Maros] belongs to Kostrad." Although Brigade 3 had been transferred to Kostrad more than a decade earlier, Prabowo's comment suggests that he viewed this as a temporary state of affairs. See, "Brigjen TNI Prabowo Subianto: Ada Kelompok Yang Mau Huru-Hara" (Brig.-Gen. Prabowo Subianto: There's a Group That Wants Chaos), *Tiras*, July 14, 1996.

[31] Two central figures in these efforts were Lieutenant-Colonel Prabowo Subianto, President Suharto's son-in-law, who was then commander of the 328th Infantry Battalion, and his military academy classmate Lieutenant-Colonel Sjafrie Syamsudin, then commander of Special Forces Infantry Battalion 1. Although no evidence is available, it seems likely that they were acting on their own initiative rather than at the behest of members of the military elite or the president.

[32] The details of the Portuguese parliamentary mission are provided in Feith, "East Timor," p. 67.

[33] A useful description, based on interviews shortly after the massacre, is Schwarz, *Nation in Waiting*, p. 212. There are reports of a second massacre in the days that followed. See "Santa Cruz Massacre: Keating, Evans deny Dili cover-up," *Sydney Morning Herald*, November 11, 1998, and "Killing continued after 1991 East Timor cemetery massacre: press," *AFP*, posted on Joyo@aol.com, November 14, 1998.

establishment of a Military Honor Board commissioned to investigate the massacre, a pretense of accountability. Suharto promptly ordered the summary and highly publicized sacking of both Military Region 9 (formerly 16) commander Major-General Sintong Panjaitan and Kolakops commander Brigadier-General Warouw.[34] A number of middle-ranking officers responsible for the units on duty in East Timor were quickly sidelined, and staff members in East Timor were replaced.[35] External battalions were hastily withdrawn and replaced by a large number of new battalions, including at least six external territorial battalions and three combat battalions from the Army Strategic Reserve Command (see Table 1, below). Finally, in August 1992, a new offensive, code-named Operation Completion, was launched, resulting in November in the arrest of Xanana Gusmaõ who, charged with masterminding the Santa Cruz demonstrations and violence, was sentenced on criminal charges (first to life, later reduced by Presidential amnesty to twenty years) and imprisoned in Jakarta. Indonesia's second attempt to normalize its rule in East Timor thus came full circle.

TRANSFORMING THE EAST TIMOR MILITARY COMMAND AND THE RISE OF TERROR

Indonesia's third attempt to normalize its rule in East Timor was initiated on April 30, 1993, when the Kolakops command was liquidated and all responsibilities for security in East Timor were transferred to the territorial Korem 164. The move was a direct response to continued international outcry over the 1991 Santa Cruz massacre and, in the context of the end of the Cold War, self-congratulatory international calls for democratization. Thus began another round of push-me-pull-me demilitarization and remilitarization in East Timor.

Once again, a shift in policy on East Timor was introduced following the successful completion of an electoral cycle in Indonesia. In 1992 national legislative elections were held, with Golkar winning a carefully targeted 68 percent of the national vote and claiming 82.6 percent in East Timor. The tally in East Timor showed an 11 percent decrease in voter turnout from the previous election, reflecting a partial reduction in electoral fraud rather than any real increase in East Timorese use of the ballot box as a means of protest. The following year the MPR convened and obediently confirmed Suharto's appointment to a sixth term in office. A new cabinet of loyalists was soon installed and, after a wide-ranging reshuffle of military personnel under the leadership of short-tenured ABRI Commander General Edi Sudradjat, the compliant General Feisal Tanjung was appointed to head the military for the next five years.[36]

---

[34] Sintong was quick to absolve Warouw of blame for the massacre, calling him "the best and most loyal officer I have ever commanded in Military Region IX/Udayana." Quoted in "'Warrouw [sic] adalah perwira terbaik'" ('Warouw is the Best Officer'), *Angkatan Bersenjata*, January 9, 1992.

[35] By contrast, the small cohort of officers most immediately involved in the massacre all fared quite well after 1991. Together, these officers were to play a central role in the disappearances of activists, anti-ethnic Chinese riots, and rapes in and around Jakarta in May 1998, that culminated in Suharto's resignation. See my "Notes," p. 70.

[36] The politics of these moves are discussed in Editors, "Current Data on the Indonesian Military Elite: January 1, 1992-August 31, 1993," *Indonesia* 56 (October 1993).

The military proudly justified the 1993 transformation of the military command in terms of the success of its mission in East Timor. The outgoing Kolakops commander, Brigadier-General Theo Syafei, explained that "the simplification of the military organization is a sign of greater stability and security" in the province. Commander of Military Region 9, Major-General Suwardi, added that the presence of rebel leader Mauhunu in the jungle no longer posed an obstacle to the cherished goal of development.[37] The abolition of Kolakops was accompanied by a reduction in the number of external battalions and total number of troops posted in East Timor. During this period military officers emphasized the "civic" nature of the military presence, discussed the possibility of further troop withdrawals, and brought in foreign journalists to relay these messages to the international community.[38] In April 1994, the number of battalions in East Timor was reduced to seven, a level at which it remained for the next three years.[39]

Closer examination reveals that the military claim that the Kolakops combat command in East Timor had been liquidated was only a partial truth, for in addition to the command staff stationed at Kolakops headquarters in Dili and external battalions regularly assigned to duty under this command, the Kolakops structure also included two combat areas, code-named Sectors A and B. Were the military truly to dismantle Kolakops, it would also have abolished combat Sectors A and B and removed their respective commanders. This was not done. Instead, at exactly the time that Kolakops was abolished, new commanders were appointed to these sectors. These officers held dual appointments as commanders of infantry brigades in the Army Strategic Reserve Command (Kostrad, Komando Strategis Angkatan Darat). In other words, the command of troops in East Timor was being shifted from a single, visible military structure within East Timor to units and officers who, formally posted thousands of kilometers away, continued what had become a phantom combat command.[40]

Meanwhile, ominous changes were taking place away from East Timor. In February 1993, Colonel Prabowo was transferred from his post as Chief of Staff of Kostrad's 17th Airborne Brigade, a position he held at the time of the Santa Cruz massacre, to command Group 3, the Special Forces Education Center located in Batujajar, West Java.[41] Based in the hills of West Java, and thus safely out of direct public view, Prabowo was in an excellent position to oversee the training of Special Forces troops for use in East Timor and, increasingly, in the military operations then in full-swing in Aceh as well.[42] Indeed, under Prabowo Group 3 quickly became the new nerve-center of the East Timor campaign, a campaign that was losing even the most rudimentary trappings of a combat mission and was taking

---

[37] Theo Syafei is paraphrased in "Kolakops Timtim segera dibubarkan" (The East Timor Kolakops To Be Immediately Disbanded), *Angkatan Bersenjata*, March 16, 1993.

[38] See, for example, "Tugas utama ABRI di Timtim 'Civic Mission'" (ABRI's Main Task in East Timor is its Civic Mission), *Angkatan Bersenjata*, March 2, 1994.

[39] Reported in "Tujuh batalyon di Timtim dapat ditarik sesuai kondisi," *Angkatan Bersenjata*, April 16, 1994. Note that the data in Table 1 are least reliable for the year 1994.

[40] The details of these appointments are discussed in my "Notes," pp. 70-71.

[41] As the group number implies, this was a reincarnation of Kopassandha Group 3, based in Maros, South Sulawesi, which was transferred to Kostrad, and in which Prabowo served during his early career.

[42] See the chapter on Aceh by Geoffrey Robinson in this volume.

on the characteristics of a simple reign of terror. In this, Prabowo and his operatives received ample support from the United States executive branch which, despite congressional resolutions ending US training of Indonesian military personnel, continued its long-standing support of the Suharto regime. As Allan Nairn writes:

> By far the main recipient of the special US training has been a force legendary for specializing in torture, disappearances, and night raids on civilian homes. Of the twenty-eight Army/Air Force exercises known to have been conducted since 1992, Pentagon documents indicate that twenty have involved the dreaded Kopassus Red Berets.[43]

From his new base in West Java, Prabowo quietly made his return to East Timor. In the face of this new official policy of normalizing the military's role in, and the status of, East Timor, Prabowo initiated a counter-movement of remilitarization outside of the formal command structure. The components of this movement involved the administrative use of terror, military training for civil servants and university students, and, most ominously, the expansion of the old combat teams, the people's defense units and youth organizations.

One of first stages in the remilitarization of East Timor were psychological operations in Dili and other urban centers. In February 1995, Dili was seized by rumors of black-clad and masked "ninjas" making nightly forays to intimidate pro-independence figures and terrorize the urban population. In 1998 a special feature article run in the *Voice of East Timor* recalled the period:

> I remember the Ninja issue in 1995. The day was February 10, 1995. In our editorial meeting, we decided to place the news about ninjas on the headline in the Saturday issue. Not having obtained verification (especially from the authorities) about the ninja issue, we tried to investigate . . . . We then returned and decided on the headline: *Ninja Issue Makes Dili Tense.*
>
> As the Saturday issue of *Voice of East Timor* was circulating, at 9.00 am the newspaper received a telephone call from Korem 164. Together with the managing editor and some friends we went to face the military. The Commander Kiki Syahnakri, the Deputy Commander Glenny Khairupan [sic], the Deputy Governor of East Timor J. Haribowo, and the staff command assistants [were all there]. [We were told that] there was no basis to the issue of ninjas and were encouraged to print news that would calm and reassure the populace.[44]

Though the label was new, there were unmistakable resemblances between these "ninja" and the *buffo* who had terrorized Dili prior to the Santa Cruz massacre.

---

[43] Allan Nairn, "Indonesia's Killers," *The Nation*, March 30, 1998, pp. 6-7. Australia also provided extensive training of the Special Forces during this period. See, for example, *Sydney Morning Herald*, March 9, 1998, and *The Australian*, March 19, 1998.

[44] J. B. Kleden, "Ninja," *STT*, July 11, 1998. The ninja episode is discussed in Arnold Kohen, *From the Place of the Dead*, p. 239.

In the wake of the ninja scare, more systematic militarization of various parts of East Timorese society was initiated. Military training sessions were held for university students belonging to the Student Regiment (Resimen Mahasiswa) at the University of East Timor.[45] Candidates for state jobs were required to attend military training held by the territorial battalions, and over a thousand civil servants were sent to the Army's Infantry Regiment Training Centers in Malang, East Java, and Denpasar, Bali, for three-month training programs (earning them the name "three-month army men").[46] Prabowo also sought to strengthen his links to, and control over, local politicians (particularly district heads) through the granting of honorary memberships in the Special Forces.[47]

The most sinister form of militarization during this period involved the establishment and expansion of paramilitary organizations. During the mid-1990s the military oversaw the formation of what were termed "traditional forces" (*pasukan adat*) at the village level for the purposes of "civil defense."[48] This was followed in urban centers by the formation of a number of paramilitaries, including Halilintar, Saka, Alfa, and Makikit.[49] In July 1995, Col. Prabowo also funded the formation of the Young Guards Upholding Integration (Garda Muda Penegak Integrasi), commonly known by the acronym Gada Paksi.[50] Though the organization was ostensibly intended to assist Timorese youths in small-scale business ventures, members quickly developed a host of illegal or semi-legal smuggling, gambling, and protection rackets. Gada Paksi developed rapidly: by early 1996 it had 1,100 members; in April it was announced that there were plans to add 1,200 members per year; and in May six hundred members were sent to Java to receive training from the Special Forces.[51] Despite its public links to these Forces,

---

[45] "Danrem Simbolon: Latsarmil Bagi Mahasiswa Bukan Untuk Membentuk Kekuatan Militer" (Korem Commander Simbolon: Military Training for Students Is Not Meant to Create a Military Force), *STT*, February 16, 1996.

[46] Reported respectively in "Gubernur Timtim, Abilio: 'Yang Tidak Disiplin Dicoret Namanya" (East Timor Governor Abilio: Violators of Discipline Will Have Their Names Struck Off), *STT*, September 5, 1995; and "Candida, dokter Timtim yang ingin Mengabdi di Daerahnya" (Candida, an East Timor Doctor Who Wants to Serve Her Region), *STT*, September 31, 1995.

[47] Examples include the Bupati of Lautem, Conceinção Silva (advertisement in *STT*, October 5, 1996) and the Bupati of Liquisa, Leoneto Martins ("Bupati Liquica Dapat Penghargaan tokoh Citra Disiplin Nasional 1997" (The Bupati of Liquica Receives an Award as Exemplary Model of National Discipline for 1997), *STT*, August 18, 1997). Contrary to the assumptions of most observers, in "trouble" areas such as East Timor, Aceh, and Irian Jaya the majority of local executives (*bupati, walikota*, etc.) were civilians, not military personnel.

[48] Reported in "Tugas utama ABRI di Timtim 'Civic Mission'." Four years later these units are reported in "Pasukan adat jadi Dan Up HUT integrasi di Manufahi" (Traditional Forces is Chief of Ceremonies Commemorating Integration in Manufahi), *STT*, July 22, 1998.

[49] The dismissal of Lieutenant-General Prabowo from the military in August, 1998, provided an opportunity for more open discussion about his activities in East Timor. A front page report in the daily *Voice of East Timor* explained: "The pro-military organizations formed by Prabowo include Halilintar, Saka, Alfa, Makikit and Gadapaksi. These organizations are armed and intended to aid military operations in Loro Sae [the local name for East Timor]." Reported in "Organisasi bentukan Prabowo memecahbelah rakyat Timtim" (Organizations Formed By Prabowo Divide the People of East Timor), *STT*, August 27, 1998.

[50] Prabowo is reputed to have spent Rp.400 million on Gada Paksi. "Gada Paksi Tegakkan Integrasi Timtim" (Gada Paksi Upholds the Integration of East Timor), *STT*, August 12, 1996.

[51] Reported in "Gada Paksi Kembangkan 17 Bidang Usaha di Timtim" (Gada Paksi Develop 17 Types of Business in East Timor), *STT*, February 14, 1996; and "HUT Kopassus Memiliki

two years after its establishment the head of Gada Paksi, Marçal de Almeida, lamented the fact that his organization was reputed to be *mauhu*—the local Tetum term for military intelligence.[52]

Prabowo also sought to integrate these paramilitary organizations into the existing territorial command. The career of Juliaõ Fraga, the former commander of Railakan I team, is again telling. In 1995 Fraga was known by the name Saka, and he commanded the three hundred-strong paramilitary of the same name. At Prabowo's request, in November 1995, he was appointed as Sub-district Military commander in Baguia, Baucau District.[53] A year later, suspected of betraying his superiors, Fraga, aka Saka, was assassinated by the Special Forces.[54] This was not the end of the case, however. In early November the *Voice of East Timor* reported that the local military commander had received a letter (allegedly) from Fretilin taking responsibility for Fraga's murder and challenging the army to "have it out at Karfak." Korem 164 commander Colonel Mahidin Simbolon commented: "I'm not sure the letter came from Fretilin, but instead from irresponsible rogues [*oknum*] who want to incite the security situation. Fretilin has never challenged the army, let alone wanted to meet at Karfak. The army doesn't even know where Karfak is."[55] The letter was a combination cover-up and provocation sent from the Special Forces, which was itself responsible for the execution.

The combination of psychological operations and the rapid militarization of Timorese society organized by members of Special Forces had an immediate impact. Tensions increased both among Timorese and between Timorese and Indonesian carpetbaggers. One consequence was a sharp increase in open social conflict in Dili and the district towns in East Timor during the mid-1990s. Riots erupted in Liquisa in early 1994, in Maliana in September 1995, in Dili in October 1995, in Baucau in June 1996, and again in Dili in October 1996. The campaign of violence had two further purposes. First, it was intended to keep military personnel in the territorial command in check, a warning of sorts, telling officers that they should not attempt to institute disciplinary measures similar to those introduced under Brigadier-General Warouw in 1989-1990. Second, continued violence necessitated maintaining the military presence, thus preventing any further personnel withdrawals. The increase in extra-legal military and paramilitary activity should thus be read against the backdrop of a third attempt to "normalize" Indonesian rule in East Timor.

Makna Refleksi dan Introspeksi" (The Special Forces Anniversary's Meaning is Reflection and Introspection), *STT*, April 17, 1996.

[52] "Mengaku Anggota Gada Paksi, Empat Pemuda Ditangkap Polisi" (Four Young Men, Claiming to be Gada Paksi Members, Arrested by Police), *STT*, August 12, 1997.

[53] Personal communication.

[54] His death is reported in "Juliao 'Saka' Fraga, Komandan Pasukan Saka Tewas Tertembak" (Juliaõ 'Saka' Fraga, Commander of the Saka Force, Shot Dead), *STT*, October 26, 1996. Team Saka was subsequently headed by a Special Forces operative named "Juanico." Personal communication.

[55] Quoted in "Menyusul Kasus penembakan Komandan Saka: GPK Kirim surat Kepada Danrem Simbolon" (Following the Affair of the Shooting of Saka's Commander: The GPK Sends a Letter to Korem Commander Simbolon), *STT*, November 2, 1996. A year later, four thousand people, including members of the Special Forces, gathered for the first anniversary of Fraga's murder and he was honored as "East Timor's best son." See "Juliao Fraga, Putra Terbaik Timtim" (Juliaõ Fraga, East Timor's Best Son), *STT*, October 27, 1997.

REFORMASI

As was the case in 1983, 1988, and 1993, the 1997-1998 national elections provided the opening salvos for another round of East Timor politics. This time, however, the crucial development was neither the "success" of the elections nor a policy shift, but rather the onset of the economic crisis in mid-1997. By early 1998 the total collapse of the Indonesian rupiah and resulting hardship prompted a massive outpouring of protests and riots in many parts of the country. Though it had been a primary concern to the brave People's Democratic Party (PRD, Partai Rakyat Demokratik) in 1995-1996, the so-called reform movement in 1998 wholly ignored the troublesome issue of East Timor, focusing instead on the dual issues of Suharto's rule and the economy. Under the banner of *reformasi* (reform), the gathering storm of protest and public dissent culminated in Suharto's resignation from the presidency on May 20, 1998 and the installation of vice-president B. J. Habibie as the country's new president. Following Suharto's resignation and the increasing demands for reform, East Timor reclaimed domestic as well as international attention.

Two days after Suharto's resignation, the *Voice of East Timor* ran a front-page article titled "The East Timor problem is homework for the new president," though it also quoted pro-Jakarta figure Florentino Sarmento calling East Timor "a minor issue" for Indonesia.[56] Several days later the head of the US Congressional Sub-committee for international affairs and human rights, Congressman Christopher Smith, met with Indonesian officials in Jakarta to discuss "new elections, the release of political prisoners, the status of the anti-subversion law, East Timor and Xanana, Irian Jaya, the disappearances [of activists], and the handling of student demonstrations."[57] Marzuki Darusman, deputy head of the National Human Rights Commission, argued that a political settlement of the East Timor problem would require releasing imprisoned Fretilin President Xanana Gusmaõ.[58] Minister of Justice Muladi pushed the issue a step further, recommending that East Timor be given "special status."[59] Pandora's box was opening.

Recognizing the long-awaited opportunity, East Timorese responded to Jakarta's political crisis and shaky new government by staging bold protests in Dili. On June 1 students at the University of East Timor held a free speech forum on *reformasi*, with wide-ranging calls for the release of political prisoners, a referendum, special status for the province, the right of self-determination, and an

---

[56] Paraphrased in "Masalah Timtim 'PR' buat Presiden baru" (The East Timor Problem is 'Homework' for the New President), *STT*, May 23, 1998.

[57] See "Amerika pertanyakan soal Timor Timur" (America Raises the East Timor Question); and "Marzuki Darusman: Xanana harus dibebaskan" (Marzuki Darusman: Xanana Must Be Released), *STT*, May 26, 1998.

[58] Ibid. This view was echoed by Sri Bintang Pamungkas, chairman of the opposition political party PUDI (Partai Uni Demokrasi Indonesia), on his release from prison. "Sri Bintang Pamungkas: Xanana dan Budiman harus dibebaskan" (Sri Bintang Pamungkas: Xanana and Budiman Must Be Released), *STT*, May 27, 1998.

[59] "Usulan Timtim diberi status Istimewa disambut positif" (A Proposal that East Timor be Given Special Status Is Received Positively), *STT*, May 27, 1998.

end to collusion, corruption, and nepotism in the provincial government.[60] This was followed by additional free speech fora, which were staged at the university campus almost every day during the first two weeks of June; at these gatherings, demands quickly coalesced around the right to self-determination and independence.[61] In Jakarta, thousands of East Timorese students from various universities in Indonesia also gathered to demonstrate at the Ministry of Foreign Affairs.[62] These expressly political rallies were accompanied by a rash of additional protests in Dili: taxi drivers and village transport employees struck for higher wages, students protested unfair high-school admissions procedures, and prisoners went on a hunger strike demanding the release of Xanana Gusmaõ.

Official responses were characteristically reactive. Realizing that the floor was falling out from under him, pro-Jakarta East Timor Governor Abilio Soares vainly sought to reposition himself and downplay the need for further change: "Indonesia used to be fascist, Indonesia used to be militarist, and whatnot; but not now, now we are a democratic people."[63] The provincial police belittled the outpouring of discontent, calling it no more than "a small explosion."[64] Military leaders, overwhelmed by the level of popular mobilization, stunned by a June 6 helicopter accident killing the territorial military commander and ten territorial staff, and uncertain about their own high command, first hesitated, then made meek requests that the popular "dialogues be held honestly and in good conscience."[65] In Jakarta, President Habibie made vague offers of "special status" and pledged a gradual troop withdrawal, positions reluctantly mouthed by Governor Abilio Soares back in Dili.[66] In accordance with Presidential Decree No. 5, political prisoners were released from the Becora jail in Dili on June 12. The following day President Habibie explained that he was "considering" freeing Xanana Gusmaõ as well, adding "if it were up to me, I'd do it as soon as possible."[67]

The student protests culminated on June 15 when leaders of the newly formed East Timorese Student Solidarity Council presented a statement to the provincial legislature and Bishop of Dili, Carlos Filipe Ximenes Belo, rejecting Habibie's

---

[60] "Mimbar bebas Untim: Tuntut bebaskan Tapol/Napol dan selesaikan masalah Timtim" (The University of East Timor Open Forum Demands Release of Political and Criminal Prisoners and Resolution of the East Timor Question), *STT*, June 2, 1998.

[61] "Ribuan mahasiswa Timtim gelar mimbar bebas: Tuntut penentuan nasib sendiri" (Thousands of East Timor Students Start Open Forum Demanding Self-Determination), *STT*, June 11, 1998.

[62] See "Kronologi Aksi Fronpetil di Deplu" (A Chronology of Actions of Fronpetil at the Foreign Ministry), issued by MateBEAN, dated June 16, 1998.

[63] Quoted in "Sabtu, Timtim gelar rapat akbar reformasi" (Saturday, East Timor Begins Mass Rally for Reform), *STT*, June 4, 1998.

[64] "Unjuk rasa di Timtim hanya letupan kecil" (Protests in East Timor Are Just a Small Explosion), *STT*, June 23, 1998.

[65] "Kasdam Udayana: Silahkan dialog, asal dengan jujur" (Udayana Chief of Staff: By All Means Dialogue, As Long As It Is Honest), *STT*, June 10, 1998.

[66] "Gubernur Abilio: Pusat Tawarkan Status Khusus Timtim" (Governor Abilio: The Center Offers East Timor Special Status), *STT*, June 12, 1998.

[67] See "Gelar spanduk saat dilepas napol dan tapol" (Banners Unfurled as Criminal and Political Prisoners Released) and the other front page news in *STT*, June 13, 1998; also "Presiden Habibie: Pemerintah mempertimbangkan [sic] pembebasan Xanana Gusmao" (President Habibie: The Government is Weighing the Release of Xanana Gusmaõ), *STT*, June 15, 1998.

offer of autonomy and demanding that a UN-supervised referendum be held on independence.[68] Xanana Gusmaõ, Ramos-Horta, and other East Timorese leaders also insisted that nothing short of a referendum would be acceptable.

One month after Suharto's resignation, East Timor had essentially become ungovernable. Despite their offers of special status and autonomy, Indonesian officials had acknowledged their inability to restore order and the necessity of a final solution. Indonesian Foreign Minister Ali Alatas now admitted that in theory a referendum was the most logical and democratic means of achieving a final settlement.[69] Habibie's motives were straightforward: he desperately needed to distance himself from Suharto, to appear reform-minded (i.e. in favor of democratization), and to increase his stature internationally. Where better to start than with a forsaken half-island two thousand kilometers away in which he had little interest?

Although ABRI as an institution seemed paralyzed, segments of the military on the ground in East Timor did take action. In early July, Dili was seized by rumors about the activities of black-clad "ninjas." The first mention of this in the Dili press reported that "people heard that certain officials [*pejabat-pejabat tertentu*] had taken advantage of the situation and conditions to drop East Timorese people in ninja disguises [*orang-orang Timor Timur ala ninja*] into residential areas." One Dili resident commented: "I don't know yet if there are ninja or not. But usually there's some truth to issues like this."[70] Over the following week the rumors of ninja activity spread rapidly, and all observers likened the terror to that in 1995.[71] There was, however, one crucial difference from 1995: this time East Timorese fought back against the ninja. In Dili, several suspected ninja were captured by neighborhood groups. In Ainaro, youths pursuing a suspected ninja attacked the Ainaro district head's house. A day later a private in the 745th infantry battalion was attacked, again because the crowd suspected they had found a ninja.[72] The military responded with "sweeps" through Dili neighborhoods to arrest suspects, ninja, and pro-independence supporters alike.[73]

---

[68] The statement is reproduced in "DPR dan Uskup terima hasil mimbar bebas" (Parliament and the Bishop Receive the Results of the Open Forum), *STT*, June 16, 1998. Fretilin's involvement in formulating the statement is not known. This, and much else, will have to await a full history to be written by East Timorese.

[69] See the extended interview in "Timtim dapat membentuk Pemerintah otonomi sendiri" (East Timor Can Form Its Own Autonomous Government), *STT*, July 21, 1998.

[70] "Isu ninja resahkan masyarakat Dili" (The Ninja Issue Disturbs Dili Society), *STT*, July 7, 1998.

[71] See the editorial, "Isu Ninja Kembali Mencuat" (The Ninja Issue Springs Back to Life), *STT*, July 8, 1998; the remarks by Kodam 9 Commander Major-General Adam Damiri in "Pangdam Adam: 'Isu ninja' rekayasa sekelompok orang" (Commander Adam: The Ninja Issue is a Manipulation by a Certain Group), *STT*, July 9, 1998; and "Ninja ala Timtim" (East Timor-style Ninja), *STT*, July 11, 1998.

[72] These cases are reported in "Diduga 'ninja', lima pemuda ditangkap" (Suspected as 'Ninja,' Five Young Men Arrested), *STT*, July 8, 1998; "Gara-gara ninja rumah Bupati Ainaro dirusak" (Because of the Ninja, the Home of the Bupati of Ainaro is Damaged), *STT*, July 9, 1998; and "Diduga ninja, Pratu Fransiskus dihajar" (Suspected as a Ninja, Private Franciscus is Beaten Up), *STT*, July 11, 1998.

[73] See "Operasi gabungan digelar, 20 warga diringkus" (Joint Operations Initiated, Twenty Locals Captured) and "Aparat lakukan sweeping, seorang pemuda tertembak" (The State Apparatus Carries Out a Sweep, One Young Man Shot), *STT* July 16, 1998; and "Amo Belo:

Throughout July, Indonesian and East Timorese leaders on both sides of the issue made repeated statements about the need for a "final solution" to the East Timor issue. Building on the free speech fora of early June, university students hosted "dialogues" in district towns throughout East Timor. Pro-independence East Timorese insisted on a referendum and demanded that all groups, including Xanana Gusmaõ and the Falintil leadership, be allowed to participate in discussions. Politicians in Jakarta and Timorese collaborators played a desperate game of catch up, vainly trying to respond to the snowballing demands and heightened mobilization in East Timor. In early August, tripartite talks were held between Indonesia, Portugal, and the United Nations in New York, at which Indonesia outlined a proposal for East Timor to become a "Special Province with Wide Autonomy."[74] The tenuousness of the Indonesian position was highlighted in late August by Nugroho Wisnumurti, the Indonesian permanent representative at the UN, who explained, "It is difficult for us to free Xanana Gusmaõ because he was tried as a criminal," but went on to add that under the Indonesian offer of autonomy "it is quite possible that Xanana could become governor."[75]

Calls for a final solution continued unabated during September and October. In early September, the resistance staged a political coup, with the five political parties that existed at the time of the 1976 Indonesia invasion announcing the establishment of a new umbrella organization, the National Council of Resistance of the People of East Timor (CNRT, Concelho Nacionale de Resistencia Timorese), with Xanana Gusmaõ elected president.[76] Given that the parties' differences had resulted in a brief civil war in 1975, the formation of the CNRT was a clear sign of East Timorese desire to exploit the new political opening. On September 10 and 11, discussions were held at the seminary in Dare, and the resulting communiqué further fueled the demand for a referendum on the territory's future. In October, Governor Soares issued an ultimatum that civil servants who did not support the Indonesian autonomy plan would be required to resign from their posts. Tens of thousands poured into the streets of Dili, Liquisa, and Baucau to support the civil servants and to demand that the governor himself resign.[77] On November 12, thousands of people from all of East Timor gathered at the Santa Cruz cemetery to commemorate the 1991 massacre, and civil servants refused to work.[78] In December, Dili was paralyzed by mass protests in which the pro-independence youth blocked

---

ABRI jangan lakukan penangkapan di malam hari" (Father Belo: ABRI Should Not Arrest People in the Middle of the Night), *STT*, July 20, 1998.

[74] "Indonesia jelaskan tawaran otonomi" (Indonesia Explains its Autonomy Offer), *STT*, August 5, 1998.

[75] "Nugroho Wisnumurti: 'Xanana Gusmao bisa jadi Gubernur Timtim'" (Nugroho Wisnumurti: 'Xanana Gusmaõ Could Become Governor of East Timor'), *STT*, September 1, 1998.

[76] "East Timorese set up new organization, name jailed rebel leader as head," Joyo@aol.com, September 9, 1998.

[77] See "Puluhan ribu massa demo di Dili: Buktikan solidaritas bagi pns" (Tens of Thousands Demonstrate in Dili: Proving Solidarity with Civil Servants), *STT*, October 12, 1998, and "Gubernur diberi batas waktu 15 hari lengser" (Governor Given 15 Days to Resign), *STT*, October 14, 1998.

[78] "Puluhan ribu massa peringati 7 tahun" (Tens of Thousands Commemorate Seventh Anniversary), *STT*, November 13, 1998.

streets and stopped all vehicles, sending civil servants home.[79] Bishops Belo and Nascimiento held joyous Christmas masses in Dili and Bacau.

East Timorese society had not only become ungovernable, but the government itself was no longer reliable. Despite continued adamant refusals to consider a referendum,[80] Indonesian behavior suggested that it had all but conceded that real change was inevitable.

MILITARY MANEUVERS

Suharto's resignation had cross-cutting implications for the Indonesian military and its policy towards East Timor. On the one hand, the military had lost its long-standing patron and found itself under vociferous attack to withdraw from the political arena. On the other hand, given the climate of political uncertainty and manner in which the military as an institution had stood aside during the tumultuous events of early 1998, the military elite in general, and ABRI Commander General Wiranto in particular, enjoyed a surprising degree of popular respect. Caught between these currents, the military leadership took the course of least resistance: it hesitated. This general stance was adopted as well in East Timor, where ABRI displayed a remarkable ambivalence, unwilling to respond to the tide of popular mobilization, yet unable to reposition itself.

Even prior to Suharto's resignation the military presence in East Timor had undergone some odd permutations. Following the abolition of Kolakops in March 1993, the number of external battalions posted in East Timor had been reduced and, if judged by appearances, regularized.[81] Allowing for gaps in the data and the uncertainty of dates, we can still conclude that during the mid-1990s there were six external battalions in East Timor at any one time. The summary of captured ABRI documents prepared by Tapol claims that in August 1998 there were only five "non-organic" (i.e. external) battalions on duty in the territory.[82] Table 1 (below), however, illustrates that beginning in late-1997 the number of battalions present increased sharply, with the total reaching thirteen. By itself this suggests a significant shift in military practice prior to Suharto's fall and the subsequent opening of the independence floodgates.

There are three reasons for this increase in military presence. First, the increasing Falintil activity and local violence during 1997 and early 1998 prompted local military officers to request that more troops be sent to East Timor.[83] Second, the heightened troop presence was intended to reassure both non-Timorese traders and civil servants, who were concerned about their security and were beginning to leave the territory. Third, a large part of this increase can be accounted for by a

---

[79] "Dili tegang diguncang demo akbar" (Dili Tense, Roiled by Mass Demonstrations), *STT*, December 18, 1998.

[80] See "Jakarta says won't budge on East Timor referendum," *Reuters,* dated October 6, 1998, posted on Joyo@aol.com, October 6, 1998.

[81] The pattern was for six external battalions to be posted in East Timor at any one time, with those from Sumatra (Kodam 1 and 2) and West Java (Kodam 3) posted in Baucau and Manatuto, those from Central Java (Kodam 4) in Viqueque, those from Kalimantan (Kodam 6) in Lautem, those from East Java (Kodam 5) in Dili and Liquisa, and those from Sulawesi (Kodam 7) and Nusatenggara (Kodam 9) in the western districts of Aileu, Ermera, Bobonaro, and Covalima.

[82] Tapol, "The Indonesian Jackboot," p. 5.

[83] *STT*, February 6, 1998.

new practice of deploying combined operations units (called Satuan Tugas Gabungan, i.e. units comprised of companies drawn from various battalions). This began in 1996 (hence the large number of battalions seen in Table 1 for that year), most likely as a means of responding to proliferation of urban riots rather than for specifically combat purposes. The use of joint battalions also served to disguise the use of combat troops from the Army Strategic Reserve Command and was a means of keeping a larger cross-section of the military actively engaged in the East Timor campaign.

In July, at the request of President Habibie, the military elite announced a series of withdrawals from East Timor, with more than one hundred Indonesian and foreign journalists flown in by the Air Force to witness the withdrawal of 1,300 troops.[84] At the same time, the Indonesian military broke off regular radio communication with Falintil. In an interview with the *Voice of East Timor*, Falintil deputy commander Taur Matan Ruak explained "[t]wo journalists filmed our communication with the Indonesian military. But they [the Indonesian military] got scared. They thought we might publicize what they said, so they cut off communications with us."[85] Indeed, transcripts of regular conversations between representatives of the military and of Falintil would not only have exposed the military as incapable of defeating what it claimed to be no more than "bandit" elements, but might also have suggested a certain duplicity in the military stand-off.

Yet while claiming to reduce troop strength in the occupied territory, the military sent fresh troops into East Timor. In September Xanana Gusmaõ claimed that since the highly publicized ABRI withdrawal, an additional 3,500 troops had secretly entered the province.[86] Indonesian activists also publicized new deployments and, contradicting military statements, claimed that the total ABRI

---

[84] This included one company from the 301st infantry battalion (based in Sumedang, West Java), one company from the 621st (Barabai, South Kalimantan), one company from the 700th Airborne (Maros, South Sulawesi), and one company and one platoon of Special Forces' paracommandos (West Java). See, for example, "Pengurangan pasukan bukti Timtim aman" (Withdrawal of Units Proves East Timor is Secure), *STT*, July 29, 1998; and "Lagi, 600 Personil ABRI Ditarik dari Timtim" (Another 600 ABRI Personnel Withdrawn from East Timor), *Media Indonesia*, July 30, 1998.

[85] It is not known when contact was opened or at whose initiative. See "Wakil Komandan Falintil Taur Matan Ruak: 'Kami Berjuang untuk Hentikan Perang'" (Deputy Falintil Commander Taur Matan Ruak: 'We are Fighting to End the War'), *STT*, September 4, 1998.

[86] Xanana Gusmaõ, "A Solution for East Timor," paper presented at the conference "Indonesia after Suharto," organized by the New Zealand Asia Institute, University of Auckland, September 10, 1998, p. 5. "Troops Sent in Despite Promises," *The Independent*, October 25, 1998, reported the arrival of "more than 700" new troops at the Com port in August.

Table 1

Battalions Posted in East Timor during the 1990s

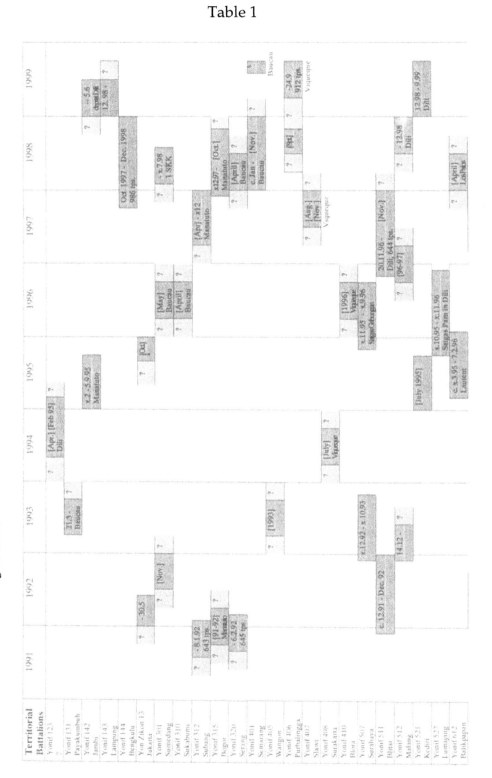

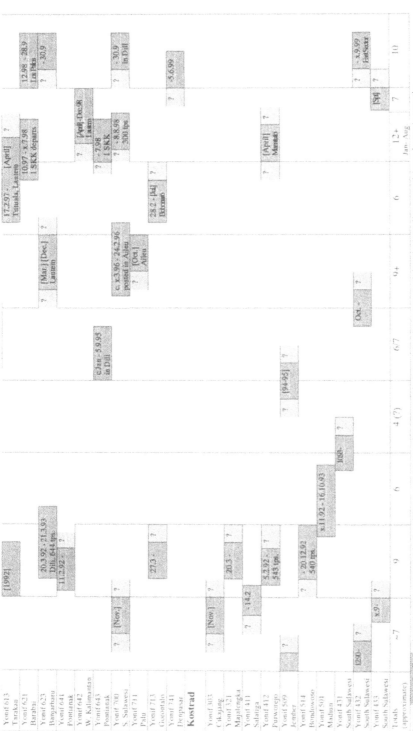

Notes: **dark shading** = battalion known to be in East Timor; when exact dates are not known, it has been assumed that the battalion served for at least six months

[July] = Battalion known to be in East Timor in that month.

light shading = indicates that the battalion may still be in East Timor

c. = circa; tps = number of troops

a Reported present for ceremony, along with troops from Yon Zipur-3 (Ujungberung) and staff from Denzipur 9, so likely a "joint unit."

b = served for three weeks.

Totals are calculated on the basis of units which served for more than 3 months in a given year

Sources: based on reporting from *Angkatan Bersenjata, Suara Timor Timur,* and other Indonesian as well as English-language sources.

presence in East Timor numbered between twenty and fifty thousand.[87] Concerned about the arrival of new troops, in mid-September Bishop Belo requested that President Habibie and ABRI Commander General Wiranto ensure that the troop withdrawals were carried out in good faith.[88] Colonel Tono Suratman in Dili responded defensively that there were only five battalions on the ground in East Timor. Though there is no way to determine for certain, the data presented in Table 1 suggest that this is roughly accurate.[89]

Soon after the July-August troop withdrawals and redeployments, the international press reported a major new Indonesian military offensive against Falintil in the eastern sector, involving twenty thousand Indonesian troops.[90] Military leaders quickly denied these reports, with General Wiranto calling them "nonsense" and Colonel Tono Suratman bleating denials in Dili.[91] While some half-hearted efforts may have been made, there is little evidence of a real offensive. Significant fighting did occur in November, however. On November 9, Falintil attacked a sub-district military command in Alas District, killing three ABRI personnel and taking seven hostages; ABRI responded to this attack with vicious reprisals against villagers in the region. Curiously, however, the ABRI offensive was launched by the two "organic" East Timor-based battalions (744 and 745) and the local District Military Command, not by external troops.[92] The use of local units largely staffed by East Timorese suggests that ABRI leaders no longer viewed a purely military solution as either possible or desirable. This reflects a belated attempt on the part of the military to portray the conflict as a "civil" affair

---

[87] See Solidamor, "Deception on a Grand Scale," press release, dated September 11, 1998. See also "'Penarikan pasukan' dari Timtim dipertanyakan" ('Withdrawal of Troops' From East Timor Questioned), *STT*, September 12, 1998. Despite claims that the data had been "cross-checked" and verified, the accuracy of these claims must be questioned. These activists claimed that members of Battalion 443 (Kostrad), the Navy, and Special Forces entered Lautem district. They also report an offensive by troops from Battalion 406 (Kostrad), and the two local battalions, 744 and 745. There is no Battalion 443 (though it is likely that they meant 433), and Battalion 406 is not a part of Kostrad. Furthermore, at least some of the new deployments are accounted for by two companies of the police Mobile Brigade. See, "Parako dan Rajawali Pulang, datang lagi dua kompi Brimob" (Paratroops and Rajawali Go Home; Two Mobile Brigade Companies Arrive), *STT*, July 31, 1998.

[88] "Uskup Belo minta Habibie dan Wiranto tinjau lagi penarikan ABRI di Timtim" (Bishop Belo asks Habibie and Wiranto to Reconsider the Withdrawal of ABRI from East Timor), *STT*, September 19, 1998.

[89] "Danrem 164/WD Dili, Tono tegaskan: Tidak ada penambahan ABRI ke Timtim" (Commander of Korem 164/Dili Tono Insists: There are No New ABRI Troops in East Timor), *STT*, September 22, 1998.

[90] "Army on the Move," *Sydney Morning Herald*, September 25, 1998. See also "Timor protests targets army," *The Australian*, October 9, 1998, which claims that two leading Falintil commanders narrowly escaped these attacks. During this period Falintil deputy commander Taur Matan Ruak gave several interviews to Dili's *Voice of East Timor*, but never mentioned anything about an offensive.

[91] See "ABRI di Timtim tak Ditambah" (No New ABRI Forces in East Timor), *Media Indonesia*, no date; and "Tak benar ABRI lakukan ofensif ke sasaran gerilyawan di sektor Timur" (It's Not True ABRI is Launching an Offensive Against Guerilla Targets in the Eastern Sector), *STT*, September 25, 1998.

[92] Reported in "More than 50 feared dead as East Timor crisis deepens," *The Age*, November 23, 1998, and November 24, 1998; and "Forces say siege of town will not be lifted," *Irish Times*, November 24, 1998.

involving East Timorese exclusively rather than as a prolonged East Timorese struggle to resist Indonesian rule.

In the political space provided by Indonesia's *reformasi*, pro-independence groups in East Timor continued a massive campaign throughout August and September calling for open talks between all segments of East Timorese society and a final solution to the twenty-three year conflict. Echoing popular sentiment expressed during district-level fora held in July and August, Bishop Belo championed the need for participation of all East Timorese, including Xanana Gusmaõ, Ramos-Horta, and the Falintil guerrilla leaders.[93] The Indonesian position continued to slide. In an attempt to counter the local dialogues and the Dare communiqué which, despite its neutral tone, clearly favored independence, pro-Jakarta East Timorese leaders announced that the fourth "All Inclusive Intra-East Timorese Dialogue" would be held in Austria, in late October. Military leaders also proved incapable of resisting the new definition of the issues; they recognized the legal right of the East Timorese National Resistance Council and agreed that dialogues would have to include the "guerrillas."[94]

These military maneuvers between July and November suggest an ambivalence on the part of the military high command. On the one hand, the military stood aside during the massive urban protests and, contrary to much reporting, did not attempt any last offensive against Falintil. When the use of troops was called for it was the local, rather than external, troops who were sent to do the dirty work. On the other hand, the military was clearly reluctant to follow the politicians' lead: renouncing East Timor was never an option, but this for reasons of internal institutional politics more than all else. In sum, the military stance reflected the hesitancy of an uncertain high command. In August 1998, Xanana Gusmaõ offered this blunt assessment: "Every military officer who has ever served in East Timor knows in his heart of hearts that the East Timorese people do not wish for *integrasi* [integration] with Indonesia, and that the only permanent solution to the problem is a referendum."[95] This reality, of course, contributed to the use of alternative means of force.

MILITIAS

The massive outpouring of protest and the July-August troop withdrawals/re-deployments set in motion a new round of paramilitary organizing and activity in East Timor's urban centers and district towns. In June, efforts were made by Governor Abilio Soares and his military colleagues to organize "pro-autonomy" counter-demonstrations, largely by drawing on military-backed organizations.[96] In mid-

---

[93] "Wawancara STT dengan Amo Belo: 'Kita sedang cari jalan agar gerilyawan aman ikut dialog'" (Interview of STT with Father Belo: 'We're Looking for a Way for the Guerillas to Join the Dialogue in Safety'), *STT*, September 23, 1998.

[94] "ABRI setuju dialog libatkan gerilyawan" (ABRI Agrees that Dialogue Should Include the Guerillas) and "Organisasi Gada Paksi tak akan dibubarkan" (Gada Paksi Will Not Be Disbanded), *STT*, September 18, 1998.

[95] Quoted in "Xanana Gusmao: 'Saya merasa sangat optimis'" (Xanana Gusmaõ: 'I'm Very Optimistic'), *STT*, August 31, 1998.

[96] "Barisan pembela integrasi pro otonomi nyatakan sikap" (The Ranks of Pro-Autonomy Defenders of Integration Declare Their Stance), *STT*, June 27, 1998, provides a detailed and graphic description of the actions. At the time Governor Soares stated that "I'm ready for

July, further "sweeps" were conducted by the military together with "armed civilian groups," resulting in more than sixty arrests.[97] In the face of protests over the activities of these groups, the Korem 164 commander, Colonel Tono Suratman, announced that the Halilintar, Saka, and Alfa teams were being placed directly under the control of the District Military Commands (Komando Distrik Militer, Kodim).[98] Several days later, he summed up these changes: "The Total People's Defense Concept [Hankamrata] will be emphasized. This is a return to the awareness and responsibility of the East Timorese people to defend against every threat and challenge, internal as well as external."[99] In other words, the pattern of using East Timorese against East Timorese and militarizing society was to be stepped-up.

We are fortunate to have several detailed reports about militia strength and activity during this period. On the basis of captured ABRI documents, the London-based Indonesian human rights organization, Tapol, released a twenty-one page report detailing the military's own figures. Tapol cites an ABRI document titled "Resistance Forces in the Province of East Timor for 1997/1998" which lists twelve paramilitary teams, named by district: "Two Saka Baucau Teams, Alfa Lospalos Team, Makikit Viqueque Team, Halilintar Atabae Team, Railakan Ermera Team, Ainaro Team, Suai Team, Same Team, Sakunar Team, Morok Manatuto Team, Liquisa Team."[100] In September 1998, activists from the Jakarta-based NGO Solidamor and the University of Indonesia provided a breakdown of the militias encountered during a research trip: Team Alpha in Lautem, with two hundred members; Team Saka in Baucau, with two hundred members; Team Sera in Viqueque, with two hundred members; Team Makikit in Manatuto, with "one battalion." They also reported a new team named "Garuda" which had recently entered East Timor via Kupang and was operating in Bobonaro.[101] But estimates on the total number of paramilitary personnel vary greatly. Tapol reports that in August 1998 the total number of "'non-ABRI' forces were just under four thousand." In July, however, Korem chief of staff Lieutenant-Colonel Supadi noted that there were "eight thousand native East Timorese sons united in militarization."[102]

---

another civil war, if that's what they [the pro-referendum forces] want." Quoted in "Delegasi Uni Eropa disambut barisan Pembela Integrasi" (European Union Delegation Received by the Defenders of Integration), *STT*, June 29, 1998.

[97] See "Pasca demonstrasi 60 warga ditangkap" (After the Demonstration, Sixty Arrested), *STT*, July 24, 1998.

[98] This is discussed in detail in "Lagi, 300 personil ABRI ditarik" (Another 300 ABRI Personnel Withdrawn), *STT*, August 6, 1998.

[99] Quoted in "600 Personil ABRI tinggalkan Timtim" (600 ABRI Personnel Leave East Timor), *STT*, August 10, 1998.

[100] Tapol, "East Timor under the Indonesian Jackboot," p. 8. Although not providing militia membership figures, an earlier section claims that there were nearly four thousand "non-ABRI" personnel. Unfortunately neither the East Timor International Support Center in Darwin nor Tapol in London have made these documents available, so it is not possible to assess their accuracy.

[101] "'Penarikan pasukan' dari Timtim dipertanyakan" ('Troop Withdrawals' from East Timor Questioned), *STT*, September 12, 1998.

[102] See Tapol, "The Indonesian Jackboot," p. 4; and "Kasrem 164/WD, Letkol. Supandi: ABRI di Timtim 80 persen putra daerah" (Lieut.-Col. Supandi, Korem 164 Chief of Staff: 80% of ABRI Personnel in East Timor are Local Sons), *STT*, July 22, 1998.

This was not simply a case of military-created paramilitary organizations wreaking havoc or acting on orders, for these actions involved collaborators threatened by—and perhaps also threatening—abandonment. Collaborators and paramilitary members were keenly aware of the threat they faced from an ABRI withdrawal, even if that withdrawal was only partial.[103] As East Timorese officials came under attack for corruption, collusion, and nepotism, they sought to protect themselves via local gangs and paramilitaries.[104] There was a crucial class dimension to these efforts, for while "high" collaborators like Governor Soares might leave the territory for Jakarta, Macau, or Portugal, militia members on the street had few such options. The Gada Paksi issue and increased activity of the old Timorese combat teams was a prelude to more systematic and directed militia activity.

The fate of Prabowo's brain-child, Gada Paksi, is particularly illustrative. In July 1998 Gada Paksi head Marçal de Almeida stated that he was not opposed to dissolving the organization so long as its members were looked after and bank credits were covered. In mid-September, Eurico Guterres, a Gada Paksi member and owner of a gambling racket (*bola guling*) in Dili, expressed his concern about being abandoned by the organization's "leaders." The Dili press reported:

> Many pro-integration youths are extremely disappointed, because the organization they embraced was dissolved and they were abandoned. . . . Eurico explained that the dissolution of the organization was not transparent and leaders did not show responsibility to the members. Rather, the members were abandoned, as too were the workshops and trades, both in Dili and throughout the rest of East Timor.[105]

Two days later, Korem 164 commander Colonel Tono Suratman fired back, insisting that Gada Paksi had not been and would not be dissolved "because it differs from the paramilitary organizations in East Timor."[106] The public row between Gada Paksi leaders and the military was revealing new tensions.

October 1998 marked a clear turning-point, as militia activity came to be directly ordered and coordinated by high-ranking ABRI officers. In 1999 a former head of the "Peace Force and Defender of Integration" militia named Tomas Aquino Gonçalves gave revealing interviews after having fled to Macau. "In 1975," he explained, "I was commander of a joint command, having been a partisan."[107] His father, Guilherme Maria Gonçalves, had served as East Timor's second governor from 1978 until 1982.[108] Tomas served as district head (*Bupati*) in Ermera from 1977

---

[103] Similar dynamics were seen in other regions of Indonesia, with military-backed youth groups hedging their bets by inciting violence (and at times even encouraging separatism) on the calculation that violence would ensure that their military backers would remain on hand.

[104] See, for example, "Diduga KKN, Bupati Norberto diminta mengundurkan diri" (Suspected of Corruption, Collusion and Nepotism, Bupati Norberto is Asked to Resign), *STT*, July 27, 1998, and the follow-up articles.

[105] "Pemuda pro integrasi kecewa" (Pro-Integration Youth Disappointed), *STT*, September 16, 1998.

[106] Ibid.

[107] "Militia defector names top generals involved," Radio Nederland Gema Warta, October 6, 1999, posted on http://www1.qzn.skyinet,net/~apcet/news-defector.htm.

[108] In 1990 he fled to Portugal.

until 1989.[109] Gonçalves explained that he attended meetings with senior military officers beginning in October and November 1998. When asked why he joined, he explained: "I had no choice. If I didn't, I would have been killed. [Korem 164] Commander Tono Suratman threatened me in October 1998."[110] At the same time, senior military officials discussed the need to "optimize" the People's Militia (Wanra).[111] It is clear then that militia activity increased sharply in the months following Suharto's resignation and was accelerated under direct military supervision in October at exactly the moment that the pro-referendum movement reached a crescendo.

FROM CONSULTATION TO REFERENDUM

The political turning point came on January 27, 1999, when President Habibie announced that he was going to make a final offer of "broad autonomy" (*otonomi luas*) for East Timor at the next tripartite meeting to be held with Portugal at the UN. To facilitate his participation in the ongoing talks, Habibie also explained that he was moving Xanana Gusmaõ from the Cipinang Prison to special house arrest. Portrayals of this offer vary greatly. The international press reported this to mean that the East Timorese would be offered the chance to vote on a choice between autonomy and independence. In Indonesia, however, Habibie's proposal came in the form of a "threat": if the Indonesian offer of autonomy was rejected in the tripartite talks with Portugal and the UN, the President would recommend to the MPR to "release" East Timor.[112] Habibie was not offering a referendum; in fact, he explicitly ruled out such a solution. "A referendum," he said, "cannot be held because East Timor became part of Indonesia not through a referendum, but through an MPR decree."[113] Nevertheless, following six weeks of talks, on March 11 an agreement was reached to hold a direct ballot among East Timorese to decide whether they would accept or reject the Indonesian autonomy proposal.[114]

Habibie's initial announcement caught all parties off guard. Though their reasons varied widely, most politically prominent Indonesians opposed Habibie's proposal. Megawati Sukarnoputri, the leader of the Indonesian Democratic Party

---

[109] Iwan Gayo, ed., *Buku Pintar Nusantara* (Handbook for the Archipelago) (Jakarta: Upaya Warga Negara, 1990), pp. 1258, 1273.

[110] "Interview: Orders to Kill," translated from the Portuguese daily *Expreso*, September 17, 1999, sent via an e-mail listserve. This appears to be the best of several versions of the interview circulating. Revealing as the interview is, there are numerous problems with Gonçalves's account and the details provided. Gonçalves is known to have been involved with the paramilitaries long before October 1998; he provides inaccurate dates for Prabowo's provision of arms; and his estimate of militia numbers is highly suspect.

[111] Colonel Tono Suratman explained that this was necessary so that the military would not have to handle the growing number of violent cases. See "Wanra di Timtim akan dioptimalkan" (The People's Militia Will be Optimalized), *STT*, November 30, 1998.

[112] See, for example, the formulation in "Timtim Dilepas Bila Status Khusus Otonomi Luas Ditolak" (East Timor will be Released if the Special Status with Broad Autonomy is Rejected), *Suara Pembaruan*, January 28, 1999; in Dili the headline read: "Terbuka peluang Timtim merdeka" (Opportunity Open for East Timor Independence), *STT*, January 28, 1999.

[113] See "Habibie rules out referendum in East Timor," *Jakarta Post*, February 5, 1999.

[114] Even then there were disputes as to whether this meant a consultation that would be forwarded to the MPR, a position adopted by Indonesian politicians, or if it would be a binding vote, an interpretation accepted by the international community.

of Struggle (PDI-P, Partai Demokrasi Indonesia–Perjuangan), and Abdurrahman Wahid, head of the country's largest Islamic organization (NU, Nahdatul Ulama), both argued against the offer, claiming that as head of a transitional government Habibie had no right to release East Timor.[115] Threatened by abandonment, East Timorese collaborators denied the seriousness of the offer and suggested that it was no more than an international relations ploy. Members of the military elite were furious with Habibie's offer, though they remained tight-lipped at the time. Even foreign governments appeared surprised by the snap announcement and expressed doubts about the possibility of actually holding a vote in the short term.

The military may have been angry, but the announcement did not come as a complete surprise. There are numerous indications that the military believed the political elite would move for a political resolution to the issue, even if it meant losing the province. Beginning in December 1998, the military had already stepped up paramilitary organizing in East Timor, overseeing the formation of several new militias including Mahidi (formed on December 17), Red and White Iron (on December 27), and Thorn (in early 1999).[116] The recruitment and arming of the militias not only continued but accelerated at the time of Habibie's announcement, with military officers openly acknowledging that they were providing weapons to the rampaging gangs.[117] Vehement protests by Bishop Belo, Xanana Gusmaõ, and Falintil commanders were ignored. On Dili's streets an increasingly deadly scenario was developing. While pro-independence forces greeted Habibie's threat/offer as a major breakthrough and staged new demonstrations, the now well-armed militias took to the streets of Dili and initiated a campaign of terror and violence.[118]

This heightened militia activity was closely coordinated and directed by the military. According to Tomas Gonçalves, he attended meetings in Bali in February at which senior military officers, including Major-General Adam Damiri and Brigadier-General Mahidin Simbolon of Military Region 9, instructed the militias "to eliminate all of the CNRT leaders and sympathizers . . . After the military commanders' proposal had been put forward, they said we had to form the militias quickly, urgently."[119] These meetings continued throughout February and March. When asked about plans to target the clergy, Gonçalves explained:

---

[115] "Gus Dur dan Megawati Tolak Pelepasan Timtim" (Gus Dur and Megawati Reject the Release of East Timor), *Kompas*, January 30, 1999.

[116] See East Timor International Support Center, "Getting away with Murder: A Chronology of Indonesian Military sponsored Paramilitary and Militia Atrocities in East Timor from November 1998 to May 1999," posted on Joyo@aol.com, May 19, 1999. See also the comments by Aniceto Gutterres in "Militias vow to rise from the ashes," *South China Morning Post*, November 19, 1999.

[117] See "1.000 Wanra resmi diterima" (One Thousand People's Military Officially Accepted), *STT*, February 8, 1999; and "Separatists [sic] fear bloodshed as military arms integrationists," *Sydney Morning Herald*, January 28, 1999.

[118] See, for example, "Pemuda Prointegrasi Lakukan Tembakan Sporadis Halau Serangan Antiintegrasi" (Pro-integration Youths Fire Sporadically on Anti-integrationists), *STT*, January 30, 1999.

[119] "Interview: Orders to Kill," *Expreso*, September 17, 1999, translated from the Portuguese. This comment is odd given that many of the militias had already been established in late 1998.

> The last meeting I went to [was] on 26 March, with the then military commander of [East] Timor, Toro Suratma [sic]. That meeting was held in Dili, and it was attended by the Governor, Abilio Osorio [Soares], and representatives of all the other militias, including Joaõ Tavares and Eurico Guterres. The meeting was held in the Governor's office. In fact, it was Osorio himself that came up with the idea of killing priests and nuns.[120]

When asked if the military commanders agreed to this, Gonçalves responded: "Absolutely! They were thrilled with the idea."[121]

Throughout March and April discussions for the consultation/referendum continued in New York while the intimidation and violence escalated in East Timor. UN officials displayed a combination of optimism and skittishness. UN representative Jamsheed Marker, for example, argued that there was "no turning back" on the referendum, yet also declared that "it's not possible to hold these consultations in an atmosphere charged with fighting."[122] Military officers at the Military Region 9 headquarters in Bali and on the ground in East Timor, who were opposed to Habibie's offer, clearly viewed the UN's nervousness as promising, and so further stepped up the violence. With official encouragement, the militias continued their campaign of terror and openly called on their followers to "conduct a cleansing of the traitors of integration. Capture them and kill them."[123]

Despite the violence and international concern, the ongoing political talks in New York culminated with the signing of the May 5 Accord between Indonesia, Portugal, and the UN calling for a popular referendum to be held on August 8. The subsequent UN resolution (No. 1236) recognized the responsibility of the Indonesian government for maintaining security, authorized the deployment of international police officers to advise the Indonesian police, and welcomed the formation of an Indonesian "ministerial team to monitor the popular consultation."[124]

Indonesia hastily established a Task Force to Oversee the Popular Consultation in East Timor. Major-General Zacky Anwar Makarim, a senior intelligence operative with long-standing East Timor experience and a relative of Foreign Minister Ali Alatas, was placed in charge, with Colonel Glenny Kairupan, an officer with extensive East Timor experience during the 1990s, as his second in command. Though formally in line with the May 5 agreement, the goals of the Task Force were not truly focused on maintenance of security. Rather, from the time of its inception in June, the Task Force sought to use intimidation and violence to secure victory. It appears that Indonesia's national election scheduled for June 6 played a crucial role in the calculations of Zacky's Task Force in East Timor. The election provided a test run by which Indonesia could gauge the prospects for the August referendum on the future of East Timor. When Golkar won 49.1 percent of the vote in East Timor, far ahead of the 34.9 percent that went to Megawati Sukarnoputri's PDI-P, this demonstrated (or at least was understood to indicate) a

---

[120] Ibid.

[121] Ibid.

[122] "No East Timor ballot if violence continues: Marker," *AFP*, posted on Joyo@aol.com, April 9, 1999.

[123] Quoted in "Second Thoughts," *Far Eastern Economic Review*, April 29, 1999.

[124] United Nations Security Council Resolution 1246 and Press Release SC/6689, June 11, 1999; and "Secretary-General's Memorandum on Security for Ballot," May 4, 1999.

clear majority in favor of Golkar and the Republic. These results were also read in comparison with the electoral results elsewhere in Indonesia. Only in Sulawesi did Golkar do better, and Zacky must have believed that this was an indication that he could "pull-off" the referendum two months later.[125] As had been the case at regular five year intervals over the previous twenty years, once again Indonesian officials viewed the East Timor issue through the peculiar lens of their own electoral politics.

Meanwhile, others in Jakarta were far less optimistic. The depths of this pessimism are revealed in a memo from the Assistant Coordinating Minister for Home Affairs, Brigadier-General H. R. Garnadi, dated July 3, that was leaked to the press. The memo "predicts the worse possibility, that Option 1 [broad autonomy] will not be accepted by the East Timorese."[126] The report goes on to predict that this would lead to widespread chaos in East Timor, with Indonesian officials, transmigrants, and carpetbaggers fleeing the territory, and cause economic paralysis. Garnadi recommended that plans be made for the evacuation of Indonesian civil servants and non-East Timorese, for the withdrawal of military units (including those from the Army, Navy and Air Force), and, finally, for the destruction of "vital facilities and objects."[127] In short, the Ministry of Home Affairs and elements of the Indonesian military, including the Task Force headed by Gen. Zacky Anwar Makarim, had arrived at divergent predictions.

Despite the overall success of the June national election in East Timor and the encouragement that this provided, the Indonesian Task Force also prepared its own contingency plans. On June 18 a meeting was held at Korem headquarters in Dili, attended by Task Force head Zacky Anwar and his deputy Glenny Kairupan, ABRI Assistant for Operations Major-General Kiki Syahnakri, Korem Commander Colonel Tono Suratman, and several of the militia heads, at which more comprehensive plans were formulated.[128] Recognizing that the outcome of the referendum remained in doubt, and that many in Jakarta were outright pessimistic about achieving electoral victory, two contingency plans were developed. The first plan proposed attempting to derail the vote, either during the three month run-up period and campaign or on polling day in August, through coordinated violence. A second, far more complex, contingency plan was prepared in case the vote was held and went against Indonesia. This involved using the militias to reject the results and to demand that East Timor be partitioned, with the western districts (particularly Covalima, Bobonaro, and Ambeno) remaining with Indonesia. Additional measures called for the forced relocation of the local population across the border into West Timor, so that there would be no population left to object, and,

---

[125] According to reliable sources, the resistance in East Timor had decided to organize a boycott of the election, but this decision was overruled by Xanana Gusmaõ, who feared that a boycott might jeopardize the UN-sponsored referendum scheduled for August.

[126] See "The report of the Politics and Security Team in Dili," No. M.53/Tim P4-OTTT/7/1999, issued under the name H. R. Garnadi, Assistant Coordinating Minister I/Home Affairs, posted on Joyo@aol.com, August 26, 1999. H. R. Garnadi is a military officer whose last known post was as Deputy Commander of the Army's Staff and Command School.

[127] It appears that this meant the destruction of government and military offices and their records, not the wholesale destruction of the territory.

[128] Personal communication, August 10, 1999. Note that both Glenny Kairupan and Kiki Syahnakri served in Dili in early 1995 at the time of the ninja activity, and therefore were not only familiar with the techniques but knew many of the paramilitary leaders as well.

potentially, for the reverse flooding of non-East Timorese back across the border to repopulate these eastern regions. Ambitious, indeed partially unrealistic, these plans lie at the root of the post-referendum events.[129]

It is necessary to underscore the point that these were contingency plans; by all appearances the Indonesian Task Force still believed that it could achieve a desired outcome. By using controlled violence and terror, the Task Force and military personnel on the ground in East Timor hoped both to intimidate East Timorese into voting in favor of broad autonomy and to scare others away from the polls. They calculated that a rough split of the vote would be grounds for the Indonesian MPR to reject the idea of releasing East Timor and that such a vote would stymie UN efforts to push independence through. On the other hand, an extremely low voter turnout would allow Indonesia to call the results into question. If Zacky Anwar did not believe that a desired outcome could be achieved, he would (and could) have simply unleashed enough massive violence to drive the UN and foreign observers from the territory and thus simply prevented the referendum from being held in the first place.

With the political agreements in place, UN staff and police advisors attached to the Indonesian police, foreign observers, and international reporters all congregated in East Timor to sponsor, supervise, monitor, and report on the referendum. They immediately encountered violence and voiced repeated concern about the militia activities and failure of the Indonesian authorities to fulfill the terms of the accord. Indonesia responded by announcing that the militias were being placed under the police as part of a civilian defense and security force.[130] This led to an extraordinary situation: individual countries which did not recognize Indonesian rule in East Timor were contributing police officers to a force under the UN, which itself did not recognize Indonesian rule, to supervise the Indonesian police which, thanks to international outcry, had now declared that the militias were formally attached to them as civilian forces.

While the UN forces on the ground faced militia activity and military indifference, little action was taken on the international front. The UN continued to issue calls for an end to the violence, but was repeatedly ignored. Canberra and Washington also insisted that the Indonesian military live up to its promises, but failed to take any meaningful action. When asked if the United States had plans to send troops to protect the East Timorese, US State Department spokesman James Rubin explained: "I don't know how to answer that . . . The military of our country has plans to do everything. That's what their job is, to have plans." He continued: "contingency plans are supposed to exist. They do exist. I'm not saying that a contingency plan exists along the lines you're just describing."[131] Remarkably, in July, Australia hosted Asia's largest regional military training exercise which involved forces from Australia, the US, and a host of Asian allies (including Indonesia) in the Timor Sea.[132] Had Canberra and Washington wanted the

---

[129] A similar version of this plan was reported after the referendum in "Revealed: army's plot to destroy a nation," *The Guardian*, September 11, 1999.

[130] See, for example, "Concern Over Status of Militias," *IPS*, posted on Joyo@aol.com, June 15, 1999.

[131] Quoted in "East Timor: How Washington has no stand-by plans, except when it does," *Sydney Morning Herald*, August 12, 1999.

[132] "Asian top guns gear up for war games off Australia," *Reuters*, July 25, 1999.

referendum to be held without military and paramilitary violence, they had the troops prepared and just off shore.

Despite two delays and massive levels of pre-referendum violence, on August 30 the people of East Timor flooded to the polling stations and voted overwhelmingly in favor of independence. While the military leadership in Jakarta remained hesitant, Zacky Anwar's Task Force neither did enough to win the referendum nor enough to prevent it from being held. With this, the well-prepared but ill-conceived contingency plans were set in motion. Massive physical destruction was the first and simplest part of the plan, facilitated in part by the forcible relocation of hundreds of thousands of East Timorese across the border into West Timor.[133] The additional stages in the plan were from the start less realistic. Though militia leaders did discuss declaring separation of the western districts,[134] this idea was soon deemed impossible and dropped in the face of the incoming UN force; plans for implementing any form of repopulation were also dropped. It is interesting to note that more than one contingency plan may have been at work in the first weeks of September, for while the Ministry of Home Affairs had plans to evacuate Indonesian officials, transmigrants, and carpetbaggers, and for the withdrawal of military personnel, Zacky Anwar had been tentatively preparing to reject the outcome, unleash wholesale destruction and violence, and perhaps even declare the separation of several districts from East Timor. These two sets of plans were partially overlapping, and may in fact have facilitated one another.

CONCLUSION

Once an integral part of international relations, in the late twentieth century territorial annexation has been replaced by punitive bombings and the establishment of puppet regimes. The reason is not necessarily that states do not wish to add to their territory (though this may in fact be a new phenomenon), but rather that such actions threaten to tarnish their legitimacy and lose them recognition. For two and a half decades Jakarta's friends and allies were willing to look away while Indonesia carried out its brutal occupation of tiny East Timor. But the issue of legitimacy and international recognition did not go away. The East Timorese resistance was incapable of defeating the aggressor, but thanks to superb leadership and commitment was able to keep the issue very much on the international agenda. Lacking international acceptance of the 1976 Act of Integration, Indonesia sought to "normalize" its rule over the occupied territory. Though at first tentative, these efforts increased over time, patterned around national electoral cycles. On each occasion, however, attempts to normalize the occupation led to increased use of covert and paramilitary tactics, in part from necessity, in part, too, at the instigation of elements within the military who were threatened by a relaxation of military rule.

The last chapter of Indonesian occupation of East Timor displayed a particular twist on this theme of "normalization." On the one hand, political leaders not only treated East Timor as normal—hence the need to extend *reformasi* to the territory,

---

[133] For an early report that provides useful regional estimates, see "East Timor's deserted outpost," *Christian Science Monitor*, October 25, 1999.

[134] See, for example, "'Bagi Dua Saja Timtim'" ('Just Divide East Timor in Two'), *Waspada*, September 6, 1999; and "Militia schemes to partition territory," *The Age*, October 5, 1999.

as well as a willingness to hold the June national elections there—but even offered it "special" status as part of Indonesia. On the other hand, the military and paramilitary violence were part of a concerted effort both to prevent any real reform or democratization from taking place and to reframe the issue as an internal East Timorese conflict, portraying the Indonesian presence as an attempt to restore order, and hence normality. Few bought this argument in 1975, fewer still in 1999.

WAITING FOR THE END IN BIAK: VIOLENCE, ORDER, AND A FLAG RAISING[1]

Danilyn Rutherford

A "NOT WHOLLY PEACEFUL" PROTEST

On July 6, 1998, just before dawn, soldiers opened fire on a group of some two hundred demonstrators, in Biak City, on Biak Island, in Biak-Numfor Regency, in the Indonesian province of Irian Jaya.[2] For four days, the demonstrators had been

[1] This essay is based on research supported by a US Department of Education Fulbright-Hays Doctoral Dissertation Research Abroad Fellowship, a Predoctoral Grant from the Wenner-Gren Foundation for Anthropological Research, a grant from the Joint Committee on Southeast Asia of the Social Science Research Council and the American Council of Learned Societies with funds provided by the Andrew W. Mellon Foundation, the Ford Foundation, and the Henry Luce Foundation, and a grant from the J. David Greenstone Memorial Fund of the University of Chicago Division of Social Sciences. A version of this essay was presented in a session entitled "Violence and the Political Economy of Terror in Irian Jaya" at the Annual Meeting of the American Anthropological Association, Philadelphia, PA, December 3, 1998. I would like to thank Stuart Kirsch for organizing this panel. I would also like to thank Benedict Anderson, Deborah Homsher, Rupert Stasch, and Mary Steedly for their helpful comments and criticisms. Any errors are, of course, my own.

[2] Advocacy organizations reporting on the Internet about the flag raising include Human Rights Watch, "Indonesia Alert: Trouble in Irian Jaya," July 6, 1998, "Irian Jaya Detainees Denied Family Visits, Medical Care," July 9, 1998, "Indonesia: Human Rights and Pro-Independence Actions in Irian Jaya," December 1998; Survival International, "Urgent Action Needed: People Shot in Biak, West Papua/Irian," July 6, 1998, "Update from Biak," July 9, 1998; TAPOL, "Situation Tense in Biak," July 5, 1998; and Buset Foker LSM, "Perkembangan Kasus Irian Jaya" (Developments in the Case of Irian Jaya), July 8, 1997. Internet press reports include (among many others) "Akibat Kurusuhan di Irja 16 Ditahan, 20 Dirawat" (As a Result of Rioting in Irian Jaya, 16 Arrested, 20 Hospitalized), *Suara Pembaruan*, July 8, 1998; "Irian Tribes Defy Slaughter," *Sydney Morning Herald*, July 8, 1998; "Indonesia's Black Death," *Sydney Morning Herald*, November 11, 1998; "Indonesian Church Groups: Two Shot Dead in

guarding a flag that flew on top of a water tower between the main market and the port. They had raised the flag before dawn on July 2. Later that morning, at an open forum, their leader, a young civil servant named Philip Karma, read an oath of allegiance to West Papua, the name of the sovereign nation that Karma and others would like Irian Jaya to become. On behalf of the Papuan people, Karma vowed not to abandon the flag and urged Kofi Annan to come to Biak to hear their case. That afternoon, when the security forces attempted to break up the demonstration, the followers wounded several policemen and burned a military truck. On July 5, after negotiations with the demonstrators broke down, authorities issued an ultimatum. If the crowd did not lower the flag voluntarily, troops would remove it by force.

The shooting is said to have lasted from 5:30 to 7:00 a.m. Just how many people were injured and killed in the operation remains unclear. Colonel Edyono, the Armed Forces commander in Biak, initially announced that there were twenty-one casualties and no fatalities.[3] Other sources have put the death toll between five and a hundred; reports of torture and disappearances abound.[4] After the Indonesian Human Rights Commission investigated the incident, the military leader finally admitted that one man, Ruben Orboi, had been killed.[5] Orboi's body had been carried out to the sea, the commander told reporters. Fearing further unrest, the soldiers had decided to conceal the death temporarily by hiding the corpse in a shallow, beachside grave. When I arrived in Biak in late July for a brief visit, bodies had begun washing up on Biak beaches. Although the government claimed to have proof that these corpses were victims of the *tsunami* that struck Papua New Guinea on July 18, the police ordered villagers to bury them immediately.[6] When I left Biak in early August, Philip Karma remained in police custody, with gunshot wounds to both of his legs.[7] It seems likely that the flag lowering cost many more than one of his supporters their lives.

Irian Jaya," *Inside China*, July 10, 1998; "Activists Rally in Indonesian Region," *Associated Press*, July 4, 1998; "Focus: Indonesian Troops Tackle Fresh Irian Rally," *Reuters*, July 7, 1998; "Indonesians Dismantle Irian Separatist Flag Pole," *Reuters*, July 8, 1998; and "Indonesian Activists Say Five Missing in Irian," *Reuters*, August 7, 1998.

[3] See "Irian Tribes Defy Slaughter," *Sydney Morning Herald*, July 8, 1998; "Focus: Indonesian Troops Tackle Fresh Irian Rally," *Reuters*, July 7, 1998; "Indonesians Dismantle Irian Separatist Flag Pole," *Reuters*, July 8, 1998; and "Indonesian Church Groups: Two Shot Dead in Irian Jaya," *Inside China*, July 10, 1998.

[4] See Human Rights Watch, "Irian Jaya Detainees Denied Family Visits, Medical Care," July 9 1998; Survival International, "Urgent Action Needed: People Shot in Biak, West Papua/Irian," July 6, 1998 and "Update from Biak," July 9, 1998. According to Human Rights Watch, the military attack resulted in three confirmed fatalities. Ruben Orboi, discussed below, died on the scene, and two more of Karma's supporters died shortly after the military released them from detention. To date, ten others have been reported missing. See "Indonesia: Human Rights and Pro-independence Actions in Irian Jaya."

[5] See *Cendrawasih Pos*, July 25, 1998, pp. 1, 4.

[6] See "Lagi Sembilan Mayat Ditemukan di Biak Timur" (Another Nine Corpses Found in East Biak), *Cendrawasih Pos*, July 29, 1998, p. 1; "Masih Dalam Penyelidikan" (Still Under Investigation), *Cendrawasih Pos*, July 29, 1998, p. 1; "Korban Tsunami PNG di Biak Ditemukan Mencapai 28 Orang" (Toll of Victims of Papua-New Guinea Tsunami Found in Biak Reaches 28), *Cendrawasih Pos*, August 1, 1998, p. 1; and "Fishermen Find Bodies Off Indonesian Coast," *Guardian Weekly*, August 9, 1998, p. 4; see also Human Rights Watch, "Indonesia: Human Rights and Pro-Independence Actions in Irian Jaya."

[7] Convicted of rebellion for his role in the flag raising, Karma was sentenced to six and a half years in prison. See "Irian Jaya Man Jailed Over Separatist Protest," *AFP*, January 31, 1999.

The Morning Star Flag, which the Biak demonstrators were guarding, was officially raised next to the Dutch flag on December 1, 1961, less than a year before the United States and Australia brokered the deal that decided the fate of Netherlands New Guinea.[8] In 1949, when the rest of the Indies gained independence, the Netherlands had retained the western half of the island of New Guinea, arguing that it was preparing its "primitive" Papuans for self-rule. In 1962, facing high deficits, heavy US pressure, and the threat of war, the Dutch agreed to relinquish the territory to Indonesia. A United Nations Temporary Executive Authority (UNTEA) was established to oversee the transfer and to assist in preparations for an "Act of Free Choice" in which western New Guinea's inhabitants would have a chance to choose between remaining within Indonesia or founding an independent West Papuan state. It soon became clear that Indonesia would not honor the principle of "one man, one vote" in the plebiscite, which was scheduled for 1969.[9] Headed by Ali Moertopo, a Special Operation for West Irian led the campaign for integration, often resorting to coercive means. When the Act was finally held, under the military's watchful eyes, 1,022 carefully selected tribal leaders unsurprisingly opted for their homeland to remain a province of Indonesia.[10] In the years leading up to the referendum, groups of urban Papuans staged demonstrations demanding genuine self-determination; others entered the forest and took up arms.[11] According to one account, it was the Indonesian

---

[8] See Robin Osborne, "The OPM and the Quest for West Papuan Unity," in *Between Two Nations: The Indonesia-Papua New Guinea Border and West Papuan Nationalism,* ed. R. J. May (Bathurst, Australia: Brown, 1986), p. 2; see also Robin Osborne, *Indonesia's Secret War: The Guerrilla Struggle in Irian Jaya* (Sydney: Allen and Unwin, 1985).

[9] For a discussion of the Act of Free Choice (AFC), as stipulated under the New York Agreement, see Peter Savage, "The National Liberation Struggle in West Irian: From Millenarianism to Socialist Revolution," *Asian Survey* 18, 10 (1978): 986. "The organization of the AFC was to include: (a) consultations with the representative councils of the nine regions on the procedures and methods to be followed for ascertaining the freely expressed decision of the people; (b) a clear formulation of whether or not Indonesia was to continue in control; (c) a guarantee of the eligibility of all indigenous inhabitants to participate in the AFC, which was to be carried out in accordance with international practice; and (d) the establishment by Indonesian-Netherlands consultation of the exact time of the AFC, which was to take place before the end of 1969. Indonesia under article XXII of the Agreement also undertook the following, without which the previous provisions would be meaningless: to guarantee the human rights of the inhabitants of West Papua New Guinea [sic], including the rights of free speech and freedom of movement and assembly."

In 1962, the head of the Indonesian mission to UNTEA and Deputy Minister of Foreign Affairs "suggested that a plebiscite through suffrage would be too difficult, and that the wishes of the people should be determined through consultation [*musjawarah*] with community leaders." Between 1962 and 1968, local leaders were pressed into signing resolutions supporting Indonesian rule and deeming the referendum unnecessary. Ibid., p. 985. See also John R. G. Djopari, *Pemberontakan Organisasi Papua Merdeka* (The Uprising of the Free Papua Organization) (Jakarta: Rasindo, 1993), pp. 72-3.

[10] Although the settlement called for UN supervision, the only observers allowed to be on hand for the plebiscite were a Bolivian diplomat—who spoke no Indonesian—and a skeletal staff. See Savage, "The National Liberation Struggle in West Irian," pp. 986-7. See also "Jayapura Tense, But Calm," *Indonesian Observer,* August 16, 2000.

[11] See "Former Governor of West Irian Interviewed by TAPOL," *Tapol Bulletin* 48 (November 1981): 9-10.

authorities who gave the budding movement its name: the Free Papua Organization or OPM.[12]

The flag raising on Biak coincided with demonstrations in several of Irian Jaya's other major cities: Sorong, Jayapura, and Wamena. The twenty-seventh anniversary of the OPM's Declaration of West Papuan Independence fell on July 1, 1998, a little over a month following the resignation of Indonesia's President Suharto after thirty-three years in office.[13] The Indonesian province of Irian Jaya was born during the same decade as Suharto's "New Order" regime. Suharto commanded a military mission intended to retake "West Irian" in 1961, four years before coming to power in the aborted coup and state-sponsored massacres that destroyed the Indonesian Communist Party and forced the Republic's first president out of office. In Irian Jaya, Suharto's sudden abdication served to revive old hopes. Irian Jayans had no doubt heard of the riots that swept Jakarta and other major Indonesian cities in May 1998, as well as the peaceful student protests that preceded them. Those with televisions may have seen images of the students who occupied the parliament building during Suharto's final days. Between rounds of chanting and singing, the protesters chatted with young soldiers, who smiled, their weapons idle at their sides. The brutal response of Indonesian troops to the pro-independence protests in Irian Jaya provided a lesson in the limits of *reformasi*, as this brave new era in Indonesian politics has been dubbed. "These people were not demanding reform; they wanted a separate state," the commander in Biak explained.[14] Against such a "betrayal of the nation," added General Wiranto, the chief of the Indonesian Armed Forces, "firm action" was required.[15]

One need not look far for a straightforward explanation of the flag raising and its aftermath on Biak. "This really isn't a new problem," said one Biak friend, voicing a sentiment widely shared in the province. "People want a fair referendum so they can decide their fate." It is not surprising that Indonesia's new rulers oppose such a proposal. Shortly after Suharto's fall, several members of the US Congress sent a letter to B. J. Habibie, the current president, and Amien Rais, his most powerful opponent, calling for dialogue on the political status of East Timor and Irian Jaya. While Indonesia proved open to negotiations on East Timor, both Habibie and Rais indicated in July 1998 that they would draw the line at Indonesia's resource-rich easternmost province.[16] In the fall, there was some softening of this stance, with plans going ahead for a "national dialogue" between Irianese leaders and the Indonesian national government.[17] But when one hundred

---

[12] See Djopari, *Pemberontakan Organisasi Papua Merdeka*, p. 100. As far as titles go, the direct precursor to the OPM was the Organisasi dan Perjuangan Menuju Kemerdekaan Papua Barat (Organization and Struggle For the Freedom of West Papua), whose leader, Terianus Aronggeor, was captured in Manokwari in 1964. The name OPM gained currency in 1965, after Permenas Ferry Awom launched a guerrilla campaign against the Indonesian army.

[13] Ibid, p. 116. See also Osborne, "The OPM and the Quest for West Papuan Unity," p. 55.

[14] See "Irian Tribes Defy Slaughter," *Sydney Morning Herald*, July 8, 1998.

[15] Ibid. See also "Focus: Indonesian Troops Tackle Fresh Irian Rally."

[16] See "Indonesia's Black Death," *Sydney Morning Herald*, November 11, 1998.

[17] See "Jakarta Ready to Hold Dialogue on Irian Jaya: MP," *AFP*, October 19, 1998; "Habibie Setuju Berdialog dengan Tokoh Irian Jaya" (Habibie Agrees To Have a Dialogue with West Irian Leaders), *Kompas*, October 27, 1998; "Irianese Want More than Pledge of Dialog," *Jakarta Post*, January 23, 1998. Spearheading the campaign for a national dialogue is FORERI, Forum Rekonsiliasi Rakyat Irian Jaya (The Forum for the Reconciliation of the Irian Jayan People),

representatives from the province presented Habibie with a demand for independence in a February 26 pre-meeting in Jakarta, the president told them to go home and think again.[18] Reports that the armed forces had a hand in orchestrating the July demonstrations in Irian Jaya are not entirely implausible. Military officers have a stake in the designation of certain provinces as "unstable." Former commanders often live out their retirement in East Timor or Irian Jaya so they can reap the harvest of profitable business deals made in the areas under their command. While the assault came later than it would have under Suharto—when flag raisings lasted minutes, not days—the brutal treatment of the demonstrators followed a familiar script, in which soldiers protect the Republic from the enemy within.

I would not want to underplay the long history of broken promises, corruption, and discrimination that has led to demands for an independent West Papuan state. Nor would I want to downplay the collusion of individual, institutional, and international interests in the continuance of Indonesian rule. At the same time, I would not want to leave the impression that the symbolic and the political aspects of the incident belong to separate domains. According to the commander in Biak, only fifty of the demonstrators were "hardcore" separatists; the other three hundred were "deluded" by promises of miraculous improvements in conditions and the belief that something religious was going on.[19] A critique of this attempt to explain away the "disturbance" must go further than asserting that religion provided a language for the protesters. An interpretation of the flag raising must pay heed to the metaphysical underpinnings of all modern states, be they imaginary or "real."

---

which came into being in the wake of the July demonstrations, following a fact-finding mission led by the deputy speaker of the national parliament, Abdul Gafur. FORERI's founding members include Herman Saud, Synod Chair of the Irian Jaya Gospel Church (Gereja Kristen Injil Irian Jaya); Leo Laba Lajar, Bishop of Jayapura; Theys Eluay, Chair of the Irian Customary Council Institute (Lembaga Dewan Adat Irian); Tom Beanal, Chair of the Foundation for Customary Consultation of the Amungme Tribe (Lembaga Musyawarah Adat Suku Amungme), Presidium member of WAHLI, Indonesia's pre-eminent environmental organization, and former delegate to the provincial parliament; Martinus Werimon, Chair of the Student Senate of Cendrawasih University; the Chair of the Student Senate of I. S. Kijne Seminary of the GKI; and feminist activist Yusan Yeblo.

[18] See "Irianese Leaders Want Control of Their Land," *Jakarta Post*, February 27, 1999; "President Habibie tentang Irian Jaya: Renungkan Lagi Tuntutan Kemerdekaan Itu" (Habibie about Irian: Contemplate Again That Demand for Independence), *Kompas Online*, February 28, 1999. For an English translation of the statement delivered to Habibie, see "West Papuans Demanding for Free West Papua," *Kabar Irian*, February 17, 1999 newsgroup posting. The statement stipulates that if their demand for independence is not met, the "people of West Papua" will boycott the general elections in 1999. Freddy Numberi, the current governor, interpreted Habibie's response as implying that the case for independence is closed; Numberi's own proposal calls for greater autonomy. See "Irian Governor Calls for 'Special Autonomy,'" *Media Indonesia*, March 11, 1999 (from a BBC Summary of World Broadcasts published on the newsgroup Kabar Irian on March 13, 1999); "Pemerintah Tolak Tuntutan Kemerdekaan Papua Barat" (Government Rejects Demand for Irian Independence), *Kompas*, March 15, 1999. On the threats received by members of the delegation upon their return to Jayapura, see Amnesty International, "Fear for Safety/Threats and Intimidation: Hermanus Wayoi, Don Flassy, Workers at ELS-HAM, a local human rights organization," AI Index: ASA 21/16/99, March 9, 1999.

[19] See *Cendrawasih Pos*, July 14, 1998, p. 1.

In an intelligent, meticulous report on the July demonstrations, Human Rights Watch notes, quite accurately, that the pro-independence actions in Irian Jaya were "not all wholly peaceful."[20] This comment confirms what upon reflection should seem obvious. Violence was not simply a means to an end in the flag raising (and flag lowering); it was crucial to the very meaning of both gestures. What was at stake in that contested piece of cloth was Indonesia's very status as a state, as defined by its ability to maintain a monopoly over the legitimate use of force.[21] This monopoly was challenged not only by the demonstrators' attack on the police, but also by the oath that legitimized the assault. The demonstration began, one should recall, with a performative: a forceful, self-fulfilling gesture.[22] Karma's declaration created its own truth by constituting its own subject, the West Papuan people, in whose name he promised never to abandon the flag. For a brief period, in one small corner of Indonesia, the demonstrators violently established the legitimacy of an alternative regime.

If the flag raising was a performative, then the shootings could be read as an attempt to prevent the founding of West Papua from becoming felicitous, that is, a speech event undertaken in a discursive context that guarantees that such an oath will shape future action. Against the soldiers' guns, the demonstrators mobilized higher powers to ground their tautological words and deeds: "God, the Father, Son and Holy Ghost," who were named as witnesses to the pledge. At the Biak water tower, as elsewhere, the violent birth of a nation entailed an appeal to the transcendent.[23] But the logic of the nation-state only captures one aspect of the confrontation, which brought together a multiplicity of conceptions of the relationship of violence to order, origins, and truth.

---

[20] "Indonesia: Human Rights and Pro-Independence Actions in Irian Jaya."

[21] See Max Weber, "Politics as a Vocation," in *From Max Weber: Essays in Sociology*, ed. H. H. Gerth and C. W. Mills (London: Routledge and Kegan Paul, 1970); see also Walter Benjamin, "Critique of Violence," in *Reflections: Essays, Aphorisms, Autobiographical Writings*, trans. Edmund Jephcott (New York: Schocken, 1978), pp. 277-300.

[22] On performatives, see J. L. Austin, *How to Do Things with Words* (London: Oxford University Press, 1976); John Searle, "What is a Speech Act?" in *Language and Social Context*, ed. Pier P. Gigioli (London: Penguin, 1965), pp. 136-54; Jacques Derrida, "Signature, Event, Context," in *Margins of Philosophy*, trans. Samuel Weber (Chicago: University of Chicago Press, 1982), pp. 307-330. The relationship between violence and order in a foundational moment, such as that posited in the flag raising, is over-determined. Some writers on violence have stressed its own performative structure, arguing that the violent act both signifies and enforces its own legitimacy by providing a pre-emptive strike that silences dissent. See David Riches, "Aggression, Warfare and Violence: Space/Time and Paradigm," *Man* N. S. 26: 281-98, and Christian Krohn-Hansen, "The Anthropology of Violent Interaction," *Journal of Anthropological Research* 50 (4): 367-382. Legally sanctioned violence, in turn, refers back to an equally performative act of force: the law-founding utterance that creates its own legitimacy, after the fact. On this problem, see Jacques Derrida, "Force of Law: The 'Mystical Foundations of Authority,'" in *Deconstruction and the Possibility of Justice*, ed. Drucilla Cornell, Michel Rosenfeld and David Gray Carlson (New York and London: Routledge, 1996), pp. 3-67.

[23] See B. Honig, "Declarations of Independence: Arendt and Derrida on the Problems of Founding a Republic," *American Political Science Review* 85,1 (1991): 97-113, and Benjamin Lee, *Talking Heads: Language, Metalanguage and the Semiotics of Subjectivity* (Durham: Duke University Press, 1997), pp. 338-341. Lee describes the double lines of authority that underwrite the US Declaration of Independence, one stretching "through the self-evident laws of nature to God, the ultimate, eternal, transcendental countersignatory"; the other "to the just announced and contested 'good people' of the colonies. The radical performativity of the latter is legitimated by the transcendent authority of the former." Ibid., p. 328.

In this essay, I explore the intersection between these multiple conceptions. I offer a tentative answer to a question many on Biak found important: what gave those young demonstrators the courage to face up to armed soldiers? I seek a response not only in Papuan nationalism and the recent experience of Indonesian rule, but also in the long tradition of Biak millenarianism. I show how this tradition finds its basis in everyday practices that transform what is foreign into a source of value, authority, and prestige. Biaks have tended to valorize objects and texts—from foreign porcelain to government slogans—that they take as traces of encounters with dangerous outsiders. The violence of a clash between worldviews is posited in many of the processes through which Biaks create their identities and seek status and power. This valorization of the foreign, taken alone, cannot account for the pro-independence protests in Biak. Nevertheless, at critical moments, a distinctively messianic vision has shaped the way Biaks envision and pursue political change.

For many Biaks, "God, the Father, Son and Holy Ghost" is really Manarmakeri, the Biak ancestor responsible for the wealth and power of outsiders. However, Philip Karma's oath may have followed a familiar model for the founding of a nation; in the very act of appealing to the divine, Karma may have allowed for a shift into a narrative premised on very different assumptions about the nature of power, space, and time. But if I approach the flag raising as a millennial moment, I also pay heed to the equally violent narratives of transformation promulgated by the Indonesian regime. To set the stage for this analysis, I begin by briefly considering the broader institutional forces that have encouraged Biaks to participate in the Papuan nationalist movement, from its earliest stages to the present day.

PAPUAN NATIONALISM AND BIAK COSMOPOLITANISM

Rising from the Pacific at the mouth of Cendrawasih Bay, roughly two hundred kilometers off the New Guinea mainland, three small islands and a scattering of atolls make up the Indonesian Regency (Kabupaten) of Biak-Numfor. Over the territory's colonial and postcolonial history, the inhabitants of these islands have sometimes appeared as exemplary of Papuan or Irianese identity, sometimes as the exception that proves the rule. Biak-speaking seafarers were among the first of New Guinea's inhabitants to confront European traders, missionaries, and officials, by virtue of their longstanding tributary relations with the Moluccan Sultanate of Tidore. By 1920, the Netherlands Indies military had pacified the islands. By the early 1930s, the vast majority of Biaks had converted to Protestantism, and almost every village featured a mission church and school. In the late 1940s, one official observed that illiteracy was "virtually nonexistent" among Biak men below the age of thirty-five.[24] At a time when the ancestors of today's Dani and Amungme had yet to encounter Europeans, Biak evangelists were spreading the Gospel along New Guinea's northern coast. Biak's longstanding experience with outsiders made islanders fodder for early Dutch descriptions of the

---

[24] See Jan Victor de Bruyn, "Jaarverslagen 1947 en 1948 van Onderafdeling Biak" (Annual Reports, 1947 and 1948, of the Biak Subdistrict), *Nienhuis Collectie van de Department van Bevolkingszaken*, Nummer Toegang 10-25, Stuk 188 (The Hague: Algemeene Rijksarchief, 1948), p. 7.

customs and character of the Papuan.[25] In the 1950s, when the Dutch retained western New Guinea as a separate colony, Biaks and other coastal Papuans continued to play a central role in colonial representations of the territory's natives, as well as in policies designed to cultivate an educated Papuan elite. Dutch propaganda featured before-and-after photographs, opposing scantily clad tribesmen from the highlands to smiling coastal workers.[26] Figures from Biak, Sentani, and other places with a long history of contact stood in for the modern Papuan whom this new civilizing mission promised to produce.

By making progress appear as the outcome of Dutch intervention, these images obscure the accidents of geography and history that have made places like Biak and Jayapura what they are today: relatively urban, cosmopolitan, multiethnic sites in a vast, sparsely populated province. During World War II, when the war in the Pacific started to turn against Japan, the Occupation forces began building what is now the longest runway in Indonesia on Biak Island; the Allies completed the project during MacArthur's famous island hopping campaign, after driving out the Japanese.[27] After the war, the Dutch expanded the airport and the surrounding settlement, building on the foundations of the American military base. Today, in addition to an international airport, Biak City boasts a port, a canning factory, a plywood mill, three markets, two supermarkets, numerous shops, hotels, restaurants, and karaoke bars, three military posts, and countless government offices. It is home to Makassarese and Sino-Indonesian merchants, officials and soldiers from Java, Bali, Sumatra, Ambon, and other distant Indonesian islands, a handful of Western visitors, and a large community of Irian Jayans from other tribes. Urban Biaks include everyone from the Regent to NGO directors to teachers, day laborers, taxi conductors (people, usually young boys, who hustle for passengers and collect fares on public minivan taxis), nurses, and low-paid government clerks. Among their numbers is a growing population of young, unemployed high school graduates and drop-outs, many of whom while away their days at the taxi terminal near the main market. Some are waiting for job openings in the civil service, which, despite its expansion under the New Order, can absorb only a fraction of those who apply. In addition, at any one time, Biak City is a temporary home to scores of rural Biaks: fishermen selling their catch, subsistence farmers marketing their extra fruit and vegetables, seasonal construction workers, and children staying with relatives while they attend school. In recent years, the Indonesian government has extended roads and bridges to distant coastal villages, making it easier for villagers to travel to market and for elite Biaks to build retirement homes on their clan land. With luck, one can make it to Biak City from almost anywhere in the islands in less than five hours. In the early 1990s, when Biak was a refueling stop on the route between Los Angeles and Jakarta, Honolulu

---

[25] "De bevolking van Biak en het kolonisatievraagstuk van Noord Nieuw-Guinea" (The People of Biak and the Question of the Colonization of Northern New Guinea), *Tijdschrift Nieuw Guinea* 1 (1936): 169-177.

[26] See, for example, *Vademecum voor Nederlands-Nieuw-Guinea* (Vademecum for Netherlands New Guinea) (Rotterdam: New Guinea Institute in cooperation with the Ministry of Overseas Territories, 1956).

[27] See Robert Ross Smith, *The US Army in World War II: The War in the Pacific*, vol. 3: *The Approach to the Philippines* (Washington, D.C.: Office of the Chief of Military History, 1953), pp. 280-396.

was less than twelve hours away. Biak bureaucrats and academics, traveling to Jakarta, Townsville or Leiden, sometimes boarded these international flights.

Below, I discuss in detail the distinctive values that orient Biaks' participation in social arenas that extend far beyond the local setting. But at this point, it is worth noting how conditions in Biak bring into sharp relief grievances shared by other Irianese groups. Biak-Numfor is the most densely populated regency in Irian Jaya, and one of the least fertile. Yet in recent years, Biaks have had to surrender clan land for a range of projects, from a satellite launcher to a transmigration site to a five-star resort. Biak fishermen complain of declining yields as commercial trawlers deplete the coastal stocks. As elsewhere in the province, non-Irian Jayans dominate the urban economy, owning everything from the taxis villagers ride into town to the shops where they buy sugar and rice.[28] Makassarese traders monopolize the choicest stalls in the central market, leaving local producers to crouch along the outer aisles or in the dirt outside. Local residents also find themselves pushed to the margins in the competition for government benefits. To the consternation of Biak parents, the children of migrants from outside the province often win jobs and scholarships reserved for the locally born. Biaks are well aware of the province's vast reserves of minerals and natural gas; some have seen the Freeport mines first hand. They are also aware that public services in the province are woefully inadequate. Even in this relatively accessible regency, classrooms stand empty, and clinics are understaffed and understocked. Above all, as I elaborate below, Biaks share with other Irian Jayans indelible memories of state terror. Some still carry scars (and in some cases bullets) from the turbulent 1970s, when the Indonesian military attacked North and West Biak villages to flush out armed guerrillas. Under the New Order, activists who criticized government policies were often accused of harboring separatist sympathies. Biaks learned from decades of extra-judicial violence that the label OPM could be the "kiss of death."[29]

But it is not enough simply to point to this *memoria passionis*, "history of suffering," to understand why the dream of self-determination has not only survived, but thrived in Biak and Irian Jaya more generally.[30] The past four decades have introduced a range of shared experiences that have made an independent West Papua imaginable for growing numbers of the province's inhabitants. On the one hand, one must consider the circumference of the administrative pilgrimages taken by the provincial elite.[31] No matter how much overseas training they may have received, the majority of Irianese bureaucrats,

---

[28] On the role of migrants in the provincial economy, see R. Garnaut and C. Manning, *Irian Jaya: The Transformation of a Melanesian Economy* (Canberra: ANU Press, 1974), and Chris Manning and Michael Rumbiak, "Irian Jaya: Economic Change, Migrants, and Indigenous Welfare," in *Unity and Diversity: Regional Economic Development in Indonesia since 1970*, ed. Hal Hill (Oxford: Oxford University Press, 1991), pp. 77-106.

[29] See "OPM is 'The Kiss of Death,' Says MP," *Tapol Bulletin* 43 (January 1980): 5.

[30] See J. Budi Hernawan OFM and Theo van den Broek OFM of the Secretariat for Justice and Peace of the Jayapura Diocese, "Dialog Nasional Papua: Sebuah Kisah 'Memoria Passionis'" (Papua's National Dialogue: A Story of 'Memoria Passionis'), *Tifa Irian*, March 12, 1998, Internet posting March 25, 1998.

[31] See Benedict Anderson, *Imagined Communities* (New York: Verso, 1991), pp. 53-56. For this analysis, I am also drawing on pp. 170-178, where Anderson explicitly considers the roots of Papuan nationalism in provincial icons and institutions.

soldiers and academics have pursued their careers in the space between Sorong (not Sabang!) and Merauke, i.e. within the borders of what is now Irian Jaya.[32] The same elite has long sustained the separatist movement, both in Irian Jaya and overseas.[33] While Biaks have no monopoly on OPM leadership—or high-ranking government posts—suitable examples emerge from their ranks. Marcus Kaisiepo, West Papua's first president-in-exile, was a graduate of the Netherlands New Guinea School for Native Administrators; Permenas Ferry Awom, leader of the 1965 Manokwari rebellion, was a member of the Papuan Volunteer Brigade; Seth Rumkorem, the brigadier-general from the OPM faction that declared independence in 1971, was an officer in the Indonesian army; Arnold Ap, promoter of Papuan culture and martyr to the separatist cause, was a lecturer at the provincial university and the curator of a museum of provincial art.[34] While it seems likely that he acted on his own, without the involvement of established separatist groups, Philip Karma, the organizer of the Biak flag raising, fits the profile of a typical OPM leader.[35] Son of the first Biak to serve as a regent, Karma was, until his arrest, a mid-level official in the provincial administration. Like so many nationalists before him, he is the product of the system he risked his life to overturn. On the other hand, one must pay heed to the unifying effects of provincial initiatives from Internet newsgroups to newspapers like the *Cendrawasih Pos* and *Tifa Irian* to government-sponsored contests promoting provincial costumes and dances. These technologies account for how Irian's highly diverse population has come to express a sense of shared purpose, despite the disunity that has often plagued the OPM.[36]

---

[32] Some Biak leaders claim that an important source of resentment lies in the fact that western Indonesians are frequently sent to serve in Irian Jaya, but Irianese officials are rarely sent to serve in western Indonesian provinces.

[33] See "Former Governor of West Irian Interviewed," *Tapol Bulletin* 49 (January 1982): 5, where D. Kafiar, a Papuan refugee, comments on the composition of the OPM in the field. "Many come from the towns. Young people and government officials from the lowest to the highest ranks." See also Amunggut Tabi, *Kabar Irian*, January 1, 1999. In this posting, which clarifies "the aspirations of the West Papuan People and the position of the OPM," one scarcely gets the sense that the provincial elite is to be criticized for working for the Indonesian state. "2. It is true that some West Papuans currently enjoy Indonesian government positions and a measure of wealth and freedom, but deep within our hearts we will never possess any real peace or satisfaction until all our people are free, and this is the essence of our struggle . . . . 8. All West Papuans will be treated equally in the new nation, including persons currently serving under the Republic of Indonesia, such as the current governor of Irian Jaya and the rector of Cendrawasih University."

[34] On the backgrounds of various OPM leaders, see Djopari, *Pemberontakan Organisasi Papua Merdeka*, pp. 100-131; Nonie Sharp with Markus Wonggor Kaisiepo, *The Morning Star in Papua Barat* (North Carlton, Australia: Arena, 1994); Anderson, *Imagined Communities*, p. 178.

[35] Neither the Papuan exiles I spoke with in Holland in September 1998, nor the human rights activists I later consulted, were aware of any connection between Philip Karma and any pre-existing separatist organizations. I was told that Karma only decided to organize the demonstration after arriving on Biak, where he had come to visit his ailing father.

[36] Recent events provide numerous examples of such expressions of shared purpose. In May 1998, Irianese college students and human rights advocates rallied in Jayapura and Jakarta for the withdrawal of troops from the Central Highlands. These demonstrations followed the widely publicized issuing of a report by Irianese religious leaders to the National Human Rights Commission documenting abuses in Mapnduma, an isolated region whose inhabitants the vast majority of Irianese will never meet. See Human Rights Watch, "Indonesia Alert: Trouble in Irian Jaya." The importance of communications technology to the Papuan nationalist movement

The new imaginings made possible by contemporary institutions and modes of communication played a crucial role in the flag raising on Biak. But there is more to the story, as the rest of this essay should confirm. My understanding of the July protest is based on the straightforward proposition that it is possible for people to invoke different identities and address different audiences, both across settings and in the course of a single social interaction.[37] Whether one has in mind the reading of a newspaper or the raising of a flag, representations are always in some sense underdetermined.[38] Although interpretations of a performance are always contextually based, no single context is ever exhaustive of all the possible meanings of an event. This is not to deny that some readings are more powerful or pronounced than others; the challenge is to consider how contrasting and even contradictory frameworks can intersect in historically grounded and systematic ways. Among Irian Jayans, one sees evidence of such an intersection on the provincial level, where nationalist pronouncements reflect the influence of a long history of mission involvement. Papuan separatists may describe themselves as members of a global order of nations, but they also depict their imagined community in explicitly Christian terms.[39] In the case of Biak, the very values that have prompted the islanders to participate in provincial struggles underwrite a resilient set of millennial expectations. Sometimes, many Biaks do seem to envision themselves as part of a politically silenced Papuan nation advancing in "homogeneous, empty time." But there is a broadly shared tendency to interpret international acknowledgment of this identity as initiating an eschatological transformation. From this perspective, independence appears as the utopian moment when Biak will be revealed as the true origin of earthly power. At other times, Biaks downplay this millennial/nationalist vision through practices that posit a very different sense of self. Nationalism is often depicted as involving the recognition of an interiorized locus of identity.[40] In Biak, this interiority stands in tension with the assumption that one gains status from being foreign: different from oneself and one's peers.

Later in this essay, I develop this argument by looking more closely at the character of Biak sociality. But first, I attend to another force of critical importance in the flag raising and its aftermath: the Indonesian state. John Djopari has noted that Irianese youths who have fled Indonesia finally feel free to express their convictions. "Perhaps when they are in Irian Jaya they restrain themselves,"

---

is reflected in a recent posting by the OPM spokesman, Amunggut Tabi, calling for support so he can establish an email network for West Papuan tribal leaders. See *Kabar Irian*, March 15, 1999.

[37] See Joseph Errington, *Shifting Languages: Interaction and Identity in Javanese Indonesian* (Cambridge: Cambridge University Press, 1998), especially pp. 4-5.

[38] See Webb Keane, *Signs of Recognition: Powers and Hazards of Representation in an Indonesian Society* (Berkeley: University of California Press, 1997).

[39] See Tabi, *Kabar Irian*, January 1, 1999. "The future nation of West Papua shall not tolerate military dictatorship of any kind, but shall be ruled by civilians. It will be the only nation on Earth to acknowledge the Bible as exclusive source for all its laws."

[40] See James Siegel, *Fetish, Recognition, Revolution* (Princeton: Princeton University Press, 1997); John Pemberton, *On the Subject of "Java"* (Ithaca: Cornell University Press, 1994), p. 134; and Marilyn Ivy, *Discourses of the Vanishing: Modernity, Phantasm, Japan* (Chicago: University of Chicago Press, 1995).

he remarks.[41] With the end of the New Order, Biaks and other Irian Jayans suddenly found themselves living in what they took to be a new and different land. Unfortunately, the changes were not as radical as they may have seemed at first— as I suggest in the following section, where I examine the logic underlying the military's brutal suppression of the demonstration. On Biak at least, state terror has persisted in uncannily familiar forms.

THE NEW ORDER AND THE ENDS OF VIOLENCE

When one considers the conditions under which President Suharto ruled, it is surprising that his fall did not come sooner. The New Order's longevity, as John Pemberton has noted, did not rest solely on open coercion or threat. To account for the quiescence that reigned in much of Indonesia for the period of Suharto's rule, Pemberton looks not to a "culture of terror," but a "relatively muted form of terror that might become culture: the repression of fear that customarily secures, over time, an appearance of normal life."[42] With fear transposed into anxiety over the specter of cultural incompletion, the Javanese population at Indonesia's core embraced the official virtues of order, stability, and progress. Seeing themselves from the perspective of the abstract authority of custom, they engaged in compulsive rounds of state-sanctioned rituals. Mobilized to create the impression of an imperishable order, the transcendent realm of culture bridged the ruptures of colonial and postcolonial history. Building museums filled with new heirlooms and improved versions of old monuments, the New Order subsumed old and new, originals and replicas, into an abstract topology of clearly demarcated regional cultures and selves.

When I was conducting fieldwork on Biak from 1992 to 1994, I found no dearth of expressions of the official narratives of culture and development that Pemberton so astutely dissects. The "security approach" had given way to the "prosperity approach," I was told, by officials committed to the revival of Biak "tradition" and the entry of the population into the ranks of orderly Indonesian subjects.[43] But alongside official discourses that assured Biaks that order and progress was what they desired was another set of narratives with a more sinister message for those who strayed from the official path. While I was free to travel to most parts of the island, I was warned against venturing to West Biak, a place that remained "disturbed" by the presence of an OPM commander who had managed to survive decades of counter-insurgency operations on the island. In 1990, Indonesian troops shot the guerrilla's nephew, who had fled to the forest after a flag raising in a West Biak village. Carrying their victim's severed head aloft on a pole, the troops marched home along the densely populated coast.[44] In this grisly spectacle, the soldiers took on the lethal power of the headhunters who once inhabited the

---

[41] See *Pemberontakan Organisasi Papua Barat*, p. 151.

[42] See Pemberton, *On the Subject of "Java,"* p. 8.

[43] See my "Of Birds and Gifts: Revising Tradition on an Indonesian Frontier," *Cultural Anthropology* 11 (4): 577-616.

[44] See Amnesty International, "Indonesia: Continuing Human Rights Violations in Irian Jaya," *Country Dossier* ASA 21/06/91, Microform E151, 1991, p. 25.

island.[45] The state had the capacity not only to annihilate their "primitive" rivals, but also to tap their savage, excessive power.

The events of last May decisively shattered the illusion that the New Order was eternal. But the logic that linked order and violence under Suharto is still not a thing of the past. Evidence has emerged of military involvement in the rape and murder of ethnic Chinese Indonesians in Jakarta and other major cities in the weeks leading up to Suharto's fall.[46] The riots could be read as an effort to repeat the violent moment of the New Order's birth, when certain factions orchestrated an eruption of local animosities, then intervened to restore the law. The military on Biak seems to have tried to follow a similar script. In the days following the flag raising, the provincial paper reported on a counter-demonstration carried out by villagers from West Biak.[47] Other sources suggest that the military not only coerced West Biak villagers into protesting the flag raising; they also set in motion a plan to bring them to the site of the demonstration.[48] Armed with axes and machetes, the West Biaks were supposed to start a battle with the demonstrators, giving the security forces an excuse to step in.[49]

Few Biaks reading of the counter-protests would have been ignorant of the heavy price West Biaks have paid for sheltering the last armed fugitive on the island. Equally few could have avoided hearing of the abuse suffered by the protesters and others unlucky enough to be near the water tower at the time of the attack. Two sets of narratives told different stories about the event, the first depicting the state's lethal power over its critics, the second assuring the faithful that chaos had been firmly, but gently, contained. The effectiveness of their interplay was evidenced in the aftermath of the shootings. Only a handful of families dared to report that their children were missing. The lack of complaints was used as evidence that no abuses had occurred. The authorities' effort to explain the sea-borne bodies as victims of a distant disaster was more than an exercise in damage control. It was an explicit demonstration of the state's monopoly over the giving and taking of identities, as well as lives.

Clearly, the *tsunami* was a stroke of good luck for the authorities; it gave them a chance to cover the traces of the massacre by providing a "natural" explanation for any recovered victims. But the argument that the corpses could not be the demonstrators because they were *not* Indonesians suited the strange logic of

---

[45] Compare James T. Siegel, *A New Criminal Type in Jakarta: Counter-revolution Today* (Durham: Duke University Press, 1998), pp. 8, 90-119. See also Janet Hoskins, "Introduction: Headhunting as Practice and Trope," in *Headhunting and the Social Imagination in Southeast Asia*, ed. Janet Hoskins (Stanford: Stanford University Press, 1996), pp. 31-37, and Anna Lowenhaupt Tsing, *In the Realm of the Diamond Queen* (Princeton: Princeton University Press, 1993), pp. 72-103.

[46] See John T. Sidel, "*Macet Total*: Logics of Circulation and Accumulation in the Demise of Indonesia's New Order," *Indonesia* 66 (October 1998): 159-196, esp. 179-182.

[47] See *Cendrawasih Pos*, July 14, 1998, p. 1; see also TAPOL, "Situation Tense in Biak," Unpublished internet posting, July 5, 1998.

[48] See Human Rights Watch, "Indonesia: Human Rights and Pro-Independence Actions in Irian Jaya."

[49] I was told that the West Biaks agreed to play their part in the drama only after the commander promised to let them recover from the forest the remains of loved ones killed by the military in earlier decades. The grim charade allowed the bereaved to demonstrate their loyalty. Otherwise, the simple act of burying the dead would have branded them as opponents of the state.

Indonesian state terror and sharpened the point of the military attack. James Siegel has recently pointed out that Indonesians have tended to "kill in their own image."[50] Extra-legal violence against separatists, communists, and criminals alike is not intended to purify the nation of alien elements, but to demonstrate the state's ability to appropriate their potency, i.e. to "nationalize death."[51] The soldiers who shot the young Biaks acted on the assumption that their victims belonged within the Indonesian state. This is not to deny that intruders of various sorts took part in the affair, including the American politicians mentioned above, whose letter reached the province, where it circulated widely. The authorities presented themselves as defusing these disruptions by translating them into manageable terms. Just as the authorities reassured the alarmed villagers by determining the true identity of the foreign corpses, they clarified the true meaning of the foreign letter, which called for limited autonomy, not independence, they claimed. Against the public secret of the state's "world destroying"—and order confirming—violence, the official version made violence alien to the law.[52]

BIAK AND THE ENDS OF ORDER

Among Biaks, one encounters a starkly different conception of the relationship between violence, order, and origins. A few months after I began fieldwork, I found myself talking with a new friend about her husband, a mild-mannered teacher whom I had met on several occasions. Jan was "*jahat*," Fransina told me, using an Indonesian word meaning "wicked" or "evil." Just as surprising as Fransina's choice of words was the boastful tone of her voice. As time went on, I met other Biaks who used the adjective, *jahat*, as a compliment. A *jahat* person, though for the most part reserved, was capable of outbursts of violent rage.[53] This capacity for violence was not only admired in fishermen or hunters. Top officials liked to describe themselves as present day *mambri*, the fearsome "warriors" for whom Biak was once renowned.

The other way that top officials liked to describe themselves was as *amber beba*, "big foreigners." A word meaning "Westerner, non-Irianese Indonesian, civil servant, or individual with special skills," *amber* also can be used as an adjective to describe the outside realms where Biaks seek wealth and prestige. From the first appearance of Biak-speaking seafarers in European records, one finds an association of the foreign with both violence and value. Powerful outsiders, ranging from the Sultan of Tidore, to whom Biaks delivered tribute, to the agents of the Dutch colonial state, attracted both fear and desire. Today's Biaks recreate the linkage between violence and value in the most intimate arenas of everyday life. Biak kinship divides the islanders into patrilineal, exogamous clans. Where same-sex siblings tend to be rivals for clan resources, cross-sex siblings regard each other with longing and love. Elsewhere I have analyzed the connection between

---

[50] See Siegel, *A New Criminal Type in Jakarta*, p. 1.

[51] Ibid., p. 108.

[52] See Elaine Scarry, *The Body in Pain: The Making and Unmaking of the World* (New York and Oxford: Oxford University Press, 1985).

[53] Such outbursts not only command respect; they are considered critical to the resolution of disputes. See Danilyn Rutherford, "Raiding the Land of the Foreigners: Power, History and Difference in Biak, Irian Jaya, Indonesia" (PhD dissertation, Cornell University, 1997), p. 202.

this affection and the inflationary logic of Biak exchange.[54] The status of a Biak brother—and his clan, more generally—depends on his and his clan's ability to give their affines more foreign valuables than they receive as bridewealth. Children become "foreigners" by virtue of the gifts their mother elicits from her brothers, who acquire this surplus through ongoing "raids" on foreign lands. Biaks speak of these gifts as motivated by a brother's "love" for his sister. But the aesthetics of the feasts that sisters host to elicit foreign valuables from their brothers portray the giving of these prestations as an act of force. Everything from the guests' noisy procession to the dance ground to the songs they sing when they arrive recalls the violence of an encounter with the new.

But it is not only at feasts that Biaks stress the violence and value of the foreign. They confirm these qualities in narratives recounting the origins of social groups. Many stories about the founding of lineages, for instance, focus on the actions of *mambri*, the warriors mentioned above. In the past, warriors offered themselves for hire to feuding clans. The offended party got the warrior drunk, then spat in his cup to insult him, before sending him off in the direction of the offending village. Like a detonated missile, the infuriated warrior killed the first person to cross his path. The victim's relatives avenged the death by hiring another warrior, thus keeping the violence in circulation. But what also circulated were alliances. Clients compensated warriors by giving them their sisters to marry; warriors gave their own sisters to their victims' clans to compensate for the loss of life. Through these unions—and the brother-sister bonds they mobilized—particular individuals and their descendants received special skills and prerogatives. A dangerous uncle and a random act of violence stood at the origins of a prestigious new line.

Clan myths also draw connections between random acts of violence and the institution of new identities. An enterprising Dutch official collected several dozen of such stories.[55] Most of them begin with a fight over a domestic animal or some other object of shared desire. A dog defecates inside a hilltop clan house, sparking an altercation between two clan brothers. A man catches a lizard; his brothers eat it; he explodes in rage. A bloody battle ensues, then the siblings disperse, naming features of the landscape as they descend to the coast. In their new homes, the siblings found new clans; eventually their descendants marry. Exploding a sibling set consisting of competing equals, the lethal violence causes a migration that sets up differences and provides a basis for exchange.

Village histories show how a particular relation to the foreign underwrites the connection between violence and origins. In 1912, Lieutenant W. K. H. Feuilletau de Bruyn arrived on Biak with a company of soldiers.[56] While his mission was ostensibly to capture the murderer of an Ambonese teacher—who had strayed into a drunk warrior's path—he used the occasion to pacify the island's north coast. Using "local methods," his troops snuck up to clan houses and took their

---

[54] See my "Love, Violence and Foreign Wealth: Kinship and History in Biak, Irian Jaya," *Journal of the Royal Anthropological Institute* 4 (2): 255-281.

[55] See de Bruyn, "Jaarverslagen 1947 en 1948."

[56] See W. K. H. Feuilletau de Bruyn, "Militaire Memorie der Schouten-eilanden" (Military Report on the Schouten Islands), August 31, 1916, *Nienhuis Collectie van de Department van Bevolkszaken Hollandia Rapportenarchief*, Nummer Toegang 10-25, Stuk 183, Algemeene Rijksarchief, The Hague. See also *Schouten en Padaido-eilanden* (The Schouten and Padaido Islands), vol. 21 of *Mededeelingen Encyclopaedisch Bureau* (Batavia: Javaasche Boekhandel, 1920).

occupants as hostages. They refused to release the men, women and children until they turned over any warriors in their midst. Soon the company was traveling with a string of prisoners, bound together by wire tied around their necks. The lieutenant scarcely cuts an endearing figure in his report on the mission. But in the stories Biaks tell about the operation, they remember him with admiration, as well as awe. "Dekna," as they call him, may have been *jahat*, but he opened a new era on the island. Ostensibly out to bring an end to heathen justice, Feuilletau de Bruyn, through these stories, has become a warrior himself.

Stories about Dekna are taken as relating a particularly treasured beginning in Biak: the dawn of Christian light in heathen darkness. It was in the 1910s that most Biak villages began the long history of mission schooling that accounts for the islanders' dominance in many arenas of provincial life. But while the flag raising undeniably could be emplotted in the colonial story of Biak's march to modernity, this story does not capture the full range of readings evoked by the act. For one thing, it cannot account for the ways that Biaks represent the military and bureaucracy as foreign: dangerous, yet available for present-day warriors who want to advance in the eyes of their peers. For another, it cannot explain the persistence of a view of national liberation as an abrupt and total transformation. As a fourth and final example makes clear, the violence and value of the foreign stands not only at the beginning of Biak identities, but also at the end.

Punctuated by a series of startling encounters and violent incidents, the myth of Manarmakeri, literally "the Itchy Old Man," lays out the origin of the foreign.[57] The story begins with the hero's discovery and loss of *Koreri*, which means "We Change Our Skin," a utopian state of unending life and pleasure also glossed by Biaks as *"Kan do mob oser,"* "We eat in one place." Disappointed by his inability to return to the cave where he witnessed *Koreri*, Manarmakeri develops a skin disease that covers his body with itching, oozing sores. The hero becomes a migrating outcast, subjected to all manner of abuse. In the key incident in the story, he regains access to *Koreri* from the Morning Star, whom he surprises when the spirit is stealing the old man's palm wine. But the old man must take a detour in order to return to *Koreri*: Manarmakeri first gains the power to impregnate a woman magically and make her his wife. The woman turns out to be the local chief's daughter, whose newborn son outrages the villagers when he identifies the old stranger as his father. Rejected again, when his affines flee the misbegotten family, the old man sets about performing miracles. He conjures up a magnificent feast and a modern steamship; he turns himself into a beautiful youth and his skin into treasure by jumping into a raging fire. But even these deeds cannot win him the Biaks' acceptance. Disappointed, Manarmakeri travels west. But someday, he will return and "open" *Koreri*. This final union with the foreign will end the world as Biaks know it. There will be no more striving, suffering, and death.

Over the course of a long history of contact with outsiders, Biaks periodically gathered to welcome Manarmakeri.[58] A leader would arise, claiming to be in contact with the ancestor; followers would abandon their gardens and gather to sing, dance, and drink palm wine, sure that *Koreri* soon would begin. While not every incident ended violently, the followers consistently posited a reversal in

---

[57] See my "Raiding the Land of the Foreigners," pp. 378-461.

[58] See F. C. Kamma, *Koreri: Messianic Movements in the Biak-Numfor Culture Area* (The Hague: Martinus Nijhoff, 1972).

existing structures of power.[59] Closing the gap between Biak and the Land of the Foreigners, the return of Manarmakeri would spell the end of a social order based on the pursuit of exogenous sources of value and power. Where New Order narratives repressed all reference to endings, for Biaks, this eschatological moment was—and remains—a focus of longing and hope.

I am certainly not the first to suggest *Koreri*'s importance to the interpretation of Papuan nationalism on Biak; prominent Papuan nationalists have done the same.[60] Scholars who take millenarianism as a stage in the "evolution of revolution" have made much of the mixture of political and religious rhetoric that *Koreri* prophets used to describe their quest.[61] The reading I would like to offer of the flag raising avoids the teleological premises of such an approach. I will not venture into debates on the millennial origins of the modern notions of progress that infuse classic accounts of millenarianism.[62] How the phenomenon looks depends on the perspective of the observer: the events of 1939-42 on Biak, called a cargo cult by some, coincided with a multitude of similar reactions that later found a place in the annals of the Indonesian revolutionary war.[63] If *Koreri* is central to my analysis, it is not because millenarianism is a precursor to "real" revolution. Using *Koreri* as a lens, we catch a glimpse of the eschatological limit that all revolutions in some sense evoke.

The Morning Star flag, which refers explicitly to an episode from the myth of Manarmakeri, first flew in 1942, during an uprising which coincided with the Japanese invasion and the collapse of Dutch colonial rule.[64] While my information on the 1998 flag raising is admittedly incomplete—and I certainly would not want to downplay the significant differences between the two historical moments— what I heard in Biak and read in reports on the previous incident suggest certain parallels. The most striking, of course, is the timing: the fall of a seemingly permanent regime. In both cases, the rupture came at the end of a period of expansion in the scope and reach of the state. A second parallel pertains to the participants. Planned by individuals with recent experience outside the island, the

---

[59] An early prophet instructed the faithful to stop traveling to Tidore; instead they should deliver their tribute to him. Ibid., p. 106. Later prophets undermined the authority of the missionaries by claiming that the Bible was really an abridged edition of Biak myth.

[60] See for example Nonie Sharp with Markus Wonggor Kaisiëpo, *The Morning Star in Papua Barat*.

[61] See Peter Worsley, *The Trumpet Shall Sound* (New York: Schocken Books, 1968), p. 48. "The urban and adjoining areas of long settlement, then, on the whole found other forms of political expression than millenarianism, and the casual labourers, peri-urban workers and small entrepreneurs had begun to develop orthodox political, economic and social organizations before World War II." Peter Lawrence also discusses the relationship between cargoism and "modern" political activism. See Peter Lawrence, *Road Belong Cargo* (Prospect Heights, IL.: Waveland Press, 1971), pp. 256-273. See also Michael Adas, *Prophets of Rebellion: Millenarian Protest Movements against the European Colonial Order* (Cambridge: Cambridge University Press, 1987).

[62] For a discussion of these debates, see Malcolm Bull, "On Making Ends Meet" in *Apocalypse Theory and the Ends of the World*, ed. M. Bull (Oxford: Oxford University Press, 1995), pp. 1-17. See also Benedict Anderson, "Further Adventures of Charisma," in *Language and Power: Exploring Political Cultures in Indonesia* (Ithaca: Cornell University Press, 1990), pp. 90-93.

[63] I make this argument in my "Raiding the Land of the Foreigners," pp. 485-87.

[64] See Osborne, *Indonesia's Secret War*, p. 51. See also Kamma, *Koreri*; and my "Raiding the Land of the Foreigners," pp. 525-565.

World War II uprising drew people from all parts of Biak, with the prophets and their close relatives forming the core of the movement. It was launched by Angganeta Menufandu, a traditional singer and healer, who had worked on the mainland as a coolie. After her arrest, the movement was carried forward by a group of young warriors who had just been released from jail. Educated in the Philippines and employed at the governor's office in Jayapura, Philip Karma had only recently returned to Biak when the flag raising occurred. Surrounded by relatives from his North Biak village, Karma attracted followers ranging from the teenagers who loiter near the Biak City terminal to villagers who made special trips to town to see the long-forbidden flag. As was the case in the earlier incident, some of the curious ended up staying on.

A third parallel can be drawn in the activities undertaken during the flag raising. At the camps set up by Angganeta and her successors, followers drank palm wine and danced in a circle, singing songs composed by their leaders. The performance genre was *wor*, a non-diatonic genre of singing once central to Biak ceremonies and feasts.[65] The leaders were helped by "peace women," as they called male and female dancers who had been possessed by the foreign and the dead. Christian imagery was central to the movement; people and places received biblical names. Last summer, the demonstrators spent their days dancing around the water tower and singing Biak and Indonesian songs. While they performed a contemporary genre, in fitting with the youth of many of the participants, the allusion to *Koreri* and Biak feasting was clear. Every hour, the entire group, led by Philip Karma, dropped to their knees and prayed. It is said that the leader even "baptized" the territory where the demonstrators exercised control. Although I heard nothing about speaking in foreign tongues, people did describe the reading of incomprehensible foreign documents: "proclamations" in English and Dutch.

A fourth parallel concerns the stress the followers placed on foreign recognition. Elsewhere I have compared the state-sponsored revival of *wor*, the above-mentioned song genre, in the 1990s to a similar revival sponsored by the mission in the 1930s.[66] In the uprisings that followed, Biaks responded to the sense that outsiders had found something unexpected in their identities. In prison, the young warriors who took over from Angganeta heard rumors of Japanese promises to honor native political parties. Upon their release, they drafted an elaborate charter for New Guinea's future, which became the basis of the movement's subsequent phase. Like the warriors, Karma and his followers acted in the belief that powerful outsiders had recognized their plight. I mentioned above the letter from the US Representatives, which circulated widely on Biak.[67] Much was made of a rumor that the protesters had appeared on CNN. As was the case in *Koreri*, this evidence of foreign attention brought to mind not only the gaze of outsiders, but also their impending presence. When one friend left for the port to meet a passenger liner during the demonstration, his neighbor asked him, in great excitement, "Has the foreigners' ship arrived?"

---

[65] See Philip Yampolsky and Danilyn Rutherford, eds., *Music of Biak, Irian Jaya: Wor, Church Songs, Yospan*, vol. 10, *The Music of Indonesia* (Washington: Smithsonian Institute/Folkways Records, 1996 compact disc).

[66] See my "Of Birds and Gifts," p. 601.

[67] Karma reputedly had other documents in his possession, including statements from the 1950s and 1960s relating to the Act of Free Choice.

A fifth parallel relates to the interplay between order and violence as the demonstration progressed. Angganeta, who called herself "the Peace Woman," gained authority from her ability to provide convincing signs of direct contact with Manarmakeri. Her successors gained prominence by claiming to represent the prophetess, the "Queen," whose troops they vowed to command. In two sites on Biak, they drilled divisions of the "New America" army. Teachers and evangelists were submitted to beatings; a policeman and a Japanese commander were killed. As the Japanese gradually assumed control of northwestern New Guinea, the new administration tried different strategies to quell the movement, including recruiting the followers of one leader to attack those of another. Finally, in October 1943, the Japanese navy opened fire on a huge crowd of unarmed believers. The bullets failed to turn to water, and hundreds of people were killed. But that was not the end of the violence. A blood bath resulted when grieving families turned on the clans who had led their loved ones to their death. Over a much shorter period, the 1998 demonstration evolved towards a violent confrontation. Early in the protest, Karma formed a security force of sorts. The protesters set up roadblocks around the water tower manned by boys wearing armbands that read "Security Guard—OPM." The demonstrators began to stockpile weapons after hearing rumors that the military was planning to attack the crowd. When news of the shootings reached young sympathizers in outlying neighborhoods, they took revenge by burning down migrants' shops.

Perhaps the strongest indication that the narrative of *Koreri* was evoked in the flag raising comes from the comments I heard after its failure. Friends spoke of Karma's movement in the same tone that they used to discuss Angganeta and the warriors'—the goal was valid, but the timing was wrong. "We can't chase it," sighed the wife of a high-ranking official, "God will give it to us in his time." Just as believers found post-hoc justifications for Angganeta's failure, they found reasons for the flag raising's tragic ending. Maybe God was on Karma's side, I was told, and the shootings were meant to happen so that more people would hear about the cause. The same friend reported how, after the incident, a Sino-Indonesian woman had had a vision of angels dancing with the demonstrators around the flag. Although Biaks envision independence in a variety of ways, many assume that divine intervention will somehow be involved in its delivery. In 1998, as in the early 1940s, the violence that will end the status quo is imagined as entailing a congress with foreigners and a triumph of prayers—if not machetes—over guns.

CONCLUSION: THE FUTURE OF THE END?

From the perspective of day-to-day life, the return of Manarmakeri must remain unpredictable. Prophets who dare to venture a forecast run a risk. Many Biaks still honor the memory of Angganeta, who turned her body into a receiver of messages from Manarmakeri. They have nothing but contempt for her successors, who actively directed the movement in her name. The comments I collected on Philip Karma seemed to range between these alternatives. Some spoke scornfully of this "big foreigner" who led others to ruin because he wanted to "make it"—i.e. independence—all by himself. But others who implied that the movement was divinely ordained spoke of the "light" in Karma's eyes.

The ambivalence Biaks expressed in their judgment of both movements' leaders reflects something of their ambivalent views on violence. If one must in some sense be dangerous to engage in exchange, when Biaks manifest their potency by inflicting bodily harm, the effect on social relations can be devastating. When the plan to involve West Biak villagers failed, the commander assigned Biak soldiers to lead the attack on the demonstrators; it may be years before the families involved mend the rift.[68] Still if Biaks generally assert that violence should be less than "real," their actions often suggest that it must refer to something more than rhetorical. The massacres that followed the collapse of *Koreri* in 1943 suggest how easily it is to slip across the line.

One way of grappling with the "not wholly peaceful" nature of episodes like the flag raising is to create taxonomies. F. C. Kamma, the Dutch missionary who wrote a well-known study of *Koreri*, spoke of a conflict between followers who truly longed for redemption and those who turned this longing to earthly ends. But the comments of those who still remember the movement suggest a more complicated dynamic. Angganeta's movement sought to collapse limits, but it also recreated them, through the brutal suppression of those who failed to follow Manarmakeri's supposed commands. In normal times, Biak justice has no room for an inexplicable death; one's misfortune is always attributable to another's misdeed. The leaders of *Koreri* violently suppressed this principle of retribution by calling for an end to all feuds. The vengeful relatives of the victims of the Japanese attack forcefully reinstated Biak law. *Koreri*'s violence was not simply the outcome of repression or the schemes of "secondary leaders."[69] The violent suppression of order elicited its violent reintroduction, in a dynamic that culminated in the movement's horrific denouement.

There is little doubt that the wartime movement, like the flag raising, involved what Walter Benjamin calls in the beginning of "Critique of Violence" "law-making" and "law-preserving" uses of force. But we get a better sense of what was at stake in *Koreri* by considering the end of Benjamin's essay, where he tells us that violence can be either mythical or divine. Mythical violence resembles that of the Biak warrior: violence not as a means, but as a manifestation, as seen in a man, "impelled by anger . . . to the most visible outbursts of a violence that is not related as a means to a preconceived end."[70] Without a pre-existing program to guide it, lawmaking, as "power-making," must take place in such a manifestation, a sign of the "existence of the gods."[71] Like the blow of a warrior or enraged clan brother, mythical violence institutes an order and produces authority by parading as an "alien" force beyond conscious, "local" control. Divine violence looks more like the moment evoked in *Koreri*: the utter annihilation of order through an imagined collapse of the distance that divides the transcendent sources of value and power from everyday life. I say "evoked" advisedly, because even Angganeta

---

[68] The soldiers were commanded by a Biak officer, who is ironically, Philip Karma's sister's husband's father.

[69] See Michael Barkun, "Introduction: Understanding Millennialism," in *Millennialism and Violence*, ed. M. Barkun (London and Portland: Cass, 1996), p. 7; Adas, *Prophets of Rebellion*, pp. 122-137.

[70] See Benjamin, "Critique of Violence," p. 294.

[71] Ibid., p. 295.

could not convey a pure vision of eschatological destruction.[72] Indeed, one could argue that Angganeta's movement served to defer the transformation of Biak notions of authority by presenting the forces of change in a locally recognizable guise. For Benjamin, divine violence is an element of all revolutions, but it is never possible to pinpoint the order-destroying moment.[73] How can one depict the elusive instant when one regime ends and another begins?

But it may be that the power of *Koreri* lies precisely in the elusiveness of its object. At moments when Biaks are drawn to see themselves from the perspective of outsiders, they evoke this figure of a millennial limit. *Koreri* portrays the submission to other orders, if fully realized, as spelling the end, not of a worldview, but of the world. On Biak, the dream of Papuan independence has proven remarkably resilient in the face of decades of repression. This is in good part due to the groundedness of *Koreri*'s messianic logic in the practices of everyday life. By valorizing the foreignness of government slogans and schemes, Biaks satisfied the demands of New Order hegemony without accepting a New Order sense of self. But one should not assume that Papuan nationalism is immune from the logic of *Koreri*, which destabilizes *any* identity defined by its place in a homogeneous order of nations. To dance around the flag is to dance with angels; it brings one into an unsustainable proximity with God.

While its roots extend deep into the colonial past, the Biak I have described in this paper is a product of the New Order. I have no way of telling what the post-Suharto era will bring to the islanders or any of the many other people who suffered under the former regime. Nonetheless, I will leave you with two thoughts to keep in mind while contemplating the future of Biak eschatology. The first is borrowed from a Biak friend who borrowed it from Kamma's book on *Koreri*.[74] The second is stolen from the title of an essay by Frank Kermode.[75] "The hope in people's heart may never die," but there is nothing so interminable as "waiting for the end."

POSTSCRIPT

Over the past two years, the Papuan nationalist movement has expanded and evolved.[76] The course of events in Irian Jaya, which President Wahid rechristened

---

[72] See Eric S. Rabkin, "Introduction: Why Destroy the World?" in *The End of the World*, ed. E. S. Rabkin, Martin H. Greenberg and Joseph D. Olander (Carbondale and Edwardsville: Southern Illinois University Press, 1983), pp. vii-xv. Rabkin points out in a study of science fiction, "there are virtually no tales of the end of the world in which all of creation ends." Ibid., p. ix. If millenarianism is a particular mode of narration, as Kermode suggests, then, as is the case with all narratives, the "conclusion" in some sense always eludes one's grasp. See Frank Kermode, *The Sense of an Ending* (Oxford: Oxford University Press, 1967).

[73] "The expiatory power of violence is not visible to men." See Benjamin, "Critique of Violence," p. 300.

[74] See Kamma, *Koreri*.

[75] See Frank Kermode, "Waiting for the End," in *Apocalypse Theory and the Ends of the World*, pp. 250-263.

[76] For an overview of the movement's recent history, see Office for Justice and Peace, Jayapura Diocese, "Description of problems in Papua: Presentation by Catholic church leaders in Papua in a personal meeting with President Abdurrahman Wahid Jakarta," unpublished internet posting, June 27, 2000; and Human Rights Watch, "Human Rights and Pro-independence Actions in Papua, 1999-2000, May 2000. See also Vaudine England, "Fight for dream of freedom," *South China Morning Post*, August 13, 2000.

"Papua" while celebrating the millennium in Jayapura, has followed something like the plot discernible in the Biak flag raising, with the entire province engaged in a symbolic refashioning of space. In a footnote of the essay, I mentioned the founding of FORERI and the meeting the group arranged between President Habibie and one hundred provincial leaders. The national dialogue sought by FORERI has yet to materialize, but the past months have seen no shortage of momentous events. Shortly following Abdurrahman Wahid's election as President, he promised to permit peaceful political expression in the province. At this moment the pro-independence movement gained a self-proclaimed leader, in the person of Theys Eluay.[77] A former legislator and chair of the province's customary council, Eluay was one of the tribal leaders chosen to participate in the Act of Free Choice in 1969. Among his colleagues is Yorrys Raweyai, the head of Pemuda Pancasila, a nationwide paramilitary organization with underworld connections, which the New Order regime used to terrorize and discredit rivals.[78] Eluay's activities began with the planning of a mass flag raising to occur in Jayapura and other cities on December 1. Some observers feared that the scheme was a trap, designed to justify a bloody crackdown.[79] But while there were shootings in Timika, in Jayapura, and elsewhere, the event went off peacefully, with security provided by the Satgas Papua, a loosely organized "task force" of uniformed youths. In February 2000, Eluay, who is from Sentani, and Tom Beanal, a well-known leader from the Amungme tribe, became the co-chairmen of a presidium convened to organize a Papuan National Congress, an initiative first discussed during President Wahid's New Year visit to the province. Wahid, who in addition to advocating the name change offered an official apology for human rights abuses in the province, supported the idea. Besides providing funding, Wahid went so far as to offer to open the Congress—an offer he later rescinded when it became clear that the proceedings were likely to result in a declaration of Papuan independence. Attended by three thousand delegates from across the province and overseas, the Congress's stated goal was the "straightening" of western New Guinea's history. Although the event, which was held in Jayapura from May 29 to June 4, 2000, took place with a remarkable lack of unrest, its conclusion—that West Papua had become independent in 1961—evoked a strong reaction from Jakarta. In an abrupt about-face, Wahid disowned the Congress, which he criticized for not representing the opinion of the majority of the province's inhabitants.[80] Other politicians went further, calling for the arrest of the organizers for treason; and, indeed, Eluay and others from the Presidium were summoned for questioning by the police.[81] In August,

---

[77] "Tokoh Irja Bertemu untuk Amankan 1 Desember" (Irian Jaya Leaders Meet to Make Sure December 1 is Peaceful), *Suara Pembaruan*, November 25, 1999. See also "IHRSTAD: No clear leadership for current resurgence in West Papua," unpublished internet posting, November 19, 1999.

[78] See Loren Ryter, "Pemuda Pancasila: The Last Loyalist Free Men of Suharto's Order?," in this volume.

[79] See TAPOL, "Critical Days in West Papua," November 25, 1999. See also Andrew Kilvert, "Irian Jaya has a dream: it may become a nightmare," *Sydney Morning Herald*, December 1, 1999.

[80] See "Government adamant Irian will remain in Indonesia," *Jakarta Post*, June 6, 2000.

[81] "House officially rejects Irian's independence,"*Jakarta Post*, June 7, 2000; "Makar, DPR Tolak Deklarasi Merdeka Papua" (Parliament Rejects the Declaration of Independence of Papua as a Manipulation), *Astaga.com*, June 7, 2000; "Irian Jaya congress organisers suspected

the Indonesian national legislature officially rejected the Congress's findings and demanded that Wahid take firm action to defend the unity of the nation. In response, Wahid pledged to fight separatism, if necessary, by "serious measures."[82]

In the midst of these developments, the Morning Star flag has become a prominent feature of the province's landscape. Following the Congress, President Wahid announced that flag raisings were to be permitted, so long as the Indonesian flag was raised alongside the Papuan flag, which should be smaller and lower than its rival.[83] This proclamation legitimized what was already in many ways the status quo. In the past two years, the flag has appeared not only atop flagpoles, but also on stickers, posters, decals, and even radio aerials sported by Papuans from all walks of life.[84] I am told that Philip Karma, who was released from jail in 1999, has shown up for meetings with the Morning Star flag affixed to his civil servant's uniform, thus combining the emblems of national and foreign power. But even in this time of tolerance, violence has occurred. In Sorong, Genyam, Timika, Nabire, and Manokwari, security forces have confronted demonstrators, and protesters and bystanders have been killed or injured. Equally troubling, there have been reports of clashes between Satgas Papua units and members of the Satgas Merah Putih, a new "task force" organized along the lines of the militias responsible for the atrocities in East Timor.[85] The situation is likely to get much worse. A military build-up is currently underway in the province.[86] In August, following the legislature's recommendation, Wahid announced that the permissive policy on flag raisings had ended, and that all Papuan flags had to be taken down.[87] At the time of this writing, riot police from Jakarta have begun to implement the order, starting in Sorong, where three protesters have died, before moving on to Manokwari and Jayapura.[88] Just as the brief period of imagined

---

of treason," *AFP*, June 20, 2000; "Papua leader meets police summons," *Indonesian Observer*, June 27, 2000.

[82] See "Indonesia's Assembly Assigns President to Curb Separatism," *Xinhua New Service*, August 15, 2000; and "Gus Dur hopeful of halting separatism," *Indonesian Observer*, August 21, 2000.

[83] See "Papuans allowed to hoist morning star flag," *Jakarta Post*, June 8, 2000.

[84] See Vaudine England, "Symbolic ritual flagged for trouble," *South China Morning Post*, August 13, 2000.

[85] See Charles Scheiner, "International Federation Warns of West Papua-East Timor Parallels in Letter to Indonesia's President," Press Release from United Nations Representative of the International Federation for East Timor, unpublished internet posting, June 13, 2000.

[86] See Paul Daley, "Concern as Indonesia dispatches troops to West Papua," *The Age*, August 10, 2000; Jackie Woods, "Megawati bad news for Papua independence hope, activist says," *Kyodo*, August 10, 2000. The build-up is said to include Kostrad and Special Forces units, along with troops from the police's Mobile Brigade. See also IHRSTAD/ELS-HAM, "Mass mobilisation to defend the state underway in West Papua," August 31, 2000; "PCRC Action Alert: Indonesian military build-up in West Papua," unpublished internet posting, August 16, 2000; "Statement by churches and NGOs: Dialogue must be pursued in Papua," unpublished internet posting, August 14, 2000.

[87] See Hamish McDonald, "Testing Time Ahead as Jakarta Tries to Pull Down Papua Flag," *Sydney Morning Herald*, August 18, 2000; "Irian Jaya police get tough on rebel flags," *Indonesian Observer*, September 7, 2000.

[88] See IRSTAD/ELS-HAM, "Morning Star Flag forcibly pulled down in Jayapura," September 12, 2000.

sovereignty under the water tower was eventually cut short, a remarkable interlude in western New Guinea's history is drawing to a close. Whether this interlude has been the work of provocateurs—or the outcome of Jakarta's bungling—something like the interplay of violence and order described in this essay appears to be unfolding in Papua. Human rights workers are justifiably concerned about what the end may bring.

RAWAN IS AS RAWAN DOES: THE ORIGINS OF DISORDER IN NEW ORDER ACEH

Geoffrey Robinson

1. INTRODUCTION

Despite its best efforts to provide a congenial environment for foreign investment and domestic corruption, over thirty-odd years the New Order regime confronted scenes of increasing chaos, violence, and political disintegration from Sabang in the west to Merauke in the east. The problem was especially acute in Aceh, Irian Jaya, and East Timor—the three regions designated by the authorities as *daerah rawan* or "trouble spots" for much of the last two decades. In each of these regions the government faced significant demands for greater autonomy or independence spearheaded by armed political movements.[1] The regime met each of these challenges with massive military operations, in the course of which hundreds of thousands of people were killed. As though to justify the harshness of its approach, the government referred to the resistance movements as *Gerakan Pengacau Keamanan* (GPK) or "Security Disruptor Movements."

In the view of New Order ideologues—and a good number of foreign experts —these independence movements were somehow a natural if regrettable consequence of the ethnic, linguistic, and geographic heterogeneity of the country. In a country so diverse, the argument ran, the primordial sentiments of diverse population groups and the traditions of enmity among them pushed inexorably in the direction of disintegration. The continued integrity and unity of Indonesia, it followed, depended ultimately on the toughness of the central state; on its capacity

---

[1] These were: The Acheh-Sumatra National Liberation Front, or Aceh Merdeka in Aceh, the Organisasi Papua Merdeka (OPM) in Irian Jaya, and in East Timor, the Frente Revolucionaria Timor Leste Independente (Fretilin), and more recently, the Conselho Nacional da Resistência Timorense or CNRT.

and willingness to use force against those who would challenge it. In this view, moreover, the experience of the 1940s and 1950s had proved that a soft, democratic, or federal state would eventually lead to the break-up of the country, along the lines of former Yugoslavia or the former Soviet Union.

My principal aim in this paper is to consider the merits of these views by examining the evidence from Aceh, where an estimated two thousand people were killed—and countless others were arbitrarily detained, tortured, and raped—after 1989 when government troops began a campaign to crush the armed independence movement, Aceh Merdeka. The inquiry is guided by two questions. First, why was Aceh so intractably unsettled, so *rawan*, in the final decade of the New Order? And second, is it destined to remain that way in the post-Suharto era? The evidence presented in this paper suggests that the problems in Aceh were not the inevitable result of the region's cultural, religious, or other primordial differences with other parts of the country, nor of its often noted "tradition" of resistance to outside authority. It also shows that, far from being the last bastion against national disunity and instability all these years, the New Order regime itself was largely responsible for the serious and protracted violence in Aceh. Accordingly, I argue that the demise of the New Order state, and its replacement by a less authoritarian, less militaristic, less centralized variant, could bring a swift end to the unsettled conditions that have plagued Aceh in recent years.

This is not to say that issues of culture and tradition were of no consequence in producing unsettled conditions in Aceh. Unquestionably they were, as the first section of the paper attempts to show. Nevertheless, I hope it will become clear that, at best, these factors provide only a partial explanation of the problem. They do not satisfactorily explain how or why the challenge from Aceh Merdeka—which was minuscule when it surfaced in 1976 and again in 1989—degenerated into widespread violence, and produced the deep-seated bitterness toward the regime that had become the norm by 1998. Nor do they explain why serious political violence, including political killings, suddenly resumed in late 1998. My argument is that two areas of New Order policy and practice were of special importance in producing these outcomes. First, its approach to the exploitation of natural resources and the distribution of the benefits; and second, the doctrine and practice of its armed forces. The New Order regime's actions in each of these realms produced a legacy of deep mistrust and animosity toward the central government, which survived the demise of President Suharto in May 1998 and appeared likely to inhibit a return to peace. To make matters worse, President Habibie seemed inclined to pursue the same policies and actions in Aceh as his predecessor, thereby accentuating rather than alleviating the underlying causes of unrest. Nevertheless, I argue that because the New Order regime's behavior in both of these spheres was shaped by underlying historical conditions, changes in those conditions are likely to alter significantly the patterns of violence and instability in the future.

While Aceh is in some respects a unique case, the argument advanced here may help to explain the growth and persistence of "trouble" in other regions as well. The fit is especially good for Irian Jaya. Despite fundamental differences in culture, religion, ethnicity, and political history, the pattern of resistance and protracted conflict there appears to be rooted in the same basic features of the New Order state that drove Aceh to a condition of chronic violence after 1989. And while the conflict in East Timor unquestionably has its own political and historical dynamic, I think the arguments made in this paper may help to illuminate certain dimensions of that struggle as well.

2. HISTORY AND REBELLION

Aceh has long been described as a center of resistance to outside authority, and a region with a strong Islamic tradition. That reputation was firmly established during the thirty-year Aceh War (1873-1903) in which an assortment of armed Acehnese bands, mobilized increasingly by Islamic leaders and inspired by the view that they were fighting a holy war, sought to resist the imposition of Dutch rule. In part because of the overwhelming military force deployed by the Dutch, but also because of the willing collaboration of many Acehnese aristocrats, known as *uleëbalang*, colonial forces eventually prevailed. Yet while the conflict officially ended in 1903, sporadic opposition to Dutch rule continued for much of the next forty years.

The traditions of political resistance and Islamic identity were further reinforced during the Japanese occupation of the Indies from 1942 to 1945, and in the period of National Revolution (1945-1949) that followed.[2] As in other parts of the archipelago, the occupation helped to invigorate an emerging consciousness of anti-colonial, Indonesian nationalism in Aceh while providing unprecedented opportunities for political mobilization, especially among the youth and reformist Islamic groups. One consequence of these developments was that, in the period after the Japanese surrender in August 1945, these groups emerged as strongly pro-Republican, raising substantial amounts of money for the fight against the returning Dutch. Equally important, the vacuum of power created by the Japanese surrender unleashed a form of anti-feudal social revolution in Aceh, in which an alliance of militant youth and Islamic organizations came close to annihilating the aristocratic *uleëbalang* class. In contrast to other parts of the Indies, moreover, Aceh was never reoccupied by Dutch or other Allied forces, so that the social revolution was never reversed, and the revolutionary forces were able to attain an unusual degree of political, economic, and military autonomy.[3] Thus, when Indonesia finally gained its independence in late 1949, the alliance that had staged the social revolution in Aceh emerged as the most powerful political and military force there.

Aceh's reputation for restiveness and Islamic militancy was further solidified in 1953, when its leaders joined groups in other parts of Indonesia in a decade-long rebellion which sought the creation of a Negara Islam Indonesia (Islamic State of Indonesia).[4] Aceh's so-called Darul Islam rebellion, nominally led by Teungku Daud

---

[2] On Aceh during the National Revolution see Anthony Reid, *The Blood of the People: Revolution and the End of Traditional Rule in Northern Sumatra* (Kuala Lumpur: Oxford University Press, 1979); and Eric Morris, "Aceh: Social Revolution and the Islamic Vision," in *Regional Dynamics of the Indonesian Revolution*, ed. Audrey R. Kahin (Honolulu: University of Hawaii Press, 1985), pp. 83-110.

[3] Clive J. Christie writes that, by the late 1940s, "Aceh had its own military force under the command of Daud Beureueh; equally, it had its own trading links—developed in the chaotic revolutionary period—that were independent of central government control. . . . [By 1949] Aceh had become accustomed to a situation where it had considerable scope for autonomous action." Clive J. Christie, *A Modern History of Southeast Asia: Decolonization, Nationalism and Separatism* (London: I.B. Tauris, 1996), pp. 147-48.

[4] The rebellion in Aceh was set in motion with a proclamation, dated September 21, 1953, declaring Aceh to be part of the Negara Islam Indonesia. Mr. S. M. Amin, "Sejenak Meninjau

Beureueh, was finally brought to an end in 1962 after years of complex negotiations, and low-level fighting, between Acehnese and central government authorities. While the rebellion failed to achieve its original goal of establishing an Islamic state in Aceh, it did win the province recognition as a *Daerah Istimewa* (Special Region) with nominal autonomy in the realms of religion, culture, and education.[5] The resolution of the Darul Islam rebellion through negotiation, and with minimal loss of life, was eased significantly by the fact that, notwithstanding their dissatisfaction with the central government in Jakarta, the rebel leaders never sought to separate from Indonesia. They had joined the movement for Negara Islam Indonesia because they were opposed to the centralizing tendencies of the regime, and to what they saw as its softness toward the Indonesian Communist Party (PKI), but there was never any serious doubt about their loyalty to a united Indonesia.

The clearest evidence of this claim is that, for roughly fifteen years after the surrender of Teungku Daud Beureueh, the province of Aceh posed no special political or security problems to the central government. Indeed, its formerly rebellious political and religious leaders joined enthusiastically with the Indonesian armed forces, political parties, and religious organizations in destroying the PKI in 1965-66.[6] And while central government authorities were somewhat anxious about the electoral successes of the Islamic-oriented United Development Party (PPP) and the corresponding weakness of government party Golkar in the 1970s, there was little doubt that the vast majority of Acehnese continued to see themselves as loyal citizens of a united Indonesia.[7]

Then in late 1976 a new rebel movement, known as Aceh Merdeka, burst onto the scene. In marked contrast to Darul Islam, the leaders of Aceh Merdeka called explicitly for the creation of an independent state of "Acheh-Sumatra," and characterized the New Order as a regime of "Javanese imperialists."[8] The movement gained strong early support in the Tiro district of Pidië, the home territory of its leader Teungku Hasan di Tiro, and on December 4, 1976 it unilaterally declared independence. The Indonesian government responded with a reasonably successful military operation aimed at capturing the movement's leaders, and in 1979 Hasan di Tiro, who had been living abroad from the early 1950s to 1976, left the country again to form a government in exile. By 1982 Aceh Merdeka appeared to have been crushed, with most of its leaders either killed, in exile, or in prison.[9]

Aceh, Serambi Mekkah" (A Glance at Aceh, Veranda of Mecca), in *Bunga Rampai tentang Aceh* (Anthology on Aceh), ed. Ismail Suny (Jakarta: Bhratara Karya Aksara, 1980), p. 80.

[5] Aceh's special status is enshrined in Republic of Indonesia, Law No.5/1974 on the Principles of Regional Government Administration.

[6] Tim Kell, *The Roots of Acehnese Rebellion* (Ithaca, NY: Cornell Modern Indonesia Project, 1995), p. 28.

[7] The PPP defeated Golkar in Aceh in the elections of 1977 and 1982, but Golkar bounced back with convincing victories in the elections of 1987 and 1992. See Dwight King and M. Ryaas Rasjid, "The Golkar Landslide in the 1987 Indonesian Elections: The Case of Aceh," *Asian Survey* 28, 9 (September 1988): 916-925.

[8] For a brief account of this early manifestation of Aceh Merdeka, see Nazaruddin Sjamsuddin, "Issues and politics of regionalism in Indonesia: Evaluating the Acehnese experience," in *Armed Separatism in Southeast Asia*, ed. Lim Joo-Jock and Vani S. (Singapore: ISEAS, 1984), pp. 111-128.

[9] Political trials of suspected Aceh Merdeka supporters continued into 1984. Kell, *The Roots of Acehnese Rebellion*, p. 66.

Nevertheless, the movement resurfaced in early 1989, launching a series of armed attacks on local military and police posts. Government authorities initially dismissed the attacks as the work of a minor criminal band with only a few weapons and little popular support. By mid-1990, however, it appeared that the rebels had gained the sympathy of a fairly wide cross-section of the population, especially in Pidië, North Aceh, and East Aceh. Moreover, civilians were now among the targets of the group's assaults, and government sources estimated that it had mobilized roughly two hundred armed fighters, some of whom were said to have received military training in Libya.[10] After an apparently unsuccessful territorial operation against the movement, in mid-1990 the Regional Military Commander was replaced and some six thousand additional troops were deployed to the region, bringing the total to about twelve thousand.[11] By late 1991 it appeared that government troops had largely succeeded in crushing the rebellion, and in killing most of its top leaders, but Aceh Merdeka supporters continued to menace Indonesian forces thereafter. One measure of the uncertainty of the central government's victory was that the military's Operasi Jaring Merah (Operation Red Net) remained in effect, and Aceh continued to be designated a Daerah Operasi Militer (DOM, Military Operations Area) until 1998.[12]

The sudden resumption of serious political violence in late 1998, just a few months after the withdrawal of most combat troops, was a further reminder of that uncertainty. On December 20, a crowd of about one thousand attacked a police post in Bayu, North Aceh, after hearing rumors that a police sergeant had sexually harassed a married woman. In the ensuing fracas, the officer in question narrowly escaped with his life, several government buildings were destroyed, an army officer and his wife were badly beaten, two marines were kidnapped, and at least two civilians suffered serious injury. Just over a week later, on December 29, a crowd in Lhok Nibung, East Aceh, beat to death several soldiers whom they had dragged from a passing bus. On January 3, 1999 a military operation called Operasi Wibawa 99, ostensibly aimed at capturing those responsible for the killings, and restoring government authority, resulted in scores of arrests and the killing of at least eleven people in the vicinity of Lhokseumawe. Although there was doubt about who had led the assaults against military and police personnel, government authorities were

---

[10] From early 1989 to April 1990 Aceh Merdeka attacks left only one civilian victim. By the end of June 1990, however, at least thirty civilians, many of them transmigrants, had been killed in attacks attributed to the group. Amnesty International, *Shock Therapy: Restoring Order in Aceh, 1989-1993* (London: Amnesty International, 1993), pp. 8-9.

[11] The President issued the order for troop deployments on July 6, 1990, and further reinforcements arrived in early August 1990. The troops deployed from outside the region included two battalions of the elite Special Forces Command, as well as units of the Marines in Jakarta, Kujang Airborne troops in Bandung, the Eighth Regional Command in East Java, the Anti-Aircraft Artillery unit in Medan, Airborne Rangers in Medan, and Police Mobile Brigades. For additional details, see Lembaga Bantuan Hukum, *Laporan Observasi Lapangan di Propinsi Daerah Istimewa Aceh* (Report on Field Observations in the Special Province of Aceh) (Jakarta: December 1990), pp. 34-35. Also see *Reuter*, July 22, 1990; August 15, 1990; and November 25, 1990.

[12] Armed Forces commander, General Wiranto, announced in early August 1998 that the DOM would be lifted in Aceh, and that all non-organic troops would be withdrawn as soon as possible. *Kompas*, August 11, 1998. Roughly nine hundred combat troops, most of them from Special Forces and Army Strategic Reserve Command units, were withdrawn from the area during the month of August. *Kompas*, September 1, 1998; *D & R*, August 29, 1998.

quick to blame Aceh Merdeka, claiming that some of the group's leaders had returned from exile in Malaysia to resume their campaign for independence. Based on that interpretation, military authorities deployed several hundred combat troops in the area, and began what many feared would be another major counter-insurgency campaign.[13]

The Limits of Tradition

So legendary is Aceh's reputation for rebelliousness and Islamic militancy, that it is tempting to view the recent Aceh Merdeka uprisings as new manifestations of an Acehnese tradition or, as some would have it, an expression of a primordial Acehnese urge to independence. There is an element of truth in these views, as the patterns of historical continuity among the different rebellions attest. The geographical base area of Acehnese resistance, for example, has remained more or less constant over the past one hundred years or so. The center of all three uprisings has been in the north-eastern coastal areas of Pidië, North Aceh, and East Aceh. There has also been a measure of continuity in the social composition of the leadership of rebellion. Aceh Merdeka leader, Teungku Hasan di Tiro, for instance, is the grandson of a hero of the Aceh War, Teungku Cik di Tiro, and was an associate of Darul Islam leader, Teungku Daud Beureueh.[14]

These historical and personal links have given Aceh Merdeka an almost automatic credibility and meaning that is difficult to distinguish from the idea of "tradition." The experience and memory of previous rebellions has also helped to consolidate a myth about Aceh—as a unique center of Islamic tradition, as a region with a glorious history of independence and resistance to outside authority, and so on—that has instilled in both leaders and followers a sense of belonging to a political community, and has given resonance to calls for Acehnese liberation and national independence. These elements of historical continuity and shared memory are an important part of the Aceh Merdeka story. Indeed, it is fair to say that without them, it would be difficult to account for the rise and popularity of the movement in the 1970s and 1980s. One might even argue that in the absence of the presumed "tradition" of Acehnese resistance, New Order authorities would have paid far less attention to the movement.

Nevertheless, the description of the recent troubles in Aceh as a mere extension of a tradition of resistance and Islamic militancy arguably obscures as much as it reveals. It obscures, first, significant differences in the aims of the different rebellions. Whereas the Darul Islam rebellion and the Aceh War aimed sincerely to promote and protect Islamic law and culture, Aceh Merdeka focused squarely on demands for political and economic independence, with religious concerns mentioned only in

---

[13] Human Rights Watch, "International Effort Needed on Aceh," January 4, 1999; Amnesty International, "Renewed Violence Plunges Aceh Back into Terror," January 11, 1999; *Meunasah*, December 23, 1998, December 30, 1998, and January 5, 1999; *Serambi Indonesia*, December 22, 1998; and *New York Times*, January 5, 1999.

[14] Hasan di Tiro, who was working for the Indonesian government at the United Nations in New York when the rebellion broke out in 1953, resigned from his post and designated himself Darul Islam's "ambassador" to the United Nations. Sjamsuddin, "Issues and politics of regionalism," p. 115.

passing.[15] This explicit demand for independence was arguably not so much an extension of Acehnese tradition as a conscious emulation—despite the very different historical and legal circumstances—of the impressive independence movement that had emerged only a few years before in East Timor. Living outside of Indonesia, and circulating in the eddies and backwaters of the international diplomatic scene, Aceh Merdeka leader Hasan di Tiro was apparently inspired by, and perhaps envious of, the power and political appeal of the East Timorese resistance, and sought for a time to coax its external spokesman, José Ramos-Horta, into an alliance. Though that initiative was rebuffed, di Tiro did his best to imitate the East Timorese resistance, in rhetoric and in method. The explicit demand for independence and the bellicose language and tactics he employed were seen as a clear provocation by the New Order and triggered a predictably harsh response.

The focus on tradition and continuity also obscures important differences in the social composition of the leaderships of the different rebellions. Whereas the earlier uprisings were led, or very strongly supported by, Aceh's *ulama*, the leadership of Aceh Merdeka has been drawn predominantly from a collection of intellectuals, local government officials, disgruntled members of the armed forces, and local businessmen. Although he uses the title "Teungku," reserved for respected men of Islam, Hasan di Tiro cannot by any reasonable measure be described as a religious leader. Indeed, as those who have met him or read his political tracts generally concur, he is far closer, sociologically and politically, to the Acehnese aristocratic *uleëbalang* class than to the *ulama* who led the earlier rebellions. He has, moreover, spent much of the past fifty years living abroad, first in the United States and then in Sweden, and in a fashion that one would not readily associate with the life of an Islamic scholar. It is hardly surprising, therefore, that very few *ulama* have given the movement their wholehearted support and some, including former supporters of Darul Islam, have been openly opposed to it.[16]

Finally, the focus on tradition and continuity obscures the long periods during which Aceh has been either super-loyal to the central Indonesian government, as it was from 1945 to 1949, or politically calm and orderly, as it was through most of the 1960s and 1970s, and even much of the 1980s. These periods of calm and order make a nonsense of the idea that Aceh has been driven to rebellion by "natural" or "primordial" urges.

Taken together, these considerations suggest that the recent Aceh Merdeka uprisings, and the extreme violence that followed from them, cannot properly be understood solely as the continuation of a tradition. Indeed, the differences between the aims and the leadership of Aceh Merdeka and the earlier rebellions, and the on-again off-again pattern of political trouble in Aceh, both suggest that the rise of Aceh Merdeka and the extreme violence after 1989 were related to changes in the broader economic and political environment—an environment which changed quite dramatically during these years.

---

[15] On this point, and for an overview of the ideas of Aceh Merdeka leader Teungku Hasan di Tiro, see Kell, *The Roots of Acehnese Rebellion*, pp. 61-66.

[16] Ibid., p. 65.

3. THE POLITICAL ECONOMY OF VIOLENCE

Aceh's historical resistance to outside authorities has always been rooted, to some degree, in conflicts over the control and distribution of economic resources. Its conflict with the Dutch in the nineteenth century, and earlier with the Portuguese and with neighboring Southeast Asian states, were not only struggles between competing worldviews but also contests for the control of trade. Similarly, the leaders of the Darul Islam rebellion of the 1950s, while sincere in their pursuit of Islamic ideals, were partly driven by a desire to maintain the considerable autonomy, in the economic and other spheres, they had come to enjoy in the late 1940s. Moreover, their resentment toward the central government was deepened by a feeling that the substantial economic contributions they had made to the Republic of Indonesia during the National Revolution had not been properly appreciated or recognized.[17]

Economic issues were also important in stimulating the New Order conflict between Aceh and Jakarta starting in the mid-1970s. In part, this was because Aceh happened to be extremely rich in natural resources—including oil, natural gas, timber, and a variety of valuable minerals—which began to be exploited to an unprecedented degree during this period. Perhaps even more significant was the manner in which New Order authorities set about exploiting those resources and distributing the benefits. One distinctive feature of that approach—and one of the reasons that massive exploitation of resources took place at all—was the very close relationship that the regime developed with foreign capital. That relationship was based partly on an ideological predisposition within the leadership group, but increasingly on the enormous material benefits that it brought both to the state and to individual officials, in the form of kick-backs, rents, fees, bribes, and so on. A second critical feature of the regime's approach was the highly centralized nature of its procedures for economic decision-making.[18]

The close nexus between state and capital, and the extreme centralization of economic decision-making, brought untold benefits to the New Order and to foreign capitalists operating in Aceh from the mid-1970s on. Simultaneously, however, it set in motion a variety of changes that generated popular support for Aceh Merdeka and contributed to the problem of unrest and violence.

---

[17] Mr. S. M. Amin, "Sejenak Meninjau Aceh, Serambi Mekkah," pp. 70-74.

[18] Kell offers the following summary of the problem of centralization: "Whatever plans the regional administration may have for the development of the Acehnese economy, the province lacks autonomy in economic matters by virtue of the highly centralized nature of state power under the New Order. Not only does the central government control the revenues that accrue from Aceh's export industries, but the concentration in Jakarta both of authority over industrial policy and of the bureaucratic agencies which grant licenses for new industrial projects also has strong 'Java-centric' effects. The pattern is accentuated by an additional 'web of informal connections' which ensures, for example, that military and government officials . . . reap the greatest reward from the negotiation of local equity in foreign owned ventures." Kell, *The Roots of Acehnese Rebellion*, p. 27.

The LNG Boom

From the mid-1970s through the 1980s, Aceh was catapulted from its status as an economic backwater into the fastest-growing provincial economy in the country.[19] The transformation has been dubbed the "LNG boom," because it was driven by the discovery and exploitation of huge deposits of liquid natural gas (LNG) and oil in the vicinity of Lhokseumawe and Lhoksukon, on Aceh's northeast coast. By the mid-1980s, as a result of the boom, Aceh's per capita GDP was equal to 282 percent of the national average, making it the third highest in the country.[20] Over the same period Aceh became one of Indonesia's most important export earners and sources of central state revenue. Through the 1980s it contributed between $2 and $3 billion annually to Indonesian exports, making it the third largest source of exports after Riau and East Kalimantan.[21] Meanwhile taxes and royalties from the oil and gas fields contributed billions of dollars annually to central government revenues.[22]

The LNG boom appears to have provided fertile soil in which the rebel movement emerged in 1976 and again in 1989.[23] In part, this was because the benefits of the boom were not equally shared. As the central government and foreign companies reaped enormous revenues, the promised "trickle down" effects of the massive investment proved to be limited. After the initial construction phase in the early 1970s, for example, employment opportunities for local people declined dramatically, and the majority of well-paid jobs were filled by Indonesians from different regions or by foreigners.[24] The problem of unemployment was especially acute in the town of Lhokseumawe, in the immediate vicinity of the major

---

[19] Aceh had by far the highest annual growth rate in the country between 1976 and 1982. Dayan Dawood and Sjafrizal, "Aceh: The LNG Boom and Enclave Development," in *Unity and Diversity: Regional Economic Development in Indonesia Since 1970*, ed. Hal Hill (Singapore: Oxford University Press, 1989), p. 111. Although it has slowed considerably since then, Aceh's growth rate has remained strong. In the period 1994-1997, for example, growth averaged 7.86 percent per annum. Bappeda Propinsi Daerah Istimewa Aceh, "Pembangunan Ekonomi di Daerah Istimewa Aceh" (Economic Development in the Special Region of Aceh), Paper prepared for symposium, Telaah Pembangunan Daerah Istimewa Aceh Memasuki Era Reformasi, Jakarta, August 22, 1998.

[20] The figure for Aceh's per capita GDP in 1983 was Rp.1,220,000, up dramatically from Rp.28,000 in 1971. Only the provinces of Riau and East Kalimantan had higher per capita GDP in 1983. Hal Hill, ed., *Unity and Diversity: Regional Economic Development in Indonesia Since 1970* (Singapore: Oxford University Press, 1989), pp. 6-7. For a synopsis of Aceh's contribution to the national economy, see Kell, *The Roots of Acehnese Rebellion*, pp. 14-16.

[21] Dawood and Sjafrizal note that, by 1984, Aceh's " . . . net exports accounted for about two thirds of the provincial GDP. Thus well over half of Aceh's production accrues, through the central government, to the rest of Indonesia." Dawood and Sjafrizal, "Aceh," p. 115. The situation has not changed significantly since then. In the mid-1990s Aceh was contributing roughly 17 percent of Indonesia's total foreign exchange earnings. See Zulkifli Husin, "Strategi Pembangunan Ekonomi Aceh Dalam Orde Reformasi" (Strategy for Aceh's Economic Development in the Era of Reform), Paper prepared for symposium, Telaah Pembangunan Daerah Istimewa Aceh Memasuki Era Reformasi, Jakarta, August 22, 1998, p.1.

[22] Dawood and Sjafrizal write that: "Virtually the entire oil and gas revenue from Aceh accrues to the central government, either through the production-sharing agreement between Mobil Oil Indonesia (MOI) and Pertamina (the state oil company), or directly through Pertamina itself." Dawood and Sjafrizal, "Aceh," p. 115.

[23] Detailed discussion of the socio-economic impact of the economic boom in Aceh can be found in Kell, *The Roots of Acehnese Rebellion*, pp. 16-21, and 52-60.

[24] Ibid., pp. 19-20.

production facilities.[25] And while the absolute level of poverty in the province was said to be relatively low by national standards, in the mid-1980s it was still the case that fewer than 10 percent of villages in energy-rich Aceh had a steady supply of electricity.[26]

Unsurprisingly, the boom also brought a number of undesirable side-effects, including the expropriation of land from small farmers without adequate compensation,[27] the failure to provide adequate social amenities and infrastructure for displaced communities and migrant workers,[28] and serious environmental degradation in the vicinity of the plants.[29] These problems were compounded by the sometimes extreme insensitivity of Indonesian government and military authorities toward local people, who were commonly described as "fanatics," whose culture and worldview were in need of modernization and improvement.[30] In return, some Acehnese blamed "outsiders" for encouraging practices they found offensive to Islam and to local custom, such as gambling, drinking, and prostitution.

Worse still, the substantial revenues generated by taxes and royalties were channeled directly to the central government, and there was a perception that very little was recycled back to the province in the form of government investment or subsidies. Of course Aceh was not alone in this regard, and it was hardly the worst off among Indonesia's provinces.[31] Nevertheless, the fact that Aceh was contributing so much to national revenues and exports helped to create a feeling of resentment that it was not getting a great deal more in return.[32] The skimming of tax and other revenues by the center was especially irritating to Acehnese intellectuals and local government technocrats, who felt that far more of the locally generated revenues ought to have been spent locally.[33]

---

[25] Dawood and Sjafrizal, "Aceh," p. 117.

[26] Ibid, p. 122. Nor has the situation improved dramatically since then. In 1997, before the economic crisis, some 51 percent of Aceh's villages were categorized as poor. See Pengurus Pusat Taman Iskandar Muda, "Kerangka Acuan Diskusi Terbatas Telaah Pembangunan Daerah Istimewa Aceh Memasuki Era Reformasi" (Frame of Reference for Closed Discussion of Research on the Development of the Special Region of Aceh at the Start of the Reform Era), Jakarta, August 22, 1998, p.1.

[27] The full extent of such expropriations began to be revealed in late 1998, as those who had lost their land began to seek compensation. In December 1998 four villagers from Desa Ampeh, Aceh Utara, brought a legal suit against Mobil Oil for land they said had been expropriated without compensation in 1977. *Waspada*, December 18, 1998.

[28] Dawood and Sjafrizal, "Aceh," p. 117.

[29] See George Aditjondro, "After Ogoniland, will it be the turn of Aceh? Notes on environmental degradation and human rights violations in Aceh" [Manuscript, n.d.].

[30] A paper prepared for the Badan Perencanaan Pembangunan Aceh (Aceh Development Planning Board) in 1971 declares: "Aceh is well known for its religious fanaticism and its cultural fanaticism . . . That condition will make it difficult for the society to progress; it will remain static, not dynamic." A. Madjid Ibrahim, "Strategi Pembangunan Daerah Aceh" (Strategy for Aceh's Development), in *Bunga Rampai tentang Aceh*, pp. 469-470.

[31] Dawood and Sjafrizal write that "government expenditure and revenue in Aceh is a surprisingly low share of GDP for a small province." They caution, however, that the figures may be misleading. Dawood and Sjafrizal, "Aceh," p. 113.

[32] Kell, *The Roots of Acehnese Rebellion*, pp. 54-55.

[33] A number of authors have described the rise of a class of technocrats in New Order Aceh, but the political role of this group remains ambiguous. While on the one hand they have been described as tools of the New Order state, it is clear that they also gave expression to many of the grievances over Aceh's unfair treatment by Jakarta. Kell writes, for example, that ". . . for

Members of Aceh's small but growing business class were unhappy for slightly different reasons. Though some benefited from the injection of private foreign investment in the region, many felt aggrieved because outsiders, particularly those with good political connections in Jakarta, or with the military in Aceh, appeared to be winning more than their share of lucrative contracts. Among the disgruntled businessmen was none other than Aceh Merdeka leader, Hasan di Tiro, whose bid for building a pipeline for Mobil Oil was reportedly beaten out by a US firm in 1974.[34] Perhaps not surprisingly, therefore, members of all these groups—intellectuals, technocrats, and businessmen—were among the strongest supporters of Aceh Merdeka.

Aceh's newfound economic importance guaranteed that the central government and military authorities would respond swiftly, and with considerable force, to any perceived threats to security in the region, especially those in the immediate vicinity of the production facilities. By all accounts, the actual military threat from Aceh Merdeka was minuscule in 1977 and only slightly greater in 1989. Though faced with only a few dozen armed insurgents, on both occasions the government deployed many thousands of troops.[35] The preoccupation with guarding the LNG facilities could also be seen in the fact that the Military Operations Command for Aceh was located in the provincial town of Lhokseumawe, right next door to the major LNG production facilities.[36] The regime's approach was neatly encapsulated by Colonel Sofyan Effendi, the Commander of Military Resort 011 in Lhokseumawe, in mid-1990. He said the military would maintain "very strict" security in the area because it "contained five major industries important to the nation's economic growth." The authorities would be taking no risks, Effendi said, because "the slightest disturbance would have a national impact."[37] The irony was, of course, that in their bid to make Aceh secure and peaceful for economic development, New Order authorities achieved precisely the opposite result.

Aceh's status as a Military Operations Area also created unrivaled opportunities for the emergence of a semi-official mafia with close links to the military, and to the Special Forces in particular. Members of units stationed in Aceh were apparently able to enrich themselves serving as enforcers, debt-collectors, security guards, and extortionists.[38] Stories of such operations began to abound in Aceh as the Special Forces became firmly entrenched in the mid-1990s. In 1997, a local human rights organization reported the case of a man named Abdul Hamid bin Itam who had been detained by three Special Forces soldiers late at night on September 14, 1996, in the town of Sigli. After being taken to the local Special Forces post, bin Itam had been badly beaten, and then shot in the head; his mutilated body was found a few days

---

the technocrats, Aceh's difficulty was that it had been denied its fair share of the national economic cake and in the process had been relegated to the status of a neglected and disadvantaged outlying region." Ibid., p. 30.

[34] Sumatra Human Rights Watch Network, "Tentang Aceh" (On Aceh) [manuscript, n.d.].

[35] On the military response in the late 1970s, see Nazaruddin Sjamsuddin, "Issues and politics of regionalism," p. 114. On the response after 1989, see below.

[36] The Commander of the Military Operations Command (*Pangkolakops*) for Aceh was simultaneously the Commander of Korem (Military Resort) 011/Lilawangsa, based in Lhokseumawe, North Aceh.

[37] *Jakarta Post*, May 14, 1990.

[38] See *Far Eastern Economic Review*, November 19, 1998, pp. 25, 18 ; and *Gatra*, August 15, 1998, p. 38.

later about two hundred kilometers from Sigli. Although at first this appeared to be a standard summary execution of an Aceh Merdeka suspect, it was later reported that the dead man had been detained in connection with a private dispute he had had with a local government official in Pidië. The official had evidently hired the Special Forces soldiers to "resolve" the dispute.[39]

Although evidence for such a military mafia remains largely anecdotal, its existence would be in keeping with patterns in other parts of the country, and in particular in other areas of long-term military operations. It would also help to account for the extraordinary reluctance of the armed forces to leave Aceh, and to end the military operation there long after Aceh Merdeka appeared to have been crushed as a military force.

The Logic of Rebellion

The conjuncture of these trends—the growing importance of Aceh's economy for the central government, the failure of the LNG boom to provide the kinds of benefits anticipated by ordinary people, the problem of military heavy-handedness, and the emergence of a military-linked mafia—led inevitably to growing tensions between Acehnese on the one hand and central government and military officials on the other. Because these trends affected a fairly broad spectrum of Acehnese society, including farmers, fishermen, laborers, unemployed migrant workers—as well as the small Acehnese political, technocratic, and economic elite—they had the effect of increasing the credibility, and broadening the appeal, of the demands made by Aceh Merdeka's leaders.

The timing of Aceh Merdeka's rise, the targets of its attacks, and its geographical focus, lend additional support to the view that the movement was stimulated by the tensions generated by New Order economic policy. It was probably not by chance, for example, that Aceh Merdeka's declaration of rebellion in late 1976 and its first military action in 1977 coincided with the opening of PT Arun, Aceh's first major facility for the extraction and processing of LNG.[40] Nor could it be mere coincidence that two of the plant's personnel, expatriate employees of Mobil Oil Indonesia (MOI), were among the first targets of rebel attacks in 1977.[41] Evidently, the Aceh Merdeka leadership viewed the plant and its personnel as symbols of what was wrong in Aceh, and calculated that assaults on the new facilities would draw the maximum possible attention to their cause. Likewise, it was probably significant that the second Aceh Merdeka uprising in 1989 began with protests against the corruption, gambling, and prostitution that were said to have been encouraged by the flood of transmigrants and other "outsiders" whose numbers had increased during the

---

[39] For this and other cases, see Sjaifuddin Gani, "Kasus Aceh: Teror Kontra Teror Sebagai Kondisi Umum" (The Case of Aceh: Terror vs. Terror as a General Condition) [manuscript, n.d.], p. 9; and Sumatra Human Rights Watch Network, "Kondisi HAM di Aceh 1995-1997" (The Human Rights Situation in Aceh, 1995-1997) [manuscript, n.d.], pp. 2-3.

[40] The massive natural gas reserves were discovered in 1971, but production did not begin until 1977. PT Arun was established as a joint venture between the state oil company Pertamina, MOI, and a consortium of Japanese companies. Dawood and Sjafrizal, "Aceh," p. 115.

[41] Aditjondro, "After Ogoniland, will it be the turn of Aceh?," p. 2.

boom.[42] Finally, it was notable that the movement's base areas in 1976 and 1989—Pidië, North Aceh, and East Aceh—overlapped closely, though not completely, with the main areas of rapid industrial development.

This is not to say that Aceh Merdeka emerged directly in response to the LNG boom in the 1970s, but rather that the changes set in motion by the state-capital link, and the extreme centralization of economic decision-making, stimulated a consciousness of shared fate that reinforced existing ideas of Acehnese identity and increased the credibility of Aceh Merdeka in the area. The fact that the main LNG and oil facilities were located in the former base areas of the Darul Islam rebellion and the Aceh War, as well as on the home turf of Hasan di Tiro, gave a special resonance to the calls for rebellion and independence in these areas. The significance of economic developments in generating the conflict in Aceh is highlighted by the remarkable quietness of the province through most of the 1960s and early 1970s. The contrast can be explained, in part, by the fact that in those years Aceh was of no great interest economically, and so was largely left alone by the center. With the start of LNG production in the mid-1970s, however, Aceh became a magnet for the greedy and the powerful, and therefore a site of economic and political contention.

Yet, while the rapid economic transformations of the 1970s and 1980s undoubtedly contributed to the rise of Aceh Merdeka, and to the heightened central government concern over stability in the area, they do not appear to account for the extreme levels of violence that engulfed the area from mid-1990 to 1993. Nor do they explain the sudden resurgence of political violence in late 1998. Part of the explanation lies in the behavior of Aceh Merdeka itself, because its ideology of explicit separatism, its bellicose anti-Javanese rhetoric, its strategy of armed resistance, and its attacks on vital industries and transmigrants have seemed designed to provoke the most hostile possible reaction from the Indonesian armed forces. Yet, when the story is told from the perspective of Acehnese who experienced these events first-hand, it becomes clear that the degree and nature of the violence in Aceh after 1990 was even more closely related to the behavior of Indonesia's armed forces. That is to say, the actions of the Indonesian military in Aceh need to be examined not simply as a response to a mature rebellion, whose "roots" lay somewhere in the socio-economic or primordial past, but as an integral part of the development of that rebellion, and of the condition of recurrent violence and instability which grew from it.

4. MILITARY DOCTRINE AND PRACTICE

The use of military force to deal with armed insurgents was not, of course, an innovation of the New Order. Dutch colonial forces behaved with conspicuous brutality in Aceh, and in some other parts of the archipelago, as they sought to extend their administrative authority to previously autonomous areas in the late nineteenth century. Under President Sukarno, combat troops had been deployed throughout the country, including in Aceh, to put down rebellions and insurrections. The soldiers of the Old Order were, on occasion, accused of serious abuses, including torture and rape. Clive Christie writes, for example, that in Aceh in the 1950s "the response of the government troops to rebel actions tended to be clumsy and

---

[42] For details of these early protests, and attacks, see Amnesty International, *Shock Therapy*, p. 8.

brutal...[and] this had the inevitable effect of increasing sympathy and support for the rebels."[43]

What was new, and distinctive, about military doctrine and practice under the late New Order was: first, the institutionalization of terror as a method for dealing with perceived threats to national security; and second, the systematic and forced mobilization of civilians to serve as auxiliaries and spies in counter-insurgency operations.[44] These features of New Order military doctrine and practice ensured that in Aceh a much broader spectrum of people came to experience the hard edge of the regime, to feel deep bitterness towards it, and to sympathize more completely with the opposition. These methods also encouraged greater violence and disruption in local society, and inflicted wounds that would prove exceptionally difficult to heal.

Terror

Mid-1990 is a critical date in this story because it marks the abrupt end of the regime's limited efforts to resolve the conflict in Aceh through political accommodation and negotiation, and the beginning of a wholly military response.[45] Once the new combat troops had been deployed, in mid-1990, and the counter-insurgency campaign known as Operasi Jaring Merah (Red Net) set in motion, the level and the nature of violence began to change almost immediately. Though there was little press coverage at the time, it later became clear that it was at this stage that the armed forces began to employ terror systematically.[46] As Amnesty International wrote in 1993: "The political authority of the armed forces, considerable even under normal conditions, now became unchallengeable. In the name of national security, military and police authorities deployed in Aceh were thereafter free to use virtually any means deemed necessary to destroy the GPK."[47]

Among the first outside troops to arrive in Aceh was an Army Strategic Reserve unit under the command of Colonel Prabowo Subianto.[48] Within a few days of its

---

[43] Christie, *A Modern History of Southeast Asia*, p. 154. One estimate from 1955 claims that 271 people were killed in the fighting between 1953 and 1954. Teungku Hadji Ali, cited in *Kompas*, August 11, 1998.

[44] The origins and evolution of these features of New Order military doctrine and practice have been analyzed in some depth by Tanter, van Langenberg, and others. See Richard Tanter, "The Totalitarian Ambition: Intelligence Organisations and the Indonesian State," in *State and Civil Society in Indonesia*, ed. Arief Budiman (Clayton, Victoria: Monash Papers on Southeast Asia, No. 22, 1990); and Michael van Langenberg "The New Order State: Language, Ideology, Hegemony," in *State and Civil Society in Indonesia*, ed. Arief Budiman.

[45] The contrast with the increasingly accommodative approach adopted by Sukarno toward the 1950s Darul Islam rebellion is instructive. As Sjamsuddin writes: "In Aceh, the political concessions granted by the Old Order regime played a great part in ending the Darul Islam rebellion in the early 1960s." Sjamsuddin, "Issues and politics of regionalism," p. 124.

[46] Detailed descriptions of the use of terror can be found in Amnesty International, *Shock Therapy*; *Kompas*, August 22, 1998; *Gatra*, August 8, 1998; *Ummat*, August, 1998; *Xpos*, August 1-7, 1998; *DeTak*, August 11-17 and August 18-24, 1998; and *Seuruenee: Bulletin Forum LSM Aceh*, July 1998.

[47] Amnesty International, *Shock Therapy*, p. 11.

[48] The unit was probably the 17th Airborne Infantry Brigade, of which Prabowo became Chief of Staff in 1989, immediately after a successful tour of duty in East Timor as Deputy

arrival by parachute in North Aceh, this unit began to burn down the houses of families suspected of supporting Aceh Merdeka.[49] That was only the start. In subsequent weeks, this and other military units began a systematic campaign to terrorize civilian populations in areas of presumed rebel strength. Their methods included armed night-time raids, house-to-house searches, arbitrary arrest, routine torture of detainees, the rape of women believed to be associated with the movement, and public execution.[50]

Among the most chilling examples of state-sanctioned terror in Aceh were targeted killings and public executions. For a period of about two years after the start of combat operations, the corpses of Acehnese victims, generally young men, were found strewn in public places—beside main roads, near village security posts, in public markets, in fields and plantations, next to a stream or a river—apparently as a warning to others not to join or support the rebels. Amnesty International reported the following patterns:

> Their thumbs, and sometimes their feet, had been tied together with a particular type of knot. Most had been shot at close range, though the bullets were seldom found in their bodies. Most also showed signs of having been beaten with a blunt instrument or tortured, and their faces were therefore often unrecognizable. For the most part, the bodies were not recovered by relatives or friends, both out of fear of retribution by the military and because the victims were usually dumped at some distance from their home villages.[51]

In technique and in evident purpose, these killings closely resembled the government-sponsored summary executions of alleged petty-criminals in the mid-1980s. Known by the acronym Petrus, the earlier "mysterious killings" had left some five thousand people dead in Java and other parts of the country. Though government and military authorities had initially denied any involvement in the Petrus killings, it eventually emerged that they had been initiated by the regime itself and carried out by a specially trained sub-unit of the Special Forces.[52] It was also revealed that the use of terror had had a deliberate strategic intent. In his memoirs, published in 1989, Suharto provided the following rationale for the killings.

> The peace was disturbed. It was as if there was no longer peace in this country. It was as though all there was was fear . . . We had to apply some *treatment*, to take some stern action. What kind of action? It had to be with violence. But this violence did not mean just shooting people, pow! pow! just like that. No! But those who tried to resist, like it or not, had to be shot . . . Some of the corpses

---

Commander of Kostrad (Army Strategic Reserve) Battalion 328. *Forum Keadilan*, August 24, 1998.

[49] Confidential personal communication from human rights lawyer, Banda Aceh, August 1998.

[50] For examples and eyewitness testimonies, see Amnesty International, *Shock Therapy*.

[51] Ibid., p. 18.

[52] On the Petrus killings, David Bourchier concludes that "The timing, the methods used and the geographical spread of the killings . . . indicate a well planned, centrally coordinated military operation." David Bourchier, "Law, Crime and State Authority in Indonesia," in *State and Civil Society in Indonesia*, ed. Arief Budiman (Clayton, Victoria: Monash Papers on Southeast Asia, No. 22, 1990), pp. 186-187.

were left [in public places] just like that. This was for the purpose of *shock therapy* . . . This was done so that the general public would understand that there was still someone capable of taking action to tackle the problem of criminality.[53]

Like the Petrus killings, the "mysterious killings" in Aceh were clearly part of a central government policy that involved the deliberate use of "shock therapy" to achieve a strategic political and security objective.[54] There can be no other explanation for the many documented instances in which military authorities severed the heads of alleged rebels and placed them on stakes in front of their command posts, or in public markets. Nor is there any other way to explain why military officers forced passersby to witness the roadside executions of rebel suspects.[55] Besides the testimony of witnesses, the evidence to support this claim comes from the statements of the military authorities involved. Commenting on the public display of corpses, for example, one military officer in Aceh admitted: "Okay, that does happen. But the rebels use terrorist strategies so we are forced to use anti-terrorist strategies."[56] Asked whether the mysterious killings were intended as "shock therapy," the Regional Military Commander, Major-General R. Pramono, said: "As a strategy, that's true. But our goal is not bad. Our goal must be correct . . . We only kill them if they are members [of Aceh Merdeka]."[57]

Many victims of summary execution were simply shot and thrown into mass graves, at least one of which reportedly contained as many as two hundred bodies. Commenting on reports of such a mass grave in late 1990, Major General R. Pramono told a journalist: "The grave certainly exists but I don't think it could have been two hundred bodies. It's hard to tell with arms and heads all mixed up."[58] But if the method of disposal was different, the intent of the mass killings was the same: to sow terror, to create an atmosphere of fear, and to ensure that witnesses to such crimes remained silent. The strategy worked, at least in the short term. As a man who lived near the site of a mass grave commented in 1998: "At that time, trucks carrying

---

[53] *Suharto: Pikiran, Ucapan dan Tindakan Saya* (Suharto: My Thoughts, Statements, and Actions) (Jakarta: PT Citra Lamtoro Gung Persada, 1989), p. 364.

[54] Amnesty International concluded that: "The timing of the worst killings in Aceh, the methods and techniques employed, and the comments made by military officers in the region, suggest strongly that extrajudicial execution was part of a deliberate and coordinated counter-insurgency strategy. Moreover, the uniformity of the pattern of human rights violations reported in Aceh and those documented in other parts of Indonesia and East Timor, indicates that, where it faces serious opposition to its authority, political killing may be a central aspect of Indonesian Government policy." Amnesty International, *Shock Therapy*, p. 18.

[55] For details of such cases, see Amnesty International, *Shock Therapy*, pp. 22-27; and Sjaifuddin Gani, "Kasus Aceh: Teror Kontra Teror Sebagai Kondisi Umum," pp. 5-8.

[56] *Reuter*, November 25, 1990.

[57] Ibid.

[58] Ibid. In late August 1998, Indonesia's National Human Rights Commission excavated several of the suspected mass grave sites. Commenting on its findings, a member of the commission said: "The discovery of the skeletal remains has convinced us beyond doubt that the reports of widespread military atrocities over the past nine years in Aceh are an undisputed fact." *Jakarta Post*, August 28, 1998. For further details of those investigations and of the mass graves, see the Commission's report, "Laporan Komnas HAM: Dari Kuburan Massal Hingga Cuwak" (The National Human Rights Commission Report: From Mass Graves to Collaborators), August 24, 1998. Also see *Kompas*, August 22, 1998; *Jakarta Post* August 22, 1998; and *Waspada*, August 14, 1998.

bodies to be buried on the peninsula or just dumped on the streets came and went at night, while people were too scared to ask what happened."[59] In the long term, however, the military's use of terror stimulated a profound anger among a broad cross-section of Aceh's population. That anger was fueled by the Habibie government's failure to take action against the military perpetrators. Under the circumstances, the assaults on military and police personnel in late 1998 were hardly a surprise.

Civil-military Cooperation

Equally important in generating political violence in Aceh was the New Order strategy of "civil-military cooperation"—a euphemism for the policy of compelling civilians to participate in intelligence and security operations against real or alleged government opponents.[60] Like the use of targeted killings, corpse display, and rape, this strategy was not unique to Aceh, having been developed and refined, for example, in counter-insurgency operations in Irian Jaya and East Timor.

Among the most notorious examples of the strategy was the "fence of legs" operations—used both in East Timor and in Aceh—in which "ordinary villagers were compelled to sweep through an area ahead of armed troops, in order both to flush out rebels and to inhibit them from returning fire."[61] The idea behind the strategy was succinctly stated by Colonel Syarwan Hamid in 1991, when he was the Commander of Military Resort 011, and simultaneously of the Military Operations Command for Aceh: "The youths are the front line. They know best who the GPK are. We then settle the matter."[62] Priests who witnessed such an operation in East Timor described it as the ". . . mass mobilization of citizens to make war on each other."[63]

More widely used in Aceh, and with similar consequences for local communities, were military-led campaigns encouraging all civilians to hunt and kill any suspected member of an alleged enemy group. This was an essential element in the dynamic of violence in Aceh. In November 1990, for example, Major-General R. Pramono, said:

> I have told the community, if you find a terrorist, kill him. There's no need to investigate him. Don't let people be the victims. If they don't do as you order them, shoot them on the spot, or butcher them. I tell members of the community to carry sharp weapons, a machete or whatever. If you meet a terrorist, kill him.[64]

---

[59] *Jakarta Post*, August 22, 1998.

[60] The strategy was officially justified by the military doctrine known as "People's total defence and security system" (*sishankamrata*).

[61] Amnesty International, *Shock Therapy*, p. 12.

[62] *Kompas*, July 11, 1991.

[63] Cited in John Taylor, *Indonesia's Forgotten War: The Hidden History of East Timor* (London: Zed Books, 1991), p. 117. The "fence of legs" strategy was used in East Timor in Operasi Keamanan (Operation Security) in 1981 and Operasi Kikis (Operation Erase) in 1986-1987. For a detailed description of these operations, see ibid., pp. 117-118 and 161.

[64] From an interview with Major-General R. Pramono, *Tempo*, November 17, 1990; translation as cited in JPRS-SEA-90-034, December 16, 1990.

Apparently seeking to reassure a western journalist that such methods were humane and appropriate, he commented: "We have written laws and unwritten laws . . . The people know the unwritten laws so they won't kill anyone who's not in the wrong. Well, one or two maybe, but that's the risk."[65]

Also commonly employed in counter-insurgency operations in Aceh were local vigilante units and night patrols made up of civilians but established under military order and supervision. They included groups such as the Unit Ksatria Penegak Pancasila (Noble Warriors for Upholding Pancasila), Bela Negara (Defend the State), Pemuda Keamanan Desa (Village Security Youth), and Laskar Rakyat (People's Militia). In the first few years of the operation alone, military authorities mobilized tens of thousands of men into such units.[66] Recruits received basic military training and, after being armed with knives, spears, and machetes, were told to "hunt" Aceh Merdeka supporters. As they had done during the anti-communist campaign in 1965-1966, and during counter-insurgency operations in East Timor, military authorities also organized mass rallies in Aceh at which civilians were exhorted to "crush the GPK," and to swear an oath that they would "crush the terrorists until there is nothing left of them."[67] The failure to participate in such campaigns—or to demonstrate a sufficient commitment to crushing the enemy by identifying, capturing, or killing alleged rebels—often resulted in punishment, and sometimes public torture and execution.[68]

The strategy of "civil-military cooperation" also entailed the recruitment of local people to serve as spies and informers for the military. One consequence of this arrangement was the reinforcement of an atmosphere of pervasive fear and silence. One simply did not know who might be listening. As an Acehnese human rights activist said in August 1998: "We have lived for years with fear. During the New Order, we kept our mouths shut, never daring to speak out . . . because in every café and street corner there were intelligence agents listening."[69]

The strategy bred terrible tensions and conflicts among Acehnese. Perhaps with honorable intentions, many Acehnese of some social standing—including members of the Majelis Ulama Indonesia (MUI, Indonesian Council of Ulamas)—joined the army's counter-insurgency campaign.[70] Others, possibly fearing the repercussions of non-cooperation, became enthusiastic spies and informants for the military. In doing so, they helped to send hundreds, perhaps thousands of fellow Acehnese to their graves. The wounds caused by such actions do not heal easily. Predictably perhaps, in the months after the withdrawal of combat troops in August 1998, Acehnese collaborators, known locally as *cuak*, were subjected to violent reprisals. At least two

---

[65] *Reuter*, November 25, 1990.

[66] In mid-1991 the Governor of Aceh, Ibrahim Hasan, estimated that some sixty thousand people had been mobilized. Kell, *The Roots of Acehnese Rebellion*, p. 75.

[67] Amnesty International, *Shock Therapy*, pp. 13-14.

[68] Confidential interviews with Acehnese refugees in Malaysia, October 1991; and Amnesty International, *Shock Therapy*, p. 13.

[69] *Kompas*, August 11, 1998. A key figure in the development of this network was the chief of the intelligence task force in Aceh in the early 1990s, Colonel Zacky Anwar Makarim. In 1997 Makarim, by then a Major-General, was appointed head of BIA, the powerful Armed Forces intelligence agency, a position he retained in late 1998. *Far Eastern Economic Review*, November 19, 1998, p. 28; *Gatra*, August 15, 1998.

[70] For more details on the role of the MUI in the counter-insurgency campaign, see Kell, *The Roots of Acehnese Rebellion*, pp. 77-78.

were beaten to death by angry crowds, while others were forced to seek protection with local authorities.[71] Like the attacks on military and police personnel, the violence against collaborators seemed likely to continue for some time, another long-term legacy of New Order military strategy.

Yet while the methods employed by the military generally helped to perpetuate a cycle of violence, they also served to stimulate a significant shift in Acehnese public discourse. Whereas in 1976-1979, and still in 1989-1990, Aceh Merdeka sympathizers rallied principally around issues of economic injustice and political self-determination, after 1991 the main focus of concern shifted to ABRI's behavior, and to its systematic violation of human rights. That change may have represented a tactical decision by the Aceh Merdeka leadership, in an effort to garner greater domestic and international support for the cause. Its effectiveness as a tactic, however, lay in the grim reality that ABRI was in fact committing the most outrageous crimes against ordinary people.

The shift in focus became even clearer after the collapse of the New Order in May 1998. Driven largely by the energetic work of a handful of NGOs, and by some unusually bold domestic media coverage, a variety of official bodies and high-ranking authorities undertook fact-finding missions to the region in mid-1998. Among the first was Armed Forces Commander General Wiranto who visited the province in early August.[72] After a series of meetings with military officials, NGOs, and community groups, Wiranto stunned the country with a public apology for human rights violations committed by ABRI over the previous nine years. He also announced that Aceh's status as a Military Operations Area would be lifted by the end of the month.[73] Wiranto's announcements appeared to be part of an effort to discredit his arch-rival, Prabowo Subianto, and to distance ABRI as an institution from any wrong-doing. Nevertheless, his remarks opened the door to further investigations of military responsibility and to more discussion in the media.

Soon, high-ranking government authorities were rushing to express their concern and their outrage over past violations. Once this had begun, it was impossible to stop the criticism from spreading. Acehnese, and other Indonesians, began to call openly *not* for Aceh's independence, and certainly not for an Islamic state, but for thorough investigations into military abuses committed over the previous ten years, for the punishment of the soldiers and officers responsible, and for compensation of the victims. While this shift did not result in the immediate punishment of those responsible for the abuses, it did substantially alter the political balance on the issue. The armed forces were clearly on the defensive for the first time, and the prospects for a proper investigation, while not great, were arguably better than they ever had been.

5. CONTEXT AND CHANGE

These recent developments highlight the importance of political and historical context in shaping both government policy in Aceh and the patterns of violence that

---

[71] *Far Eastern Economic Review*, November 19, 1998.

[72] Wiranto's visit came shortly after a fact-finding team from the national parliament (DPR) announced that serious human rights violations had indeed occurred in Aceh. See reports in *Waspada*, July 29, 1998; and *Jakarta Post*, August 6, 1998.

[73] See reports in *Kompas*, August 11 and 26, 1998; and *Jakarta Post*, August 7 and 8, 1998.

stem from it. Three factors appear to have been especially important in shaping New Order strategy in Aceh after 1989: a national and international political context conducive to terrorist methods; tensions within the military itself that encouraged a full-scale intervention by the center; and backgrounds in counter-insurgency and intelligence shared by the key military figures responsible for the operation. This section examines each of these factors in turn, considering first how they influenced the course of events after 1989, and then how recent changes might influence the likelihood of future political violence in Aceh.

Models and Opportunities

The authorities who plotted the New Order's response to the Aceh Merdeka rebellions were influenced by contemporaneous events, both within Indonesia and abroad, and by memories of recent successes and failures. The models of action available to them, that is, were framed and limited by the historical circumstances and the timing of the events in question.

We have noted, for example, how Aceh Merdeka's emulation of the resistance in East Timor in the late 1970s must have caused considerable alarm among the authorities in Jakarta, moving them to respond more forcefully than they might otherwise have done. At the same time, the fact that the regime was then in the midst of a major military campaign in East Timor meant that it could not afford to launch a full-scale counter-insurgency operation in Aceh as well. Moreover, many of the most brutal tactics and methods that would later be employed in Aceh had not yet been fully developed or perfected when Aceh Merdeka launched its first rebellion in the late 1970s. By the time of the second uprising in 1989, the regime's counter-insurgency repertoire had expanded considerably. Techniques like the "mysterious killings" and the "fence of legs" had by then been tried and proven in the field and were available for "export" to Aceh and other trouble spots. The availability of these techniques meant that a type of systematic terror was possible in the early 1990s that would have been difficult to institute in the late 1970s.

The timing of the government response to the second Aceh Merdeka uprising was significant in other ways as well. It should be recalled that the crackdown in Aceh began more than a year before the November 1991 massacre at Santa Cruz, East Timor, and the unprecedented criticism at home and abroad that stemmed from it. That criticism would eventually send shock waves through the regime and the Armed Forces, but in the years and months before the Santa Cruz massacre the regime's leading figures displayed a remarkable confidence about the success of their terrorist methods. It may be recalled that 1989 was the year East Timor was "opened up" to tourists and journalists for the first time in fifteen years. It was also the year President Suharto published the autobiography in which he took credit for, and gloated over, the success of the Petrus killings of the mid-1980s.

This was a time, too, when international criticism of the New Order's human rights record had reached a low ebb. Stimulated by a desire to capitalize on the then burgeoning economies of the region, Western governments were reluctant to voice concern about, or to take concrete measures in opposition to, the violations committed by Indonesian government forces. In these years, Western governments routinely argued that the human rights situation in East Timor was improving, and that it was pointless and irresponsible to question the territory's political status. There was even less concern about human rights violations occurring in Indonesia itself. When Indonesian troops killed scores of Muslim villagers in the province of Lampung in February 1989, for example, there was scarcely a murmur of protest from the international community.

In short, the counter-insurgency campaign in Aceh was set in motion at a time when the New Order leaders had reason to believe that the brutal methods used in East Timor, Irian Jaya, Java, Lampung, and other "trouble spots" had worked. Under the circumstances, they undoubtedly felt confident that the same methods could be used to good effect, and without serious political cost, in Aceh as well. That confidence was bolstered by their judgment that the international community would exhibit little sympathy for the victims in Aceh, if they could be successfully portrayed as dangerous Muslim fanatics.

That assessment was not far wrong. Long after the Santa Cruz massacre had forced recognition of the seriousness of the problem in East Timor, and at least some sort of response from the New Order, the widespread violations of human rights in Aceh received scarcely a mention either abroad or within Indonesia. The silence within Indonesia was not surprising, because legitimate fears of military retribution inhibited both the gathering of accurate information and its public dissemination. The inaction of the international community, on the other hand, was inexcusable. Most Western and Asian governments maintained a deliberate silence on the subject even though they had credible information about what was happening, both from their own embassy officials, and from human rights organizations such as Amnesty International and Human Rights Watch. Among Asian governments, Prime Minister Mahathir's Malaysia was conspicuous for its hypocrisy. While berating Western governments for their failure to come to the aid of Muslims in Bosnia, Malaysian authorities returned dozens of Acehnese asylum-seekers to Indonesia against their will, in violation of the internationally recognized principle of non-refoulement.[74] The decision to maintain that unseemly silence, to conduct business as usual with the New Order, and to cooperate actively in the persecution of Acehnese, unquestionably helped to ensure that military operations, and human rights abuses, would continue in Aceh for nearly a decade.

By contrast, changes in the wider political context after May 1998 provide some grounds for optimism about Aceh's future. Notwithstanding the extreme reluctance of the Habibie government to take action, in late 1998 the domestic political climate was arguably more conducive to the investigation of human rights violations, and the punishment of those responsible, than at any time in the preceding three decades. The same was true of the international political climate, which appeared not only to support a shift toward democratization in Indonesia but also the punishment under international law of those responsible for egregious violations of human rights.[75] The continuing economic crisis, moreover, left the Habibie regime vulnerable to, and dependent on, the demands of foreign creditors, and there was no indication in late 1998 that the latter favored a return to the corrupt authoritarian system which many blamed for the crisis. In any case, the avalanche of evidence of past wrong-doing by the military had left international actors with little choice but to support the process

---

[74] On the Acehnese asylum-seekers in Malaysia, see Amnesty International, *Shock Therapy*, pp. 53-56.

[75] Among the most notable developments in this regard in 1998 were the agreement to establish an international criminal court, and the initiation by a Spanish magistrate of legal proceedings against General Pinochet of Chile for crimes against humanity.

of reform and democratization. Indeed, the United States and other governments appeared to have given notice that any overt move toward the reassertion of military control of political life would not be welcome.

Intra-military Tensions

The logic of the national and international context notwithstanding, it would be a mistake to imagine that the decision to launch a counter-insurgency campaign in Aceh in mid-1990 was reached through consensus among the military and political leadership.[76] In fact, there is reason to believe that both the military campaign in Aceh, and the sudden growth of Aceh Merdeka in 1989, were stimulated by a conflict between the central military command and regional military and police authorities.

Looking first at the government side, we find several pieces of evidence that the military campaign coincided with an effort to restore central authority over the regional command structure. First, as noted earlier, the operation launched in mid-1990 involved the deployment, on the direct orders of President Suharto, of some six thousand centrally commanded troops from *outside* the military operations area. This move suggested that the central command could not, or preferred not to, entrust the task of dealing with the rebels to the territorial command, despite its more than ample troop strength.[77]

Second, the full-scale counter-insurgency campaign began within a few days of the replacement of the old Regional Military Commander, Major-General Joko Pramono. When isolated rebel attacks and bombings began in early 1989, Joko Pramono had responded in a *relatively* low-keyed fashion. Rather than initiating armed intervention, he had first sought the assistance of Muslim community leaders to nip the incipient movement in the bud.[78] By mid-1990, however, Joko Pramono had been replaced by R. Pramono, and the concerted campaign of political violence began in earnest.

Third, this centrally directed military operation began shortly after the replacement of the old commanders of Military Resorts 011 and 012, both located in Aceh, by new men with close links to the center. After their removal, the military careers of these Military Resort commanders essentially ground to a halt. The dismissed Commander of Military Resort 011, Colonel H.M. Ali Hanafiah, for example, became the Bupati of Labuhan Batu, North Sumatra, while the old Commander of Military Resort 012, Colonel Soehardjono, simply disappeared from the screen.

---

[76] We know that conflicts among the Indonesian military elite have historically been important in stimulating serious political violence. In an analysis of the Indonesian military elite published in early 1992, for example, the Editors of *Indonesia* argued that the Santa Cruz massacre in East Timor may have been triggered by a festering conflict between elements of a local military-civilian "mafia" and representatives of the central military command installed to bring it under control. The Editors, "Current Data on the Indonesian Military Elite: July 1, 1989-January 1, 1992," *Indonesia* 53 (April 1992).

[77] Recent comments by Aceh's then Governor, Ibrahim Hasan, lend support to this interpretation. In an interview in August 1998, Hasan explained that his decision to ask Jakarta to deploy extra troops was taken after Regional Military Commander Joko Pramono and the two Military Resort commanders in Aceh told him, somewhat implausibly, that they did not have sufficient troops to deal with the rebels. *Republika*, August 12, 1998.

[78] Kell, *The Roots of Acehnese Rebellion*.

These changes came close on the heels of other moves by the center aimed at "cleaning up" the regional military apparatus. In early 1989 at least forty-seven Aceh-based military officers were dismissed on disciplinary grounds. The dismissals took place in the context of a centrally coordinated anti-narcotics campaign, called Operasi Nila (Operation Indigo), which had resulted in the capture of thousands of tons of marijuana and the exposure of key figures in the syndicate, including unnamed military and police officials. The timing of the disciplinary measures against the Aceh-based officers strongly suggested that those dismissed had been involved in the drug business. This fact might account for the government's somewhat curious initial insistence that the trouble in Aceh in these years was the work of criminal rather than political elements, and that central military operations there were part of an anti-crime campaign.[79]

The central government crackdown on the drug racket in Aceh in 1989 may also help to explain the sudden increase in the armed strength of Aceh Merdeka and its renewed capacity and propensity for violence at this time. According to political observers in Aceh, in 1989 dozens of disgruntled ex-military and police—some of whom had been dismissed and others who had deserted—joined forces with Aceh Merdeka and began to launch coordinated assaults on military personnel and installations.[80] The link between ABRI and Aceh Merdeka is confirmed by the fact that, of the fifty or so alleged Aceh Merdeka members or supporters tried in Indonesian courts by the end of 1992, no fewer than ten were ex-ABRI.[81] It is perhaps noteworthy in this regard that marginalized military and police officers also formed an important fighting core of the Darul Islam rebellion in the 1950s, and of the OPM in Irian Jaya in the 1960s.[82] Without the experience of such men on the side of the

---

[79] Speaking before the United Nations Commission on Human Rights in August 1991, the government said, for example: "What occurred in Aceh was that armed criminals spread terror and intimidation which caused social unrest . . . These occurred after the local authorities took stringent measures to eradicate the cannabis cultivation. Against these [sic] background the Indonesian authorities was [sic] forced to take action to restore peace and public order." Republic of Indonesia Right of Reply under Item 10, United Nations Commission on Human Rights, February 1991.

[80] *Reuter*, July 22, 1990.

[81] Amnesty International, *Shock Therapy*. One of the ex-ABRI men who bolstered Aceh Merdeka as a fighting force was the field commander, Robert Suryadarma, a former Army sergeant from Battalion 111 based in East Aceh who had reportedly been dismissed for his involvement in the drug trade. Acehnese refugees in Malaysia have reported interesting details about Robert, who went into hiding in Kuala Lumpur shortly after the government launched its full-scale military campaign in mid-1990. They have claimed, for example, that he was a follower of a certain Rizal Gading, a rival of Hasan di Tiro within Aceh Merdeka. Rizal Gading, in turn, is alleged to have had close ties to the former Indonesian intelligence boss, General Murdani. Given the serious tensions between Murdani and the Palace that developed in the late 1980s, it is not beyond the realm of possibility that Murdani lent his support to certain disgruntled elements in the military at this time. Nor is it entirely implausible that the center's moves to clean up the regional command in 1989 were aimed, in part, at weakening the grip of men with links to Murdani.

[82] Referring to the Darul Islam rebels, the former Governor of North Sumatra, Mr. Amin, writes: "It was very well understood at the time that the rebellion would mean serious bloodshed, considering that those leading the resistance were men with military experience dating from the time of the struggle for independence." Amin, "Sejenak Meninjau Aceh, Serambi Mekkah," pp. 86-87.

rebels, it may be argued, the Darul Islam, the OPM, and Aceh Merdeka rebellions might not have amounted to very much militarily.

If the military action initiated in mid-1990 can be understood, in part, as a campaign by the center and its allies in Aceh to oust a mafia with links to the military, developments after about 1993 may plausibly be seen as an effort by the center—and by the Special Forces in particular—to maintain the central military control that had by then been established. This is certainly the view of many informed observers in Aceh,[83] who have noted that, since 1993, all demands for the ending of military operations have been thwarted by acts of violence, some of them apparently instigated by the military itself.

Such acts have continued in recent times. Shortly after General Wiranto announced that Aceh's status as a Military Operations Area would be abolished in August 1998, a number of highly provocative incidents occurred in rapid succession, including an Aceh Merdeka flag-raising at a school just days after the announcement, and a wild stone-throwing attack (in which nobody was injured) on a unit of departing Special Forces troops. The latter incident was later reported to have been staged by a Special Forces-trained vigilante youth organization, Pemuda Keamanan Desa, and there was a general perception that at least some of the other incidents, too, had been orchestrated to justify a reversal of the announced plan to end the military operation. Similar allegations were made in connection with the violence that erupted in late 1998, though it is too early to say whether these allegations were true. Yet, whatever its root causes, the recent violence did serve to justify the redeployment of combat troops in the province, leading many Acehnese to the pessimistic conclusion that a second counter-insurgency campaign was set to begin.

On the other hand, certain developments after the demise of President Suharto in May 1998 made possible a cautious optimism about Aceh's future. While there was every likelihood that some officers would continue to seek a return to Aceh's status as a Military Operations Area, the dramatic nationwide decline in respect for and trust in the military, and the depth of public outrage over past human rights abuses, seemed likely to encourage the central command to resist that temptation. While such an act of restraint could not be expected to resolve immediately all outstanding problems, it would help to limit the chances for a dramatic re-escalation of violence.

Profiles in Terror

While the decision to launch a counter-insurgency campaign in Aceh in mid-1990 may be attributable to military doctrine, and to tensions within the Indonesian military as an institution, the actual character of the operation must be understood in part as the responsibility of specific individuals, and more precisely the key military figures posted there at the time. A preliminary analysis of the training and experience of those men provides insight into the reasons for the peculiar savagery of the operations in the period 1989 to 1993. Simply stated, the officers responsible for operations in Aceh during these years were overwhelmingly men who had been trained in, or had first-hand experience with, the use of such tactics.

Mention has already been made of Colonel Prabowo Subianto, Suharto's notorious son-in-law and protégé, whose arrival in Aceh in mid-1990 as an Army

---

[83] The information in this paragraph is based on a confidential personal communication from an Acehnese human rights lawyer, Banda Aceh, August 28, 1998.

Strategic Reserve unit commander coincided with the onset of the worst violence. Though, as we have seen, he was responsible for ordering acts of brutality in Aceh, Prabowo's significance in the story extends beyond his personal actions. His dramatic rise through the military hierarchy starting in the late 1980s arguably signaled President Suharto's endorsement of and enthusiasm for officers who had demonstrated their personal loyalty and who had a background in counter-insurgency and intelligence. Accordingly, when in 1989-1990 the Palace decided that there was a job to be done in Aceh, it appears to have turned to men of this ilk.

Virtually all of the commanders of Regional Military Command (Kodam) 1, within which Aceh lay, had experience in one of the elite combat or counter-insurgency units—RPKAD (Army Paratroop Regiment), Special Forces, and Army Strategic Reserve—or a background in military intelligence, or both. Most also had close links with the Palace. A similar tendency is evident for the Chiefs of Staff of Kodam 1, and for the Commanders of the two Military *Resorts* (Korem) in the immediate area of military operations.[84]

Of the two Korem in question, Korem 011/Lilawangsa, with its headquarters in Lhokseumawe, was arguably the more important because the Commander there doubled as Commander of the Military Operations Command, and therefore had direct responsibility for all combat and intelligence operations in Aceh. In the critical period from August 1989 to January 1991, the Commander of Korem 011 was Colonel Sofyan Effendi, who had previously served with the RPKAD and as Deputy Commander of the Special Forces. After Effendi, most Korem 011 Commanders were also men with experience in intelligence or counter-insurgency. Colonel Sridono, who held the position from late 1992 to early 1994 had previously served as Assistant for Intelligence in Kodam 1, while his successor, Colonel Djoko Subroto, had served in Manatuto, East Timor, from 1987 to 1988, and as the commander of the Core Infantry Regiment of Kodam 1 from 1993 to 1994.[85] Effendi's immediate successor in the post of Commander of Korem 011, Colonel Syarwan Hamid, who held the job from January 1991 to December 1992, was somewhat atypical in the sense that his experience was mainly in socio-political affairs rather than counter-insurgency or intelligence. Nevertheless, his career trajectory both before and after his time in Aceh suggests that he had the trust of both the central military command and the Palace.[86]

Turning to Chiefs of Staff of Kodam 1, in the key years 1989 to 1993, we find again a pattern of domination by officers with intelligence and counter-insurgency backgrounds. The Chief of Staff from March 1989 to January 1991, Brigadier-General R. Soerjadi, had served with the elite paracommando regiment, RPKAD, from 1965 to

[84] The information in the following paragraphs is drawn from various editions of "Current Data on the Indonesian Military Elite," compiled by the editors of *Indonesia*. A listing of the key military figures posted in Aceh is provided in Appendix 1.

[85] The same pattern was evident for commanders of Korem 012/Teuku Umar, with its headquarters in Banda Aceh. From April 1989 to August 1992, the Commander of Korem 012 was Colonel Muhammad Chan whose previous position had been Assistant for Intelligence in Kodam 2 (North Sumatra). His successor, Colonel Rudy Supriyatna, who held the post from August 1992 to February 1995, had previously served as Assistant for Intelligence to the Chief of Staff of Kodam 6 (West Java).

[86] In the years before his appointment as Commander of Korem 011, for example, Hamid had served as Assistant for Territorial Affairs in the important Greater Jakarta Regional Military Command. After his tour of duty in Aceh, he served, among other posts, as Head of the Armed Forces' Information Service (Kapuspen ABRI), Armed Forces Chief of Social and Political Affairs, and Minister of Home Affairs.

1970, during which time it formed the backbone of the savage assault on real and alleged communists. Soerjadi's successor, the former Commander of Korem 011 Brigadier-General Sofyan Effendi, who was Kodam 1 Chief of Staff from January 1991 to September 1992, had a strong counter-insurgency background, as noted above.[87]

A similar pattern is evident among the Regional Military Commanders of Kodam 1. Major-General R. Pramono, who held the post from June 1990 to April 1993—thus during the very worst of the violence in Aceh—had served as Assistant for Intelligence in Kodam 4 (Central Java) in the early 1980s (in the lead-up to the *Petrus* killings) and as Army Strategic Reserve Chief of Staff for the two years before his appointment as Commander of Kodam 1.[88] His successor, Major-General Pranowo, who held the position from April 1993 to September 1994, also had counter-insurgency experience. For two years immediately prior to his time in Aceh, he had been Chief of Staff of Kodam 8, based in Irian Jaya. Pranowo had also served as commander of the Presidential Security Force from 1985 to 1987, a post which would have brought him regularly into contact with the President and his immediate circle.

If the background of the key military officers in Aceh helps to explain the pattern of violence there in the early 1990s, a glimpse at the subsequent careers of these men leaves room for doubt that the immediate future will be much brighter. The most obvious cause for concern is that a number of the officers posted in Aceh during the worst of the violence subsequently moved swiftly up the military and political ladder, and by 1998 had assumed positions of considerable political power. They included Syarwan Hamid, who became Minister of Home Affairs in the Habibie government, and Zacky Anwar Makarim, who became Head of BIA in 1997. Another officer with Aceh experience still in a position of some influence in 1998 was Agum Gumelar, who was then Governor of the National Defence Institute (Lemhannas). All of these men were well placed to resist efforts to investigate military abuses in Aceh. They could, moreover, rely on the support of people in the military and political elite who had reason to fear that inquiries about Aceh might lead to revelations about wrongdoing in other parts of the country.

On the other hand, the career trajectory of a number of other figures responsible for the violence in Aceh provides reason for greater optimism. By late 1998, many of those in charge during the worst of the violence—Suharto, Prabowo Subianto, R. Pramono, R. Soerjadi, and Sofyan Effendi—had either been ousted or no longer held positions of real political or military power. This development arguably improved the prospects for a proper vetting of military responsibility in Aceh. Moreover, the fate of Prabowo and many of his closest allies, and the precipitous decline in the prestige of the Special Forces in 1998, may help to ensure that terrorist methods will

---

[87] While Effendi's two immediate successors as Chief of Staff did not have counter-insurgency backgrounds, both were his classmates at the Military Academy (AMN), having graduated together as members of Class 6 in 1965. No automatic inference can be drawn from this fact, but these collegial ties may well have encouraged Effendi's successors to maintain and pursue the approach he had helped to set in motion. In any case, the tradition of filling the Chief of Staff post with a counter-insurgency man was resumed in 1994, with the appointment of Brigadier-General Agum Gumelar, who had served with the Special Forces for some twenty-five years, two of them (1993-1994) as Commander.

[88] *Angkatan Bersenjata*, August 9, 1988.

no longer be regarded as career-enhancing options, a change that could lead to a general decline in state violence in the coming years.

6. CONCLUSIONS

I began by asking why Aceh was so unsettled, so *rawan*, under the New Order, and whether it is destined to remain that way in the post-Suharto era. The broad answer to the first question is that the violent conflict in Aceh after 1989 was not the inevitable consequence of primordial Acehnese sentiments, nor a manifestation of a venerable Acehnese tradition of resistance to outside authority or of Islamic rectitude. Instead, I have argued that it was the unintended, but largely inevitable, consequence of certain characteristic policies and practices of the New Order state itself. The argument is not that the culture and traditions of the people of Aceh were of no importance in stimulating demands for independence there, or in generating the conflict that followed. Rather, I have tried to show how the policies and practices of the New Order regime, and the unique historical circumstances which shaped them, gave these incipient demands a much wider credibility than they might otherwise have had, and also ensured a rapid escalation from resolvable political disagreement to widespread violence and political conflict.

Both the Aceh Merdeka rebellions and the violence that followed appeared to be integrally linked to the New Order's management of the exploitation of Aceh's natural resources and the distribution of economic benefits, especially as these policies developed after the discovery of oil and LNG in the 1970s. Driven by a highly centralized system of decision-making, by its close association with foreign capital, and by the opportunities for public and private revenue generation that these arrangements provided, the New Order's own economic policy in Aceh kindled support for Aceh Merdeka among a broad cross-section of the population in the late 1970s and 1980s. The regime's heightened efforts to ensure security in the area from the mid-1970s, largely through repressive means, paradoxically produced the opposite effect, generating still greater resentment and instability, and stimulating Aceh Merdeka's resurgence in 1989. Although Aceh Merdeka appeared to have been defeated militarily by the mid-1990s, the underlying economic and social grievances that made it popular had not been resolved by 1998. This was immediately evident when, with the fall of Suharto, Acehnese of diverse social backgrounds began again to express their views openly again.

As fundamental and persistent as these grievances were in generating support for Aceh Merdeka, they do not appear to account for the unprecedented levels of violence that followed the movement's re-emergence in 1989 and persisted for nearly a decade thereafter. Aceh Merdeka was partly responsible for that development in the sense that its explicitly separatist objectives, bellicose language, resort to arms, and sense of timing seemed calculated to provoke a harsh government response. Nevertheless, the escalation and persistence of violence and instability after 1989, I have argued, was primarily the result of the specific doctrines and practices employed by the Indonesian armed forces in their efforts to quash the incipient rebellion—in particular the use of systematic terror and the forced mobilization of civilians as military auxiliaries.

In the short term, terror and "civil-military cooperation" worked rather well. By terrorizing the population, the military ensured that all but the most foolhardy would abandon the rebellion and remain silent about what they had witnessed. And by forcing the population to join in military and intelligence operations against members of their own communities, they divided those communities and effectively weakened the social base of the resistance. At the same time, however, Indonesian military policy and practice in Aceh produced a range of disastrous medium and long-term consequences. First, through the systematic use of terror, it generated levels of insecurity and political violence far greater than anything that ever was, or ever could have been, achieved by Aceh Merdeka itself. Second, by compelling civilians to participate in its intelligence and combat operations, it laid the foundation for bitter conflicts among Acehnese which surfaced in late 1998, and appeared likely to inhibit a return to peace. Third, by designating Aceh as a Military Operations Area for almost a decade, it may have fostered the emergence of a military mafia that could be expected to resist all efforts to change the status quo. Finally, by resorting to the use of provocation and terror against civilian populations, it stimulated a deep-seated anger among an ever-widening circle of Acehnese. As human rights activist Munir noted in August 1998, "The excesses committed during the military operation in Aceh have given birth to a seed of popular hatred toward the armed forces."[89] That hatred, and the new cycle of violence it helped to generate in late 1998, were depressing reminders that the legacy of the military strategy used in Aceh might survive long after its principal architect, Suharto, had left the scene. The failure of the Habibie government to address widespread concern about past military abuses, and its apparent inclination to pursue similar strategies in Aceh, further fueled popular anger and appeared likely to impede the prospects for peace.

The strategy and tactics employed in Aceh after 1990 were not the product of a rigid and unchanging Indonesian military doctrine. Rather they were shaped by the specific historical context within which both the rebellion and the response to it occurred. Three factors were especially important in facilitating the violence: an international and domestic political climate that together encouraged a sense of confidence and impunity among Indonesia's leaders in the use of terrorist methods; the existence of tensions within the Indonesian military, and in particular between the central command and local units deemed insufficiently loyal to the center; and finally, a pattern of domination of key military posts in Aceh by officers with close ties to the Palace and experience in counter-insurgency and intelligence.

To the extent that the methods used by the military in Aceh were shaped by unique historical conditions, it may be argued that changes in those conditions will alter the pattern of violence in the future. In this respect, a number of recent developments offer some grounds for optimism that Aceh, and other "trouble spots," may be spared a future of chronic violence. One potentially positive change, I have argued, is the decline in the power and prestige of the Special Forces, and of other units specializing in counter-insurgency and terror. Another is the dismissal of Prabowo, and the fact that the careers of many of the key figures responsible for military operations in Aceh have gone nowhere. Although they must be set against the Habibie government's strong disinclination to investigate and punish past abuses, these developments may nevertheless serve to weaken the propensity for the use of official violence in Aceh and elsewhere in the future.

Perhaps the greatest reason for optimism, however, lies in the remarkable changes in the domestic and international political climate that have come with the collapse of the New Order. Within a few months of the Suharto regime's demise the

---

[89] *Tajuk*, August 20, 1998.

mysterious killings, the rapes, the mass graves, and a litany of other crimes committed by the armed forces in Aceh over almost a decade became the focus of wide-ranging public scrutiny and debate. Key members of the international community, so long complicit in hiding these and other New Order crimes, appeared ready to support moves toward genuine democratization. Notwithstanding serious doubts about the sincerity of the Habibie government's commitment to reform, these shifts appeared to offer a rare opportunity to pursue investigations into past military wrong-doing, to prosecute the authorities responsible, and thereby to break the cycle of impunity that had for so long encouraged abuses to continue.

An important implication of these recent developments, and of the historical evidence presented in this paper, is that continued conflict in Aceh, and perhaps in other "trouble spots" as well, is by no means inevitable. On the contrary, if I am right in locating the problem of instability and violence in the distinctive policies and practices of the late New Order state, and in the particular historical context within which they were played out, then a change in those policies and in that context could conceivably bring an end to the violence, and perhaps even to demands for independence. The evidence also suggests that national disintegration will not be the automatic result of an end to authoritarian rule in Indonesia. In fact, I think it can be argued that, far from jeopardizing the political future of the country, a shift toward a less authoritarian political system—and one which is less wedded to the use of terror—may provide the best possible guarantee of its continued unity and viability.

APPENDIX 1: KEY MILITARY FIGURES IN ACEH, 1988-1995

Regional Military Commanders – Kodam 1

12 Aug 88 – 9 Jun 90	Maj.-Gen. Joko Pramono
9 Jun 90 – 1 Apr 93	Maj.-Gen. R. Pramono
1 Apr 93 – 1 Sep 94	Maj.-Gen. A. Pranowo
1 Sep 94 – 2 Aug 95	Maj.-Gen. Arie Kumaat

Chiefs of Staff – Kodam I

22 Mar 89 – Jan 91	Brig.-Gen. Soerjadi
Jan 91 – 10 Sep 92	Brig.-Gen. Sofyan Effendi
10 Sep 92 – 8 Jan 94	Brig.-Gen. R. Karyono
8 Jan 94 – 23 Sep 94	Brig.-Gen Makmun Rasyid
23 Sep 94 – 1 Mar 96	Brig.-Gen. Agum Gumelar

Military Resort Commanders – Korem 011/Lilawangsa

? – 12 Aug 89	Col. H.M. Ali Hanafiah
12 Aug 89 – Jan 91	Col. Sofyan Effendi
Jan 91 – Dec 92	Col. Syarwan Hamid
Dec 92 – 19 Apr 94	Col. Sridono
19 Apr 94 – 6 Mar 95	Col. Djoko Subroto

Military Resort Commanders – Korem 012/Teuku Umar

? – 4 April 89	Col. Soehardjono
4 April 89 – 10 Aug 92	Col. Muhammad Chan
20 Aug 92 – 11 Feb 95	Col. Rudy Supriyatna
11 Feb 95 – ?	Col. Ahmad Yourda Adnan

GLOSSARY

ORGANIZATION NAMES

ABRI | Angkatan Bersenjata Republik Indonesia, Armed Forces of the Republic of Indonesia.

Aceh Merdeka | Acheh-Sumatra National Liberation Front.

Balatkom | Bahaya Laten Komunisme: "latent communist danger" doctrine.

Bimmas | Bimbingan Masyarakat: "Guidance of Society" division of the police force.

CNRT | Concelho Nacionale de Resistencia Timorese, National Council of Resistance of the People of East Timor), formed in 1995.

DOM | Daerah Operasi Militer, Military Operations Area: the designation used by the military for any region where armed resistance to the state existed—eg. East Timor, Aceh, and Irian Jaya/Papua. Officially dissolved in 1998.

DPR | Dewan Perwakilan Rakyat, People's Representative Assembly: i.e. the national parliament.

DPRD | Dewan Perwikilan Rakyat Daerah: the provincial congress.

Fretilin | Frente Revolucionaria Timor Leste Independente, Revolutionary Front for an Independent East Timor.

Falintil | Forças Armadas de Libertação Nacional de Timor Leste, The National Liberation Armed Forces of East Timor: Fretilin's armed wing.

G30S | The September 30th movement: so-called "communist" coup cited by Suharto as his reason for intervening and, hence, seizing power, beginning the New Order.

Gada Paksi   Garda Muda Penegak Integrasi, Young Guards Upholding Integration: Prabowo-formed paramilitary organization in East Timor.

Golkar   Golongan Karya (Functional Groups): chief political party during the New Order, Suharto's political machine for winning elections.

GPK   Gerakan Pengacau Keamanan or "Security Disruptor Movements": New Order name for resistance movements in, for example, East Timor, Aceh, and Irian Jaya.

ICMI   Association of Indonesian Muslim Intellectuals: Islamic organization formed by Suharto in order to expand his political power base; initially headed by B. J. Habibie.

IPKI   Ikatan Pendukung Kemerdekaan Indonesia, League of the Supporters of Indonesian Independence.

KNPI   The Indonesian National Youth Committee.

Kodam   Komando Daerah Militer, Regional Military Command.

Kolakops   Komando Pelaksana Operasi, East Timor Operations Implementation Command.

Komnas HAM   Indonesian Human Rights Commission.

Koopskam   Komando Operasi Keamanan, Security Operations Command.

Kopassus   Komando Pasukan Khusus, Special Forces Command.

Kopkamtib   Komando Pemulihan Keamanan dan Ketertiban, Operational Command for the Restoration of Order and Security: the special security command initiated by Suharto in 1965. With almost unlimited powers, it was used in the 1960s and 1970s to eliminate "communists," and later to repress all kinds of groups regarded as enemies by the New Order state. Formally abolished in September 1988 and replaced by Bakorstanas (Badan Koordinasi Bantuan Pemantapan Stabilitas Nasional, Body for Assisting in Preserving National Unity).

Korem   Komando Resort Militer, Sub-Regional Military Command.

Kostrad   Komando Strategis Angkatan Darat, Army Strategic Reserve Command.

Lemhannas   Lembaga Pertahanan Nasional, National Defense Institute.

MPR	Majelis Permusyawaratan Rakyat, People's Consultative Assembly: the highest organ of the state.
NU	Nahdatul Ulama: the country's largest "orthodox" Islamic organization.
OPM	Organisasi Papua Merdeka, Free Papua Organization.
PDI	Partai Demokrasi Indonesia, The Indonesian Democratic Party.
PDI-P	Partai Demokrasi Indonesia-Perjuangan, The Indonesian Democratic Party of Struggle.
PDR	Partai Rakyat Demokratik, People's Democratic Party.
Pemuda Pancasila (PP)	Pancasila Youth. Semi-official, semi-criminal organization used by Suharto for much of his regime's "dirty tricks."
Petrus	Pembunuhan Misterius, "Mysterious Killings" (1982-1983).
PKI	Partai Komunis Indonesia, Indonesian Communist Party.
PNI	Partai Nasional Indonesia, Indonesian National Party.
PPP	Partai Persatuan Pembangunan, the Unity Development Party.
Siskamling	Sistem keamanan lingkungan, environment security system. Term coined by the head of the Indonesian police in the early 1980s to describe a new way of organizing the local security apparatus so as to give police responsibility for coordinating and supervising neighborhood security.
Trikora	Tri Komando Rakyat: when Sukarno called for the crushing of Dutch colonialism in West Irian and prepared for popular mobilization of volunteers to be sent to Irian. December 19, 1961.

TERMS

dwifungsi	official doctrine that the Indonesian military was to have both a military and sociopolitical role in Indonesian society.
gali-gali	gabungan anak-anak liar. Gangs of wild kids, often involved in criminal behavior.
globalisasi	globalization
ilmu	magical powers

jahat	"wicked" or "evil"
jawara	Also *jago, jegger,* and *bromocorah.* Traditional charismatic toughs, in recent times often professional criminals.
kertubakaan	openness—meaning the periodic loosening of the New Order's tight control of the mass media.
kewaspadaan	vigilance
mahasiswa	university students
mambi	fearsome "warriors" for whom Biak was once renowned
massa	"the masses"
masyarakat madani	civil society
operasi	operation
orang pintar	a person with special occult powers
Pancasila	Five Principles: invented by Sukarno in 1945, the official doctrine of the Indonesian State. The principles are belief in God, nationalism, internationalism or humanitarianism, democracy, and social justice.
pembangunan	development
pemuda	youth
perjuangan	heroic struggle
preman	"street hoodlums"
pribumi	"native," "not Chinese"
rakyat	"the people"
rawan	troubled
reformasi	reform: rallying point for the opposition to the residues of the New Order after Suharto's resignation as president.
ronda	neighborhood watches, surveillance
satpam	Satuan Pengamanan: security unit, used to refer to private security guards

uleëbalang	Acehnese aristocrat
ulama	Muslim teacher or scholar
Negara Islam Indonesia	Indonesian Islamic State: goal of various "extremist" Islamic groups from the late 1940s on. Found support especially in West Java, Aceh, and South Sulawesi.
"LNG Boom"	Rapid transformation of Acehnese economy due to the discovery and exploitation of large deposit of liquid natural gas (LNG) and oil in the vicinity of Lhokseumawe and Lhoksukon on Aceh's northeast coast.

SOUTHEAST ASIA PROGRAM PUBLICATIONS
Cornell University

Studies on Southeast Asia

Number 32   *Fear and Sanctuary: Burmese Refugees in Thailand*, Hazel J. Lang. 2002. 204 pp. ISBN 0-87727-731-1.

Number 31   *Modern Dreams: An Inquiry into Power, Cultural Production, and the Cityscape in Contemporary Urban Penang, Malaysia*, Beng-Lan Goh. 2002. 225 pp. ISBN 0-87727-730-3.

Number 30   *Violence and the State in Suharto's Indonesia*, ed. Benedict R. O'G. Anderson. 2001. Second printing, 2002. 247 pp. ISBN 0-87727-729-X.

Number 29   *Studies in Southeast Asian Art: Essays in Honor of Stanley J. O'Connor*, ed. Nora A. Taylor. 2000. 243 pp. Illustrations. ISBN 0-87727-728-1.

Number 28   *The Hadrami Awakening: Community and Identity in the Netherlands East Indies, 1900-1942*, Natalie Mobini-Kesheh. 1999. 174 pp. ISBN 0-87727-727-3.

Number 27   *Tales from Djakarta: Caricatures of Circumstances and their Human Beings*, Pramoedya Ananta Toer. 1999. 145 pp. ISBN 0-87727-726-5.

Number 26   *History, Culture, and Region in Southeast Asian Perspectives*, rev. ed., O. W. Wolters. 1999. 275 pp. ISBN 0-87727-725-7.

Number 25   *Figures of Criminality in Indonesia, the Philippines, and Colonial Vietnam*, ed. Vicente L. Rafael. 1999. 259 pp. ISBN 0-87727-724-9.

Number 24   *Paths to Conflagration: Fifty Years of Diplomacy and Warfare in Laos, Thailand, and Vietnam, 1778-1828*, Mayoury Ngaosyvathn and Pheuiphanh Ngaosyvathn. 1998. 268 pp. ISBN 0-87727-723-0.

Number 23   *Nguyễn Cochinchina: Southern Vietnam in the Seventeenth and Eighteenth Centuries*, Li Tana. 1998. Second printing, 2002. 194 pp. ISBN 0-87727-722-2.

Number 22   *Young Heroes: The Indonesian Family in Politics*, Saya S. Shiraishi. 1997. 183 pp. ISBN 0-87727-721-4.

Number 21   *Interpreting Development: Capitalism, Democracy, and the Middle Class in Thailand*, John Girling. 1996. 95 pp. ISBN 0-87727-720-6.

Number 20   *Making Indonesia*, ed. Daniel S. Lev, Ruth McVey. 1996. 201 pp. ISBN 0-87727-719-2.

Number 19   *Essays into Vietnamese Pasts*, ed. K. W. Taylor, John K. Whitmore. 1995. 288 pp. ISBN 0-87727-718-4.

Number 18   *In the Land of Lady White Blood: Southern Thailand and the Meaning of History*, Lorraine M. Gesick. 1995. 106 pp. ISBN 0-87727-717-6.

Number 17   *The Vernacular Press and the Emergence of Modern Indonesian Consciousness*, Ahmat Adam. 1995. 220 pp. ISBN 0-87727-716-8.

Number 16   *The Nan Chronicle*, trans., ed. David K. Wyatt. 1994. 158 pp. ISBN 0-87727-715-X.

Number 15   *Selective Judicial Competence: The Cirebon-Priangan Legal Administration, 1680–1792*, Mason C. Hoadley. 1994. 185 pp. ISBN 0-87727-714-1.

Number 14   *Sjahrir: Politics and Exile in Indonesia*, Rudolf Mrázek. 1994. 536 pp. ISBN 0-87727-713-3.

Number 13	*Fair Land Sarawak: Some Recollections of an Expatriate Officer*, Alastair Morrison. 1993. 196 pp. ISBN 0-87727-712-5.
Number 12	*Fields from the Sea: Chinese Junk Trade with Siam during the Late Eighteenth and Early Nineteenth Centuries*, Jennifer Cushman. 1993. 206 pp. ISBN 0-87727-711-7.
Number 11	*Money, Markets, and Trade in Early Southeast Asia: The Development of Indigenous Monetary Systems to AD 1400*, Robert S. Wicks. 1992. 2nd printing 1996. 354 pp., 78 tables, illus., maps. ISBN 0-87727-710-9.
Number 10	*Tai Ahoms and the Stars: Three Ritual Texts to Ward Off Danger*, trans., ed. B. J. Terwiel, Ranoo Wichasin. 1992. 170 pp. ISBN 0-87727-709-5.
Number 9	*Southeast Asian Capitalists*, ed. Ruth McVey. 1992. 2nd printing 1993. 220 pp. ISBN 0-87727-708-7.
Number 8	*The Politics of Colonial Exploitation: Java, the Dutch, and the Cultivation System*, Cornelis Fasseur, ed. R. E. Elson, trans. R. E. Elson, Ary Kraal. 1992. 2nd printing 1994. 266 pp. ISBN 0-87727-707-9.
Number 7	*A Malay Frontier: Unity and Duality in a Sumatran Kingdom*, Jane Drakard. 1990. 215 pp. ISBN 0-87727-706-0.
Number 6	*Trends in Khmer Art*, Jean Boisselier, ed. Natasha Eilenberg, trans. Natasha Eilenberg, Melvin Elliott. 1989. 124 pp., 24 plates. ISBN 0-87727-705-2.
Number 5	*Southeast Asian Ephemeris: Solar and Planetary Positions, A.D. 638–2000*, J. C. Eade. 1989. 175 pp. ISBN 0-87727-704-4.
Number 3	*Thai Radical Discourse: The Real Face of Thai Feudalism Today*, Craig J. Reynolds. 1987. 2nd printing 1994. 186 pp. ISBN 0-87727-702-8.
Number 1	*The Symbolism of the Stupa*, Adrian Snodgrass. 1985. Revised with index, 1988. 3rd printing 1998. 469 pp. ISBN 0-87727-700-1.

SEAP Series

Number 19	*Gender, Household, State: Đổi Mới in Việt Nam*, ed. Jayne Werner and Danièle Bélanger. 2002. 151 pp. ISBN 0-87727-137-2.
Number 18	*Culture and Power in Traditional Siamese Government*, Neil A. Englehart. 2001. 130 pp. ISBN 0-87727-135-6.
Number 17	*Gangsters, Democracy, and the State*, ed. Carl A. Trocki. 1998. Second printing, 2002. 94 pp. ISBN 0-87727-134-8.
Number 16	*Cutting across the Lands: An Annotated Bibliography on Natural Resource Management and Community Development in Indonesia, the Philippines, and Malaysia*, ed. Eveline Ferretti. 1997. 329 pp. ISBN 0-87727-133-X.
Number 15	*The Revolution Falters: The Left in Philippine Politics after 1986*, ed. Patricio N. Abinales. 1996. Second printing, 2002. 182 pp. ISBN 0-87727-132-1.
Number 14	*Being Kammu: My Village, My Life*, Damrong Tayanin. 1994. 138 pp., 22 tables, illus., maps. ISBN 0-87727-130-5.
Number 13	*The American War in Vietnam*, ed. Jayne Werner, David Hunt. 1993. 132 pp. ISBN 0-87727-131-3.
Number 12	*The Political Legacy of Aung San*, ed. Josef Silverstein. Revised edition 1993. 169 pp. ISBN 0-87727-128-3.

Number 10   *Studies on Vietnamese Language and Literature: A Preliminary Bibliography*, Nguyen Dinh Tham. 1992. 227 pp. ISBN 0-87727-127-5.

Number 9   *A Secret Past*, Dokmaisot, trans. Ted Strehlow. 1992. 2nd printing 1997. 72 pp. ISBN 0-87727-126-7.

Number 8   *From PKI to the Comintern, 1924–1941: The Apprenticeship of the Malayan Communist Party*, Cheah Boon Kheng. 1992. 147 pp. ISBN 0-87727-125-9.

Number 7   *Intellectual Property and US Relations with Indonesia, Malaysia, Singapore, and Thailand*, Elisabeth Uphoff. 1991. 67 pp. ISBN 0-87727-124-0.

Number 6   *The Rise and Fall of the Communist Party of Burma (CPB)*, Bertil Lintner. 1990. 124 pp. 26 illus., 14 maps. ISBN 0-87727-123-2.

Number 5   *Japanese Relations with Vietnam: 1951–1987*, Masaya Shiraishi. 1990. 174 pp. ISBN 0-87727-122-4.

Number 3   *Postwar Vietnam: Dilemmas in Socialist Development*, ed. Christine White, David Marr. 1988. 2nd printing 1993. 260 pp. ISBN 0-87727-120-8.

Number 2   *The Dobama Movement in Burma (1930–1938)*, Khin Yi. 1988. 160 pp. ISBN 0-87727-118-6.

Translation Series

Volume 4   *Approaching Suharto's Indonesia from the Margins*, ed. Takashi Shiraishi. 1994. 153 pp. ISBN 0-87727-403-7.

Volume 3   *The Japanese in Colonial Southeast Asia*, ed. Saya Shiraishi, Takashi Shiraishi. 1993. 172 pp. ISBN 0-87727-402-9.

Volume 2   *Indochina in the 1940s and 1950s*, ed. Takashi Shiraishi, Motoo Furuta. 1992. 196 pp. ISBN 0-87727-401-0.

Volume 1   *Reading Southeast Asia*, ed. Takashi Shiraishi. 1990. 188 pp. ISBN 0-87727-400-2.

CORNELL MODERN INDONESIA PROJECT PUBLICATIONS

Cornell University

Number 75   *A Tour of Duty: Changing Patterns of Military Politics in Indonesia in the 1990s*. Douglas Kammen and Siddharth Chandra. 1999. 99 pp. ISBN 0-87763-049-6.

Number 74   *The Roots of Acehnese Rebellion 1989–1992*, Tim Kell. 1995. 103 pp. ISBN 0-87763-040-2.

Number 73   *"White Book" on the 1992 General Election in Indonesia*, trans. Dwight King. 1994. 72 pp. ISBN 0-87763-039-9.

Number 72   *Popular Indonesian Literature of the Qur'an*, Howard M. Federspiel. 1994. 170 pp. ISBN 0-87763-038-0.

Number 71   *A Javanese Memoir of Sumatra, 1945–1946: Love and Hatred in the Liberation War*, Takao Fusayama. 1993. 150 pp. ISBN 0-87763-037-2.

Number 70   *East Kalimantan: The Decline of a Commercial Aristocracy*, Burhan Magenda. 1991. 120 pp. ISBN 0-87763-036-4.

Number 69   *The Road to Madiun: The Indonesian Communist Uprising of 1948*, Elizabeth Ann Swift. 1989. 120 pp. ISBN 0-87763-035-6.

Number 68   *Intellectuals and Nationalism in Indonesia: A Study of the Following Recruited by Sutan Sjahrir in Occupation Jakarta*, J. D. Legge. 1988. 159 pp. ISBN 0-87763-034-8.

Number 67   *Indonesia Free: A Biography of Mohammad Hatta*, Mavis Rose. 1987. 252 pp. ISBN 0-87763-033-X.

Number 66   *Prisoners at Kota Cane*, Leon Salim, trans. Audrey Kahin. 1986. 112 pp. ISBN 0-87763-032-1.

Number 65   *The Kenpeitai in Java and Sumatra*, trans. Barbara G. Shimer, Guy Hobbs, intro. Theodore Friend. 1986. 80 pp. ISBN 0-87763-031-3.

Number 64   *Suharto and His Generals: Indonesia's Military Politics, 1975–1983*, David Jenkins. 1984. 4th printing 1997. 300 pp. ISBN 0-87763-030-5.

Number 62   *Interpreting Indonesian Politics: Thirteen Contributions to the Debate, 1964–1981*, ed. Benedict Anderson, Audrey Kahin, intro. Daniel S. Lev. 1982. 3rd printing 1991. 172 pp. ISBN 0-87763-028-3.

Number 60   *The Minangkabau Response to Dutch Colonial Rule in the Nineteenth Century*, Elizabeth E. Graves. 1981. 157 pp. ISBN 0-87763-000-3.

Number 59   *Breaking the Chains of Oppression of the Indonesian People: Defense Statement at His Trial on Charges of Insulting the Head of State, Bandung, June 7–10, 1979*, Heri Akhmadi. 1981. 201 pp. ISBN 0-87763-001-1.

Number 57   *Permesta: Half a Rebellion*, Barbara S. Harvey. 1977. 174 pp. ISBN 0-87763-003-8.

Number 55   *Report from Banaran: The Story of the Experiences of a Soldier during the War of Independence*, Maj. Gen. T. B. Simatupang. 1972. 186 pp. ISBN 0-87763-005-4.

Number 52   *A Preliminary Analysis of the October 1 1965, Coup in Indonesia (Prepared in January 1966)*, Benedict R. Anderson, Ruth T. McVey, assist. Frederick P. Bunnell. 1971. 3rd printing 1990. 174 pp. ISBN 0-87763-008-9.

Number 51   *The Putera Reports: Problems in Indonesian-Japanese War-Time Cooperation*, Mohammad Hatta, trans., intro. William H. Frederick. 1971. 114 pp. ISBN 0-87763-009-7.

Number 50   *Schools and Politics: The Kaum Muda Movement in West Sumatra (1927–1933)*, Taufik Abdullah. 1971. 257 pp. ISBN 0-87763-010-0.

Number 49   *The Foundation of the Partai Muslimin Indonesia*, K. E. Ward. 1970. 75 pp. ISBN 0-87763-011-9.

Number 48   *Nationalism, Islam and Marxism*, Soekarno, intro. Ruth T. McVey. 1970. 2nd printing 1984. 62 pp. ISBN 0-87763-012-7.

Number 43   *State and Statecraft in Old Java: A Study of the Later Mataram Period, 16th to 19th Century*, Soemarsaid Moertono. Revised edition 1981. 180 pp. ISBN 0-87763-017-8.

Number 39   Preliminary Checklist of Indonesian Imprints (1945-1949), John M. Echols. 186 pp. ISBN 0-87763-025-9.

Number 37   *Mythology and the Tolerance of the Javanese*, Benedict R. O'G. Anderson. 2nd edition 1997. 104 pp., 65 illus. ISBN 0-87763-041-0.

Number 25	*The Communist Uprisings of 1926–1927 in Indonesia: Key Documents*, ed., intro. Harry J. Benda, Ruth T. McVey. 1960. 2nd printing 1969. 177 pp. ISBN 0-87763-024-0.
Number 7	*The Soviet View of the Indonesian Revolution*, Ruth T. McVey. 1957. 3rd printing 1969. 90 pp. ISBN 0-87763-018-6.
Number 6	*The Indonesian Elections of 1955*, Herbert Feith. 1957. 2nd printing 1971. 91 pp. ISBN 0-87763-020-8.

LANGUAGE TEXTS

INDONESIAN

Beginning Indonesian through Self-Instruction, John U. Wolff, Dédé Oetomo, Daniel Fietkiewicz. 3rd revised edition 1992. Vol. 1. 115 pp. ISBN 0-87727-529-7. Vol. 2. 434 pp. ISBN 0-87727-530-0. Vol. 3. 473 pp. ISBN 0-87727-531-9.

Indonesian Readings, John U. Wolff. 1978. 4th printing 1992. 480 pp. ISBN 0-87727-517-3

Indonesian Conversations, John U. Wolff. 1978. 3rd printing 1991. 297 pp. ISBN 0-87727-516-5

Formal Indonesian, John U. Wolff. 2nd revised edition 1986. 446 pp. ISBN 0-87727-515-7

TAGALOG

Pilipino through Self-Instruction, John U. Wolff, Maria Theresa C. Centeno, Der-Hwa V. Rau. 1991. Vol. 1. 342 pp. ISBN 0-87727—525-4. Vol. 2. 378 pp. ISBN 0-87727-526-2. Vol 3. 431 pp. ISBN 0-87727-527-0. Vol. 4. 306 pp. ISBN 0-87727-528-9.

THAI

A. U. A. Language Center Thai Course, J. Marvin Brown. Originally published by the American University Alumni Association Language Center, 1974. Reissued by Cornell Southeast Asia Program, 1991, 1992. Book 1. 267 pp. ISBN 0-87727-506-8. Book 2. 288 pp. ISBN 0-87727-507-6. Book 3. 247 pp. ISBN 0-87727-508-4.

A. U. A. Language Center Thai Course, Reading and Writing Text (mostly reading), 1979. Reissued 1997. 164 pp. ISBN 0-87727-511-4.

A. U. A. Language Center Thai Course, Reading and Writing Workbook (mostly writing), 1979. Reissued 1997. 99 pp. ISBN 0-87727-512-2.

KHMER

Cambodian System of Writing and Beginning Reader, Franklin E. Huffman. Originally published by Yale University Press, 1970. Reissued by Cornell Southeast Asia Program, 4th printing 2002. 365 pp. ISBN 0-300-01314-0.

Modern Spoken Cambodian, Franklin E. Huffman, assist. Charan Promchan, Chhom-Rak Thong Lambert. Originally published by Yale University Press, 1970. Reissued by Cornell Southeast Asia Program, 3rd printing 1991. 451 pp. ISBN 0-300-01316-7.

Intermediate Cambodian Reader, ed. Franklin E. Huffman, assist. Im Proum. Originally published by Yale University Press, 1972. Reissued by Cornell Southeast Asia Program, 1988. 499 pp. ISBN 0-300-01552-6.

Cambodian Literary Reader and Glossary, Franklin E. Huffman, Im Proum. Originally published by Yale University Press, 1977. Reissued by Cornell Southeast Asia Program, 1988. 494 pp. ISBN 0-300-02069-4.

HMONG

White Hmong-English Dictionary, Ernest E. Heimbach. 1969. 8th printing, 2002. 523 pp. ISBN 0-87727-075-9.

VIETNAMESE

Intermediate Spoken Vietnamese, Franklin E. Huffman, Tran Trong Hai. 1980. 3rd printing 1994. ISBN 0-87727-500-9.

* * *

Southeast Asian Studies: Reorientations. Craig J. Reynolds and Ruth McVey. Frank H. Golay Lectures 2 & 3. 70 pp. ISBN 0-87727-301-4.

Javanese Literature in Surakarta Manuscripts, Nancy K. Florida. Vol. 1, *Introduction and Manuscripts of the Karaton Surakarta*. 1993. 410 pp. Frontispiece, illustrations. Hard cover, ISBN 0-87727-602-1, Paperback, ISBN 0-87727-603-X. Vol. 2, *Manuscripts of the Mangkunagaran Palace*. 2000. 576 pp. Frontispiece, illustrations. Paperback, ISBN 0-87727-604-8.

Sbek Thom: Khmer Shadow Theater. Pech Tum Kravel, trans. Sos Kem, ed. Thavro Phim, Sos Kem, Martin Hatch. 1996. 363 pp., 153 photographs. ISBN 0-87727-620-X.

In the Mirror: Literature and Politics in Siam in the American Era, ed. Benedict R. O'G. Anderson, trans. Benedict R. O'G. Anderson, Ruchira Mendiones. 1985. 2nd printing 1991. 303 pp. Paperback. ISBN 974-210-380-1.

To order, please contact:

Cornell University
SEAP Distribution Center
369 Pine Tree Rd.
Ithaca, NY 14850-2819 USA

Online: http://www.einaudi.cornell.edu/bookstore/seap

Tel: 1-877-865-2432 (Toll free – U.S.)
Fax: (607) 255-7534

E-mail: SEAP-Pubs@cornell.edu

Orders must be prepaid by check or credit card (VISA, MasterCard, Discover).

Milton Keynes UK
Ingram Content Group UK Ltd.
UKHW030131020824
446387UK00009B/390